D0712933

Art Center College of Design
Library
1700 Lida Street
Pasadena, Calif. 91103

ART CENTER COLLEGE OF DESIGN

3 3220 00178 3377

This book presents an innovative analysis of the role of imagination as a central concept in both literary and art criticism. Dee Reynolds brings this approach to bear on works by Rimbaud, Mallarmé, Kandinsky and Mondrian. It allows her to redefine the relationship between Symbolism and abstract art, and to contribute new methodological perspectives to comparative studies of poetry and painting.

The late nineteenth/early twentieth century is a crucial period in the emergence of new modes of representation, and is currently at the forefront of critical enquiry. This is the first book to examine Symbolism and abstraction in this way, and the first to treat these poets and painters together. It is an original contribution to interdisciplinary scholarship in art history, literary history and comparative aesthetics.

Art Center College of Design
Library
1700 Lida Street
Pasadena, Calif. 91103

CAMBRIDGE STUDIES IN FRENCH 51

SYMBOLIST AESTHETICS AND
EARLY ABSTRACT ART

Art Center College of Design
Library
1700 Lida Street
Pasadena, Calif. 91103

CAMBRIDGE STUDIES IN FRENCH

General editor: Malcolm Bowie (*All Souls College, Oxford*)

Editorial Board: R. Howard Bloch (*University of California, Berkeley*), Terence Cave (*St John's College, Oxford*) Ross Chambers (*University of Michigan*), Antoine Compagnon (*Columbia University*), Peter France (*University of Edinburgh*), Christie McDonald (*Harvard University*), Toril Moi (*Duke University*), Naomi Schor (*Harvard University*)

Recent titles in this series include

A complete list of books in the series is given at the end of the volume.

759.0652
R462
1995

SYMBOLIST AESTHETICS
AND EARLY
ABSTRACT ART

Sites of imaginary space

DEE REYNOLDS

Lecturer in French, University of Bristol

Art Center College of Design
Library
1700 Lida Street
Pasadena, Calif. 91103

CAMBRIDGE
UNIVERSITY PRESS

Published by the Press Syndicate of the University of Cambridge
The Pitt Building, Trumpington Street, Cambridge CB2 1RP
40 West 20th Street, New York, NY 10011–4211, USA
10 Stamford Road, Oakleigh, Melbourne 3166, Australia

© Cambridge University Press 1995

First published 1995

Printed in Great Britain at the University Press, Cambridge

A catalogue record for this book is available from the British Library

Library of Congress cataloguing in publication data
Reynolds, Dee.
Symbolist aesthetics and early abstract art: sites of imaginary space / Dee Reynolds.
p.   cm. – (Cambridge studies in French; 51)
Includes bibliographical references and index.
ISBN 0 521 42102 0 hardback
1. Imagination. 2. Symbolism (Literary movement)–France.
3. Rimbaud, Arthur, 1854–1891 – Aesthetics.
4. Mallarmé, Stéphane, 1842–1898 – Aesthetics.   5. Art, Abstract.
6. Kandinsky, Wassily, 1866–1944 – Aesthetics.
7. Mondrian, Piet, 1872–1944 – Aesthetics.
8. French poetry – 19th century – History and criticism.
I. Title.   II. Series.
BH301.I53R49   1995
759.06'52–dc20   94-7453 CIP

ISBN 0 521 42102 0   hardback

Contents

Illustrations

PAINTINGS

Illustrations are reproduced by kind permission of the
institutions named and by licence from the Design and Artists
Copyright Society, London (Kandinsky) and International
Licensing Partners, Amsterdam (Mondrian). The Mondrian
material is © 1994 ABC/Mondrian Estate/Holtzman
Trust.

Preface

The initial impetus for this book was my reaction to what I judged to be reductionist accounts, based on structuralist premisses, of Rimbaud's and Mallarmé's poetry. I was seduced by the suggestive power of the extraordinary language of their poetry and by the writings of phenomenologically inspired critics such as Jean-Pierre Richard, which espoused its imagery and heightened its impact. Structuralist accounts, on the other hand, insisted on the self-contained nature of these texts, which were held to 'refer' only to themselves. When I subsequently became interested in non-figurative images in painting, which, like the poetry, opened up new and unexplored worlds, I was both intrigued and irritated to find in art criticism similar affirmations of the 'self-referential' character of these images.

Although the endless search for models and formulas within structuralist and semiotic approaches held a certain appeal, I was keenly aware of the issues which they left out of account, particularly the role of the receiver's imagination in reading the text/looking at the picture. This 'receiver factor' meant that content could never be equated with allegedly 'objective', quantifiable properties of the poetic/pictorial medium. However, structuralism's *mise en cause* of the mediation of coded meanings/lived experience by verbal and visual signs drew my attention to the problematic nature of this relationship, which had not been addressed by phenomenological criticism. Later, my encounters with poststructuralism and deconstruction confirmed my suspicion that a 'naïve' approach to the analysis of signifying processes and the position of the subject within them was no longer possible. Moreover, it had become apparent to me that the discourses of structuralism and in turn of poststructuralism themselves had close links with and were directly derived from radical experimentation in literature, in particular the writing of Mallarmé, and, to a lesser extent, Rimbaud.

It was precisely when analysing such 'disruptive' texts, which upset accepted codes of communication and relationships to reality and lived experience, that the claims of post/structuralist critics concerning self-referentiality became most extreme. However, I remained convinced that while these claims might be true of certain texts, there was a crucial category of avant-garde poetry and painting where this disruption served a different purpose. Its function here was to appeal to the reader's/spectator's imagination, using sensory, and especially visual imagery (through words in the poetry, through forms and colours in the painting) to challenge the limits of conceptual logic. This invitation to the receiver to unlock and activate the imaginary space within the medium was being occluded by the 'self-referential' school. Such art does not reflect reality, but neither does it reflect itself: it sets itself the task of producing and proposing new models for experience. In so doing, it transforms the status of the poetic/ pictorial medium. In a Mallarmé sonnet or a Kandinsky canvas, the substance of words and of colours and forms itself becomes the starting point for constructing new imaginary spaces.

The poems and paintings which take this process to its furthest extreme are those which inaugurate movement away from previous communicative norms, but without becoming purely formalistic, experimenting with the medium for its own sake. Kandinsky and Mondrian appeared very close to Rimbaud and Mallarmé in this respect, and I was excited to discover, on reading their theoretical writings, many significant points of contact with Symbolist poetics. These connections became the starting point for my exploration of the role of imagination in the reception of semantically disruptive poems and paintings.

Acknowledgements

The writing of this book was greatly facilitated by the resources provided by the Library and staff of the University of Warwick, to whom I owe a debt of gratitude. I have received generous financial assistance from the British Academy, which has enabled me to make research trips to France, Holland, Germany and the United States, and has contributed substantially towards the costs of copyrights on the paintings. The K. Blundell Trust has also provided a significant sum for this purpose. I am most grateful to the art galleries and private collectors who have waived reproduction rights for the purposes of this publication.

My interest in the field of comparative aesthetics was nurtured in its early stages by David Scott, for whose intellectual stimulus and enthusiastic encouragement I will always be grateful. Clive Scott provided valuable guidance when I was writing my Ph.D. thesis. I am most grateful to the editor of this series, Malcolm Bowie, for his constructive and diplomatic comments on the manuscript. I would also like to thank those friends and colleagues who have contributed their critiques, in particular Christine Battersby and Roger McLure. Neil Crawford provided valuable information on typography. Last but certainly not least, I would like to thank my parents, whose encouragement and practical support were crucial in enabling me to develop the interests which led to this book, and my husband Stephen, for his continuing generosity and wizardry.

Abbreviations

RIMBAUD

RO   *Œuvres*, ed. S. Bernard and A. Guyaux.(Paris: Gallimard, 1981.)

SARTRE

IM   *L'Imaginaire, psychologie phénoménologique de l'imagination.* (Paris: Gallimard, 1940.)

Introduction

The principal aims of this book are threefold: firstly, to reinstate imagination as a central concept in literary and art criticism; secondly, to redefine the relationship between Symbolism and abstract art in this light; and thirdly, to contribute to renovating the methodology of comparative studies of poetry and painting.

Rimbaud and Mallarmé, the Symbolist poets selected for special study here, are well known for having achieved new extremes of difficulty in poetry and for their radical questioning of the relationship between the linguistic sign, reality and coded meanings. These two writers are, of course, extremely different, with Mallarmé usually being thought of as more 'formalist', and Rimbaud as anticipating/influencing aspects of Surrealism. Kandinsky and Mondrian, the early abstract artists whose work I shall be examining here, are also often thought of as opposites, with Kandinsky breaking into abstraction in a lyrical outburst of colour, while Mondrian 'geometrizes'. Kandinsky is generally regarded as the pioneer of abstraction, but although the milieu in which Mondrian worked was influenced by Kandinsky's ideas of the 'spiritual' in art, the path Mondrian followed into abstraction was quite independent of and different from Kandinsky's. It would have been interesting to include discussion of Malevich and Suprematism in this context, but considerations of space have imposed limitations. However, all four poets and painters in question here radically disrupted established codes within their respective art forms and provoked awareness of the problematic nature of the relation between sign and object. Roman Jakobson (a leading figure of Russian Formalism and of Prague Structuralism) affirmed: 'Dans une certaine mesure aucun mot poétique n'a d'objet. Ce à quoi pensait le poète français [Mallarmé] qui disait que la fleur poétique est l'absente de tous bouquets.'[1] Jakobson, who was also influenced by abstract painters (including Kandinsky), declared that: 'the tendency to make the sign independent of the object . . . is the grounding principle of the whole of modern art'.[2]

These poetic and artistic practices, then, raised new questions concerning the nature of meaning and reference, and seemed to many to be asserting the autonomy of the linguistic/pictorial sign, causing it to refer to nothing outside itself. I shall argue, however, that this disruption of communicative codes is not in fact an end in itself, but a means to new modes of signifying, in which the imagination of the receiver performs a central role. Imagination is central to all three key areas of this book, which is why I will devote considerable space to discussing it in the first chapter. Imagination, as I propose to use the term, involves experiencing according to a sensory mode of apprehension, but in a way which surpasses empirical knowledge. As a response to signifying processes which transgress logical/representational norms, imagination can operate in a manner which defies definition in conceptual and empirical terms, and gestures towards an impossible 'other' space. Imagining activity is a process which cannot take place without a consciousness, embodied in a receiving subject or subjects. As a mode of response to poems and paintings, it is dependent upon linguistic and/or pictorial signifying systems, but it is not reducible to them and cannot be equated with purely textual/pictorial features. However, there can be no question of simply substituting the autonomous consciousness of a receiver for that of a creator. Although the term 'imagination' resonates with associations that come to us from Romanticism and also from the phenomenological 'imaginaire', my project is fundamentally different from both these traditions.

My use of the term 'imaginary' is much closer to the spirit of phenomenology than to that of Lacanian psychoanalysis, where the 'imaginary' presents a different set of problems.[3] However, it differs from phenomenological usages in challenging concepts of imagination which are rooted in idealist/humanist models of subjectivity and meaning. These concepts had already been undermined by poetic/pictorial practices themselves, even before the recent onslaught of deconstruction. Reader-response criticism, which has been heavily influenced by phenomenology, is compatible with structuralist approaches, but has not so far met the challenges of deconstructionist critique.[4] It is necessary to elaborate a view of imagination which can take account of its dependence on and 'inscription' in the poetic and pictorial signifying processes and the loss of autonomy this implies. Such a view does not therefore involve return to an ethos of unity, synthesis and identity, often conveniently labelled as a 'metaphysics of presence'. Imagination can be described in terms analogous to the signifying process as it is seen in poststructuralism, in other words, as a *process* of image production which does not culminate in the formation of a final, stable and coherent image. Imagining activity causes the fissuring of an image's presence, through awareness of what the image does not contain, its lack of totality and wholeness. An 'image', whether it be a mode of consciousness generated by a linguistic description or a visual image in a painting, is not 'imaginary' unless it negates itself by exceeding its own powers of presentation, suggesting more that it can explain or make visible. The challenge to interpretation posed by the poems and paintings of Rimbaud, Mallarmé, Kandinsky and Mondrian does not involve, as is frequently supposed, an attempt to replace represented objects in the world outside the work with the medium of the work itself. Rather, these poems and paintings evoke indefinable imaginary 'objects', which are constructed by the receiver's response to the medium. This means that their content needs to be conceptualized in a new way, which involves rethinking the projects of literary and art criticism as elucidating the interaction between the poetic/pictorial medium and the imagining activity of the receiver. I shall use the term 'imaginary space' to refer to the 'sensory unreality'[5] generated by this inter-action. Moreover, although the medium does not become an object of reference, it does become an object of imaginary trans-formation: the goal of imagining activity is to effect a synthesis of textual/pictorial and imaginary space. This goal is unrealizable, however, and the medium as a 'site' of imaginary space remains both semantically and ontologically 'undecidable'.[6]

A considerable obstacle to the enterprise of redrawing the boundaries of imagination in this way is the extent to which canonical theories of imagination seem to point in the opposite direction to the one which I propose to take here. For many postmodernists and poststructuralists, imagination has been dis-credited, owing to its associations with humanist ideas of an individual, autonomous subject and with identity and synthesis.[7] I will therefore begin in chapter 1 below by analysing a number of 'key moments' in aesthetics,[8] in order to explore opportunities for dissociating imagination from humanist perspectives where the subject is in control of meaning, and where the 'image' is defin-able in conceptual terms. Kant's *Critique of Judgement* lays the basis for a view of imagination which is not dependent on defin-able concepts, and where imagination undermines its own powers of representation. I shall develop an account of imagination which draws on Kant's theory of the 'mathematical sublime', in which imagination confronts its own limits by becoming involved in a process of 'negative presentation'. However, Kant's theory privileges inner mental processes rather than engaging with the subject's relationship to external sensory phenomena, and in seeking to move beyond Kant, I shall draw on Lipps' theory of empathy, and will argue that the supremacy of the subject can be undermined by the reflexive relationship of imagination with the medium. I will also emphasize the projective function of imagining activity which exceeds and transcends the given, transforming it into a site of imaginary space which is directed towards the not yet realized, whose im/possibility is constitutive of its imaginary character.

It has often been pointed out that there is a connection between Symbolism and the aesthetics of early abstract painting.[9] However, although some research has been done on the background to this connection, it has never been examined in terms of the aesthetic project which, I argue here, is shared by Rimbaud, Mallarmé, Kandinsky and Mondrian: the transformation of the medium itself through the imagination of the receiver. If the relationship between Symbolism and abstraction has not previously been examined in this way, this is partly because Symbolist poetics has not been considered in terms of how textual structures can themselves become 'symbolic' through their connection with a non-conceptual imaginary dimension evoked by the text, and partly because links between the work of early abstract artists and Symbolist painting have been made on the level of iconography rather than form, and have not therefore been investigated in the abstract paintings. Morever, although Kandinsky's and Mondrian's theoretical writings clearly locate the motivation behind their move into abstraction in the desire to transform the spectator's perception and experience of the medium itself, their didactic and mystical overtones have alienated many critics and have fostered a polemical response to this crucial aspect of their work.[10]

The significant parallels between the poetics and aesthetics of these poets and painters are connected with similarities in their intellectual backgrounds, and we shall see that the most crucial link here is the emphasis on the medium of the art work itself as an object of imaginary and aesthetic transformation. They do not, however, share a theory of imagination which they consciously apply to their work. The theory of imagination presented here to elucidate their projects is a *retrospective* construct, although it draws on the views of the poets and painters concerned. Moreover, this study of poetry and painting differs from many other comparative projects in that its main aim is not to trace the influence of theories of imagination on these poets and painters or their influence on each other, but to explore the central role attributed in their work to the imagining activity of the receiver.

The goal of transforming the receiver's perception of the medium is by no means common to all Symbolist poets or to all abstract artists. Within Symbolism, it is the culmination of a process involving the transformation of the subject-object relation through imagination, which has roots in Romanticism and in German Idealism, and which, in Rimbaud and Mallarmé, comes to be focussed on the poetic medium itself. In abstract art, on the other hand, this aim furnishes the initial impetus, the motive and the justification for an art without objects. The pioneers of abstract art were acutely aware that only the spectator's imaginative response to the pictorial elements of form and colour could prevent them from being seen as purely material marks on the canvas. Their goal, which is characteristic of early Modernism, is to elevate the function of the medium itself to a means of transcending the immediately visible, not through subject matter (as in the case of religious iconography, for instance), but by challenging the limits of logic and of experience through new forms of signifying.

In Rimbaud's and Mallarmé's poetry, the challenge to conventional logic and to interpretation comes about first of all on a semantic level, through poetic imagery which has a sensory – mainly visual – content, but which defies logical and empirical categories. Imagining does not involve representation of known images, but rather innovative activity which remains open-ended. Analogies between rhythmic features of the imaginary space evoked and visual and spatial patterns in the text enable the latter to be experienced as sites of imaginary space. The reader's recognition of metapoetical implications in the imagery draws his/her attention to the relationship between the textual and the imaginary, and causes imagining activity to become reflexive. In Kandinsky's and Mondrian's semi-abstract and abstract painting, the pictorial images do not represent known objects, and can be experienced in terms of imaginary rhythms and relationships which exceed the purely visual and enable the spectator to experience pictorial space itself as a site of imaginary space. Metapictorial implications within the paintings, as well as titles and theoretical writings, encourage reflexive awareness of this interaction.

Two key characteristics associated with imagination since the Romantics are involved here. Firstly, imagination is activated through suggestion of relationships which defy definition in terms of particular concepts or objects and which are non-finite. Secondly, imagining activity creates connections between consciousness and sensory objects: here, the medium itself. Instead of being a 'sign' of absent ideas or objects which could exist independently of it, the medium is perceived as a 'mirror' of the imagining process of the receiver. Through this reflection, the poetic/pictorial medium can be experienced as imaginary, while at the same time it undermines the autonomy of imagining activity. The transgression of linguistic and figurative codes is not an end in itself, but a means of altering the receiver's perception of poetic/pictorial space.

The approach adopted in this study has been evolved by relating personal experience of the works concerned to relevant theories of imagination and of signs, and remodelling the latter in the light of this experience. I have also sought to take account of what might be called the 'ideal receiver' constructed by the work itself (not primarily by the theories of its creators, though I shall also discuss these). The character of the 'ideal receiver' is in fact inseparable from the circumstances of the art work's production and from prevailing cultural attitudes. Moreover, the ideal receiver is not gender-free and could in many cases be demonstrated to be (predictably) male. A wider-ranging study would have devoted more space to these highly significant issues and would also have debated the gendering of imagination itself.[11] To discuss such questions in depth would have strained the limits of an already very broad and diverse agenda. However, there will be some discussion in chapter 6 below of the ideal receiver, including gender, in relation to the utopian dimension of the work of Rimbaud, Mallarmé, Kandinsky and Mondrian.[12]

This project also has significant consequences for the methodology of comparative studies of poetry and painting. My discussion of the interpenetration of the textual and the imaginary in Rimbaud and Mallarmé both draws on and develops the implications of David Scott's *Pictorialist Poetics* concerning the 'auto-illustrative' nature of certain poetic texts.[13] Moreover, many interesting attempts have been made to analyse visual images using semiotic models derived from linguistics.[14] However, it emerges clearly from the analyses undertaken here that logico-linguistic structures do not constitute a suitable model for aesthetic modes of signification and reception, and that comparisons based on seemingly direct parallels are in fact undermined by the radical semiotic differences between the mediums of poetry and painting.

· The final chapter includes discussion of the relation between Symbolism and Impressionism and of connections between experimental poetry and avant-garde art in the twentieth century. Here it is shown that despite similarities between certain aspects of the poetry of Rimbaud and Mallarmé and the work of Symbolist and Impressionist painters, differences between the mediums concerned render these parallels problematic. The same is true of developments in twentieth-century poetry which appear to have direct parallels with abstract painting. Moreover, the specificity of the poetic and pictorial mediums is vital in explaining why abstract art did not emerge sooner, and why experimentation in poetry which happened at the same time as abstract art led to very different results in terms of their effects on the receiver.

I shall begin here, in the first chapter, with a discussion of the problematic of imagination and imaginary space, which will lead into consideration of the intellectual backgrounds to Symbolism and abstract art. Subsequent chapters (2–5) will consist mainly of in-depth 'readings' of the works of Rimbaud, Mallarmé, Kandinsky and Mondrian, while the final chapter will focus on the utopian dimension of imaginary space.

CHAPTER I

Imagination and imaginary space

[L'imagination] décompose toute la création . . . elle crée un
monde nouveau, elle produit la sensation du neuf . . . elle est
positivement apparentée avec l'infini.
                    (Baudelaire, 'La Reine des facultés')[1]

The sublime . . . is to be found in a formless object, so far as
in it or by occasion of it *boundlessness* is represented, and yet
its totality is also present to thought.
                    (Kant, *Critique of Judgement*)[2]

I am proposing here an account of imagination which emphasizes
its capacity to operate in a sensory mode while exceeding knowledge derived from experience, and which also recognizes its
inscription in and dependence on signifying processes which
disrupt access to logical meanings and definable objects. This will
enable imagination to be deployed as a critical concept in discussing the reception of texts and pictures which embody such
disruptive signifying processes. I shall begin by exploring ways in
which existing theories allow for or even anticipate the possibility
of dissociating imagination from humanist, subject-centered
accounts of logic and meaning. This is not the place in which to
engage in a full-scale survey of the history of imagination, and I
shall focus on three main areas: the Kantian sublime, the
phenomenological 'imaginaire', and the theory of empathy as
elaborated by Theodor Lipps.

Kant's theory of imagination is important to my argument
because imagination here exceeds conceptual definition and, in
the sublime, bridges the gap between the 'sensible' and the
'supersensible'. Moreover, it is self-subverting and undermines its
own powers of representation. However, it is only by reading
Kant against the grain that the senses can be seen to play a
positive role in the experience of the sublime. Moreover, imagination is seen here in terms of a faculty, a 'compartment' of the
mind. Phenomenological approaches, on the other hand, explore
the 'imaginaire' as a mode of consciousness. Sartre conceives of

the 'imaginaire' as an 'irréel' which is both sensory and unreal, like imaginary space as I describe it here. For Sartre, however, the 'irréel' remains tied to definable objects and negates material presence, whereas I shall argue that imaginary space, as a product of disruptive signifying processes, cannot be defined in terms of pre-coded, recognizable objects, and interacts reflexively[3] with the concrete space of the medium. Theodor Lipps' theory of empathy analyses the subject-object relation in ways which are useful in conceptualizing the interaction between the receiver and the work of art, especially because of the links between Lipps' theories and the emergence of abstract painting. For Lipps, however, the subject remains central, and I shall argue that the reflexivity of imagination undermines this position. Reflexivity and semiotic changes in the poetic and pictorial mediums will be discussed with reference to the semiotics of C. S. Peirce. I shall then move on to examine the intellectual backgrounds to Symbolism and the emergence of abstraction, with particular emphasis on the influence of theories which explore interconnections between matter and consciousness.

KANT

In the Kantian sublime, imagination transgresses the boundaries which separate sensible experience from knowledge of the supersensible, which is the province of reason. Moreover, whereas Kant usually describes imagination and the process of cognition itself in terms of unity and synthesis, in his account of the 'mathematical sublime' (*CJ* p. 86/94 ff.), imagination is said to be unable to meet the demand for synthesis which emanates from reason. Here, imagination feels its inability to present ideas of reason, which lie outside the boundaries of experience. The weight of Kant's critical philosophy, which aims to delineate the boundaries of knowledge (he argues that speculative reason ought not to attempt to 'soar beyond' the limits of possible experience),[4] now falls on imagination itself. In the face of a spectacle which overwhelms the subject's capacity to represent it, imagination is made painfully aware of its own limitations. Imagination's serial mode of apprehension can continue to infinity, but cannot meet reason's demand for 'absolute totality' (*CJ*, p. 98/108): discouraged, it 'sinks back into itself' (*CJ*, p. 91/100). What is peculiar to the experience of the sublime, however, is that this very lack of presentation itself functions as a 'negative presentation' (*CJ*, p. 115/127) of what lies beyond the power of imagination to present. The mind 'feels itself raised' (*CJ*, p. 95/105) by the awareness of the unpresentable produced by the recognition of its own powerlessness. In this way, imagination undergoes an 'extension . . . by itself' (*CJ*, p. 87/96). Its *telos* is the reflexive consciousness of the subject, which recognizes its own failure, thereby producing a 'split' consciousness where the breakdown of imagination can itself be objectified and transcended and where the supersensible is experienced as a negative dimension of the sensible.

As is well known, Kant maintains that the sublime is a property of the state of mind of the person experiencing it, not of an object (*CJ*, p. 89/98). Moreover, although he argues that the art of genius requires the invention of new rules (*CJ*, p. 161/180), and is therefore formally innovatory, the 'formless' is said to be characteristic of the sublime, not the beautiful, which must be formally pleasing. For these reasons, and because Kant links the sublime with natural spectacles rather than with art, it is often held that sublimity is not a characteristic which can properly be attributed to works of art. However, in the sublime, the supersensible is experienced by means of objects. Although imagination surpasses the sensible and reaches a negative awareness of the supersensible, this experience is triggered off by a sensory object in the first place. 'This idea of the supersensible, which we can no further determine – so that we cannot *know* but only *think* nature as its presentation – is awakened in us by means of an object whose aesthetical appreciation strains the imagination to its utmost bounds' (*CJ*, p. 108/120). As other commentators have pointed out, one can discriminate between objects which are liable to cause this experience and those which are not.[5] In fact, Kant himself says that the sublime 'is to be found *in a formless object*' (see epigraph to this chapter, emphasis mine). He allows for some overlap between the sublime and the realm of art, speaking of 'the presentation of the sublime, insofar as it belongs to beautiful art': (*CJ*, p. 170/190), although he does specify that in this case, the sublime must be toned down. 'The artistic presentation of the sublime in description and embellishment . . . may be and ought to be beautiful, since otherwise it would be wild, crude and repulsive, and, consequently, contrary to taste.'[6]

The Kantian sublime is in fact doubly subversive: its 'formlessness' is opposed to the formal harmony of the beautiful, and its pleasure is a paradoxical one, inseparable from the pain experienced through the failure of imagination to achieve its goal. In the mathematical sublime, imagination is overwhelmed by the 'excess' of a sensory object, and is unable to perform its synthetic function and grasp the object as a totality. However, although the sublime is the antithesis of classical aesthetic criteria of formal coherence and harmony, imagination forms a link between beauty and sublimity. Indeed, the sublime is arguably a logical consequence of eighteenth-century theories of beauty where imagination plays a vital role. In the discipline of aesthetics as founded by Alexander Baumgarten in 1750, beauty is seen as affording a kind of knowledge which is derived from, yet superior to, other forms of sensory cognition. Beauty is associated with the perfection of sensory cognition[7] obtained by increasing the 'density'[8] of images, whose suggestiveness stimulates imagination. The complexity and vividness of poetic images, which are formed in imagination, can suggest 'a relation to the inconceivable'.[9] Kant rejects Baumgarten's theories on the grounds that beauty involves a pleasurable relationship between imagination and understanding brought about by beautiful objects, rather than the perfection of sensory cognition as such. However, Kantian aesthetical ideas are said to occasion 'more thought . . . than can be grasped or made clear' (*CJ*, p. 158/177). Indeed, there are significant similarities between the 'extensive clarity' of sensory cognition described by Baumgarten and the 'extension' of imagination which takes place in the Kantian sublime, where it is the excessive suggestiveness of a sensory object (for example its grandeur or strength) which, by overwhelming imagination, causes it to exceed and transcend itself.

The fact that in the sublime, the supersensible is experienced through imagination as a negative dimension of the sensible raises the question of the role of imagination in Kantian epistemology. For Kant, knowledge is confined to possible experience, and 'ideas' of reason are beyond the reach of experience. The mind synthesizes and processes sensory data according to *a priori* rules: synthesis of intuition[10] is the task of imagination, but it is through the understanding, which 'bring[s] this synthesis *to concepts*' (*CPR*, A 78: B 103, p. 112), that we attain knowledge. Whereas intuition 'relates directly to the object and is single', the concept 'refers to it mediately by means of a feature which several things may have in common' (*CPR*, A 320: B 377, p. 314). Concepts are therefore more general and abstract. Intuition can also take the form of 'pure' intuition, space and time, which are themselves the conditions of the appearance of objects. Kant distinguishes between reproductive and transcendental (*a priori*) functions of imagination. 'The *image* is a product of the empirical faculty of reproductive imagination; the *schema* of sensible concepts, such as of figures in space, is a product, and, as it were, a monogram, of pure *a priori* imagination, through which, and in accordance with which, images first became possible' (*CPR*, A 141–2: B 181, p. 183).

In the first edition of the *Critique of Pure Reason* (1781), Kant had accorded a very prominent role to imagination. Here, he affirmed that productive imagination mediates between and is the root of both sensibility and understanding, and that 'a pure imagination, which conditions all *a priori* knowledge, is . . . one of the fundamental faculties of the human soul' (*CPR*, A 124, p. 146). Heidegger argues that the implications of Kant's work were that 'human pure reason is necessarily sensible reason'.[11] Alarmed at this outcome, Kant drew back from the 'abyss' into which the foundation of metaphysics threatened to disappear. 'How can sensibility as a lower faculty be said to determine the essence of reason? Does not everything fall into confusion if the lower is put in place of the higher?'[12] According to Heidegger, in the second edition of the *Critique* (1787), the role of imagination is modified to the extent that 'the transcendental imagination is present only in name' and 'the function of the transcendental imagination is transferred to the understanding'.[13] In fact, imagination can still represent an object without its presence in intuition, and the distinction between the empirical and the transcendental functions is maintained, but there is now relatively less emphasis on the autonomy of imagination as an independent faculty and more emphasis on its status as a function of the understanding (see *CPR*, A 118–24, pp. 142–6, and B 150–4, pp. 164–7).

In *The Critique of Judgement* (1790), Kant again accords considerable prominence to imagination. Here, imagination is discussed firstly in relation to understanding, in judgements of taste, and secondly in relation to reason, in the sublime. In judgements of taste, it is understanding which is 'at the service of imagination, and not vice-versa' (*CJ*, p. 79/88).[14] Imagination engages in 'free play' in harmony with understanding, which is experienced through sensation independently of concepts (*CJ*, p. 53/59–60). Here, the freedom of imagination from understanding means that aesthetic experience is envisaged in terms of disinterested pleasure rather than of knowledge. We have seen that in the sublime, on the other hand, there is a conflict between imagination and reason, owing to the incapacity of imagination to perform the synthesis desired by reason. It is through this conflict that the subject is made aware of the supersensible as a negative dimension of the sensible. In this way, there is a transgression of the boundaries between the knowable and the unknowable, which is not mediated by the abstract, logical concepts of the understanding.

Moreover, there are close correspondences between Kant's

descriptions of the sublime and of symbols in poetry, where nature can function as a schema for the supersensible (*CJ*, p. 171/192). He argues that the art of poetry is the most suited to expanding the mind by 'setting the imagination at liberty' (*CJ*, p. 170/191) and by suggesting 'a wealth of thought to which no verbal expression is completely adequate' (*CJ*, p. 171/191). Here, it is symbols which trigger the 'passage' from the sensible to the supersensible. Symbols function by means of analogy, supplying intuitions (i.e. sensory images) which correspond to the form of reflection on a rational idea, not on its content. Like symbols, aesthetical ideas are 'representations of the imagination' which 'strive after something which lies beyond the bounds of experience and so seek to approximate to a presentation of concepts of reason' (*CJ*, p. 157/176). Rational ideas, which are by definition outside the realm of experience, can in fact be experienced *only* through indirect representations (*CJ* p. 197/221).[15] Symbols aesthetically 'enlarge' concepts 'in an unbounded fashion'. Aesthetical attributes give 'occasion to the imagination to spread itself over a number of kindred representations that arouse more thought than can be expressed in a concept determined by words' (*CJ*, p. 158/177). Imagination is stimulated to think 'more . . . than could be comprehended in a concept and therefore in a definite form of words' (*CJ*, p. 159/178). In this way, the symbol/aesthetical idea functions as a 'negative presentation' (*CJ*, p. 115/127) of a rational idea to which no intuition can directly correspond.

Thomas Weiskel points out that 'the sublime comes to be associated both with the failure of clear thought and with matters beyond determinate perception'.[16] Writing on the sublime, Burke argued that in nature, 'dark, confused, uncertain images have a greater power on the fancy to form the grander passions than have those which are more clear and determinate'.[17] These criteria could also be applied to art. In fact, far from being perceived as faults, during the course of the eighteenth century, density and obscurity were increasingly seen as augmenting the suggestive power and thereby the aesthetic value of the work of art. Moreover, the central role accorded to impact on imagination as a criterion of beauty raised interesting questions concerning the relative merits of poetry and painting. The importance of sensory images in stimulating imagination favoured painting, which could create a more direct visual impact, but the desirability of complexity and synthesis favoured poetic images, where, according to Baumgarten, 'more things tend towards unity than in pictures. Hence, a poem is more perfect than a picture'.[18] However, he conceded the superior sensory impact of painting, citing Horace: 'less vividly is the mind stirred by what finds entrance through the ear, than by . . . what one can see for oneself'.[19] Like Baumgarten, Lessing, in his famous *Laocoön* of 1766, explicitly compared poetry and painting in terms of their effect on imagination. Lessing placed greater emphasis than Baumgarten on the role of imagination rather than direct sensory cognition, and, while stressing the limitations and specificity of poetic and pictorial signs (the former being temporal, the latter spatial), insisted that these limitations could be compensated for by the powers of suggestion of the medium concerned. 'Now that alone is fruitful which gives free play to the imagination. The more we see, the more must we be able to add by thinking. The more we add thereto by thinking, the more can we believe ourselves to see.'[20]

In recent years the sublime has once again been in vogue. Owing largely to attacks on conventional aesthetic values from within avant-garde artistic practices, the concept of 'beauty' has become problematic, whereas the sublime has come to the forefront of contemporary art theory, to the extent of being a 'buzz-word'.[21] Jean-François Lyotard argues that 'modern' aesthetics is an aesthetic of the sublime which is inhabited by 'the nostalgia for presence',[22] where 'the unpresentable is put forward only as the missing contents', whereas the 'postmodern' imparts a sense of the unpresentable through the disruption of form itself.[23] Kant's reference to the sublimity of 'formless' objects can indeed be related to the violation of formal rules, which impedes the receiver's perception of the work as an ordered whole. However, the sublime is predicated on unfulfilled desire, and a more crucial distinction than the problematic one between form and content is that between nostalgia for the 'unpresentable' posited as really existing outside the sensible, and the 'unpresentable' as a construct of the receiver's response to the (aesthetic) object, which produces a desire for the 'unpresentable'. In the latter case, the receiver is at once frustrated and gratified by the sense that the work contains 'more' than can be directly presented and intuitively grasped or conceptually defined, but here, the unpresentable is a product of interaction between the medium and imagination, and exists only as a fiction, not in a 'noumenal' realm beyond the work. The desired *telos* of imagining activity, the fusion of the medium with imaginary space, cannot be fully achieved, but this unrealizable *telos* maintains the dynamism of imagining activity and creates ontological ambiguity.

THE *IMAGINAIRE*

In many respects, twentieth-century phenomenology represents an advance on previous theories of imagination. In particular, imagination is no longer regarded as a 'faculty', with the image being conceptualized as an object 'in' consciousness. Rather, it is an act of consciousness, which is directed towards an intentional object. Sartre's theory of imagination is grounded in Husserl's account of the image as an act of consciousness, rather than as a thing 'in' consciousness (the 'illusion d'immanence'[24]). Phenomenology, with its emphasis on the interaction between consciousness and object in the construction of experience, has provided a valuable theoretical basis for several strands of reader-response criticism.[25] In France, phenomenologically inspired approaches have been enormously influential, and have interacted fruitfully with structuralist methods in the work of critics such as Richard and Poulet.[26] This interaction was possible because structuralist methods could be applied to the study of the imaginary as it emerged in thematic patterns. A major difference, however, is the role of the author and of lived experience, or the 'vécu'. The importance accorded to the 'vécu' of the author and the role of intentional objects in the 'imaginaire', together with the emphasis on dialectical synthesis and on presence and revelation, meant that this kind of criticism was incompatible with post/structuralist critiques. It was in fact in the context of the phenomenological tradition of literary criticism that the 'imaginaire' came to be associated with the privileging of the producer's experience[27] and to be seen as dependent on representation to the extent that a challenge to representation could be interpreted as a challenge to the imaginary. Although critics such as Richard and Iser both recognize and value the polyvalence and disruption of familiar models of meaning which characterize many modern texts, they see the task of the reader as that of re-establishing semantic unity and coherence.[28]

Merleau-Ponty privileges the fullness of lived experience: poets and painters are called upon to creatively deform abstract, logical categories in order to interpellate the receiver, who is enabled to enter their 'monde imaginaire'.[29] Similarly, in *La Poétique de la rêverie*, Bachelard describes his project in terms of communicating, via the poetic image, with the 'conscience créante du poète',[30] an approach which has strongly influenced literary critics' treatment of the image as a means of access to the poet's 'vécu'.[31] Moreover, Bachelard declares that 'la phénoménologie de l'image nous demande d'activer la participation à l'imagination créante'.[32] The receiver can therefore participate in the creative act, which is often conceptualized on a model of transcendental subjectivity. Jacques Garelli, for instance, describes imagining as an 'acte libre, unique et originelle'.[33] Paul Ricoeur's theory of the herme- neutical imagination emphasizes its revelatory function. Imagin- ation is 'an insight into likeness' which 'is both a thinking and a seeing':[34] to imagine 'is not to have a mental picture of something but to display relations in a depicting mode'.[35] In metaphor, the writer/reader imagines in this way by contributing to the *epoche* or suspension of 'ordinary descriptive reference and to the *projection* of new possibilities of redescribing the world'.[36] Imagination contributes actively to 'the completion of the *meaning* of meta- phor', which involves 'the emergence of a new semantic con- gruence or pertinence from the ruins of the literal sense shattered by semantic incompatibility or absurdity'.[37] The imagination brings about a dialectical synthesis which is seen in terms of revelation and unconcealment of a pre-existing 'presence'. Poetic meaning 'constitutes the primordial reference to the extent that it suggests, reveals, unconceals . . . the deep structure of reality'.[38]

This foregrounding of originality, completeness and revelation has been a target of deconstructionist critique. Moreover, the prominence accorded to sensory imagery in phenomenological criticism has come under attack as being tied up with a transpar- ent model of language which allows access to the 'vécu' of the producer. However, such imagery can just as well be seen as a function of the interaction between the medium and the receiver, without reference to the experience of the producer. Moreover, it does not have to be dependent on a known object as its intention- al correlate, a dependence which negates its capacity for episte- mological innovation. In Sartre, the 'imaginaire' has no inno- vatory potential. The mental image is constructed out of previously acquired knowledge. 'On ne se représente en image que ce qu'on sait d'une façon quelconque . . . Une image ne saurait exister sans un savoir qui la constitue' (*IM*, p. 116). It is always related to the absence of a known object. 'Une image n'est pas le monde nié, purement et simplement, elle est toujours *le monde nié d'un certain point de vue*, précisément celui qui permet de poser l'absence ou l'inexistence de tel objet qu'on présentifiera "en image"' (*IM*, p. 355). Even a non-figurative picture must be seen as an analogon of new objects: it is 'un ensemble irréel de choses neuves' (*IM*, p. 366).[39]

On the other hand, for Sartre, the image does have ontological specificity: it is a way of being conscious of an object which is distinct from those of perception and conceptual meaning. When we have a mental image, the 'object' itself is absent, but it is envisaged 'à la façon des choses' (*IM*, p. 130), i.e. in a sensory manner. The mental image is a paradoxical combination of absence and presence (*IM*, p. 145). The capacity to imagine is the capacity to negate the world, which constitutes the transcendental freedom of consciousness (*IM*, p. 358). This means that the image is incompatible with sensory perception. 'La formation d'une conscience imageante s'accompagne . . . d'un anéantissement d'une conscience perceptive et réciproquement' (*IM*, p. 232). The existential type of the work of art is an 'irréel' (*IM*, p. 362), and its aesthetic value is located entirely in the 'imaginaire'. 'Le réel n'est jamais beau. La beauté est une valeur qui ne saurait jamais s'appliquer qu'à l'imaginaire et qui comporte la négation du monde dans sa structure essentielle' (*IM*, p. 372). We shall see below when discussing the theories of Lipps that the dimension of 'sensory unreality' which Sartre attributes to the 'imaginaire' can be achieved without this negation of the material presence of the medium.

It is largely the dependence on intentional objects which Derrida attacks in the 'imaginaire'. Writing on Husserl, he points out that the imaginary, which is seen here as a lived, pre-linguistic experience, has to be compatible with the 'ordre logique de la conceptualité'.[40] This logical order is itself constrained by the possibility of a relationship to a known object: 'le sens ne s'ouvre que dans l'intentionnalité *connaissante* par rapport à l'objet'.[41] The difference between sense and nonsense is determined linguistically by whether 'la forme grammaticale permet la possibilité d'un rapport à l'objet', regardless of the fact that, as Derrida points out, 'il y a dans les formes de signification non discursives . . . des ressources de sens qui ne font pas signe vers l'objet possible'.[42] Derrida also sees the 'imaginaire' as a space of dialectical synthesis which is held to transcend the text. He argues that the process of signifying is 'undecidable' and that there can be no thematic content outside writing itself, and therefore no 'imaginaire'.[43] He declares himself opposed to the 'projet phénoménologique, herméneutique et dialectique du thématisme'. It is impossible to find 'un thème ou un sens au-delà des instances textuelles dans un imaginaire, une totalité ou un vécu'.[44]

Derrida's critique is directed at specific aspects of the phenomenological 'imaginaire'. There are, however, more radical and critical aspects to these approaches. For Bachelard, the image is independent of 'savoir'.[45] It is at once material and dynamic, sensory and self-metamorphosing. It is an impulse, a 'mouvement de l'âme',[46] which 'met en branle toute l'activité linguistique'.[47] The poetic image, which is itself linguistic ('un nouvel être du langage')[48] is the origin of both consciousness and language.[49] Moreover, the dynamic, self-metamorphosing character of the Bachelardian imagination performs a critical, iconoclastic function which 'serves to demystify not only the immobilizing prestige of reality but also the fascinating power of imagination itself'.[50] Both Bachelard and Ricoeur place great emphasis on the future-orientated character of the poetic image/metaphor, which is not a looking back to something already known or experienced, but a looking forward, an opening of undetermined possibilities. Ricoeur distinguishes between imagination which 'stages a process of identification that mirrors the order', where imagination 'has the appearance of a picture', and imagination which has a 'disruptive function': 'its image in this case is productive, an imagining of something else, the elsewhere'.[51] The distinction between these two kinds of imagination corresponds to 'the polarity between picture and fiction and ideology and utopia'.[52]

Commenting on Bachelard, Foucault remarks that 'mieux que personne, M. Bachelard a saisi le labeur dynamique de l'imagination', but continues: 'mais devons-nous le suivre encore quand il montre ce mouvement s'accomplissant dans l'image et l'élan de l'image s'inscrivant de lui-même dans le dynamisme de l'imagination?'. For Foucault, the conflict between the dynamism of imagining and the stasis of the image (understood in the Sartrean sense as an 'irréel' which re-presents an absent object) makes them mutually exclusive. The image, which is a 'forme cristallisée', 'ne s'offre pas au moment où culmine l'imagination mais au moment où elle s'altère . . . l'image mime la présence de Pierre, l'imagination va à sa rencontre. Avoir une image, c'est donc renoncer à imaginer'.[53] On this account, the act of imagining is irreducible to static 'pictures' and/or definable concepts, and is essentially negative and self-subverting. These are precisely the characteristics of imagination as I have described it here. Imagining activity operates in a sensory mode, but is a movement towards a fullness which is never fully realized and which, if it were, would put an end to the activity of imagining.

Imagination as a dynamic and self-subverting activity has much in common with the Derridean concepts of 'différance' and 'supplément'. 'Différance' (a term which combines the meanings of 'difference' and 'deferral') is not subject to synthesis 'dans la présence à soi d'une synthèse ontothéologique ou onto-téléologique. La différance doit signer . . . le point de rupture avec le système de l' "Aufhebung" et de la dialectique spéculative.'[54] It is irrecuperable and non-progressive, without an origin or *telos* which could be separated from the shifting network of differences which characterizes the signifying process. 'La langue et en général tout code sémiotique . . . n'ont pas pour cause un sujet, une substance ou un étant quelque part présent et échappant au movement de la différance . . . il n'y a pas de présence hors de et avant la différance sémiologique.'[55] Although it is precisely 'différance' as the dispersive, anti-discursive character of writing which he sees as incompatible with the 'imaginaire', Derrida invokes 'différance' in his discussion of imagination in Rousseau. 'Si nous désirons au-delà de notre pouvoir de satisfaction, l'origine de ce surplus et de cette différence se nomme imagination . . . l'imagination, origine de la différence entre la puissance et le désir, est bien déterminée comme *différance*.'[56]

The activity of imagining is bound up with the 'différance' of the signifying processes of the text, both stimulating desire for and deferring imaginary 'presence' and completeness, on whose very elusiveness the continuing activity of imagination depends. Derrida distinguishes between the impossibility of 'la totalisation' where finitude is inadequate to grasp infinity, and a finite ludic field whose lack of totality is due not to infinity, but to the absence of a centre 'qui arrête et fonde le jeu des substitutions', where 'la nature du champ . . . exclut la totalisation'.[57] Imagining activity can operate in both these fields, but, unlike 'différance', it is oriented towards an unfulfilled goal which is in excess of that which is/can be presented. Moreover, although it is not located in a space 'outside' the text, since it is irreducibly 'differed/deferred' from itself through its interaction with the poetic/pictorial medium, imagining activity involves the agency of a receiving subject and cannot be described in terms of signifying systems alone. By contrast, 'différance' is described in purely textual terms, writing out references to consciousness[58] or experience and resulting in a kind of textual anthropomorphism, where the effects of desire are attributed to the text itself. Derrida argues that 'la différance n'est pas précédée par l'unité originaire et indivise . . . Ce qui diffère la présence est ce à partir de quoi au contraire la présence est annoncée ou désirée *dans son représentant, son signe, sa trace* . . .'[59]

EMPATHY, IMAGINARY SPACE AND REFLEXIVITY

Although we have discussed theories of imagination in which it is seen as a dynamic and self-subverting activity, we have not yet explored the role within this activity of the signifying processes of a poetic or pictorial text. This is a difficult problem to resolve in that previous accounts of imagination have tended to be subject-centered and to treat the work of art as an object to be transcended, or even, as in Sartre, to be 'negated' in terms of its sensory presence, owing to the incompatibility of the 'conscience imageante' with sensory perception (*IM*, p. 232). Post/structuralist theories resort to the opposite extreme, where the signifying processes are analysed in isolation from consciousness. However, the poetic/pictorial object can itself become an 'object' of imagining activity, undergoing an ontological transformation by being experienced as a site of imaginary space, while at the same time retaining a difference and otherness which prevent its 'Aufhebung' into consciousness, and through which imagining activity recognizes its own 'différance' and dispersal through the signifying processes.

Theodor Lipps' theory of 'Einfühlung' (literally 'feeling into') or 'empathy'[60] explores the dynamics of imagining activity in relation to the object of perception. If one allows (as Lipps himself does not) that this relation can become reflexive, then the interaction between imagining activity and the medium of the work can be seen as one of difference and deferral, as well as of ontological transformation. Lipps' theories are also of interest because of the considerable influence they exerted on the artists of Kandinsky's circle. 'Einfühling' is an imagining activity (a 'Phantasietätigkeit'), in which the subject experiences the sensation of living 'in' an external object, and where characteristics of the subject are transferred onto the object. A line, for instance, can be perceived as moving, when the dynamism of the act of perception is transferred onto the line itself. 'The straight line runs, extends, or stretches itself from A to B or from B to A, or from the middle to both sides. It does the one or the other, *depending on my observation*. If it is vertical, then it rises up or sinks down.'[61] In the process of 'Einfühlung', the subject feels totally at one with the object, and the object (for example colour) can be experienced as a living being (*AS* I, p. 441). Lipps ascribes to objects of 'Einfühling' dynamic potential ('Kraft') and mood ('Stimmung'). However, these properties are neither completely subjective nor objective, but are functions of the interaction between subject and object. For instance, a colour which seems to attract the spectator towards it is experienced as containing a certain energy, which comes from the spectator as well as being inextricably bound up with the qualities of the particular colour:

The 'strong' colour pulls me with a certain energy towards itself, i.e. I experience in myself . . . a *striving*, to turn towards it. This striving is my striving, but I experience it directly [*unmittelbar*] as coming, not from me but from the colour and its particular quality, as bound up with it, as 'belonging' to it. And this striving has a certain energy ['*Kraft*']. The energy of colour is therefore the energy of my striving, but of a striving which 'belongs' to the particular quality of the colour, i.e. directly linked with it, in and with its directly given striving. (*AS* I, p. 442).

The energy which is experienced as a property of the colour is a product of the interaction between colour and consciousness. Lipps distinguishes between the energy of colours and the moods with which they can be associated. He emphasizes that these moods vary from person to person and cannot be defined linguistically. He also emphasizes that the moods are not inherent in the colours themselves, but are experienced as belonging to them through empathy: 'the mood . . . is "felt into" the colour' ["*in die Farbe eingefühlt*"]' (*AS* I, p. 445).[62] Interestingly, Lipps remarks that he has deliberately discussed the effects of colours in their own right, but that 'if they are colours of objects, then the aesthetic effect of the object to which the colour belongs will compete with the aesthetic effect of the colour' (*AS* I, p. 448). The stronger the connotations of the object to which the colour is attached, the weaker the independent effects of the colour will become.[63] 'Einfühlung' is closely bound up with dynamism, and involves an inner mimesis or 'Nachahmung' (*AS* I, p. 120), where the subject's identification with the object is indissociable from his/her imaginary enactment of its dynamics. In watching an acrobat, for instance, 'I feel myself in the optically perceived movement of the acrobat, so that in the acrobat as I perceive him, I feel myself striving and inwardly active' (*AS* I, p. 123). Because of this imaginary identification, contemplation of the object becomes inseparable from contemplation of the subject's own inner 'activity'. So, for instance, 'my pleasure in architectonic forms is without doubt above all a pleasure in my inner expansion and concentration, in the whole *inner movement* which I perform while contemplating the forms' (*AS* II, pp. 97–8, emphasis mine).

In this way, aesthetic experience becomes an 'objectified self-enjoyment' (*AS* II, p. 102). According to Lipps, in aesthetic 'Einfühlung', there is no division between subject and object. 'The object and subject of aesthetic contemplation are not separated . . . The I, which lingers in this aesthetic contemplation, is superindividual [*überindividuelles*] . . . It lives in the contemplated object' (*AS* II, p. 87). Although the subject of aesthetic contem-

plation retains a sense of identity (i.e. while I am empathizing
with the acrobat, I don't really think that I have become the
acrobat), s/he does not consciously reflect on the difference
between the real I and the empathizing I, which Lipps refers to as
the ideal ('ideelles') or experienced ('erlebtes') I. Aesthetic
experience leads to a 'freeing of the I from itself', first of all
through the transition from the real I to the 'ideelles' I, but also
through a further transition, where the 'ideelles' I itself becomes
'a stronger, richer I, unified in a special way by the unity of the
work' (*AS* II, p. 88). The project of the aesthetic experience
thereby becomes the aggrandizement of the subject. Significantly, in elaborating a theory of the aesthetic sublime, Lipps
excludes the experience of sensory excess, where 'what I must
comprehend exceeds the limits of my ability to comprehend'. This
negative experience induces self-consciousness and 'catapults me
out of aesthetic contemplation' (*AS* I, p. 534). Lipps' aesthetic
sublime involves 'Einfühlung' with the object and is a wholly
pleasurable experience, without the pain which is an inevitable
component of the sublime in Kant.

The process of 'feeling oneself into' or 'living with' (Lipps uses
the term 'Miterlebnis') an object, in the sense of imaginatively
enacting textual/pictorial rhythms and experiencing dynamic
interactions between imagining activity and textual/pictorial
space,[64] is crucial to the imaginary transformation of textual and
pictorial space as it will be described here. However, I argue that
this relationship between imagining consciousness and textual/
pictorial space does not take the form of a hierarchical 'Aufhebung', where the text/picture is penetrated and absorbed by
consciousness, or, to use another Hegelian term, 'vergeistigt'
('spiritualized'),[65] but is rather one of non-hierarchical similarity
and difference. It is significant that Lipps, who does not wish to
compromise the supremacy of the subject, refuses any possibility
of 'Einfühlung' becoming reflexive. It is essential to the 'Aufhebung' or sublation of the object that the subject should 'inter-
nalize' it to the extent of losing awareness of its presence.
However, the receiver's reflexive awareness of the process of
'Einfühlung' destroys any illusion that the external, sensory
object has been merged with consciousness.[66]

This theory of reflexivity is radically different from formalist
accounts according to which the work, having disrupted external
reference (for example through semantic incoherence or subversion of figurative representation), internalizes it by 'referring'
to its own signifying structures (i.e. by becoming 'self-
referential'). There, the text/picture is treated as if it were self-

sufficient, with the textual/pictorial 'object' replacing an object of references in the external world. On the view outlined here, however, reflexivity is not internal either to the text/picture or to consciousness, but involves dynamic interaction between them, of which the receiver can become aware. Such reflexivity does not end the imagining process, as claimed by Lipps, but enables the receiver to perceive the tension of similarity and difference between imaginary and textual/pictorial space and to recognize that imagining activity is not autonomous but is an effect of the text/picture itself. An art work which stimulates this response can escape definition in terms of recognizable objects or conceptual meanings without becoming 'self-referential' because its content consists, not in ideas which can be defined in conceptual terms, but rather in an *event*: the modification of its relationship with the consciousness of the receiver through which it can be experienced as a site of 'imaginary space'.

This modification necessitates changes in the functioning of poetic and pictorial signs. C. S. Peirce's semiotics provides a useful means of conceptualizing these changes because it is concerned not merely with the taxonomy but with the ontology of signs, their mode of being, and because for Peirce, the 'interpretant' is a crucial part of the sign. Peirce's by now well-known division of signs into icons, indices and symbols is based, not on distinctions such as those between 'pictures' and 'words', but on the categories of 'Firstness', or quality (requiring one element only), 'Secondness', or reaction/experience (requiring two elements) and 'Thirdness', or representation/mediation (requiring three elements).

Firstness is the mode of being of that which is such as it is, positively and without reference to anything else. Secondness is the mode of being of that which is such as it is, with respect to a second but regardless of any third. Thirdness is the mode of being of that which is such as it is, in bringing a second and a third into relation to each other.[67]

It is often thought that the Peircean icon refers in the first instance to pictures, especially of the figurative kind, since an icon signifies by virtue of its resemblance to its object. A figurative image can indeed be described as 'iconic'. An icon, however, is first and foremost a sign which belongs to the category of Firstness. Pure Firstness is an 'unanalyzed total impression' (VIII.329), and a pure icon 'by virtue of it being an immediate image . . . strictly speaking, exists only in consciousness' (IV.447). An icon does not require its object to have real existence. Whereas an icon is immediate, an index is particular, and a symbol is general. An index (for example a photograph) is a sign which has a real relation to its object and which is affected by it (IV.531, II.248). Indices belong to the category of Secondness, which involves reaction and consciousness of otherness (see 1.324 ff. and II.283 ff.). Indices are not necessarily causally connected with their objects: they can also be defined by their function of 'forcing the attention to the thing intended', (VIII.368, n. 23). The signifying capacity of icons is determined by the characteristics possessed by the sign itself, which it shares with its object. Indices signify through an existential connection with a real object. Symbols, however, can function as signs only by virtue of their relation to an interpretant, which links sign and object (II.304). The 'interpretant' is the sign created in the mind of the person to whom the sign is addressed (II.228) and can be described as 'a modification of consciousness' (V.485). Symbols belong to the category of Thirdness, and refer to their object by virtue of a law or convention (IV.448, II.249) or by consequence of habit or natural disposition: they enable us to generalize and create abstractions (IV.531).

Strictly speaking, the terms 'icon', 'index' and 'symbol' should be used only to describe the relation of signs to their dynamic objects (VIII.314), as Peirce employs different classifications to define relationships to interpretants.[68] However, I shall use the term 'iconic' to indicate a sign where Firstness predominates, 'indexical' for a sign where Secondness predominates, and 'symbolic' for a sign where Thirdness predominates, in relation to the interpretant as well as to the object. I confine my discussion to these terms, partly because Peirce's classifications are immensely complex, but also because, in the examples we will be discussing here, the sign-object relationship is inseparable from the sign-interpretant relationship. In fact, Peirce specifies that in icons, the interpretant can itself be the object (II.311). Peirce's classifications are not mutually exclusive: signs can combine different elements. Verbal language, for instance, is more 'symbolic' than figurative painting, but it too can contain 'iconic' elements. For Peirce, the most perfect signs are those which combine characteristics of all three categories (IV.448). He cites the 'diagram' as an example of a sign which, though mainly iconic, also contains symbolic and indexical characteristics. Here, not only can the object and the interpretant be the same, but the object is not a particular thing or idea, but a 'form of relation', which 'is the very form of the relation between the . . . corresponding parts of the diagram' (IV.530).

The use of Peircean terminology will be kept to a minimum in the discussions of the poetry and painting of Rimbaud, Mallarmé,

Kandinsky and Mondrian, but we shall see how each acquires a more synthetic, 'diagrammatic' mode of signifying which focusses, not on individual, definable objects, but on 'forms of relations' (IV.352), which create close links between the medium itself and the imagining activity of the receiver. These links foreground the element of Firstness. However, metadiscursive elements can perform an indexical function by drawing the receiver's attention to the relationship of similarity and difference between the interpretant and the medium, inducing an awareness of the 'not-self' in the self (1.324), the presence of the textual/pictorial in the imaginary. Moreover, this awareness causes imagining activity itself to become reflexive, involving an element of representation, or 'Thirdness', where textual/pictorial space mediates between imagining activity as subject and object of its own critical reflection.

Peirce himself locates 'Esthetic Feeling' in 'Category the First' (V.111), which is evoked in his description of painting.[69] 'In contemplating a painting, there is a moment when we lose the consciousness that it is not the thing, the distinction of the real and the copy disappears, and it is for the moment a pure dream – not any particular existence, and yet not general. At that moment we are contemplating an *icon*' (III.362). However, he also specifies that aesthetic enjoyment involves generalization, and is 'a consciousness belonging to the category of Representation, though representing something in the Category of Quality of Feeling' (V.114). Reflexivity in the form of self-consciousness is a kind of Firstness, but also involves Thirdness (representation), where 'we conceive a mere quality of Feeling, of Firstness, to represent itself to itself as Representation' (V.70).

The long held associations between the image and representation of known objects and between imagination and subject-centred philosophies have led to the view that the 'imaginary' is incompatible with subversive signifying processes. The foregoing discussions have shown, however, that it is possible to conceive of imagination as an activity which is stimulated by the medium itself to defy conceptual definition and synthesis. As a response to semantically disruptive poems and paintings, imagination can operate in the sensory mode of the 'irréel', projecting an imaginary space which is irreducible to coded, known objects. Moreover, through its 'Einfühlung' with the object of contemplation, imagination can experience its own activity as a property of the object, here, the medium of the work. This also means, however, that imagining activity is itself 'other'; textual/pictorial as well as imaginary. Lipps emphasizes the role of dynamism in 'Einfühlung', and we shall see that it is in fact largely through rhythm that connections are forged between the concrete space of the textual/pictorial medium and the 'sensory unreality' of imaginary space. Rhythmic patterns can replace coded objects and act as a 'bridge' between the medium and imagining activity. Rhythmic interactions between textual/pictorial and imaginary space can be described in terms of the Peircean 'diagram', which will be discussed further in chapter 6 below.

SYMBOLISM AND ABSTRACTION

As stated in the introduction, Rimbaud, Mallarmé, Kandinsky and Mondrian do not share a theory of imagination which they consciously apply to their work. However, the concept of inter-action between matter and consciousness, based on rhythm or vibration, is central to the intellectual contexts of both Symbolism and early abstraction. Although my analyses here are based on my own theories of imagining activity and imaginary space, the importance accorded to rhythm in these contexts as a means of bridging the gap between matter and consciousness reinforces my argument, in that the medium itself comes to be seen as an 'object' which can interact directly with the imagination of the receiver. The remainder of this chapter will be devoted to discussion of this background.

Rimbaud has written very little on his poetics, though what little he wrote is justly famous. Mallarmé has produced fasci-nating and idiosyncratic texts on many topics, very often related to writing itself, but (unlike Baudelaire) not directly on imagin-ation. Both Kandinsky and Mondrian produced an extensive body of theoretical writings, whose function is generally didactic and polemical, in which they do refer to imagination.[70] My account of the relationship between imagining activity and signi-fying processes differs from Kandinsky's and especially from Mondrian's in several respects, notably concerning the degree to which imaginary space is held to be derived from the medium itself, rather than expressing the artist's experience or conveying *a priori* ideas. Rimbaud and Mallarmé in fact display greater awareness of the active role played by the medium, which reduces the degree of control exercised by the producer and accords increased 'initiative' both to the signifying processes and to the reader/spectator.

The label 'Symbolist' encompasses so many diverse character-istics that it is not a very helpful critical term. It is particularly important to distinguish between 'allegorical' and 'symbolic' tendencies. Moréas' Symbolist Manifesto, published in 1886, claimed in Neoplatonic language that Symbolist poetry aimed to 'vêtir l'Idée d'une forme sensible'.[71] Albert Aurier's article on 'Le Symbolisme dans la peinture; Paul Gauguin', which officially launched the Symbolist movement in painting, was published in 1891, although painting which could be termed Symbolist was in fact well established by then, notably through the works of Gustave Moreau, Puvis de Chavannes and Odilon Redon. Aurier described Symbolist painting as '*synthétique*, puisqu'elle écrira ces formes, ces signes, selon une mode de compréhension générale' and '*subjective*, puisque l'objet n'y sera jamais considéré en tant qu'objet, mais en tant que signe d'idée perçu par le sujet'.[72] He cited Baudelaire's famous 'Correspondances' sonnet, but maintained that 'le signe, pour indispensable qu'il soit, est rien en lui-même . . . l'idée seule est tout'.[73] Both of these manifestos were couched in terms which could more properly be applied to allegory than symbol, if allegory is seen as an illustration of the general by the particular, which is definable, while the symbol is a particular which contains the general and which is characterized by a 'processus signifiant inépuisable'.[74] According to Thomas Carlyle, 'in a Symbol, there is concealment and yet revelation . . . in the Symbol proper, there is ever . . . some embodiment and revelation of the Infinite'.[75] Todorov cites Humboldt as saying that whereas in allegory, 'une idée clairement pensée est attachée arbitrairement à une image', authentic symbols 'arrivent aux idées qu'ils ne connaissaient pas d'avance, qui même restent éternellement insaisissables en elles-mêmes'.[76]

It is clearly the symbol which has the closest affinities with the theory of imagining activity outlined here and which forms the basis of the continuity between Symbolism and abstraction. The symbol's inexhaustibility undermines the capacity of the subject to define or control it within the sphere of discursive meaning. In Romantic writing, this view of the symbol, and the role of imagination as the creator and receiver of symbols are often associated with a mystical vision of the universe as mysteriously interconnected in all its parts. According to Baudelaire, whose thought on this subject was influenced by Swedenborg and Fourier, the poet can see into 'l'inépuisable fonds de l'immense analogie' (*BOC* II, p. 133). He writes that 'Swedenborg . . . nous avait déjà enseigné . . . que tout, forme, mouvement, nombre, couleur, parfum, dans le *spirituel* comme dans le *naturel*, est significatif, réciproque, converse, *correspondant*' (*BOC* II, p. 133). Baudelaire believes that it is possible to experience interactions between the senses. He cites Hoffmann: 'je trouve une analogie et une réunion intime entre les couleurs, les sons et les parfums' (*BOC* II, p. 425). These correspondences cannot be apprehended through rational thought, but only through imagination. 'L'imagination . . . perçoit tout d'abord, en dehors des méthodes philosophiques, les rapports intimes et secrets des choses, les correspondances et les analogies' (*BOC* II, p. 329). The true artist and poet should treat nature, not as an object to be copied, but as a dictionary, from which elements are chosen and recombined in new ways (see *BOC* II, p. 625).[77] Baudelaire's strong hostility to what he calls 'copying' nature is a direct consequence of his belief in the capacity of imagination to reconstruct reality. Moreover, the implications are far more radical than a mere idealizing of nature, because the material medium of the work of art can interact directly with the imagination of the producer/receiver, rendering representation of an 'external' subject superfluous.

Baudelaire sees both language and colour as physical mediums with which imagination can interact directly. He writes of Hugo that 'le lexique français, sortant de sa bouche, est devenu un monde, un univers coloré, mélodieux et mouvant' (*BOC* III, p. 133). A picture by Delacroix, placed at too great a distance to perceive the subject, can create a powerful effect by its colours alone (*BOC* II, p. 753). Colours and forms can affect the spectator independently of objects. Baudelaire writes of Delacroix's painting: 'il semble que cette couleur . . . pense par elle-même, indépendamment des objets qu'elle habille' (*BOC* II, p. 595). Similarly: 'Une figure bien dessinée vous pénètre d'un plaisir tout à fait étranger au sujet. Voluptueuse ou terrible, cette figure ne doit son charme qu'à l'arabesque qu'elle découpe dans l'espace' (*BOC* II, p. 753). Although the major influence on Baudelaire's art theory, and especially his theory of colour, was Delacroix, who did in fact depict subjects, a tendency is clearly emerging here to consider the suggestive effects of the medium itself independently of its representational function. Roger Shattuck points out: 'Baudelaire institutes a line of thinking and looking that would eventually lead to nonfigurative or abstract painting . . . He is asking us to consider the pure play of colour.'[78]

Baudelaire's analysis of the effects of colours could be considered 'allegorical', in that he connects them with particular moods: 'tout le monde sait que le jaune, l'orangé, le rouge, inspirent et représentent les idées de joie, de richesse, de gloire et d'amour'. However, he emphasizes that the individual tones are modulated and modified by the art of composition, which links painting with mathematics and music. 'L'art du coloriste tient par de certains côtés aux mathématiques et à la musique' (*BOC* II, p. 625). The link between the arts is both structural and synaesthesic: 'la musique donne l'idée de l'espace: tous les arts, plus ou moins; puisqu'ils sont *nombre* et que le nombre est une traduction de l'espace' (*BOC* I, p. 702). Baudelaire is fascinated by rhythmic structures in time and space. In 'Fusées', he attributed the charm of a ship in motion to 'la multiplication successive et . . . la génération de toutes les courbes et figures imaginaires opérées dans l'espace par les éléments réels de l'objet', and continues: 'l'idée poétique qui se dégage de cette opération du mouvement dans les lignes est l'hypothèse d'un être vaste, immense, compliqué, mais eurythmique' (*BOC* II, p. 663).

The ideas developed by Baudelaire had in fact already begun to take shape in early Romanticism. Music was seen as a model for both painting and poetry because of its direct impact on the listener, who is moved by its rhythms: ideally, forms and colours should be able to communicate directly with the spectator, without the intermediary of representational forms and their frequently 'literary' associations. Moreover, music achieved its effects through a rhythmic ordering of tones, which meant that for the Romantics, it had a universal as well as a subjective value, since rhythm was seen as the organizing principle of a universe pervaded by dynamism and change. Novalis saw all life as rhythm. Runge regarded the world as process, as eternal becoming.[79] Novalis and Tieck envisaged the possibility that painting might be able to create content independently of objects. Comparing music and painting, Novalis said that although music seemed to be free of imitation, while the painter was constrained to copy nature, in reality, the art of the painter was just as autonomous as that of the composer. He spoke of 'visual music' consisting of 'arabesques, patterns, ornaments'.[80] He saw poetry as an effect of the action of language, a 'mystery of language'.[81] Tieck's novel, *Franz Sternbald's Wanderungen* (1798), features an artist-hero, who sees his task as the expression of subjective feeling and mood instead of the depiction of external reality and believes that in the interests of expressivity, painting should renounce conventional action and composition in favour of a play of colours without 'meaning in the usual sense of the word'. He imagines a picture which would be 'no more than an artificial, almost trifling play of colours', but would none the less also be 'action, ideal, perfection'.[82] Later, in Gottfried Keller's *Der Grüne Heinrich* (1851–3), the artist-hero, who follows the dictates of feeling in his painting, arrives at an almost non-objective picture, which is described by a critic as attaining 'the perfect freedom of beauty'.[83]

Rimbaud and Mallarmé greatly admired Baudelaire, whom Rimbaud called 'le premier voyant, roi des poètes, *un vrai Dieu*' (*RO*, p. 351). Both poets emphasized the positive effects of obscurity and disruption of meaning,[84] as well as the power of the verbal medium to initiate thought independently of the conscious intention of the writer. The controversial 'Voyelles' sonnet is often cited in connection with Rimbaud's 'Symbolism', and the numerous synaesthesic effects in his poems show his search for a new 'language' in the spirit of Baudelaire's 'Correspondances'. Mallarmé's poetics of suggestion ('*nommer* un objet, c'est supprimer les trois quarts de la jouissance du poëme qui est faite de deviner peu à peu: le *suggérer*, voilà le rêve') are quintessentially 'Symbolist', although the 'maître' himself declared his opposition to literary 'écoles'.[85] It is sometimes argued that Rimbaud's poetics are not 'Symbolist' in the sense of using the poetic sign to 'point' away from and beyond the material world. However, this is to adopt an 'allegorical' view of Symbolism. Moreover, it would be wrong to characterize Mallarmé himself as an intellectual or abstract poet. He claimed to experience even the 'Néant' through sensation,[86] and his imagery is highly sensuous, while at the same time exploring the negative dimension of concrete objects, their 'presque disparition vibratoire' (*MOC*, p. 368). Rimbaud, on the other hand, aims to invent a new sensory reality (including language) of heightened intensity: 'J'ai essayé d'inventer de nouvelles fleurs, de nouveaux astres, de nouvelles chairs, de nouvelles langues!' (*RO*, p. 240).

For both poets, the poetic enterprise is one of radical destruction and reconstruction, which involves a restructuring of language itself, challenging the boundaries of conventional logic and inaugurating a new 'reality' of rhythmic relationships. Rimbaud is fascinated by rhythm, number and harmony: 'Toujours pleins du *Nombre* et de *l'Harmonie* ces poèmes seront faits pour rester. – Au fond, ce serait encore un peu la Poésie grecque . . . La Poésie ne rythmera plus l'action; elle *sera en avant*' (*RO*, p. 350). Rhythm – and rhythmic movements evoked in his poetry – takes on for Rimbaud a quasi-magical function, having an active influence on the world. Mallarmé sees the task of poetry as freeing both objects and words from contingent, individual existence by transposing them into a network of reciprocal relationships. Poetry itself should ultimately become the supreme form of Music, where music signifies 'Idée ou rythme entre les rapports'.[87] In fact, Mallarmé's supreme and unrealizable ambition was to 'transpose' the world into a rhythmic, permutational structure, the 'Livre'.[88]

Like Kandinsky and Mondrian, both Rimbaud and Mallarmé were interested in esoteric theories which explored mysterious, hidden connections between phenomena. Rimbaud's view of the role of the poet as a 'voyant' is likely to be connected with his readings on the occult.[89] He appears to have been conversant with many aspects of magic, alchemy and the cabbala, and to have been influenced by the poetic, anti-authoritarian and utopian writing of Jules Michelet and by the utopian socialism of Fourier, who, like Rimbaud, was intrigued by theories of number and harmony.[90] Mallarmé's library included books by Michelet and by Edouard Schuré, to whom he wrote admiringly of *Les Grands initiés*.[91] He was certainly influenced by occultism,[92] and the performances of the 'Livre' as he describes them resemble a magical ritual. He compares his attempt to produce a 'Grand Œuvre' with that of the alchemists[93] and refers sympathetically to the cabbalists (*MOC*, p. 850). The esoteric tradition, especially that of the cabbala, appealed to Mallarmé's sense of the mystery of language. In the cabbalistic tradition, letters had numerical and symbolic significance, and the word possessed creative power.

For Mallarmé, creative power resided in language itself: Valéry said of Mallarmé that he was 'un homme qui n'allait . . . à rien de moins qu'à diviniser la chose écrite'.[94] The 'Livre' is an 'expansion totale de la lettre' and the 'miracle . . . doué d'infinité jusqu'à sacrer une langue' (*MOC*, p. 380) is contained in the alphabet itself. 'Avec ses vingt-quatre signes, cette Littérature exactement dénommée les Lettres . . . système agencé comme spirituel zodiaque, implique sa doctrine propre, abstraite, ésotérique comme quelque théologie' (*MOC*, p. 850). Discussing the suggestive power of letters in the 'antiques grimoires', Mallarmé affirms that 'Le tour de telle phrase ou le lac d'un distique, copiés sur notre confirmation, aident l'éclosion, en nous, de caractères et de correspondances' (*MOC*, p. 646). Mallarmé is often thought of as a philosophical poet. Camille Mauclair even described him as 'l'applicateur systématique de l'hégélianisme aux lettres françaises'.[95] However, there is no evidence that he engaged in any systematic study of philosophy. Mallarmé wrote to Aubanel in 1866 of 'des monceaux de livres que je scrute et feuillette sans courage . . . Il est vrai que ce sont des livres de science et de philosophie, et que je veux *jouir* par moi de chaque nouvelle notion et non l'apprendre.'[96]

By the end of the nineteenth century, an extraordinarily wide range of sources was available to those who wished to explore 'correspondences' between matter and consciousness. Scientific approaches themselves seemed to lend credence to the substance of esoteric theories. Baudelaire referred almost in the same breath to Swedenborg and to the physiognomist Lavater who, 'limitant au visage de l'homme la démonstration de l'universelle vérité, nous avait traduit le sens spirituel du contour, de la forme, de la dimension' (*BOC* II, p. 133).[97] In fact, the use of 'scientific' methods was a central feature of nineteenth-century aesthetic theories. The Symbolists' search for a 'language' of colour and form and the Neo-Impressionists' interest in discovering laws determining the workings of colour and form found common ground in the discipline of psychophysics, a branch of psychology concerned with the relationship between physical stimuli and their effects on the organism, which gave 'scientific' status to investigations of the interaction between physical and psychic states. Psychophysics aimed at establishing empirical bases for the 'correspondences' between the sensual and the spiritual which were the leitmotiv of Symbolist theory.

The landmark in the founding of psychophysics as an experimental science was the publication of Gustav Fechner's *Elemente der Psychophysik* in 1860, but of more importance for painters were the works of Charles Blanc, whose *Grammaire des arts du dessin* appeared in 1867, and Charles Henry, who wrote prolifically on the psychophysical foundations of aesthetics in the 1880s and nineties.[98] Both Henry and Blanc drew substantially on Humbert de Superville's *Essai sur les signes inconditionnels dans l'art* (Leiden: C. van der Hoek, 1827), which claimed that the expressive value of the lines of the human face, whose 'direction' indicates emotions, is a source of 'unconditional' graphic signs.[99] De Superville, whose diagrams were reproduced by Henry, aimed to outline a universally valid system of pictorial signs based on the expressive lines of the human face.[100] Henry had close Symbolist connections and cited Baudelaire's sonnet 'Correspondances'.[101] His theories strongly influenced Sérusier and also Seurat and his followers. Henry set out to establish correlations between sensory stimulation and psychological effects. He argued that forms and colours are experienced as more or less pleasurable depending on the movements which they suggest (which he claimed to be able to measure): all reality could be expressed in terms of 'direction',[102] and the task of a scientific aesthetics was to determine which directions are associated with pleasure and which with displeasure.

These 'scientific' approaches to pictorial aesthetics sought to establish direct correlations between the physical properties of the pictorial medium and its suggestive and expressive effects. In contrast to Aurier, who denied any autonomous role to the material sign, many of the Symbolist painters themselves insisted on the importance of the sensuous qualities of colour and form. Maurice Denis protests that Aurier's Platonic formulas could not be applied to painters who were 'trop avides de sensation directe pour s'installer dans "le spirituel et l'intangible"'.[103] Denis wishes to distinguish between 'literary' or 'allegorical' Symbolism (from which he withholds the term 'Symbolist') and Symbolism proper, where the expressive force of the medium itself takes precedence over subject matter. 'Nous nous étonnons que des critiques renseignés . . . se soient plu à confondre les tendances mystiques et allégoriques, c'est-à-dire la recherche de l'expression par le sujet, et les tendances symbolistes, c'est-à-dire la recherche de l'expression par l'œuvre d'art'.[104] Gauguin argues against an 'allegorical' interpretation of his painting 'D'où venons-nous', on the grounds that 'mon rêve ne se laisse pas saisir, ne comporte aucune allégorie; poème musical, il se passe de libretto) citation Mallarmé' [sic].[105] Moreover, the painters emphasize the possibility of creating content through colour and form alone. Van Gogh wrote to Bernard: '. . . pour te rappeler que pour donner une impression d'angoisse, on peut chercher à le faire sans viser étroit au jardin de Gethsemane historique'.[106] For him, colour carries emotional charge. 'Exprimer l'amour de deux amoureux par un mariage de deux tons complémentaires, leur mélange et leur opposition, les vibrations mystérieuses de tons rapprochés. Exprimer la pensée d'un front par le rayonnement d'un ton clair sur un fond sombre.'[107] Early Symbolist painters, notably Redon and Moreau, had also spoken of the autonomous suggestive power of the pictorial medium. Moreau referred to the absence of a subject and to 'la plastique pure',[108] and Redon emphasized that the content of his pictures would depend on the imaginative response of the spectator to the medium itself. 'L'action [des lignes] qui en dérivera dans l'esprit du spectateur l'initiera à des fictions dont les significations seront grandes ou petites, selon sa sensibilité et selon son aptitude imaginative à tout agrandir ou rapetisser.'[109]

There can be no doubt that the aesthetics of Symbolist painting tended strongly towards abstraction, in theory if not in practice. Gustave Moreau is an interesting case in point. Moreau's commentary on his painting *Les Filles de Thespius* (1853, repainted 1883) shows that he believed that mythological themes could co-exist with 'la plastique pure'. 'Il n'y a pas de sujet, pas d'idée précise. C'est de la plastique pure.'[110] It has been suggested that Moreau went further than this and actually produced abstract works.[111] Clearly, some of the paintings in question are simply 'ébauches', studies for finished paintings, in which Moreau is working out the colour composition. It is impossible to say whether any of them were intended to be finished paintings. It seems unlikely, since this would have been such a radical departure from convention, but these paintings (oils and watercolours) are in any case extraordinary works, which show how close to abstraction Moreau had come.[112] His fascination with expressive colour must have been of great interest to his students Matisse and Rouault. Moreover, features of some Symbolist and also Impressionist paintings, such as flattening of perspective and non-realistic use of colour, directly influenced the emergence of abstraction.[113] The early work of both Kandinsky and Mondrian is, not surprisingly, heavily influenced by Neo-Impressionist techniques, notably Fauvism, as well as by Symbolist tendencies. It is interesting to observe the parallel between Baudelaire's response to the effect of a Delacroix painting placed at a distance and Kandinsky's reactions to a Monet *Haystack* canvas where he was unable to perceive the object, and to the sight of one of his own canvases placed on its side. (See *KCWA*, p. 363 and 369.) Kandinsky, like Baudelaire, was overwhelmed by the power of colour to affect him independently of the subject of the picture.

A major obstacle to the 'breakthrough' to abstract art was the fear that exclusion of the object would lead to art which was mere 'decoration'. Kandinsky saw clearly that going so far as to completely exclude objects meant finding new ways of ensuring that forms and colours would not be perceived as purely decorative. It was not enough simply to sever forms and colours from a figurative function: it was necessary to find new ways of creating content. Writing in 1911, Kandinsky maintained that:

If, even today, we were to begin to dissolve completely the tie that binds us to nature, to direct our energies toward forcible emancipation and content ourselves exclusively with the combination of pure colour and independent form, we would create works having the appearance of geometrical ornament, which would – to put it crudely – be like a tie or a carpet . . . Precisely because of the elementary state of our painting today, we are as yet scarcely able to derive inner experience from compositions with wholly emancipated forms and colours . . . the vibrations of the spirit, the movement of the soul that they conjure up, are too weak. (*KCWA*, p. 197)

Like the Symbolists, early abstract artists were anxious to establish a basis for the existence of connections between matter and consciousness which would support their belief in the possibility of creating content without reference to figurative objects or even, ultimately, to iconographical codes. Sources of such support ranged from the occult to scientific theories which questioned the immutability of matter. Kandinsky declared that when even 'positivistic science' is caught up in the 'spiritual revolution' and 'stands on the threshold of the dissolution of matter, then we can maintain that only a few "hours" separate us from this pure composition' (*KCWA*, p. 197). Later he would confirm that the splitting of the atom removed one of the most important obstacles from his path (probably a reference to Rutherford's discoveries of 1902). His friend Franz Marc declared that 'the theory of energy was a more powerful artistic inspiration to us than a battle or a rushing torrent'.[114] The concept of matter as energy both challenged the 'solidity' and indissolubility of objects in painting and pointed to connections between matter and the dynamics of 'inner' consciousness.

Kandinsky's and Mondrian's interest in Theosophy[115] is well documented but also controversial, being frequently seen as retrograde and also as marginal to their pictorial practices. For both painters, however, abstraction had a distinctly utopian dimension which was linked with Theosophy and its eschatological vision of the epoch of the 'great Spiritual'. Kandinsky led the way here, and his book *On the Spiritual in Art* (1911) was highly regarded by the artists of Mondrian's circle. It is well known that a sense of the apocalyptic and the eschatological was crucial to the Expressionist aesthetic.[116] These currents provided a powerful catalyst for Kandinsky's move into abstract art by encouraging his belief in the ephemeral nature of the material world (the 'object') and by providing him with a mission of spiritual regeneration. He closed *On the Spiritual in Art* with a reference to the coming of a new age, the 'epoch of the great spiritual' (*KCWA*, p. 219), a belief which found support in Blavatsky's prophecy that 'in the twenty-first century this earth will be a paradise by comparison with what it is now' (*KCWA*, p. 145) and in Steiner's apocalyptic imagery. Destruction was seen as a positive, creative force which would lead to the end of a materialistic era and to the birth of a better world. Kandinsky was doubtless also aware of the propagandistic value of these ideas in persuading the public of the value of his work. Interestingly, when *Reminiscences* was published in Russian in 1918, he saw fit to purge it of mystical elements. H. L. C. Schoenmaekers, the Dutch Theosophist, whose ideas interested Mondrian, wrote that: 'Our deliverance can only come about through a plastic force . . . deliverance is nothing but the dying away of our particular individuality in order to be resurrected . . . The positive mysticist knows for certain that this new world is a reality . . . it is a new earthliness, a

Art Center College of Design
Library
1700 Lida Street
Pasadena, Calif. 91103

new heaven.'[117] When he was exiled to London during the Second World War, Mondrian wrote to his brother: 'I kept feeling that it all showed a kind of guidance, and still think there is a form of higher control.'[118]

Kandinsky's and Mondrian's attraction to these mystical ideas was inseparable from their belief that colour and form could convey content independently of figurative representation. There are striking similarities between Kandinsky's descriptions of colour and those of Rudolf Steiner, whose colour theories were influenced by Goethe. Steiner argued that in the higher state of awareness which he called 'Imagination', sense impressions such as colours, sounds and smells could be experienced as creations of the soul or spirit, independently of objects in the real world. Kandinsky noted these ideas.[119] Steiner also describes the interaction between colour and consciousness, where the observer feels as if he is located *inside* the colour image. 'This sensation can only be described by saying that one no longer feels outside, but *inside* the colour image, and one is conscious of taking part in its emergence.'[120] He declared that 'I must live spiritually with colour, I must be able to rejoice with yellow, to experience the solemnity and gravity of red . . . I must be able to permeate matter with spirit, if I want to develop its inner capacities.'[121] Kandinsky owned a copy of *Die Kräfte der Farben* ('Colour Energies') by the chromotherapist A. Osborne Eaves,[122] and annotated Eaves' descriptions of the effects of blue and red with remarks and diagrams which are closely related to his description of the effects of blue and yellow in *On the Spiritual in Art* (*KCWA*, p. 178). He also owned a copy of Besant and Leadbeater's *Thought Forms*.[123] Here, as in Kandinsky's writings, the interaction between invisible thoughts and visible auras is described in terms of 'vibrations'. If the vibrations are powerful enough, the aura can be detached and becomes an independent 'being'. Besant and Leadbeater's book shows pictures of these 'thought forms', which are similar to shapes in some of Kandinsky's paintings, notably 'Woman in Moscow' (1912).

In 1921, Mondrian wrote to Rudolf Steiner that he had read several of his books and that Neo-Plasticism was the art of the future for true Anthroposophists and Theosophists.[124] Among the publications found in Mondrian's possession after his death were a speech by Steiner and a book by Krishnamurti. There was also a copy of *Het Nieuwe Wereldbeeld* (*The New Image of the World*) by M. H. J. Schoenmaekers, with whom Mondrian was acquainted.[125] Seuphor reports that Mondrian was also very enthusiastic (as was Mallarmé) about Edouard Schuré's *Les Grands initiés*.[126]

Theosophy provided Mondrian with an epistemological frame-work which influenced and/or corroborated his pictorial theories, including his notorious sets of binary oppositions, which were sum-marized by van Doesburg in 1929 as 'The equations of Mon-driaan': 'Vertical = Male = Space = Statics = Harmony. Hori-zontal = Female = Time = Dynamics = Melody.'[127] Blavatsky spoke of 'the celestial perpendicular and the terrestrial horizontal base line' and observed that 'the vertical line being the male prin-ciple, and the horizontal being the female, out of the union of the two at the intersection is formed the *cross*'.[128] Schoenmaekers, who called his system 'positive mysticism' or 'plastic mathematics', was fascinated by hidden structures: he asserted that 'we want to pene-trate nature in such a way that the hidden construction of reality is revealed to us,'[129] and held that contraries were real only in rela-tion to one another. Similarly, Mondrian affirmed that things could only be known through their opposites. ('*In time, opposite becomes known by opposite.*'[130]) Schoenmaekers too saw the cross as an essential symbol of the intersection of contrary forces. 'The figure, which objectivates the conception of a pair of absolute entities of the first order, is that of absolute rectangular construction: the cross.'[131] It embodies the contrast between vertical, active move-ment and horizontal, passive movement. Schoenmaekers wanted to discover the general behind the particular. He wrote: 'In art, it [positive mysticism] creates what we call, in the strictest sense "style". Style in art is: the general in spite of the particular. By style, art is integrated in general, cultural life.'[132] This could almost be Mondrian writing. The passages on colour are remarkably similar to Mondrian's views. 'The three principal colours are essentially yellow, blue and red. They are the only colours existing.'[133]

Mondrian and Kandinsky also drew on other sources of support for their views and/or their didactic aims. Mondrian cites Hegel, Schopenhauer, Spinoza and Bolland.[134] His interest in the concept of the 'new' is connected with the emerging discourses of modernism in the Netherlands, where, 'between 1890 and 1919, "the new" is re-articulated within an argument around the concept of the modern'.[135] Kandinsky refers to Nietzsche and was an admirer of Wagner and of the Belgian Symbolist poet and dramatist, Maeterlinck. Both Kandinsky and Mondrian were interested in psychophysical theories of colour and form. Mon-drian refers in *De Stijl* to the ideas of De Superville. Kandinsky was especially attracted to Goethe's colour theories, which emphasized the moral ('sittlich') effect of colour, and to theorists who followed Goethe in singling out yellow and blue as com-plementary colours. In his Bauhaus courses, he often refers to the optical theories of Wilhelm Ostwald (also cited by Mondrian and published in *De Stijl*), whose colour system has been described as 'n'étant lui-même, dans le langage de la science naturelle, qu'une transcription des idées de Goethe'.[136] Like Goethe, and Edward Hering, whose ideas he followed, Ostwald regarded yellow and blue as contrasting primaries.[137] Eugène Chevreul's *De la loi du contraste simultané des couleurs et de l'assortiment des objets colorés*, which had been published in 1839 and which influenced Neo-Impressionist painters, had analysed sensory data in terms of their effect on the perceiver. Adolf Hölzel claimed that the effects of simultaneous contrast of colour described by Chevreul were of an 'immaterial' nature, since the colours perceived by the subject could not be equated with the actual physical pigments.[138] Chevreul's theories were discussed by von Helmholtz, a physiologist, whose *Popular Scientific Lectures* (1876) were very widely read and to whom Kandinsky referred in his Bauhaus lectures. Helmholtz, like Goethe, stressed the psychological phenomenon of the irradiation of colours.[139] The physicist von Bezold, whose works, indirectly at least, were known at the Bauhaus (where Kandinsky taught from 1922 to 1933), wrote of the advancing and retreating movements of colours.[140] Line, too, was seen as dynamic. Helmholtz cited the geometrical definition 'that a point in moving describes a line, and that a line in moving describes a surface'.[141]

The factor widely seen in this period as uniting 'outer' form and 'inner' response was rhythmic movement. The works of Robert Delaunay, which are very relevant to this discussion, but which space does not allow me to discuss here, are explorations of 'rhythmic simultaneity'.[142] The notions of movement, rhythm and vibration were central to the *Jugendstil*[143] and Symbolist milieux with which Kandinsky was associated in Munich,[144] and it is precisely these concepts which were used by Kandinsky and others to justify the possibility of a kind of painting which could create content without recourse to representation. According to George Fuchs, director of the Munich Künstlertheater, 'the work of art . . . is not object, and not subject, rather it is *movement*, a movement which springs out of the contact and saturation of the subject with the "object"'. Fuchs wrote that the drama 'transforms itself . . . at the curtain line from a physical movement-rhythm into a spiritual movement-rhythm'.[145] Rhythm and movement in fact came to be considered the most crucial features of works of art, experienced directly by the receiver through the medium of the work itself, and potentially taking the place of conceptual meaning. Meschonnic cites Hervarth Walden, writing in *Der Sturm*: 'La décharge d'âme dégagée par l'œuvre d'art

dépend de celui qui la reçoit . . . La fonction d'une œuvre d'art
n'est pas d'avoir un sens ou de dégager certains sentiments. Une
œuvre d'art a pour effet, où le sens n'intervient pas, de provoquer
du mouvement dans le corps et dans l'âme . . . c'est pourquoi
l'essence de toute œuvre d'art est dans son rythme.'[146]

Jugendstil artists such as Hölzel, Obrist and Endell came to the
conclusion that linear and ornamental elements could produce
strong effects on the spectator independently of subject matter. Peg
Weiss has pointed out that Hölzel (whom Kandinsky knew) had
begun to make abstract line drawings before the beginning of the
century, and that there are remarkable similarities between some
of Hölzel's and Kandinsky's semi-abstract paintings in the early
years of the twentieth century.[147] Hölzel, Obrist and particularly
Endell (who was a student of Lipps, and who influenced Kandinsky) were amongst the many artists interested in Lipps' theory
of kinetic empathy. Although not mentioned by him, Lipps' ideas
were in fact very close to Kandinsky's.[148] Lipps was an important
influence on Wilhelm Worringer's *Abstraction and Empathy*, which
appeared in 1908.[149] Worringer restricted the application of 'Einfühlung' to objects of the 'real' world and saw abstraction as a
withdrawal from the external world. What he – unlike the artists –
failed to recognize was that empathy with the pictorial elements of
form and colour provided the basis for a new kind of content in art,
based on the spectator's response to the medium itself.[150]

Already in 1897, Endell had written of 'the beginning of a
totally new art, an art with forms that mean nothing and represent nothing and remind one of nothing; yet that will be able to
move our souls so deeply, as before only music has been able to do
with tones'.[151] He suggested that in perceiving line in time, the
observer experiences a sensation similar to that of perceiving an
object in movement, and that lines could express feelings associated with dynamic tensions.[152] For Hölzel, a common dynamism
united exterior perception and inner images and feelings: the
rhythmic movement of thought was accompanied by graphic
gestures of an intuitive, unpremeditated nature, which were later
subjected to conscious elaboration. Arthur Roessler affirms that
in Hölzel, 'the line in itself, running forward or drawing back into
itself, or as the contour of a form, can very well be significant not
only as ornament or as organically constructive necessity, but also
as expression, as a graphic sign, as the gesture of a thought or
feeling'.[153] Writing on the expressive force of line, Roessler echoes
van de Velde, who, like Lipps, conceived of line in dynamic
terms: 'line is a force [*Kraft*]', which embodies 'the sensuously
perceptible expressions of movements of the mind or soul'.[154]

***

We have seen that there is a widespread concern, in the intellectual environments of Symbolism and early abstraction, with mystical phenomena and with positivistic, pseudoscientific explanations of the rhythmic relation between consciousness and material objects. The foregrounding of rhythm is crucial both to challenges to conventional modes of meaning and representation and to interactions between 'matter' (here, the medium of the work) and imagining activity. Rhythmic structures which create these interactions effect changes in the way the receiver experiences the medium, and it is these changes, rather than conceptually definable subject matter, which constitute the principle content of the work. Rhythm can be conceived of as *a priori* and ineffable: in Romanticism, it took on a quasi-mystical significance as an expression of the hidden life of the cosmos, and the foregrounding of rhythmic features is frequently accentuated by 'cosmic' connotations. Rhythm can, however, be interpreted as an effect of the interaction between signifying processes and imagining activity rather than as a revelation of 'universal' truths. Imaginary space is a fiction grounded in the interaction of imagination with the medium itself and not in any 'noumenal' sphere.[155]

As a mode of response to disruptive signifying processes, imagination can be 'reconstructed' as an activity of the mind operating in a sensory mode, but exceeding conceptual and linguistic definitions, constituting an imaginary space of 'sensory unreality'. Although it draws on sensory elements derived from experience, in imaginary space these elements are combined in new ways and detached from representational or logical functions. Moreover, imagining activity can be separated from both metaphysical presuppositions and humanist models of an autonomous subject. Imaginary space can never be fully present to itself, because it is not purely imaginary, but also textual/pictorial, and the reflexive relationship between imagining activity and textual/pictorial space means that the receiver is made aware of this interaction and cannot effect a synthesis or 'Aufhebung' whereby the 'otherness' of this space would be fully absorbed into imagining consciousness. The medium is experienced as 'imaginary' at the same time as imagining activity itself is experienced as 'other', differed/deferred from itself through its inscription in poetic/pictorial space. Reflexivity enables the receiver to be positioned both 'inside' and 'outside' imaginary space, becoming – as we shall see in a moment with Rimbaud – both actor and spectator, conscious of the ephemeral and fictive status of imaginary space, which none the less infinitely expands the possibilities of the medium.

CHAPTER 2

Verbal hallucination: Rimbaud's poetics of rhythm

Je m'habituai à l'hallucination simple . . . Puis j'expliquai
mes sophismes magiques avec l'hallucination des mots!
(Rimbaud, 'Alchimie du verbe', *RO*, p. 230)

Toutes les possibilités harmoniques et architecturales
s'émouvront autour de ton siège . . . Ta mémoire et tes sens
ne seront que la nourriture de ton impulsion créatrice.
(Rimbaud, 'Jeunesse IV', *RO*, p. 298)

INTRODUCTION

Rimbaud's first poems were published in 1870, when he was
sixteen. By 1872 at the latest, he had started to write prose poetry.
Most of the *Illuminations* (nearly all of which are prose poems)
were published in 1886, but there has of course been considerable
controversy about when exactly these texts were written and their
chronological relationship to *Une saison en enfer*, which could be
interpreted as a rejection of the experiment of the *Illuminations*.[1]
The quite astounding diversity of critical responses to the *Illuminations* is indicative of the eclecticism of the texts themselves. It is
unlikely that any single approach could do justice to their extraordinary range of tones, intertextual references, formal patterns
and imagery. The controversies which they continue to provoke
in contemporary criticism are intimately related to the problems
we have been discussing here concerning imagining activity and
its relation to the text. The seeming incoherence of these texts has
frequently been accounted for by analysing them as expressions or
translations of a 'visionary' experience which has taken place
prior to the writing of the poem. According to many critics,
however, the incoherence of the *Illuminations* means that they are
irreducible to lived experience and can be described only in
purely textual terms, as 'self-referential' or 'autothematic'. This
attitude is in large part a direct reaction to the excesses of
reductive biographical criticism, and it is also a function of

hostility to a phenomenological 'ontology of vision' associated with the 'hope for a more revelatory visual experience'[2] and to the 'imaginaire' seen as a category prior and external to the signifying processes. In the eyes of several critics, the 'triumph of an opaque and self-referential language' goes hand in hand with 'the weakening of ocular primacy'[3] central to a humanist, subject-centred episteme.

What is particularly fascinating about the *Illuminations*, however, is precisely that they explode presuppositions about the centrality of the subject and fixed meanings at the same time as they create a new kind of 'visionary' writing – 'verbal hallucination' – which is intensely visual and sensory in terms of the 'imaginary' as we have defined it here. Imagining activity breaks away from mimetic models which allow 'picturing' of realistic images: the reader is not invited to mentally picture potentially realistic scenarios, but to engage in a process of projecting new, hitherto unthought of and ungraspable sensory spaces. Imaginary space is indefinable: it interacts with textual rhythms, but cannot be identified with them. It is fragmentary, highly sensory, and kaleidoscopically dynamic. The impossibility of grasping imaginary space and of synthesizing it with the text is experienced as both painful and pleasurable, since this indefinite 'deferral' enables imagining activity to continue indefinitely.

CRITICAL APPROACHES

The semantic disruption in these poems and the unrealistic quality of their imagery liberate imagination from the constraints of logic and mimesis. For most recent critics, however, the notion of 'image' is too closely tied up with outdated models of expressivity and a poetics of 'presence' to be seen as compatible with the semantic subversion and the decentred subjectivity of Rimbaud's texts. In fact, writing on Rimbaud, Jacques Plessen has suggested that the term 'image' should be replaced by 'signe', 'ce qui impliquerait . . . qu'on placerait le point de départ stratégique de l'explication dans la lecture du texte, vaste tissu sémiotique'.[4] There is a striking contradiction between the undeniable presence of a great deal of sensory, especially visual imagery, which has attracted the attention of many critics, and which has led to numerous comparisons between Rimbaud's imagery and painting (Suzanne Bernard, who has written about the *Illuminations* in relation to Impressionism and Symbolism, says that Rimbaud writes 'pour suggérer des impressions, pour nous faire "voir"'),[5] and the insistence on the part of many critics that these poems, because their meaning is undecidable, work against visualization and must be read in purely textual terms. Some have recognized the paradoxical combination of suggestiveness and disruption in Rimbaud's imagery, which can only be understood in the context of a non-mimetic imagination. According to Frohock, for instance, 'each word seems to create the beginning of a new spectacle, but no single one is allowed to grow',[6] and Houston points out that 'Rimbaud's visions generally include effects which are, strictly speaking, unrealizable in material terms, his medium being words and his esthetic postmimetic to an ample degree.'[7]

Earlier critical approaches to the *Illuminations* often sought to 'explain' the texts in terms of lived experience ('le vécu'), whether this be of a biographical and empirically verifiable, or of a purely 'spiritual' nature. This method, which 'traverse instantanément le texte à la recherche d'indices sur le monde réel',[8] is the first type of criticism singled out for attack by Tzvetan Todorov, who cites Rimbaud's assertion: 'ta mémoire et tes sens ne seront que la nourriture de ton impulsion créatrice' ('Jeunesse IV') in support of his view that the origin of a text should not be confused with its meaning. Given the difficulty of Rimbaud's texts and his enig-matic and colourful life, it is perhaps not surprising that there is an abundance of Rimbaud studies where, in the words of Plessen, 'au fond, le texte n'est traité que comme un prétexte pour nous parler des expériences supposées extraordinaires du poète'.[9] There is at present widespread agreement on the limitations of using the texts as data for biographical analysis. As Todorov points out, one serious drawback of this approach is its unsatis-factory circularity, since the texts themselves are often used to reconstruct biographical details.[10] However, the poems can also be read as accounts of a lived reality of an imaginary kind. Mario Richter rejects the notion that the text recounts what he calls a 'réalité biographique', and says of the poem 'Aube' that it inter-ests him as a '*réalité faite de mots écrits*'. But he sees this verbal reality as an 'aventure seconde', the first adventure being a '"réalité vécue", c'est-à-dire *passée*, expérimentée dans la vie passée'.[11] So the text is still seen here as 'secondary' to a lived experience.

Jean-Pierre Richard, arguably the most brilliant and seductive of the critics to explore the 'imaginaire' in literary texts, has analysed superbly the rich sensory texture of Rimbaud's imagery. Interestingly, however, certain facets of Rimbaud's texts appear to offer less suggestive potential in Richard's terms than do those of Baudelaire. Richard says of Rimbaud that: 'Ses visions s'étalent sur un écran sans épaisseur. Il n'y a rien derrière, ni épaisseur, ni abîme, ni être, ni néant, ni infini; elles ne laissent aucune place pour la divination, ni l'annonciation, ni la "conjecture" – c'est-à-dire pour la Beauté au sens baudelairien du terme.'[12] Writing on Baudelaire, Richard describes the 'analogie universelle' as an invitation to the imagination to 'suivre, à travers le réseau sensible des correspondances, le trajet d'une signification unique qui circulerait et s'approfondirait d'objet en objet pour revenir enfin, toute gonflée d'une richesse accumulée, se perdre en sa source première'.[13] Rimbaud, by contrast, 'ne remonte plus aux sources'.[14] Richard recognizes in the *Illuminations* a 'poésie objective', where 'l'imagination rimbaldienne se place à l'intérieur des choses mêmes'.[15] However, he does not explore the effects of the semantic disruption and the iconoclastic force of these texts, nor does he engage with the relationship between imagining activity and language itself which Rimbaud's subversive poetics creates.

For Todorov, the uniqueness of the *Illuminations* lies in their 'incohérence de surface'.[16] The *Illuminations* are, and are intended to be, incoherent, and to attempt to clarify them is to undermine this uniqueness, which consists in their lack of reference and of meaning. Reference is undermined by undecidability and discontinuity, and effectively eliminated by frankly contradictory affirmations.[17] 'Paradoxalement, c'est en voulant restituer le sens de ces textes que l'éxégète les en prive – car leur sens, paradoxe inverse, est de n'en point avoir. Rimbaud a élevé au statut de littérature des textes qui ne parlent de rien, dont on ignorera le sens – ce qui leur donne un sens historique énorme . . . leur message essentiel . . . est précisément l'affirmation d'une impossibilité d'identifier le référent et de comprendre le sens.'[18] According to Todorov, the main drawback of what he calls 'la critique paradigmatique', which aims at explaining syntagmatic incoherence through coherent paradigmatic structures, is that since any text can be analysed in these terms, this approach overlooks the precious uniqueness of the *Illuminations*. However, the view that incoherence can suffice as a criterion of literary worth is itself extremely dubious, and Rimbaud was not alone in inaugurating the category of 'difficult' texts.[19] The incoherence which Todorov regards as proof of this 'uniqueness' is in fact a commonplace of avant-garde writing.

This emphasis on incoherence focuses attention on the text as an end in itself. Other critics, notably Wing and Riffaterre, have argued that incoherence is merely a temporary obstacle on the way to interpretation and that interpretants *can* be found. These interpretants are themselves of a purely textual nature. Like

Todorov, Wing regards ambiguity as a positive attribute, because it is a means of internalizing reference. A poem which does not have a logically coherent subject must refer to itself. 'Ambiguity in an obscure context sets up a tautology, since semantic elements cancel normally appropriate associative links . . . Obscurity, then, is . . . a positive element of the poetic function . . . The words . . . enter into systems of association which establish the text as its own referent.'[20] Wing goes on to say that the texts of the *Illuminations* 'generate meaning in terms of purely verbal patterns of association'.[21]

In his *Semiotics of Poetry*, Riffaterre affirms that the 'literary' status of the text is dependent on its relationship to an intertext. 'To perceive the text as a transform of an intertext is to perceive it as the ultimate word game, that is, as literary.'[22] In literary language, the sign refers at once to its object and its interpretant, which is an intertext. According to Riffaterre, 'the reader's perception of what is poetic is based wholly upon reference to texts'.[23] Ungrammaticalities perceived when following the linear, syntactical development of the text can be resolved by paradigmatic readings which link seemingly incongruous words with other words in the same text or in different texts. The relevant reading of a text is not the first, but this subsequent, 'retroactive' reading,[24] in which the ungrammaticalities spotted in the first reading are related to one another in a paradigmatic network which constitutes the *significance* of the text. The semiotic reading, forced by the distortion of mimesis, is paradigmatic: the text functions as a signifying unit, and not as a signifying syntagm. The paradigmatic perspective causes the text to be read as an 'overdetermination' of an intertext which may be actual or hypothetical, and the new combinations discerned through this type of reading reveal the text's transformation of 'semic features, stereotypes, or descriptive systems'.[25] The poem can be read as an idiolect which results from the poet's 'wilful misreading of the sociolect's semantic relationships'.[26] The referent may be hidden, but 'in practice', claims Riffaterre, 'it can be found'.[27]

The purpose of hiding the referent is to jerk the reader from passivity to activity, to alert him to the relationship between text and intertext, to the 'constants' which link the 'ungrammaticality' to the intertext. This paradigmatic, intertextual dimension is a semiotic function which is diametrically opposed to 'mimesis', and therefore to visualization in Riffaterre's terms. 'The sign's dual reference [syntagmatic and paradigmatic] . . . sees to it that reading can never yield a stable, secure grasp of the whole meaning, *can never, above all yield visualization*.'[28] Literary language necessarily precludes visualization: 'The text hardly permits a visualization of what goes on. This alone . . . would suffice to establish . . . literariness . . . for cognitive language allows or at least seems to promise visualization.'[29] Riffaterre chooses Rimbaud's poetry 'to test out the relevance of semiotics to interpretation',[30] firstly because critics (he mentions Baudry and Kittang) are tending more and more towards the conclusion that Rimbaud's poetry allows of no stable interpretation, and secondly because it has given rise to theoretical generalizations, Todorov having deduced from it that there exists a category of 'undecidable texts' which are by definition inaccessible to interpretation. Riffaterre's analyses of 'Barbare'[31] and of 'Promontoire'[32] stress the purely verbal nature of the text's reference, explicitly opposing the textual to the visual, to the detriment of the latter.

Intertextuality, where individual texts function as 'rewritings' of other texts, is indeed a prominent feature of the *Illuminations*.[33] The problem with Riffaterre's account, however, is that the text/intertext functions as a privileged interpretant, allowing no space for imagining activity, whose sensory dynamics are an *effect* of language which cannot be equated with their cause. The dynamic and sensory mental processes involved in reading cannot be reduced to a purely textual play, any more than the text can be reduced to a pure 'expression' of a pre-existing imaginary space. The reflection of imagining activity in the space of the text itself, where linguistic patterns mirror the rhythms of imaginary space, does not mean either that imaginary space is 'blocked out' by the text or that the text is 'absorbed' into imagining consciousness. Analogies between textual structures and imaginary space do not collapse the imaginary into the textual by establishing the text as its own referent, but combine similarity with difference, maintaining a tension between text and imagination. Perception of analogies between textual and imaginary space causes the reader to become conscious of the imaginary dimension of the textual, and *also* of the textual dimension of the imaginary. Awareness of the textual dimension of imaginary space means that the 'I/eye' of imagining consciousness is experienced as 'other' (textual), while recognition of the imaginary dimension of textual space means that the text is not seen in purely linguistic terms, but also in relation to the sensory dynamics of imaginary space, and can be perceived as 'other' (imaginary). The interpenetration of textual and imaginary rhythms creates a 'diagrammatic' relationship between textual and imaginary space.

THE SPATIAL AND THE VISUAL

One of the most ingenious and original Rimbaud critics to date, Atle Kittang, while upholding the view that the text is essentially autotelic (reflexive and self-referential), deals with the problem of visual imagery by replacing the notion of the 'visual' with that of the 'spatial', which can more easily be assimilated to textual structures. The epithet 'spatial' applied to poetry can operate on many different levels.

On the structural level, 'spatial' characteristics have come to be associated with modernist writing in which disruption of syntax and of causal, chronological sequence privileges paradigmatic, simultaneous relationships over syntagmatic, sequential links. Saussure's linguistic theories and Jakobson's model of poetic language have strongly influenced critics' views of this 'spatial' dimension of language. Genette says that in defining language as 'un système de relations purement différentielles où chaque élément se qualifie par la place qu'il occupe dans un tableau d'ensemble et par les rapports qu'il entretient avec les éléments parents et voisins, il est indéniable que Saussure et ses continuateurs ont mis en relief un mode d'être du langage qu'il faut bien dire spatial'.[34] Jakobson connects this dimension of language with the poetic function when he declares that '*the poetic function projects the principle of equivalence from the axis of selection into the axis of combination*'.[35] In a poetic sequence, the choice of words which follow one another is based, not on logical progression, but on the principle of equivalence, on the relationships of the words to one another, for example similarity of sound patterns. In texts which are too long to be perceived in one glance, repetitions and symmetries which invite re-reading create a virtual spatial structure which causes the linear progression of the text to fold back on itself.

Semantically, the principle of equivalence normally governs selection of words which do not appear together in the same sequence. Applying this principle to the axis of combination (sequence) rather than to the axis of selection (substitution) can lead to juxtaposition of words which one would not normally find together. Spatial metaphors can be used to describe semantic 'écarts' which are opened up between signifieds in the figurative use of language and to designate kinds of writing which play with semantic 'spacing' rather than aiming to communicate meaning in a 'linear' fashion. Moreover, the concrete space of writing is also *visual*. A short text can be perceived as a single spatial unit on the page. Genette points out that 'la spatialité manifeste de

l'écriture peut être prise pour symbole de la spatialité profonde
du langage'. He goes on to say that since Mallarmé, we have
become more attentive both to the visual aspect of writing and to
its 'spatiality' in terms of atemporality and simultaneity.[36] For the
purposes of our study, 'textual space' will designate both the
concrete space of the text constituted by its visual and auditory
signifiers and the virtual space suggested by its spatio-temporal
rhythmic structures, which can generate a visual 'subtext'.

The concept of space is fundamental to Kittang's view of the
Illuminations as ludic, autotelic texts: the space of writing is seen as
autonomous and non-expressive, based on a 'poétique du faire'
rather than a 'poétique du dire'.[37] According to Kittang, the
subject of the *Illuminations* is a decentred, schizophrenic 'I', and
the oxymoronic semantics of these texts prevents them from being
the 'expression' of any subject-centred visionary experience.
Visualization is said to be dependent on semantic coherence:
Kittang refers to a 'confusion sémantique' (in 'Les Assis') which
'empêche tout effort de *visualisation* d'une image concrète quelconque'.[38] Discussing 'Barbare', he connects rejection of meaning
with rejection of vision. 'La lente constitution d'une vision com-
plète, d'un sens isotope, d'un message à communiquer, – voilà ce
telos que "Barbare" refuse de servir.'[39] 'Spatial' writing, on the
other hand (especially the rhetorical space of the oxymoron)
disrupts semantic coherence. Kittang explains the discrepancy
between the importance accorded in the *Illuminations* to descriptions, portraits and landscapes, which appear to draw attention
to a 'chose signifiée' and his own view of Rimbaud's writing as
leading to 'le retrait de la chose signifiée, et l'autonomisation du
signifiant'[40] by arguing that these descriptive genres can be seen
as *spatial* rather than visual, which means that they are 'en
correspondance parfaite avec la force spatialisante de l'écriture
rimbaldienne'.[41] In 'Génie', for instance, the emphasis on
opening and immensity on the level of the signified is said to be
reflected in the 'spatialization' of the writing, which foregrounds
dispersal and metonymy.[42] The 'thematic' level of the text – for
example in 'Barbare', the challenge to spatio-temporal constructs
with which the text opens – in fact designates 'l'espace propre,
multidimensionnel, du jeu scriptural',[43] which blocks the vision.
Kittang argues that this results in a 'retrait du signifié' and of the
visual element, even in the poems which are frequently described
as 'paysages' or 'architectures' and compared with Impressionism, such as 'Marine'. 'Promontoire' is singled out as the best
example of 'l'épaisseur textuelle des poèmes descriptifs, et de

l'évanouissement de la "vision" derrière la substance du signi-fiant'.[44]

The real 'theme' of these texts, then, is not the object(s) to which they appear to allude, but the very texts themselves, which are 'autothématiques'. Semantic structures are said to designate the form of writing in a given text. 'Le poème se met à refléter dans les structures sémantiques . . . la forme spécifique de sa propre écriture spatialisée.'[45] Kittang rejects thematic criticism because he considers its premises to be too close to the Romantic model of subjectivity which Rimbaud reacts against, and he cites Genette's objections to its 'postulat sensualiste, selon lequel le fondamental (et donc l'authentique) coincide avec l'expérience sensible'.[46] He none the less agrees with its structuralist method, according to which themes are treated as '[des] schémas con-ceptuels'.[47] Unlike sensory experience, conceptual schemas are reducible to abstract textual structures.

However, texts cannot be at once 'non-thematic' and 'auto-thematic', as Kittang claims: if a poem does not have a theme, it cannot take itself as a theme. He describes 'Barbare' as a 'jeu pur et extatique, loin de tout miroitement thématique, discursif ou référentiel', but argues that the musical imagery is to be read as 'un reflet *auto-thématique* de cette structuration répétitive com-plexe et musicale'.[48] Moreover, his subordination of the visual to the spatial and of the space of the signified to that of the signifier results in a hierarchical absorption of 'imaginary' into 'textual' space, where the sensory superabundance of imaginary space is translated into an abstract spatial vocabulary. The *Illuminations*, however, as their very title suggests, are highly visual, rather than purely 'spatial' texts. The title draws attention both to their visual/visionary qualities and to the connection between visual and verbal artistry. According to Verlaine, 'Illuminations' is an English word meaning 'coloured plates', which was the subtitle which Rimbaud had given his manuscript.[49] This explanation of the title clearly indicates connections with the visual arts. Indeed, there are several references to painting in the *Illuminations*, includ-ing a specific reference to 'gravures' in 'Après le Déluge', although the only painter mentioned by name is Boucher, in 'Fête d'hiver'. Moreover, the *Illuminations* have provoked comparison with extremely diverse painters and styles, ranging from Man-tegna to abstract painters, including Kandinsky.[50] Read as an English word, the title *Illuminations* suggests ornamentation of manuscripts, combining visual and verbal art.

'Illuminations' also evokes a combination of visual and

visionary experience. Both in French and in English, the primary meaning of the verb 'illuminer' concerns the action of casting light or of enlightening, depending on whether the action is sensory or spiritual: in French, the latter implication is particularly strong. (This possibility is reinforced by Rimbaud's interest in mystical, 'illuminist' thought.) Both the act of seeing and the presence of light are frequently evoked in the *Illuminations*. Light is associated with mystical experience because of its power to make things visible, to expand subjective awareness. It also has festive and decorative connotations, as in street illuminations. Interestingly, when describing the type of artefacts that he likes, Rimbaud mentions 'enluminures populaires' (popular engravings), and also other items which combine text and image, such as 'enseignes' and 'petits livres d'enfance': 'J'aimais les peintures idiotes, dessus de portes, décors, toiles de saltimbanques, enseignes, enluminures populaires; la littérature démodée, latin d'église, livres érotiques sans orthographe, romans de nos aïeules, contes de fées, petits livres de l'enfance, opéras vieux, refrains naïfs, rythmes naïfs' (*RO*, p. 228). This shows Rimbaud's interest in the bizarre, the artificial, the naïve and the erotic,[51] and also his predilection for eclectic and marginal artefacts rather than conventional 'high art'. He goes so far as to say, in typically iconoclastic fashion: '[je] trouvais dérisoires les célébrités de la peinture et de la poésie moderne' (*RO*, p. 228). The types of theatrical performance which he mentions are similarly unconventional: 'opéras vieux', and a little further on, 'vaudeville'. His declaration that 'un titre de vaudeville dressait des épouvantes devant moi' (*RO*, p. 230) suggests a 'hallucinatory' response to a verbal stimulus.

TEXTUAL AND IMAGINARY RHYTHMS

If the imagining process is in fact independent of identifiable objects and can take place both despite and because of semantic disruptions, then it does not 'vanish', as Kittang claims, behind the signifier. Disruption of logical coherence frees imagining activity and enables it to make new, unforeseen combinations, while its reflection in the text creates dynamic interactions between textual and imaginary space. Imaginary space in the *Illuminations* is both intense and unreal: in the words of Hugo Friedrich, it can be described as a 'sensory unreality'.[52] Incongruity and unreality here increase the vividness of sense impressions, leading to a heightened reality or 'surreality'. This is particularly noticeable in colour notations where the colour is strong, detached from objects, and animated by an autonomous dynamism, as in the description of 'Being Beauteous': 'des blessures écarlates et noires éclatent dans les chairs superbes. Les couleurs propres de la vie *se foncent, dansent et se dégagent* autour de la Vision' (emphasis mine). Synaesthesia, too, has the effect of both intensifying and 'de-realizing' sensation, as in the image 'les parfums pourpres du soleil des pôles' ('Métropolitain').

The *Illuminations* abound with references to auditory as well as visual sensation, and the richness and variety of sensory evocation are highlighted by the allusions, not just to one, but to several art forms. As well as painting and architecture, there are many references to music, theatre and dance. Rimbaud aims to construct a new language, which will embody the 'dérèglement de *tous les sens*' (*RO*, p. 346), semantic *and* sensory: he wants to find a 'langue [qui] sera de l'âme pour l'âme, résumant tout, parfums, sons, couleurs, de la pensée accrochant la pensée et tirant' (*RO*, p. 349). The *Illuminations* are markedly different from Rimbaud's earlier poetry, and it is significant that changes in content coincide with exploration of new forms. Rimbaud is not seeking simply to subvert conventional forms, but to draw on the auditory, visual, spatial and rhythmic resources of language in order to create interactions between textual and imaginary space. 'Le poète . . . devra faire sentir, palper, écouter ses inventions . . . inspecter l'invisible et entendre l'inouï . . . les inventions d'inconnu réclament des formes nouvelles' (*RO*, pp. 349–51).[53] Rimbaud's description of the relationship between what he calls 'l'hallucination simple' and 'l'hallucination des mots' may seem to confirm the view that the text is an expression of a pre-verbal 'hallucination'.

Je m'habituai à l'hallucination simple: je voyais très franchement une mosquée à la place d'une usine, une école de tambours faite par les anges, des calèches sur les routes du ciel, un salon au fond d'un lac; les monstres, les mystères; un titre de vaudeville dressait des épouvantes devant moi. Puis j'expliquai mes sophismes magiques avec l'hallucination des mots! (*RO*, p. 230)

A closer look, however, implies that there is a more complex relationship between 'l'hallucination simple' and 'l'hallucination des mots'.

The very term 'hallucination des mots' implies a mysterious complicity between verbal and visual hallucination. 'Visual' hallucination is described in terms which indicate ingenuousness: 'simple'; 'je voyais très franchement'. This ingenuousness is subsequently belied by the description '*sophismes* magiques' (emphasis mine). The word 'sophismes' connotes rhetoric and artifice, pointing up the fictive nature of the hallucination and suggesting that it may be a product of verbal magic: 'sophismes magiques' are a form of 'alchimie verbale'. This section of *Une saison en enfer* is entitled 'Alchimie du verbe'. Just as the directness and simplicity of visual hallucination are simultaneously affirmed and denied, the discursive clarity which appears to be attributed to words in '*j'expliquai* mes sophismes magiques avec l'hallucination des mots' (emphasis mine) is belied by the very term 'hallucination'. Words will not 'explain away' hallucination by distilling it into logical form, but will 'illuminate' it through a process of *verbal* 'hallucination'. (Synonyms of 'expliquer' are 'éclairer' and 'montrer': 'to shed light on' and 'to show'.) In the compositional process, then, one may surmise that 'l'hallucination simple' is not a purely visionary/visual experience which is then translated into verbal form, but that language plays an essential role throughout. In the process of reading (arguably more important, and certainly more accessible to examination), 'simple hallucinations' (imagining activity stimulated by verbal artifice) are created through associations between signifieds which suggest 'dérèglements de tous les sens' in both semantic and sensory terms, and 'verbal hallucinations' (textual 'illustrations' of this process) are created by textual structures – syntactical patterns, sound repetitions etc. – which indirectly suggest correspondences with imaginary space. The texts are 'illuminations' both because they open up new areas of imagining experience for the reader and because textual structures themselves reflect this imaginary 'scène'.

Although the sensory dimension of imaginary space is irreducible to linguistic structures, through textual rhythms, its dynamics can be experienced in the process of reading. In the *Illuminations*, Rimbaud forges new forms of poetic rhythm. In verse, rhythm is created, not only by metrical regularity, but also through interactions between the regular patterns imposed by metre and the natural diversity of linguistic texture.[54] In French, stress patterns are determined largely by syntactical structures, and prosodic divisions (which are based on syllable count) tend to coincide with syntactical units. However, as poets began to experiment with variations on fixed structures, they explored the possibility of creating tensions between syntactical and poetic divisions (for example through more daring use of *enjambement*). Such tensions and expectations based on fixed patterns do not occur in prose poems in the same way as in verse. None the less, the techniques which Rimbaud uses, while giving him greater flexibility, operate on similar principles. Indeed, rhythmic patterns in the *Illumi-*

nations often draw on conventional syllabic and formal structures.[55] ('Aube', for instance, opens and closes with a perfect octosyllable.)

Although it is frequently held that rhythm is a characteristic pertaining exclusively to temporal phenomena, in fact rhythm involves time *and* space, where 'space' can be understood both as a metaphor for simultaneity and as a concrete, physical space. As W. J. T. Mitchell points out, 'we cannot experience a spatial form except in time; we cannot talk about our temporal experience without invoking spatial measures'.[56] The etymology of the word 'rhythm' suggests that it was originally applied to the 'physical act of drawing, inscribing, engraving and was used to mean something like "form", "shape" or "pattern"': it was not until later that it was applied to the temporal arts, possibly through dance, where the positions of the body were related to patterns in the music.[57] Rhythmic structures involve spatio-temporal tensions which are experienced and activated by the receiver. Valéry has written of the impossibility of reducing rhythm to a question of 'l'observation objective'. 'Il est impossible à mon avis de *réduire le rythme à l'observ[ation] objective* . . . C'est ce que J'ajoute à la suite des perceptions enregistrables qui construit le rythme [*sic*].'[58] He describes the temporal experience involved in perception of rhythm as a 'liaison passé-futur, avec annulation du présent'.[59] The temporal dimension is essential to rhythmic patterns, which transform each present moment into a connection between past and future, but this mode of apprehension also involves simultaneous, 'spatial' perception. A crucial aspect of rhythm in verse forms is the establishment of a pattern which sets up expectation of fulfilment, for example for completion of a line with a rhyming word. These expectations encourage a 'spatial' mode of reading, where different layers of time are superimposed. A rhyme word, for instance, is linked in one's mind with previous rhyme words and leads one to anticipate the next. Rhythm, according to Valéry, is 'un système tel que la réponse régénère la demande'.[60]

In the *Illuminations*, syntactical units create structures of repetition and variation which, accentuated by sound patterns, constitute the basis of poetic form and encourage perception of the text in simultaneous, 'spatial' terms. Analogies between different parts of the text emphasize its paradigmatic, 'spatial' structure and interact with, rather than replace, the syntagmatic linear sequence which is followed in reading. Instead of metrical units countering syntactical progression, syntax itself becomes non-linear, reinforcing the anti-discursive semantics, and suggesting potentially 'spatial' readings. The relationship between syntactical units is not 'periodic', as in regular verse, where each element is perceived in the context of a formal (spatial and visual) structure of which the reader has prior knowledge. In the *Illuminations*, this structure is discovered in the course of reading. The paradigmatic dimension, which links each 'present' element with past and future, must be found by the reader in each poem. In this way, s/he participates more fully in the enactment of rhythmic structures.

André Guyaux has pointed out the privileged role played by individual lines in the structure of many texts in the *Illuminations*, a prominence which is reflected in the visual layout of the poems written in Rimbaud's hand.[61] Moreover, the 'spatial' dimension of rhythm in the *Illuminations* also takes on a virtual visual dimension, linking textual rhythms to the dynamics of imaginary space. Rhythmic structures, while not forming a visible shape on the page as in lines of verse, frequently suggest spatial patterns which can be visually transcribed: the poem thereby generates a visual 'subtext'. (This will be explained further below.) Unlike calligrammatic poetry, where the actual shape of the text on the page forms a 'picture', these correspondences between textual and imaginary space are based on rhythmic analogies which link imaginary movements with the dynamics of reading and create an ontological ambiguity which enables the text to be experienced as a site of imaginary space. The absence of direct pictorial depiction and of explicit metalinguistic or autothematic references emphasizes the autonomy of the text's imaginary dimension.

'BARBARE'

The texts chosen for analysis here have been selected because they exemplify a type of relationship between textual and imaginary space which is not equally in evidence in all texts of the *Illuminations*, but which is certainly a highly significant feature of the poetics of the collection as a whole.

The remarkable sensory suggestiveness of the imagery in 'Barbare' is intensified by the incongruous juxtapositions which remove it from any known reality. This imagery draws on real sensations but abstracts them from familiar contexts, resulting in the creation of a 'sensory unreality' which defies logical explanation. Riffaterre argues that the stereotyped discourse of 'barbarity' (he points out that 'barbare' can mean 'barbaric', 'barbarous', or 'barbarian') here plays the role of intertext. The text is the opposite of the pejorative stereotyped discourse of

barbarity, its 'parallel meliorative derivation', a message which is
unique to the poem's idiolect: it is 'a reinterpretation of *barbare*'.[62]
Wing, Todorov and Kittang also account for the text's violation
of discursive norms in terms of its metalinguistic implications.[63]
The mistake here is to assume that the challenge to logical
meaning nullifies the suggestive function of the imagery and
necessitates a purely textual interpretant. The challenge to
logical meaning liberates the suggestive force of the sensory
imagery and ensures that the text can never coincide with itself,
because at the very same moment that it points to itself, it also
points to an 'other', imaginary space. The intensity and incongruity of some of the semantic juxtapositions could be described
as 'surreal', and the unwillingness of critics to recognize the visual
import of the imagery is all the more surprising given that
surrealist poetry is known to be both irrational and visually
suggestive, and of course has close links with painting. The
suggestive force of this imagery can be fully appreciated only in
the context both of its semantic contradictions and of its sensory
import, which cannot be accounted for by paradigmatic patterns
or reduced to purely textual structures.

A striking example of suggestive, non-mimetic imagery here is
the sequence 'Les brasiers pleuvant aux rafales de givre, –
Douceurs! – les feux à la pluie du vent de diamants jetée par le
cœur terrestre éternellement carbonisé pour nous. – O monde!'.
Riffaterre explains this sequence in the context of his theory that
the poem is to be read as an idiolectical rewriting or reversal of
the stereotyped discourse of 'barbarity': this reversal takes place
within the text itself, and syntagmatic sequences are intended to
be read paradigmatically, linking cognates in different lines. The
'proper' reading is retroactive and vertical; there is a 'veritable
nullifying of linear reading'. The 'sole purpose' of the 'nonsensical
succession' of 'feux', 'pluie', 'vent' and 'diamants' is said to be its
'positive' transformation of 'brasiers' to 'feux', 'pleuvant' to
'pluie', 'rafales' to 'vent', and 'givre' to 'diamants' (the positive
character of the transformation is in fact apparent only in 'diamants'), where the first line is 'retroactively perceived as the
negative intertext of the second'.[64] In this way, the contradictions
of the imagery are resolved into a logical pattern.

However, a paradigmatic reading cannot replace the syntagmatic one, in which the reader experiences the shock of contrasts
and correspondences between the radically different sense
impressions associated with the images: heat, redness and
liquidity interact with cold, whiteness and crystalline hardness.
Fire successively coalesces with rain, wind, frost and diamonds in

a series of dynamic interactions which at once intensify contrasting sensations and force a shifting of the semantic boundaries which separate them. In 'les brasiers, pleuvant', and 'les feux à la pluie', the *rapprochement* of fire and rain, which causes a logical conflict, both intensifies their respective sensory associations and causes them to interconnect. The unity of 'fire' and 'rain' as homogeneous and distinct images is exploded as the heat of fire interacts with the coldness of rain and the rising motion of flames with the falling of water, suggesting liquid fire and molten rain, yet never crystallizing into a single image. The association of contradictory terms forces the reader to attempt a connection (there is a tendency towards synthesis), but this connection cannot be fully realized, since it defies logical categories and visual models derived from known reality. The demands made on imagination to envisage contradictory combinations mean that the *process* of imagining, rather than the formation of a definite image, becomes an end in itself.

The opening sequence of 'Barbare', 'Bien après les jours et les saisons et les êtres et les pays', forces imagination outside fixed categories of time and space. In 'le pavillon en viande saignante sur la soie des mers et des fleurs arctiques', the polyvalence of 'pavillon' (nautical flag, tent – possibly military – pavilion), and the ambivalence of 'sur' (suggesting 'down upon', 'over', or 'silhouetted against') encourage the reader to envisage interacting images which do not stabilize into a coherent whole. The 'pavillon' is not any particular, definable object, but a collection of characteristics which can be dispersed and re-combined with sense impressions associated with other objects. If read as 'pavilion', its connection with 'viande saignante' suggests an enclosed space of bleeding flesh – with possible sexual connotations – but its location at a height above the sea draws out the lexical implications of 'nautical flag', reinforced by 'soie'. The image is irreducibly bizarre, and suggests interaction between contrasting sensory experiences.

Blood pours down onto the sea, bringing together the oppositions of red and blue, hot and cold: 'la soie des mers' evokes the smooth texture of liquidity (and possibly the material of the flag), but also a softness which differs sharply from the implications of butchery in 'viande saignante'. Although the redness of the 'pavillon en viande saignante' contrasts with the blue of the sea, they are linked through softness and liquidity. 'La soie des mers *et* des fleurs arctiques' (emphasis mine) connects the flowers with the silky softness of the seas, while 'arctiques' suggests a crystalline whiteness which contrasts with the flow of blood which falls on them. The statement 'elles n'existent pas' indicates clearly the purely fictive status of the flowers, which are both 'present' and 'absent', making the reader aware that the 'fleurs' are a product of the interaction between language and imagination.

The third *verset*,[65] however, speaks of the unwelcome intrusion of a violent past which has partially receded but is still present in 'encore': 'Remis des vieilles fanfares d'héroïsme – qui nous attaquent encore le cœur et la tête – loin des anciens assassins –.' A further ambiguity is the relationship between different forms of 'barbarity', notably past and present. The 'vieilles fanfares d'héroïsme' and the 'anciens assassins' suggest a barbaric militarism and violence located in the past, from which the subject ('nous') wishes to be freed. But the second *verset*, which appears to be located after and beyond this earlier time, continues to evoke violence in the image of 'le pavillon en viande saignante'. The new epoch is itself violent, and there is no clear-cut distinction between a negative 'barbarity' and a positive opposite. However, whereas the old violence is based on militaristic and aggressive heroism, involving affirmation of opposition, the new epoch is marked by interpenetration of opposites and affirmation of difference as harmony rather than conflict. The dynamism of this interchange between apparently conflicting sense impressions and logical attributes is mirrored in imaginary physical movements which suggest increasing build-up and release of energy. The dripping motion of 'la viande saignante' is repeated and emphasized in the 'rain' of 'les brasiers, pleuvant': descent is associated with 'liquidifying'. This cascade is whipped up in 'rafales' (suggesting rapidity, as well as movement of air) and, as the interchange of sensations and cosmic substances is intensified, downward movement is redirected in a climactic ascent where the diamonds are shot upwards: 'jeté[s] par le cœur terrestre éternellement carbonisé pour nous'. The upward shower of diamonds involves imaginary interaction between fire, water, air and earth: the 'brasiers pleuvant aux rafales de givre' and the 'feux à la pluie du vent de diamants' combine these elements in a mood of increasing ecstasy, expressed by the exclamations 'Douceurs!' (*verset* 5), ' – Douceurs! – ' and ' – O monde! – ' (*verset* 6).

The diamonds are the culmination of these interactions in that they combine the transparency of water with the hardness and coldness of ice, yet they are also the product of great heat and 'flash' with the flickering light of fire ('les feux d'un diamant'). However, they are not a final synthesis: the combustion is 'eternally' repeated, as are the interaction between sensations and movement in different directions. The 'vieilles retraites' and the 'vieilles flammes' of the next *verset* (7) are a reminder of former times (echoing the 'vieilles fanfares' of *verset* 3), and are followed in *verset* 8 by a repetition of 'brasiers', which, as in *verset* 6, is followed by a liquid element, 'les écumes', suggesting again the presence of the sea. In 'la musique, virement des gouffres et choc des glaçons aux astres', the icicles, like the diamonds, are sent soaring upwards to join their celestial counterparts, the stars. The association of diamonds, icicles and stars highlights their glittering, crystalline qualities and the interchange between earth and sky, where downward motion involves liquidity and dispersal, and upward motion involves crystallization and synthesis.

'La musique', in apposition to 'virement des gouffres' and 'choc des glaçons aux astres' seems to be produced by this cosmic movement: dynamism thus becomes literally harmonious, and a further synaesthesic element is implied in the association of music with 'virement', which can refer to change in colour tone, as well as to change in direction and circular, whirling motion. The choice of the word 'virer' is interesting here, since it is a nautical term which reinforces the nautical implications of 'pavillon', and also because its indication of change in direction precedes the ninth *verset*, where the ascent of the 'glaçons' to the stars (the ecstatic implications of which are expressed by the exclamation which opens the ninth *verset*, 'O Douceurs, o monde, o musique!'),[66] is followed by a descent to the surface of water (presumably 'la soie des mers'), and then a further descent to the 'fond des volcans et des grottes arctiques'.

'Et là' does not designate any particular location, but 'sueurs', 'larmes', and 'flottant' indicate a return to a liquid medium, associated with the sea mentioned earlier. The second exclamation of 'o douceurs!' is occasioned, not by crystallization and synthesis, but by dissolution and dispersal. In the line 'et là, les formes, les sueurs, les chevelures et les yeux, flottant', the multiplicity and dismemberment of parts of the human body and their dissolution in a liquid landscape (emphasized by 'les larmes blanches, bouillantes') evoke an extraordinary dreamlike spectacle, in which dismembered organs merge with the landscape: 'Et là, les formes, les sueurs, les chevelures et les yeux, flottant. Et les larmes blanches, bouillantes, – o douceurs! – .' 'Et là' is at once definite and vague, implying a precise but unnamed location, and the plurality of 'les', together with the lack of an individual subject whose presence could unify these physical attributes, intensifies the impression of randomness and the breakdown of individual identity in a merging of self and world. The references to 'chevelures' and 'yeux', parts of the female anatomy so often praised by poets, suggest here a female presence. This is reinforced by the mention of tears in 'larmes blanches, bouillantes' and the 'voix féminine' which follows, emphasizing the sexual, maternal and emotional connotations of the imagery in the poem. The descent of 'la voix féminine' to the depths of the 'volcans' and the 'grottes arctiques' brings together these places of extreme heat and cold, and repeats the descent of the falling blood at the beginning.

The combination of whiteness, heat and liquidity in 'les larmes blanches, bouillantes' is significant, since earlier, whiteness had been associated with cold, crystalline qualities. By the end of the poem, such oppositions no longer operate. Here, a state of utopian pleasure has been achieved, where desires have been gratified through dynamic interaction between contrasting qualities. The liquidity of this *verset*, with its 'sueurs', 'flottant', and 'larmes blanches, bouillantes', evokes both bodily fluids (including milk from the breast) and 'la soie des mers' of the refrain ('mer' of course suggesting 'mère'). There is a preponderance of liquid over crystalline imagery, and a return to the downward movement of the 'refrain' in the descent of the female voice. One could perhaps see here a triumph of feminine gentleness over masculine 'barbarity'. However, masculine and feminine paradigms interact in a way which suggests that what is taking place is rather a breaking down of these distinctions, like that between distinct semantic and sensory attributes.

The ideal state sought after in 'Barbare', then, is one where differences are mobilized into dynamic interactions. Violence is no longer opposed to gentleness, since instead of being aggressive and confrontational, as in the case of the 'anciens assassins', violence (or 'barbarity') becomes an affirmation of life forces which are both powerful and loving. Connotations of masculinity and femininity, strength and gentleness, fiery energy and liquid softness are organically interconnected. These 'barbaric' forces also operate on the level of semantic structures: the oxymoronic imagery of 'Barbare' challenges boundaries between separate semantic attributes. This reading can be linked with contextual data which confirm on different levels the utopian quality of this imaginary space. The 'anciens assassins' are probably connected with the sect of drug-crazed assassins ('Haschischins') written about by Michelet and Baudelaire,[67] and also with Rimbaud's poem 'Matinée d'ivresse', whose images of 'fanfares atroces' and 'assassins' echo 'Barbare', and where torture is exalted as a means to 'démence', sought after by Rimbaud as a source of poetic

a

1

Bien après les jours et les saisons, et les êtres et les pays,

b

2

Le pavillon *en viande saignante sur la soie des mers et des fleurs arctiques;*

(elles n'existent pas.)

4

Oh! *Le pavillon en viande saignante sur la soie des mers et des fleurs arctiques;*

(elles n'existent pas)

c

3

Remis *des vieilles fanfares d'héroïsme -*

qui nous attaquent **en**core le *cœur* et la tête -

loin des **anciens** assassins -

5

Douceurs!

7

(Loin des vieilles retraites et des vieilles flammes,

qu'**on** **ent**end,

qu'**on sent**,)

10

Le pavillon...

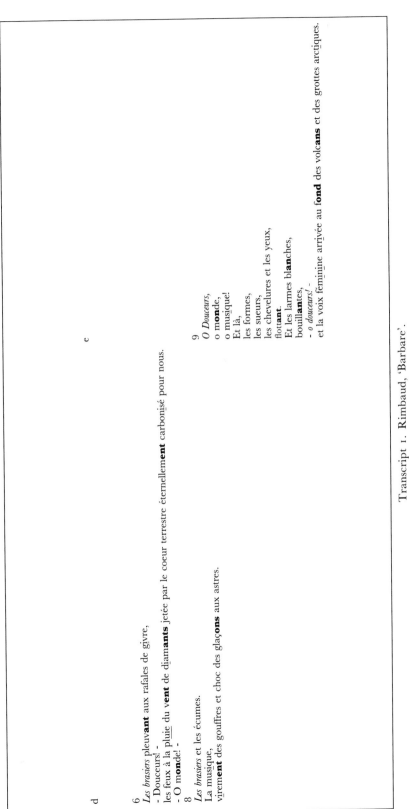

d

e

6
Les brasiers pleuvant aux rafales de givre,
- Douceurs! -
les feux à la pluie du **vent** de diamants jetée par le coeur terrestre éternellement carbonisé pour nous.
- O monde! -

8
Les brasiers et les écumes.
La musique,
virement des gouffres et choc des glaçons aux astres.

9
O Douceurs,
o **monde,**
o musique!
Et là,
les formes,
les sueurs,
les chevelures et les yeux,
flottant.
Et les larmes blanches,
bouillantes,
- *o douceurs!* -
et la voix féminine arrivée au **fond** des volcans et des grottes arctiques.

Transcript 1. Rimbaud, 'Barbare'.

inspiration. The rejection of 'fanfares d'héroïsme' and 'anciens
assassins' in 'Barbare' seems to herald a new epoch where mental
states can be altered without the self-inflicted torture of which
Rimbaud speaks in one of his famous 'lettres du voyant'.[68]
Moreover, it has often been pointed out that Rimbaud was
attracted to primitive, barbaric forms of existence which he saw
as more civilized, in a sense, than 'la barbarie moderne' of
contemporary society ('Villes II'). Michelet, whose work
Rimbaud admired, speaks of the contemporary tendency to
compare the progress of 'le peuple' (as opposed to the nobility or
the bourgeoisie) to the barbarian invasion. He regards this term
as a compliment, and wishes to identify himself with the 'chaleur
vitale' of the Barbarians, which is opposed to the 'culture' of the
higher classes.[69] The notion of barbarity can have positive as well
as negative connotations, and in 'Barbare', the positive aspects
are seen as following on the negative ones, which, it is hoped, can
be discarded.

One of the most remarkable characteristics of imaginary space
in the *Illuminations* is its highly orchestrated dynamism. Rhythmic
correlations beween the movements which take place in imaginary space and textual patterns can themselves be envisaged in
spatial terms which contribute to the reader's reflexive awareness
of the imagining process. Through the dynamic interaction
between the textual and the imaginary, the process of reading
itself participates in the dynamization of difference which constitutes the utopian dimension of the text.

In 'Barbare', as in other texts of the *Illuminations*, rhythmic
structures are created by relationships between syntactical units,
which are 'framed' by punctuation and linked through parallel
formal and semantic patterns. Here, however, the text is also
divided into *versets*, which form visible units on the page and
create a periodic structure based on the repetition of the second
verset, 'Le pavillon . . .'. Both of these rhythmic structures can be
transcribed in visual terms (see transcript 1). In the transcript,
different syntactical units are written on separate lines, to highlight the spatial structure which they suggest. The recurrent nasal
vowels [ɔ̃] and [ɑ̃] are indicated in bold type and the narrow
vowel [i] is underlined, while italic type indicates repetition of
entire words or phrases in the same column. These repetitions
consolidate the tripartite structure of the text, which is also shown
in the transcript, where the *versets* follow one another in series of
three. *Verset* 4 is a repetition of *verset* 2 (suggesting a 'return' to this
part of the text). Similarly, *verset* 7 contains many repetitions of
verset 3, suggesting another 'return', and so on for another group

of three, which suggests a parallelism between 6 and 8 (both of which open with the words 'les brasiers'). After 9, the longest *verset*, the recurrence of 'le pavillon' suggests a return to *versets* 2 and 4, creating a cyclical, rotating structure.

This cyclical structure is especially significant because of the 'circular' trajectory followed in imaginary space, where the falling of blood and of rain is succeeded by the rising movement of the diamonds, in turn followed by the descent of the female voice to the depth of the 'volcans' and the 'grottes arctiques' and then a return to the height of 'le pavillon', which completes the 'circle' and starts the cycle again. The pattern of *versets* in 'Barbare' forms a three-part structure, where the second element of one sequence becomes the first of the next (similar to *terza rima*), which can be represented spatially as follows:

$$a \quad b \quad c$$
$$b \quad c \quad d$$
$$c \quad d \quad e$$
$$b$$

The movement suggested here indicates alternating progression and regression, where the 'return' movement creates a vertical or paradigmatic axis, which indicates a possible 'direction' of reading. As in the 'pantoum' form, which is composed in 'rimes croisées', and where the second and fourth lines of the first stanza become the first and third of the second, the structure of 'Barbare' combines an alternating pattern (a b c b c d c d e b) with a circular, enclosed one (a b c b c d c d e b). Morier's description of the 'pantoum' form emphasizes its connection with movement by describing it as 'twirling', and comparing it with certain dances where three steps forward are followed by two backwards[70] (in 'Barbare', three 'steps' forward are followed by one backwards).

The visual transcript of 'Barbare''s rhythmic structures shows the iconic and 'diagrammatic' relationship between movements in imaginary space and the dynamics of reading. Rhythmic patterns create a textual 'space' which reflects the movement and position of objects in imaginary space. In addition to the cyclical structure of the text which highlights circular movement, the transcript foregrounds the relationship between horizontal and vertical axes, suggesting the height and depth which are essential to the position and movement of objects in imaginary space. The 'le pavillon' series, for instance (*versets* 2, 4 and 10), forms a vertical line, which suggests movement both up and down: down as the poem progresses, and up at the end, leading on from 'le pavillon' of *verset* 10 back to 'en viande saignante' of *verset* 2. The ninth contains far more short units than the other *versets* (again, this is made visible by the transcript), indicating the fragmentation which is in fact taking place in imaginary space, and the vertical column of text suggests the downward trajectory of the voice, which leads to the lowest point in the text, both in imaginary and textual space, as the voice arrives 'au fond des volcans et des grottes arctiques'. (The final 'le pavillon' appears further down, but since it is a repetition of *versets* 2 and 4, it also invites an 'ascent' to the first 'le pavillon' at the top of the page.)

Rimbaud exploits the freedom of the *verset* form to create strong rhythmic contrasts, where long sequences alternate with shorter ones. These contrasts exist both within individual *versets* and between one *verset* and another, and can be observed in visual form in the transcript. It is noticeable that the longest lines in the text ('le pavillon . . .', 'les feux à la pluie . . .', 'virement des gouffres . . .', 'et la voix féminine . . .') are also those which suggest movement through space. 'Les feux à la pluie du vent de diamants jetée par le cœur terrestre éternellement carbonisé pour nous' is both the most dramatic movement and the longest line in the text, and its length is emphasized by the position of this line between the short exclamations 'Douceurs!' and 'O monde!'. 'Douceurs' is in fact a key word in the text, which is repeated four times. It even occupies a whole *verset* to itself (*verset* 5), whose place in the transcript indicates a strategic position. 'Douceurs' contains an anagram of 'cœur': in the transcript, 'cœur' appears in *verset* 3, above *verset* 5, and also in *verset* 6, which follows it. The notion of 'heart' is crucial both in terms of emotion and of a central point (the centre of the earth), in each case associated with heat, figurative and literal and melting. In the 'textual space' shown by the transcript, 'Douceurs!' appears in a central cavity, at the 'heart' of the text.

The second exclamation of 'Douceurs!', in *verset* 6, again plays a pivotal role, occurring just before the dramatic reversal of the direction of 'pluie' to the upward shower of diamonds. Here, its centrality is also emphasized by the semantic correspondences mentioned above between 'brasiers' and 'feux', 'pleuvant' and 'à la pluie', 'aux rafales' and 'du vent', and 'de givre' and 'de diamants', forming an interlocking circular pattern with ' – Douceurs! – ' at the centre:

brasiers/pleuvant/rafales/givre/Douceurs/feux/pluie/vent/diamants

The sequences 'les brasiers, pleuvant aux rafales de givre' and 'les feux à la pluie du vent de diamants' are in fact isosyllabic, and if the ending of 'brasiers' is read as a diaeresis and the mute 'e' in 'pluie' is sounded,[71] then both are alexandrines. This reading emphasizes the semantic paradigms discussed above, where the 'hemistichs', 'les brasiers, pleuvant' and 'aux rafales de givre' correspond to 'les feux à la pluie' and 'du vent de diamants'. 'Douceurs!' is thereby set apart in a central position, which is highlighted by punctuation.

Like ' – O monde! – ' in the same *verset*, and ' – o douceurs! – ' in *verset* 9, ' – Douceurs! – ' is isolated for special attention, 'set' between dashes, like stones in a ring, around which imaginative associations can crystallize. Here, punctuation is used to graphically suggest a circular, ternary structure, where the repetition of the first dash in the third position suggests movement around a central element (here, the word 'Douceurs'). Curvature is also indicated in the repeated capital 'D' of 'Douceurs', and in the letter 'o', which recurs in the lyrical exclamations: 'Oh! le pavillon' (in the fourth *verset*), ' – O monde! – ', 'O Douceurs, o monde, o musique!', and ' – o douceurs! – '. Punctuation plays an important role in 'Barbare', as in many texts of the *Illuminations*, largely because syntax is based on juxtaposition rather than logical co-ordination and subordination. The use of dashes is particularly noticeable: they appear in *versets* 3, 6 and 9. Dashes do not explain the nature of the connection between clauses, and they indicate fragmentation and the omission of logical links. This sense of incompleteness is emphasized by the syntactical structure of 'Barbare', where the opening adverbial clause, 'Bien après les jours et les saisons' is followed by 'le pavillon en viande saignante' rather than by a clause with a finite verb, as one would expect, and the series of statements of which the rest of the poem consists are juxtaposed without ever leading to a logical conclusion. The anti-linear syntax is accentuated by parentheses, which occur in the repeated *verset* 2, and in *verset* 7. In '(elles n'existent pas)', they are a graphic indication of the intervention of critical reflection which provokes awareness of the purely fictive nature of imaginary space. The sequence '(Loin des vieilles retraites . . .)' in *verset* 7, also in brackets, again suggests critical reflection and comparison between 'real' flames (those which can be heard and felt) and those which do not really exist.

The effect of the repeated use of 'et' to link nouns and clauses in apposition is similar to that of the dashes, since it merely juxtaposes, without explanation. The repetitions of 'et' 'les' and 'des' also contribute to the dense harmonic pattern of the text. The sounds which conclude the first and second 'lines' of *verset* 1, 'sais*ons*' and 'p*ays*', are echoed very frequently throughout (see transcript), and whole words and phrases are also repeated. The sound patterns based on repetition of 'et' emphasize the symmetries created by juxtaposition of parallel syntactical units. In the first *verset*, symmetry is both syntactical and phonetic: 'Bien après les jours et les saisons' is picked up in '*et les* êtres *et les* pays'. In *verset* 9, '*Et là*' introduces a tripartite anaphoric sequence, '*les* formes, *les* sueurs, *les* chevelures', followed in turn by '*et les* yeux . . . *et les* larmes . . . *et la* voix' (where 'et la' echoes the first 'et là'). It is significant that *verset* 9, which is the most ecstatic in tone, with its triple exclamation of 'O Douceurs, o monde, o musique!', should have a particularly dense harmonic texture.

.The 'vertical' correspondences between *versets* 2, 4 and 10, 3, 5 and 7, 6 and 8, are reinforced by repetitions and symmetries. 'Remis des vieilles fanfares' corresponds to 'Loin des vieilles retraites' ('vieilles' recurs again in 'vieilles flammes'), while 'loin' itself echoes 'loin' of *verset* 3. There are also semantic similarities, which do not involve repetition of the same words. The effect of the 'vieilles fanfares d'héroïsme', which 'nous attaquent encore le cœur et la tête' is comparable to that of 'des vieilles retraites et des vieilles flammes', which can be heard and felt (each emphasizes sensory impact), all the more so since the vocabulary of both sequences has strong military connotations. The opening words of *verset* 8, 'les brasiers', repeat those of *verset* 6. Moreover, in *verset* 8, the sequence 'Les *brasiers* et les *écumes*. La musique, virement des gouffres et choc des *glaçons* aux *astres*' corresponds to 'brasiers/ pleuvant/rafales/givre: feux/pluie/vent/diamants' in *verset* 6, and the ascent of 'glaçons' to the stars at the end of *verset* 8 is a symmetrical reversal of the descent of 'givre' at the beginning of *verset* 6. In retracing this connection, the reader in fact moves 'backwards' and 'upwards' in the text. Just as objects are released from gravitational pull, the reader is liberated from the linearity of language.

The textual space suggested by repetitions and symmetries is multidimensional, involving syntactical, semantic, phonetic and graphic patterns and suggesting rhythms of reading which are both temporal and spatial. In discovering and observing textual structures, the reader can become the spectator of his/her imagining processes, reflected in textual space, which are thereby also experienced as 'other' and 'fictive'. In 'Les Ponts', as in 'Barbare', textual rhythms suggest a correlation with positions and movements in imaginary space (see transcript 2). 'Les Ponts' is a particularly interesting text from the point of view of imaginary space, since it foregrounds descriptive and visual registers without

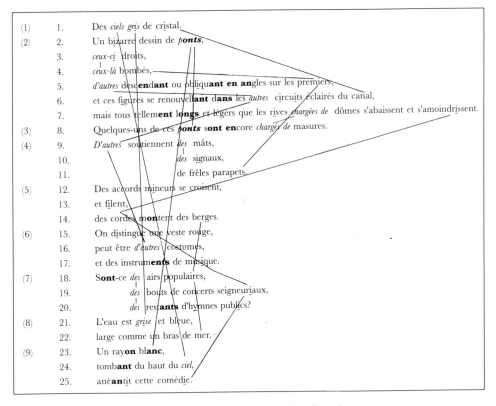

(1)   1.   Des *ciels gris* de cristal.
(2)   2.   Un bizarre dessin de ***ponts***,
       3.   *ceux-ci* droits,
       4.   *ceux-là* bombés,—
       5.   *d'autres* desc**end**ant ou obliqu**ant en an**gles sur les premiers;
       6.   et ces figures se renouvell**ant dans** les *autres* circuits éclairés du canal,
       7.   mais tous tellem**ent longs** et légers que les rives *chargées de* dômes s'abaissent et s'amoindrissent.
(3)   8.   Quelques-uns de ces *ponts* sont en**core** *chargés de* masures.
(4)   9.   *D'autres* soutiennent *des* mâts,
     10.   *des* signaux,
     11.   de frêles parapets.
(5)   12.   Des accords mineurs se croisent,
     13.   et filent,
     14.   des cordes mont**ent** des berges.
(6)   15.   On distingue une veste rouge,
     16.   peut être *d'autres* costumes,
     17.   et des instrum**ents** de musique.
(7)   18.   **Sont**-ce *des* airs populaires,
     19.   *des* bouts de concerts seigneuriaux,
     20.   *des* rest**ants** d'hymnes publics?
(8)   21.   L'eau est *grise* et bleue,
     22.   large comme un bras de mer.—
(9)   23.   Un ray**on** bl**anc**,
     24.   tomb**ant** du haut du *ciel*,
     25.   ané**ant**it cette comédie.

Transcript 2. Rimbaud, 'Les Ponts'.

depicting objects in a realistic manner. The imagery in 'Les Ponts' is unrealistic in a different way from that of 'Barbare'. In 'Barbare', contradictory sense impressions are combined in ways which work against the formation of stable, coherent images, while in 'Les Ponts', the 'unreal' quality of the imagery stems also from its evocation of forms and movements rather than of individual, identifiable objects.

Here, perhaps because of the implied pictorial references, critics have in fact been more responsive to the visual images which the text contains, even if they are not of a conventional kind, and some commentators have suggested similarities with abstract painting. Broome describes 'Les Ponts' as 'a "paysage" writing and re-writing itself inconclusively before the imaginative eye: lines criss-crossing, intertwining, describing different shapes and angles as an excitement to the structural sense; some aspects expanding and coming into prominence, others shrinking: a dance of planes and perspectives; a dynamic arrangement of fragments of shape, sound and colour'.[72] According to Hugo

Friedrich, in 'Les Ponts', 'the objects are distilled into pure movements and geometric abstractions'.[73] Wing writes that in 'Les Ponts', 'the term "dessin" suggests the abstractness of the vision: it is evidently the sequence of relations between objects, related by an affectively charged vocabulary, not the objects themselves, which will be the subject of description'.[74] Felsch says of the language here that 'it is not pictorial in the same way as that of "Après le Déluge" and yet to a certain extent it evokes stronger pictorial associations, with a modern, abstract painting'.[75]

It has been speculated that Rimbaud may have been influenced by Impressionism, and comparisons with abstraction have also been made. Felsch continues: 'We were referring to the emphasis on the linear structure of the bridges. The effect of the individually specified objects is more like that of the elements highlighted by painterly technique in an Impressionist painting.'[76] Albert Py compares the opening of 'Les Ponts' with 'the tonality, the fog which drowns so many paintings by Monet and Sisley'.[77] These comparisons with both Impressionism and abstract painting are apparently contradictory, since Impressionism is often contrasted with abstraction, as indicated by Wing's remark that description in Rimbaud is 'anti-impressionistic and anti-representational'.[78] However, this juxtaposition is particularly interesting in view of the tendencies towards abstraction within Impressionism, to which contemporary viewers were particularly sensitive.[79]

Moreover, Friedrich points out that the term 'abstract', used of 'Les Ponts', 'is not limited to the non-perceptual and the non-objective', but refers rather to the foregrounding of form which disrupts connections 'between the subject matter and reality'.[80] In other words (and this could also be said of abstract painting), the emphasis is on the presence of forms rather than on the absence of objects. Forms are foregrounded at once in the text and in imaginary space and are both sensory and dynamic, suggesting patterns of movement. The principle of using rhythmic structures, rather than individual objects, as the source of pictorial significance, is fundamental to the emergence of abstraction, and the discovery of this principle in linguistic and poetic forms links Rimbaud's poetry to abstraction in painting. Description of realistic objects becomes secondary to the creation of rhythmic correspondences between textual and imaginary space. However, as will be argued in chapter 6 below, the linguistic medium of poetry does not lend itself to the exclusion of meanings in the same way as the exclusion of objects in painting (although, as we shall see, even 'abstract' painting frequently re-introduces 'objects'). In Rimbaud, 'abstract' structures are foregrounded, not through exclusion of reference to objects, but through semantic ambiguities and focussing on processes and movements in ways which cause them to be seen primarily from the point of view of rhythmic relationships.

There are several terms in 'Les Ponts' which point to a connection with the visual arts: 'ciels', 'dessin', 'figures'. ('Ciels' is a plural form used only with reference to painting.) 'Figures' is particularly suggestive: as well as a pictorial figure, it could mean, for instance, a rhetorical figure of speech (emphasizing the connection between visual and verbal 'hallucination'), an illustration, such as an engraving,[81] or the path traced by a dancer's movements. The 'on distingue' of line 15 (see transcript 2)[82] indicates the presence of a spectator, and the references to music and costumes and the word 'comédie' at the end of the text suggest a theatrical performance. The movement attributed at the beginning of the text to the lines of the bridges, which one would presume to be static, could be explained by transference of the dynamism of the act of seeing onto the lines themselves.[83]

Like many other images in the *Illuminations*, the capacity of the 'bridges' for regeneration and metamorphosis deprives them of any stable identity. Their strangeness is apparent from when they first appear: their proliferation, their varying shapes, their apparent dynamism and their spatial ambiguity prevent them from forming a coherent picture. The vision exerts a fascination arising from the complexity of the network of lines and forms and crystalline textures which unfold before us. Paradoxically, the spatial illogicalities and semantic uncertainties in the description of the bridges which make it impossible to resolve the conflicting visual data in a coherent image actually increase the intensity of the desire to visualize, as the reader is teased and tantalized by the seductive forms and textures which elude the possession and control of the imagining gaze.

It has of course been suggested that the 'objects' referred to in 'Les Ponts' are in fact the structures of the text itself. According to Kloepfer and Oomen, 'the text names bridges and their forms, but they are not realized in a concrete, precise visual impression which corresponds to something existing in reality – the bridgelike quality is realized rather in the linguistic structure'.[84] As in 'Barbare', however, the lack of a 'concrete, precise visual impression' stimulates open-ended imagining activity, which cannot be reduced to textual referents. The metapoetical implications of 'les ponts', which are referred to as 'ces figures', draw the reader's attention to the connections between textual and imaginary space which are enacted by imagination itself.

The transcript shows the visual space suggested by the syntactical and phonetic patterns of the text. This transcript follows principles similar to 'Barbare', except that in lines 9–11 and 18–20, instead of starting a new line, parallel syntactical units have been placed directly under one another, to emphasize their symmetry. Repeated words or phrases are indicated in italics and linked with lines. Repetition of [i] sounds is indicated by underlining, and that of the nasal vowels [ɔ̃] and [ɑ̃] by bold print. Lines also connect similar sounds occurring at the line endings. The short first sentence contrasts with the long second sentence (which has been described as 'bridgelike'), and the repetition of the first 'ciels' in 'ciel' of the final sentence of the text suggests a 'framing' of the central 'picture'. Especially in the second sentence, syntactical and phonetic structures correspond to patterns of movement in imaginary space. Like the bridges, the second sentence seems to move by means of some mysterious inner power, propelled by the expanding force of its syntactical structures: it is drawn out by juxtaposition of subordinate clauses, by the conjunctions 'et' and 'mais', and its momentum is built up and maintained by the repetition of present participles, which emphasize continuation. 'Ceux-ci droits' and 'ceux-là bombés' indicate the shape of the bridges' contours, but these shapes also imply movement (the extension of straight lines, the swelling of curved lines), which is emphasized in line 5 by the description of geometrical movement in dynamic terms: 'd'autres descendant ou obliquant en angles sur les premiers'. The connection between form and movement is highlighted by the dynamic 'obliquant'; 'oblique' is in fact normally an adjective qualifying position (form), and is not used as a verb.

The relationship of the bridges to one another is ambiguous. 'Obliquant en angles' could indicate, not only two-dimensional diagonal movement, but also recession into three-dimensional space, especially since the other bridges are seen first (they are described as 'les premiers'), perhaps because they are positioned in the foreground. At the same time, 'sur les premiers' suggests that the oblique forms in fact project down over and even in front of 'les premiers', emphasizing their length. Both the extension of these bridges and the zigzagging movement suggested in 'obliquant en angles sur les premiers' are paralleled in the structure of this syntactical unit (line 5), which is much longer than the preceding ones, and where the ending of 'premi*ers*' leads back to 'bomb*és*' (see transcript 2). Reverse movement is also suggested by the frequent 'return' to similar sounds in 'descendant ou obliquant en angles'. (The shape of the letter 'z' in 'bizarre' reflects the zigzag pattern of the bridges.) These nasal sounds also suggest a return to 'ponts', and the continuation and repetition of visual forms indicated by the phrase 'et ces figures se renouvell*ant*' is also enacted phonetically in the 'renewal' of these sounds in 'se renouvellant dans'.

This segment (line 6) is somewhat longer, suggesting the expanding horizon of 'les autres circuits éclairés du canal', while the circularity implied by 'circuits' is enacted in the return from 'les *autres* circuits' to 'd'*autres*' in line 5 (see transcript 2). ('Circuits' can also mean 'circumlocution', linking up with the rhetorical meaning of 'figures'; 'oblique' also has rhetorical connotations.) 'Autres' will again be repeated in lines 9 and 16. This phrase also suggests that the bridges are seen reflected in the water of the canal ('et ces figures se renouvellant dans les autres circuits éclairés du canal'). The crystalline quality of the sky in 'des ciels gris de cristal' could refer to its refracted reflection in the water (a very 'Impressionistic' effect). If the linear structures are reflections, this could account for their complexity and dynamism. The ending of the final word of line 6, 'can*al*', echoes the final word of line 1, 'crist*al*', creating a textual 'reflection' which reinforces the suggestion that the 'ciels gris de cristal' are reflected in the canal, as are the bridges themselves.

The 'longs et légers' which qualifies the bridges in line 7 is reflected in the elongation of this very long section of the sentence. Sound patterns and isosyllabism connect 'mais tous tellement longs et légers', suggesting the rising movement of the bridges, with 'dans les autres circuits éclairés' (both nine syllables) in line 6, which in transcript 2 appears further up than line 7, where the 'rives' are sinking. This sinking of the banks is presented as a direct consequence of the length and lightness of the bridges: 'mais tous tellement longs et légers que les rives chargées de dômes s'abaissent et s'amoindrissent'. As frequently occurs in the *Illuminations*, illogical happenings are presented in a highly logical manner, just as the pattern of the bridges is described with formal precision and yet is spatially confusing. There is no obvious reason why the length and lightness of the bridges should have such a negative effect on the banks, or why the banks should be described as 'still' loaded with hovels. However, if a picture or visual scene is being evoked, then the sinking and shrinking of the banks could be an optical effect, created by the contrast between the long, dynamic and 'light' lines of the bridges (bare geometrical forms, unburdened by

objects) with the more highly ornamented, 'heavy' banks, which
are 'chargés de dômes'.

Sentences 3 and 4, however, bring about changes in the bridges
themselves, some of which are described as 'chargés de masures',
and others as 'supporting' 'mâts', 'signaux', and 'frêles parapets'.
Some of the bridges are encumbered with objects which weigh
them down, and this suggestion of weight, as well as the rather
unpleasant connotations of 'masures' and the fragility of the
'parapets', introduce a negative note. The piling up of objects is
reflected in the anaphorical structure of 'des mâts, des signaux, de
frêles parapets', which can be seen in visual form in the transcript.
Both 'mâts' and 'signaux' have nautical connotations (masts and
ships' signals). As noted above, the bridges are described in line 6
as 'ces figures', suggesting that the term 'ponts' can be read as a
figure of speech. Since 'mâts' and 'signaux' are both objects which
one would expect to find on ships, this implies that the 'ponts' can
also be seen as ships' bridges.

These 'figures', moreover, are infinitely flexible, and in the
second half of the text, the linear dynamism of the bridges takes a
musical form. Music is well known as a model for non-represen-
tational art forms, and its presence here emphasizes the abstract
quality of the linear pattern of the bridges. The fifth sentence of
the poem, 'Des accords mineurs se croisent, et filent, des cordes
montent des berges', where 'croiser', 'filer' and 'monter' recall the
movement of the bridges, adds a synaesthesic, musical dimension
to the dynamism of the bridges. The verb 'filer' is quite extraordinarily suggestive in this context, where it can be read in
several relevant ways, for example to pay out rope (linking up
with 'cordes'), to go at a speed of (nautical), to pass by quickly
(dynamism), to go in a straight line (visual), to hold a note
(musical), to extend a metaphor (poetic). If 'cordes' is read as
'ropes', then it ties in with the nautical vocabulary, and brings
together the visual image of '*cor*des' with the auditory sensation of
'des a*cor*ds'. However, it can also be read as 'strings', prefiguring
the 'instruments de musique' of the next sentence.

The connection between musical sound and visually perceived
movement in 'des accords mineurs se croisent, et filent', where
musical patterns are described in visual terms, suggests rhythmic
patterns which are visual, auditory and also non-figurative in
that they cannot be linked with any specific object. The last word
of line 13, 'filent', echoes the last words in lines 7, 17, 19, 20 and
25: 's'amoindr*i*ssent', 'mus*i*que', 'seigneur*i*aux', 'publ*i*cs', and
'coméd*i*e', forming a textual counterpart to the network of
connections and movements in imaginary space. The phonetic

symmetry of '*des* ac*cor*ds' and '*des cor*des' also forms a textual
'chord', whose structure is parallel to that of the anaphoric
sequences 'des mâts, des signaux, de frêles parapets' and 'des airs
populaires, des bouts de concerts seigneuriaux, des restants
d'hymnes publics', which also suggest chordlike simultaneity, and
whose visual pattern in the transcript is similar to that of a
musical chord.

Musical associations are increasingly strong: 'des accords' and
'des cordes' are followed by 'instruments de musique', 'airs populaires', 'concerts', and 'hymnes publics'. 'Costumes' suggests that
this may be a theatrical performance. (In fact, the last word of the
text is 'comédie'.) However, there is a marked contrast between
the gravity-defying, dynamic movement of the 'ponts', the
'accords' and the 'cordes', and the stasis and hesitancy which
follow. ('Mineurs' already suggests a certain melancholy and
instability.) This alteration is connected with a change of perspective, in 'on distingue': whereas previously, the multiplicity of
perspectives and angles allowed for no privileged point of view
'outside' the image, the spectator is now external, looking in, and
his vision is limited and uncertain: 'on distingue . . . peut-être . . .
sont-ce . . . ?' These rational, analytical enquiries seek to identify
and classify specific objects, contrasting with the flexible sensory
dynamism of the earlier part of the text. Under this scrutinizing
gaze, the music becomes more incomplete, dissolving into fragments: 'des bouts de concerts seigneuriaux, des restants d'hymnes
publics'.

As these images disintegrate, water reappears ('l'eau est grise et
bleue, large comme un bras de mer'), reinforcing the implication
that all these fictive images had 'appeared' in the mobile, reflecting surface of the water itself. The grey colour of the water recalls
and reflects the grey skies of the opening sentence, and the sky
also appears in the last sentence: 'Un rayon blanc, tombant du
haut du ciel, anéantit cette comédie.' The connection between
'des ciels *gris* de cristal' and 'l'eau est *grise* et bleue' suggests a
reflexive circularity and a downward movement from earth to
sky, enacted in textual space along a vertical axis linking 'gris'
and 'grise' (see transcript 2). This downward movement prefigures the descent of the 'rayon blanc' in the next sentence. Also,
the fact that the water is 'grise et bleue', whereas the 'ciels' in line
1 were 'gris', suggests that the sky has cleared, preparing for the
advent of the 'rayon blanc'.

The 'rayon blanc', rather than a welcome alternative to grey-
ness, is an intrusion which disintegrates the closed, autonomous
space of the vision. The dash which sets this sentence apart from

the rest of the text emphasizes its exteriority, and its whiteness and position in the sky suggest sunlight, a natural source of illumination which contrasts with the refracted luminous quality of the painted crystalline skies at the beginning and the possibly artificial light of the 'circuits éclairés du canal'. 'Reality' and 'artifice' have been closely intertwined throughout, where the terms 'ciels', 'dessin', 'figures', followed by the theatrical terminology, have made it difficult to ascertain whether the scene is 'real' or 'artificial'. The separation of viewer and viewed in 'on distingue' suggests a distinction between the 'real' world of spectators and the 'artificial' world of art, whose final 'splitting', brought about by the destructive intrusion of the 'external' world in the 'rayon blanc', provokes the (possibly) ironical description of the 'vision' as a 'comédie'.

This duality provokes the reflexivity of self-consciousness, whose 'lucidity' reveals the fictitiousness and the textual dimension of imaginary space. Moreover, this unmasking is itself part of its textual *mise en scène*. The 'rayon blanc' is in fact both outside the vision framed by the grey sky above and the grey water below, and inside it, in that it forms part of the imaginary 'paysage'. In case the reader had missed the close parallels between the rhythmic structures of textual and imaginary space, at the end of the poem, with consummate artifice, the self-destruction of imaginary space through the dissolving action of the 'rayon blanc' is synchronized with the dissolution of the text into the blank space of the page. 'Un rayon blanc, tombant du haut du ciel, anéantit cette comédie.' Paradoxically, the textual inscription of imaginary rhythms prevents imaginary space from coinciding with itself by constituting it as both textual and imaginary, never fully present either in the text or in imagining consciousness. It is therefore not surprising that the *same* sentence which confirms the synchrony and isomorphism of imaginary and textual space also dismisses this 'mimesis' as a 'comédie'.

It is not a coincidence that so many poems of the *Illuminations* contain theatrical imagery: the enactment of textual in imaginary space is paralleled in imaginary space, enhancing the reader's awareness of the performative aspect of reading itself. There are many reasons why one would expect Rimbaud to be interested in theatre: stage sets ('décors') create spaces which are both real and artificial, and theatrical performances can be highly eclectic in both content and tone, even involving circuslike entertainment, as in vaudeville. Most importantly of all, perhaps, the movement of the actors and the changing of sets gives theatre a dynamic and self-transforming quality which is an essential characteristic of the imaginary space of the *Illuminations*.[85] Theatrical elements in the *Illuminations* have been closely studied by critics.[86] In addition to allusions to performance, such as 'comédie' ('Les Ponts'), 'costumes', 'pièces', 'comédie' ('Parade'), 'scène', 'jouer', 'chefs d'œuvre dramatique' ('Vies I'), 'opéra-comique' ('Fête d'hiver'), 'théâtre' ('Villes II'), 'l'ancienne Comédie', 'tréteaux', 'scènes lyriques', 'l'opéra-comique' and 'notre scène' ('Scènes'), the *Illuminations* abound with 'theatrical' characteristics, such as settings which evoke stage scenery (for example, 'Fête d'hiver', 'Fleurs') and suggestions of role-playing, as in 'Fairy' ('l'ardeur de l'été fut confiée à des oiseaux muets'), and 'Enfance IV', where the roles are played by 'je' ('je suis le saint . . . je suis le savant . . . je suis le piéton . . . je serais bien l'enfant abandonné'), as they are in 'Bottom' ('je me trouvais . . . en gros oiseau bleu'). These allusions to theatre play on the tensions in the *Illuminations* between belief and disbelief in the reality of the vision, where the reader is alternately positioned as 'actor' and 'spectator', 'enacting' imaginary rhythms in textual space and acting as a spectator of his/her own 'performance'.

As mentioned above, 'Promontoire' is singled out by Kittang as being the best example of 'l'évanouissement de la "vision" derrière la substance du signifiant'.[87] Arguably, however, the non-mimetic, oxymoronic and eclectic imagery of this text liberates imagining activity from logical constraints, while analogies between imaginary and textual space invest the complex textual structures with an imaginary dimension. 'Promontoire' is a particularly striking instance of textual density and complexity, corresponding to the architectural structures described. The word 'Promontoire' does not name the text itself as a referent, but, as with 'Les Ponts', the metapoetical implications of this 'figure' draw the reader's attention to the parallels between textual and imaginary space. The text is presented in one long paragraph of continuous prose, which emphasizes its density, and the recurrence of capital letters also foregrounds the density and impenetrability of the textual surface. The first sentence divides into four segments, the first of which is very long, and the last three of which gradually diminish in length, a curious contrast to the extension of the 'promontoire' being described. The 'promontoire' is composed of 'cette Villa' and 'ses dépendences', which becomes 'cet Hôtel' in line 15 and 'Palais. Promontoire [*sic*]' in line 25 (see transcript 3). The second sentence is immense, composed of twenty-one sections, and the process of finding one's way through it is similar to exploring an enormous labyrinthine structure, whose complexity defies comprehension. The complex

1.   L'aube d'or et la soirée frissonnante trouvent notre brick en large *en face* de *cette Villa* et de ses dépendances,
2.   qui forment *un promontoire* aussi étendu que l'Epire et le Péloponnèse,
3.   ou que la grande île du Japon,
4.   ou que l'Arabie!
5.   Des fanums qu'éclaire la rentrée des théories,
6.   d'immenses vues de la défense des côtes modernes;
7.   des dunes *illustrées* de chaudes fleurs et de bacchanales;
8.   de grands canaux de Carthage et des Embankments d'une Venise louche;
9.   de molles éruptions d'Etnas et des crevasses de fleurs et d'eaux des glaciers;
10.   des lavoirs entourés de peupliers d'Allemagne;
11.   des talus de parcs singuliers penchant des têtes d'Arbre du Japon;
12.   *les façades* circulaires des 'Royal' ou des 'Grand' de Scarbro' ou de Brooklyn;
13.   et leurs railways flanquent,
14.   creusent,
15.   surplombent les dispositions de *cet Hôtel*,
16.   choisies dans l'histoire des plus élégantes et des plus colossales constructions de l'Italie,
17.   de l'Amérique et de l'Asie,
18.   dont les fenêtres et les terrasses à présent pleines d'éclairages,
19.   de boissons et de brises riches,
20.   sont ouvertes à l'esprit des voyageurs et des nobles-
21.   qui permettent,
22.   aux heures du jour,
23.   à toutes les tarentelles des côtes,–
24.   et même aux ritournelles des vallées *illustres* de l'art,
25.   de décorer merveilleusement *les façades* du Palais. *Promontoire.*

Transcript 3. Rimbaud, 'Promontoire'.

articulations of this sentence with its subordinate clauses, which suggest the 'dépendences' of the villa-promontory, can be seen clearly from the transcript.

The oxymoronic opening image, 'l'aube d'or et la soirée frisso-nante' prevents any concrete visualization and is yet character-istically evocative of a sensory imaginary space, filled here with the delicate, shimmering light of the transition from dawn to day and/or from dusk to night. ('Frissonner' suggests in particular the reflection of light on water; it could also refer to a very slight breeze, and can indicate trembling caused by emotion.) This pattern of 'non-mimetic' imagery continues throughout the text, where images drawn from an immense variety of contrasting places and epochs, referred to in the plural even when they are proper nouns (for example, 'de molles éruptions d'Etnas') explode any possibility that a 'real' landscape is being referred to, yet the imagining gaze is treated to a colossal, kaleidoscopic feast of changing vistas, comprising landscapes, vegetation, processions, railways, ornaments, geological spectacles and architectural extravaganzas, combining the natural and the man-made, from mythological times to the present and extending to all corners of the globe. The effect of the eclecticism and immensity of the spectacle is overpowering in that the scene cannot be grasped as a single image, but this merely adds to its fascination.[88]

Vision is foregrounded throughout the text: the evocation of light in 'l'aube d'or et la soirée frissonante' is followed by 'des fanums qu'éclaire la rentrée des théories' (line 5), and then 'd'immenses vues' (line 6), 'des dunes illustrées' (line 7), and 'pleines d'éclairages' (line 18). Moreover, the 'promontory' is a prime vantage point. 'Notre brick' locates a subject/spectator, situated 'en large en face de cette Villa et de ses dépendances'. The size and complexity of the villa-promontory suggests the overpowering and exclusion of the spectator/reader. However, the seemingly impenetrable 'Hôtel' is then 'hollowed out' by the railways. Following on the dense anaphorical structure of lines beginning with indefinite articles which designate a static accumulation of objects, the conjunction 'et' in line 13 signals a turning point: the static nominal structure is dynamized by the introduction of three finite verbs following 'et leurs railways': 'flanquent', 'creusent', and 'surplombent', which have the effect of opening up both the sentence structure and the 'Hôtel'. 'Creusent' is the shortest line in the text (line 14), followed in the transcript by an open space, which emphasizes the hollowing action of the railways.

The 'Hôtel', which is now described in aesthetically superlative terms, opens up to the outside world: its windows and terraces are filled with lights, inviting the '*voyageurs*' (recalling the 'brick' of the first line and suggesting '*voyeurs*') to gain access to this 'visionary' space: 'cet Hôtel . . . dont les fenêtres et les terrasses à présent pleines d'éclairages, de boissons et de brises riches, sont ouvertes à l'esprit des voyageurs et des nobles'. This illumination and 'opening up' of the 'Hôtel' lead to a final aesthetic transformation, in which the 'heures du jour' (suggesting daylight, a return to the 'aube d'or' of the beginning), tarantellas (a dance to very rhythmic music, or the dance music itself) and ritornellos (a short piece of instrumental music repeated before verses in a song or recurring motifs in a dance), which are associated with the 'vallées illustres de l'art', combine in order to 'décorer merveilleusement les façades du Palais. Promontoire', where the word 'Palais' is itself a 'decoration' which imbues the 'promontoire' with royal splendour.

'Tarentelles' and 'ritournelles' both evoke repetitive, circular structures. In textual space, this circularity is enacted in phonetic patterns, where 'façades' (line 25) echoes 'façades circulaires' (line 12) and 'en face' (line 1), while 'Palais. Promontoire' refers back to 'promontoire' (line 2), which is in turn connected with 'cette Villa' (line 1) and 'cet Hôtel' (line 15). 'Heures du jour' also suggests a return to line 1, and 'illustres' echoes 'illustrées' (line 7). The 'decoration' of the 'Hôtel' through references to visual, musical, and choreographical art forms evokes a syn-aesthesic, aesthetic imaginary space which is enacted in poetic structures which draw on the graphical, phonetic and spatial resources of language. The aesthetic transformation of the imaginary architecture in 'Promontoire' reflects the interpenet-ration of textual and imaginary rhythms which transforms the reader's perception of textual space.

Rimbaud is fascinated by the possibility of experiencing environments which are at once natural and artificial, spon-taneous and artistic, and whose hallmark is excess, the super-lative, superabundance of life. The combination of their capacity for movement and their excessive size and complexity makes Rimbaud's imaginary architectural structures seem to come alive (as in 'Les Ponts' and 'Promontoire'), while the geometrical and symmetrical ordering of 'natural' landscapes (as in 'Fleurs' and 'Mystique') renders them simultaneously artificial. Like 'Prom-ontoire', 'Villes II' evokes enormity ('les plus colossales . . . un goût d'énormité singulier') and interpenetration of the natural and the artificial ('les parcs représentent la nature primitive travaillée par un art superbe'). As in 'Villes I', the enormity and complexity of imaginary space disorientate the visitor/reader. 'C'est le prodige dont je n'ai pu me rendre compte: quels sont les niveaux des autres quartiers sur ou sous l'acropole? Pour l'étran-ger de notre temps, la reconnaissance est impossible.' The mythological, temporal and geographical eclecticism which char-acterizes these texts distances imaginary space from any possible reality. The terms in which it is evoked resemble the discourse of the sublime (wonder, disorientation, the feeling of being over-whelmed, which is both pleasurable and painful), and its enact-ment in the text means that the receiver can experience the pain and the pleasure of dislocation in the space of the text itself.

Rimbaud's iconoclastic attitude towards conventional art works (as expressed in 'Alchimie du verbe') contrasts with the utopian aspect of many texts of the *Illuminations* which envisage the advent of a new beauty, opening up 'toutes les possibilités harmoniques et architecturales' ('Jeunesse IV'). Texts such as 'Antique', 'Being Beauteous', 'A une Raison', and 'Génie', are

Promène-toi,
la nuit,
en mouvant doucement cette cuisse,
        cette seconde cuisse et cette jambe de gauche.

Transcript 4. Rimbaud, 'Antique', excerpt.

written in praise of figures who embody these harmonic principles. 'Being Beauteous', as mentioned above, contains a superb image of the liberation of colour: 'Les couleurs propres de la vie se foncent, dansent et se dégagent autour de la Vision'. The fabulous creatures of 'Antique' and 'Being Beauteous' exhibit an ideal superabundance, as does 'Génie', who is 'l'amour, mesure parfaite et réinventée, raison merveilleuse et imprévue, et l'éternité'. In 'Conte', the Prince 'prévoyait d'étonnantes révolutions de l'amour' which he himself prefigures: 'De sa physiognomie et de son maintien ressortait la promesse d'un amour multiple et complexe! d'un bonheur indicible, insupportable même!'

'Antique' ends with a sentence which evokes perfection of rhythmic movement in both imaginary and textual space (see transcript 4). Slow deliberation and graceful balance ('Antique' is described as the 'gracieux fils de Pan') are suggested by the gradual expansion of the syntactical structure and by the symmetrical repetitions. The echoing of '*mouvant*' in '*doucement*' makes the movement seem almost imperceptible: the phonetic change in 'cette cuisse' signals a clear alteration in position, although balance is maintained by the link with 'n*uit*' in 'c*uisse*'. The first repetition of 'cette' returns the 'gaze' in both imaginary and textual space to the point of departure of the first step, in anticipation of the step to follow, and the interposition of 'seconde' between 'cette' and 'cuisse' suggests extension in both imaginary and textual space, while the 'et' preceding 'cette jambe de gauche' indicates further expansion. The slow unfolding of the sentence and the emphasis on modulation of phonetic patterns (especially alternation of 'š' and 'č' sounds) encourage pronunciation of the mute 'e's, so that close attention is paid to each syllable, just as to each intimation of movement. 'Promène-toi, la nuit, en mouvant doucement' is a perfect alexandrine, and 'cette seconde cuisse' has six syllables, while 'et cette jambe de gauche' has seven, again emphasizing the extension of this step.

A very short 'illumination', the fifth section of 'Phrases', links textual space with imaginary choreographic and cosmic movements.

> J'ai tendu des cordes de clocher à clocher;
> > des guirlandes de fenêtre à fenêtre;
> > des chaînes d'or d'étoile à étoile,
> et je danse.

This apparently very simple little text has a dense rhythmic structure, and evokes a synaesthesic and celebratory imaginary space. The action of 'j'ai tendu' involves moving through space and linking objects in a way which emphasizes the spaces between them, across which the 'cordes', 'guirlandes', and 'chaînes d'or' are hung. The first line suggests musical connections, while 'guirlandes' evokes colourful flowers, and 'chaînes d'or', linking stars, evokes light. At the same time, the symmetry of the anaphorical syntactical structure suggests synesthaesic correspondences between 'cordes', 'guirlandes', and 'chaînes d'or' ('*cordes*' is also linked with '*or*') and connects 'clocher', 'fenêtre' and 'étoile'. The splendour of the garlands reaches a climax in 'chaînes d'or', where they rise to the sky: the dance takes place among the stars. The non-teleological, symmetrical movement of dance is suggested by the rhythmic structures of the text, where the movement of the reader through textual space parallels the rhythms of movement in imaginary space. This motion is framed by the opening and closing sequences of the text, which suggest a weaving, circular motion. 'J'ai tendu' and 'et je danse' are trisyllabic, and have criss-crossing sound patterns: 'J'ai tendu . . . et je danse', or a b c b a c. The past tense of 'J'ai tendu' is balanced by the continuous present of 'et je danse', which suggests indefinite continuation of the dance in time and space.

These analyses have shown that non-mimetic imagery in the *Illuminations*, where disruption of semantic norms prevents the reader from 'picturing' a coherent image, far from blocking access to imaginary space, opens up processes of imagining activity which are dynamic and sensory and whose rhythms can be reflected in textual space, thereby enabling the reader to become the 'spectator' of his/her imagining processes. In these poems, the texts themselves become 'illuminations' because they 'illustrate', in textual terms, the rhythms experienced in imaginary space, and because the imagining process in turn 'illuminates' the text, casting a new light on linguistic structures, as in the 'cosmic choreography' of this 'Phrase', a perfect 'hallucination des mots'.

CHAPTER 3

Reflections in black and white: Mallarmé and the act of writing

A savoir, s'il y a lieu d'écrire   (*MOC*, p. 645)

L'homme poursuit noir sur blanc   (*MOC*, p. 370)

TEXTUAL AND IMAGINARY SPACE

Mallarmé's obsession with perfection in his writing meant that his output was small, but highly refined. Most of his life was spent in obscurity, but by 1880 he had won recognition in poetic circles and had begun to hold his famous 'mardis', which gathered leading writers and artists at his house in the Rue de Rome. His late poetry reached unprecedented, and perhaps unparalleled degrees of concentration and suggestiveness. The relationship between textual and imaginary space in this poetry has significant parallels with the *Iluminations*. In both cases, the imagining activity provoked in the reader is reflected in the rhythmic structure of the text itself, enabling textual space to be experienced as 'imaginary' and imagining activity as 'textual'. In both cases too, the revolt against linguistic logic and description shows a desire to exceed the constraints imposed by language and by empirical reality. However, in certain texts by Mallarmé, the connections between textual and imaginary space are developed even further than is the case in Rimbaud. Moreover, although Rimbaud already manifests a surprising degree of self-awareness about his poetic enterprise, Mallarmé takes this reflexive awareness much further, scrutinizing writing itself as an act of existential and ontological significance. In his words: 'l'acte, par moi choisi, a été d'écrire' (*MOC*, p. 883) and 'l'acte d'écrire se scruta jusqu'en l'origine. Très avant, au moins, quant au point, je le formule: – A savoir, s'il y a lieu d'écrire' (*MOC*, p. 645).

Mallarmé's writing has strongly influenced the development of structuralist and poststructuralist approaches to language and texts.[1] As with Rimbaud, his challenge to conventional modes of meaning and interpretation has led recent critics to emphasize the role of the textual in his work at the expense of the imaginary. The opposition between thematic and textual approaches takes a rather different form here to the one we have seen in Rimbaud. From the outset, it was clear to critics that writing itself was Mallarmé's central preoccupation, and his conventional lifestyle did not hold the same appeal for biographers as did Rimbaud's adventures. In 1922, Thibaudet observed that 'Mallarmé n'a eu qu'un sujet, n'a fixé que sur un point ses yeux interrogateurs et rêveurs: le fait littéraire, l'existence et la vie du vers, du poème, du livre.'[2] However, his writing could still be read as an account of an imaginary lived experience, or 'vécu'. Thematic critics have tended to treat Mallarmé's preoccupation with writing as a theme alongside others, whereas textual critics argue that writing has a special status, since the Mallarmean text revolves around reflexivity and intertextuality, which exclude the phenomenological 'imaginaire', including writing itself as a 'theme'.

The most brilliant thematic readings of Mallarmé in the phenomenological/structuralist tradition are undoubtedly those of Jean-Pierre Richard.[3] Richard follows the traces of Mallarmean reveries through the interweaving of sensory images, revealing their complex and fascinating inter-relationships. This approach to the Mallarmean 'imaginaire' is highly seductive, but has been criticized for its emphasis on the lived experience of the author (especially his search for 'bonheur'), for its privileging of sensory experience (seen as a Bachelardian heritage) and for seeking to resolve differences and discontinuities in a grand synthesis. Genette voiced doubts about these aspects of Richard's approach as early as 1966, referring to Richard's 'postulat psychologiste' and 'le postulat sensualiste, selon lequel le fondamental (et donc l'authentique) coincide avec l'expérience sensible, et le postulat eudémoniste qui pose une sorte d'instinct du bonheur sensible au fond de toute l'activité de l'imagination'. He cites Richard: 'Le bonheur poétique – ce qu'on nomme bonheur d'expression – n'est past autre chose sans doute que le reflet d'un bonheur vécu'.[4] This importance accorded to lived experience undermines the role of Mallarmé's 'travail poétique'.[5] Moreover, Genette is sceptical about Richard's desire to 'embrasser une totalité des choses et des formes'.[6]

It is this view of the 'imaginaire' which Derrida rejects so vehemently in his well-known text, 'La Double séance',[7] whose critique is aimed directly at Richard. Here, the 'imaginaire' is seen as a thematic 'totalité' which can be extracted from the text.[8] Derrida rejects at once the 'psychologisme' which 'constitue le texte en expression, le réduit à son thème signifié', the dialectic which he links with Platonic and Hegelian metaphysics (in particular the Hegelian *Aufhebung* which all of Derrida's work seeks to deconstruct), and the phenomenology to which in his early work he had opposed the problematic of the 'undecidable'.[9] According to Derrida, there can be no 'imaginaire' in the Mallarmean text: the themes are not 'outside' the text because they cannot be separated from writing, which is present everywhere through the text's reflexivity, which ensures that there can be no 'hors texte'.[10] For Derrida, Mallarmé's concept of 'fiction' (which we shall discuss further below) is itself a textual operation, in which writing 'mimes' an event which does not really take place, the only 'event' being writing itself: 'le contenu thématique ou l'événement mimé . . . finalement n'est autre, malgré l'effet de contenu, que l'espace de l'écriture . . . tout . . . décrit la structure même du texte et en effectue la possibilité'.[11] In this way, the imaginary is effaced: 'Le référent étant levé, la référence demeurant, il ne reste plus que . . . la fiction sans imaginaire'.[12]

Derrida links the thematic approach with the notion of visibility: the hegemony of textuality is marked by the disappearance of the visual image. The 'supplément' of 'écriture' is said to effect the demise of images both as representations of the writer's lived experience or 'vécu' and as visualizations by the reader. In images of white, for instance, 'tous les "blancs" s'ajoutent le blanc comme espacement de l'écriture'.[13] In this way, whiteness becomes invisible and inaccessible to thematic criticism. It loses 'l'éclat du phénomène': 'dans le repli du blanc sur le blanc, le blanc . . . devient . . . son propre fond incolore, toujours plus invisible . . . texte dans le texte, marge dans la marque, l'une dans l'autre indéfiniment répétée: abîme. Or – la pratique de l'écriture en abîme, n'est-ce pas ce dont la critique thématique – et sans doute la critique – en tant que telle – ne pourra jamais rendre à la lettre compte?'[14] Also, the repeated insistence in 'La Double séance' that there can be no 'imaginaire' in the Mallarmean text is premissed on a concept of the imaginary as being 'outside' textuality: since there is no 'hors-texte', there can be no 'imaginaire'. The 'imaginaire' is clearly aligned with reference: 'Le référent étant levé, la référence demeurant, il ne reste plus que l'écriture du rêve, la fiction sans imaginaire.'[15] Moreover, it is seen as an internal, mental space, which is not compatible with the 'espacement' of writing. 'Le spacieux de l'écriture, pourvu qu'on prenne en compte l'hymen de la mimique, interdit de ranger la *fiction* mallarméenne dans la catégorie de l'imaginaire.'[16]

Derrida is right to point out the limitations of thematic criticism in the face of texts which indeed defy interpretation in terms of unified themes which lie beyond or outside of writing. However, this is not to say, as he does, that the only 'event' which takes place in the text is writing itself. The text can evoke an imaginary space which is visual and sensory without being reducible to a 'vécu', susceptible to dialectical synthesis, or definable in logical terms. Coming from a very different angle to Derrida (opposing rather than championing the notion of undecidability), Riffaterre also argues that reading Mallarmean texts is a purely textual affair. We have already discussed this intertextual approach in relation to Rimbaud, and the premisses are similar here. According to Riffaterre, a poem by Mallarmé allows of only one interpretation, which is 'verbal and within the limits of literary experience'.[17] He produces a reading of Mallarmé's 'Don du poème' which argues that 'the entire piece is derived from its title, which constitutes the semantic given'.[18] In this case, the semantic given is also a genre, that of the dedicatory epistle, and the poem is structured around a semiotic transformation of this genre, of which Riffaterre finds a particularly salient example in Hugo's 'Envoi des feuilles d'automne'.

Although both Derrida and Riffaterre, in very different ways, provide valuable insights into the functioning of the Mallarmean text, writing in Mallarmé cannot be accounted for in purely (inter)textual terms. It activates the reader's imagination and invites interrogation of its own ontological status. This imagining activity is semantically open-ended, sensory and reflexive: it disrupts the 'imaginaire' as an object of intentional consciousness, susceptible to thematic interpretation, and opens up an imaginary space which is analogous to textual structures without being reducible to them, thereby making the text ontologically as well as semantically ambiguous, at once 'textual' and 'imaginary'. The much maligned 'postulat sensualiste' of Richard is not tied to a pre-textual 'vécu' of the writer, but can bring into play a *new* 'vécu' in the reader, which does not correspond to pre-existing logical or empirical categories. Imagining activity can be stimulated by the sensory characteristics of language itself. Mallarmé's poetry is an example of art where the imaginary dimension arises out of the medium. In relation to Mallarmé, Valéry speaks of 'la musique déduite des propriétés des sons; l'architecture déduite de la matière et de ses forces; la littérature, de la possession des mots . . . en un mot, la partie réelle des arts créant leur partie imaginaire'. He says that 'le nouveau devoir lui était apparu d'exercer et d'exalter la plus spirituelle de toutes les fonctions de la Parole, celle qui ne démontre, ni ne décrit, ni ne représente quoi que ce soit: qui donc n'exige, ni même ne supporte, aucune confusion entre le réel et le pouvoir verbal de combiner, pour quelque fin suprême, *les idées qui naissent des mots*'.[19]

The text itself can become an object of imaginary transposition. 'Cette visée, je la dis Transposition – Structure, une autre'; '*La divine transposition*, pour l'accomplissement de quoi existe l'homme, *va du fait à l'idéal*' (*MOC*, p. 366 and p. 522). Mallarmé speaks of 'l'abolition du texte, lui soustrayant l'image' (*MOC*, p. 403). At the same time, like the 'fait de nature' which is held in a state of 'presque disparition vibratoire' which releases its 'notion pure' (*MOC*, p. 368), the text oscillates between presence and absence, between the textual and the imaginary. Mallarmé congratulates A. Mockel in these terms: 'Oui, vous êtes arrivé à ce point très miraculeux . . . que votre texte . . . se prête comme à une disparition de lui-même encore qu'on ne cesse de subir son délice; et s'évanouit, toujours présent en une sorte de silence qui est la vraie spiritualité.'[20] The purpose of this operation on the text is to distil the 'notion pure' (*MOC*, p. 368) of the text itself, its 'autre chose'. 'Autre chose . . . ce semble que l'épars frémissement d'une page ne veuille sinon surseoir ou palpite d'impatience, à la possibilité d'autre chose' (*MOC*, p. 647). The 'notion pure', however, like the 'idéal', does not exist, or rather it exists only by virtue of its pure fictionality. The concept of 'fiction' is crucial to Mallarmé's aesthetics and cannot be reduced, as it is by Derrida, to a *mise en abîme* of representation where nothing takes place but the process of representation itself. The 'fiction' is constituted not only by the process of miming representation without an object or event (where representation itself is fictive), but also by the construction of an imaginary event/object, which might have happened or existed in a different, impossible set of circumstances. In its ultimate form, the fiction is an 'empty transcendence',[21] an illusory absolute, pursued both despite and because of its fictionality. This status is encapsulated in Mallarmé's use of the conditional perfect in his comment on a lithograph by one of his favourite artists, Odilon Redon: 'Mon admiration tout entière va droit à ce grand Mage inconsolable et obstiné chercheur d'un mystère qu'il sait ne pas exister, et qu'il poursuivra, à jamais pour cela, du deuil de son lucide désespoir, car *c'eût été* la Vérité!'[22]

This lucid despair and obstinate pursuit of the impossible underlie Mallarmé's view of poetry as a linguistic creation which abolishes reality as we know it by its inscription of absence: 'Nous savons, captifs d'une formule absolue que, certes, n'est que ce qui

est . . . Mais, je vénère comment, par une supercherie, on pro-
jette, à quelque élévation là-haut et de foudre! *le conscient manque
chez nous* de ce qui là-haut éclate . . . Quant à moi, je ne demande
rien de moins à l'écriture et vais prouver ce postulat.' (*MOC*,
p. 647, emphasis mine). The problem for the poet is that reality
already exists and that writing cannot add to it ('La Nature a
lieu, on n'y ajoutera pas': *MOC*, p. 647). The architect can add
cities or railways: the poet, however, can add to reality only by
showing what it lacks. 'Tout l'acte disponible, à jamais et
seulement, reste de saisir les rapports . . . d'après quelque état
intérieur et que l'on veuille à son gré étendre, simplifier le monde
. . . A l'égal de créer: la notion d'un objet, échappant, qui fait
défaut' (*MOC*, p. 647).

THE 'LIVRE'

The supreme entity missing from reality is what Mallarmé called
the 'Livre', which he saw as the destiny of the world. One of his
most famous sayings is that 'le monde existe pour aboutir à un
livre' (*MOC*, p. 378). The relationships which 'summarize'
reality could exist only in the form of the Book which was to have
been the culmination of his life's work, but which was never
written. In fact, the ambitiousness of the project – no less than a
synthesis of the universe – made it unrealizable, and the idea took
on mythical dimensions, becoming the supreme Mallarmean
Fiction. The first title which he envisaged for his 'volume lyrique'
was '*La Gloire du mensonge, ou Le glorieux Mensonge*'.[23] Mallarmé's
obsession with the act of writing was directly connected with the
importance he attached to his 'mission' of writing the Book. In
1869, he wrote to his friend Cazalis: 'J'ai fait un vœu, à toute
extrémité, qui est de ne pas toucher à une plume d'ici à Pâques
. . . le simple acte d'écrire installe l'hystérie dans ma tête, ce que
je veux éviter à toute force pour vous, mes chers amis à qui je dois
un Livre et des années futures.'[24] Valéry says of Mallarmé that 'il
en est venu à vouloir donner à l'acte d'écrire un sens universel, *une
valeur d'univers*, et . . . il a reconnu que le suprême objet du monde
et la justification de son existence . . . était, ne pouvait être qu'un
Livre'.[25]

Mallarmé's conception of the Book evolved in progressive
stages. He began by referring to his project as his 'œuvre' or
'volume lyrique', and only later used the terms 'livre', 'Livre' and
'Grand Œuvre', terms which are used with reference both to his
own project and to a universal Book 'tenté à son insu par quicon-
que a écrit' (*MOC*, pp. 662–3). After his death, a collection of

notes was found which, although untitled, appear to be notes for the 'Livre', and were published under the title of *Le 'Livre' de Mallarmé* in 1957.[26] Perhaps the most remarkable aspect of these notes is their overwhelming concern with numerical structure. The manner of the Book's presentation and its numerical permutations were worked out in far more detail than its contents. Most of the pages consist entirely of numerical calculations and structural diagrams.[27] The idea for this project originally took shape while Mallarmé was undergoing a spiritual crisis, when he felt that he had succeeded in losing his individual identity in order to become an impersonal presence, 'une aptitude qu'a l'Univers spirituel à se voir et à se développer'; his 'œuvre' was to have been 'l'image de ce développement'.[28] Although in the 1870s this project seems to have acquired a more concrete, down-to-earth dimension,[29] a text of 1885, 'Autobiographie', shows that it had by then taken on even more mythical characteristics, being described as 'l'explication orphique de la Terre, qui est le seul devoir du poëte et le jeu littéraire par excellence'. At the same time, Mallarmé here recognizes the impossibility of actually writing this book in its entirety: he can only hope to produce fragments: 'prouver par des portions faites que ce livre existe, et que j'ai connu ce que je n'aurai pu accomplir' (*MOC*, p. 663).

In Mallarmé's plans for the 'Livre' we can see his 'mythology' of the text in its most extreme form. 'Impersonnifié, le volume, autant qu'on s'en sépare comme auteur, ne réclame approche de lecteur. Tel, sache, entre les accessoires humains, il a lieu tout seul: fait, étant. Le sens enseveli se meut et dispose, en chœur, des feuillets' (*MOC*, p. 372). Mallarmé's attractiveness to post/ structuralist critics is due above all to his attribution of the 'initiative' to words themselves, which disrupt logical categories and decentre writing and reading subjects. The poetics of the 'Livre' are the culmination of his view that the author should be absent from the text: 'l'œuvre pure implique la disparition élocutoire du poëte, qui cède l'initiative aux mots, par le heurt de leur inégalité mobilisés; ils s'allument de reflets réciproques' (*MOC*, p. 366). Mallarmé is fascinated by the relationship between text and consciousness. The ideal text (the 'Livre') is a model of reflexive consciousness. In reality, text and reader have need of each other to create this reflexivity. The modern reader, Mallarmé believes, wishes the text to function as a mirror: 'voilà ce que, précisément, exige un moderne: se mirer' (*MOC*, p. 375). His poetry affords the reader an opportunity of self-contemplation, where the structure of textual space reflects imagining processes. 'Il y a lieu, en lisant, d'imaginer . . . les caractères initiaux de l'alphabet . . . par le fait de feuillets entre-bâillés pénètrent, émanent, s'insinuent, *et nous comprenons que c'est nous'* (*MOC*, p. 375). The blank space surrounding the text becomes emblematic of the 'espace spirituel' of the reader's conscious-ness, which is filled with 'mille rythmes d'images': 'refléter, au dehors, mille rythmes d'images . . . L'armature intellectuelle du poème se dissimule et tient – a lieu – dans l'espace qui isole les strophes et parmi les blancs du papier: significatif silence qu'il n'est pas moins beau de composer, que les vers' (*MOC*, p. 872).

SCENES OF WRITING

The visual image of writing on the page is not a purely material configuration, but a 'mise en scène spirituelle' (*MOC*, p. 455) where one can perceive the enactment of one's own spiritual drama: 'un Lieu se présente, scène, majoration devant tous du spectacle de Soi' (*MOC*, p. 370). The 'au-delà magiquement produit par certaines dispositions de la parole'[30] is recognized as a figment of language and of the imagination, like the divine in religious ceremonies: 'Sommairement il s'agit, la Divinité, qui jamais n'est que Soi' (*MOC*, p. 391). Through this interaction, the 'place' of writing can be imagined as 'un lieu abstrait, supér-ieur, nulle part situé' (*MOC*, p. 656). The space of the page can be imaginatively transposed into the expanse of the sky (the 'folio du ciel': *MOC*, p. 294), and writing into the stellar pattern of the 'alphabet de la Nuit' (*MOC*, p. 303).

Like dance, the art of poetry requires a concrete space, that of the page. 'La danse seule, du fait de ses évolutions, avec le mime me paraît nécessiter un espace réel, ou la scène' (*MOC*, p. 315). Mallarmé frequently compares dance with writing: it is an 'écri-ture corporelle' (*MOC*, p. 304), and the dancer is a 'Signe' (*MOC*, p. 307) or 'hiéroglyphe' (*MOC*, p. 312). However, the physical presence of a dancer or actor may prevent spectators from recognizing the drama as their own. In a wonderfully ironic passage, Mallarmé describes the complacency of spectators who, with an absent-minded glance towards the stage, can casually assert: 'Ce n'est pas moi dont il est question' (*MOC*, p. 315). The reader, on the other hand, creates his own 'mise en scène'. The epigraph to 'Igitur' reads: 'Ce Conte s'adresse à l'intelligence du lecteur qui met les choses en scène, elle-même' (*MOC*, p. 433). The space of the page can become a 'scène intérieure': 'le livre essaiera de suffire, pour entrouvrir la scène intérieure' (*MOC*, p. 328). 'A la rigueur un papier suffit pour évoquer toute pièce:

aidé de sa personnalité multiple chacun pouvant se la jouer en dedans, ce qui n'est pas le cas quand il s'agit de pirouettes' (*MOC*, p. 315). It follows that poetry has no need of illustration. 'Je suis pour – aucune illustration, tout ce qu'évoque un livre devant se passer dans l'esprit du lecteur' (*MOC*, p. 878).[31]

Poetry itself could become a supreme form of dance, and also of music and theatre. Mallarmé was rather disconcerted when Debussy set his 'L'Après-midi d'un faune' to music, since he believed that the poem already comprised its own music.[32] Many of Mallarmé's claims for poetry were made specifically in opposition to Wagner, whom he perceived as an arch rival. Mallarmé sees poetry as the supreme art form: 'aux convergeances des autres arts située, issue d'eux et les gouvernant' (*MOC*, p. 335). Poetry is 'music' in its purest form: 'ce n'est pas de sonorités élémentaires . . . mais de l'intellectuelle parole à son apogée que doit avec plénitude et évidence, résulter, en tant que l'ensemble des rapports existant dans tout, la musique' (*MOC*, p. 368). Mallarmé's use of the term 'musique' recalls the status of music in Romantic writing as the supreme art form and as a metaphor for universal rhythms.[33]

Mallarmé was immensely jealous of the power of music to captivate its audience. 'Le miracle de la musique est cette pénétration, en réciprocité, du mythe et de la salle' (*MOC*, p. 393). Valéry recounts that at the Lamoureux concerts, which he used to attend every week, Mallarmé used to sit absorbed 'non pas à écouter la musique pour elle-même, tant qu'à essayer de lui dérober ses secrets. On le voyait le crayon aux doigts, qui notait ce qu'il trouvait de profitable à la poésie dans la musique, essayant d'en extraire quelques types de rapports qui pussent être transposés dans le domaine du langage.'[34] Music is an unusually privileged form, since it has its own special notation ('ces successions macabres de signes sévères, chastes, inconnus': *MOC*, p. 257) accessible only to the initiated, and yet it also has the capacity to move crowds. Mallarmé is often seen as an élitist who deliberately made his poetry obscure in order to protect it from profanation by the masses. However, the much-discussed obscurity and difficulty of his writing is aimed not only at surrounding his texts with an aura of mystery in order to protect them from prosaic, insensitive readers, but also at encouraging readers to participate actively in the signifying process. Valéry remarked that: 'Mallarmé créait . . . en France la notion d'*auteur difficile*. Il introduisait expressément dans l'art l'obligation de l'effort de l'esprit. Par là, il relevait la condition de lecteur.' He also notes that the Symbolists began the tradition of works which create their public, instead of passively reflecting existing tastes: 'Loin d'écrire pour satisfaire un désir ou un besoin préexistant, ils écrivent avec l'espoir de créer ce désir et ce besoin.'[35] The participation which Mallarmé's texts require from their readers is not purely intellectual, but also (and above all) imaginative. '*Nommer un objet, c'est supprimer les trois quarts de la jouissance du poëme qui est faite de deviner peu à peu: le suggérer,* voilà le rêve.' Poetry should give readers 'cette joie délicieuse de croire qu'ils créent' (*MOC*, p. 869).

Although the 'Livre' was never completed and there is controversy over which, if any, of Mallarmé's finished poems would have formed part of it, there is a sense in which all of his work is informed by the ambition to encapsulate 'l'ensemble des rapports existant dans tout' and embodies the characteristics of the 'Livre' in microcosm. The 'transposition du fait à l'idéal' involves the transformation of the text itself from a finite and static arrangement of words to a network of virtually infinite dynamic relations. Given Mallarmé's fascination with the contrast between black and white,[36] whose decorative qualities are enhanced by its associations with the relationship between writing and the page and between darkness and light, it is not surprising that black/white contrasts should be at the heart of relationships between textual and imaginary space in the two poems where this transformation is most crucial, 'Ses purs ongles' and 'Un coup de Dés'. In other poems too, however, structural and visual analogies between the textual space of the poetic signifiers and the imaginary space conjured up by the connections between signifieds allow the text itself to be experienced as a 'mirror' of imagining activity and as oscillating between textual and imaginary space.

WHITE SIGNS

By analogy with Gautier's 'Symphonie en blanc majeur', 'Le vierge, le vivace et le bel aujourd'hui' has been described as a 'sonnet en i majeur', in recognition of the predominance of the 'i' sound which corresponds to the prominence of the colour white.[37] Semantic ambiguities, negations and proliferating analogies mean that imaginary space is fragmentary and dynamic, while evocation of objects and of sense impressions (for example coldness, light and the colour white) ensures its sensory quality. The role of whiteness in imaginary space is related to the concrete space of the text, and this relationship affects the way in which textual space is perceived by the reader. Just as the 'fait de nature' is suspended in a 'presque disparition vibratoire', so the text is suspended between textual and imaginary space. As opposed to a simple naming which establishes language/writing/ the poem/poetry/the poet as a 'referent', the reflexivity of the Mallarmean text is a performative one, which transforms the reader's perception of the text itself. The final 'Cygne' suggests but does not name a textual 'sign'. As Timothy Hampton has pointed out: 'Were Mallarmé to end the sonnet with "le Signe", it would lose all interest for us as a poem, as an enigma celebrating its own polysemous mystery, and degenerate into a lifeless anecdote about writing.'[38]

By choosing the word 'Cygne' rather than 'Signe', Mallarmé opts for an imaginary rather than a graphical gesture towards the sinuous neck of the swan, and creates a tension between the textual 'signe' and the imaginary 'Cygne', which by the end of the poem no longer names an object but has instead become the focal point of the 'reflets réciproques' evoked throughout the text. The curious combination of opposition and affinity which characterizes the relationship of the swan with his surroundings in 'Le vierge, le vivace'[39] reflects the reader's experience of the connections between the textual and the imaginary: like the swan in the lake, imaginary space is 'caught' in the text, which cannot become 'other', and yet by virtue of this very aspiration the text is already 'other', distanced from itself. This effect is not a meaning in the conventional sense: it is an 'operation' performed by the interaction between text and consciousness.

The opening two lines indicate the 'rapprochement' between 'aujourd'hui' and bird on which the poem is to be based. Already the imagination is struggling: bird and dawn illuminate aspects of each other (the bird picks up the brightness of dawn, the dawn picks up the dynamism of the bird), and yet they refuse to coalesce entirely. Moreover, these entities are as yet only suggested: of the future 'cygne' only the 'coup d'aile' is mentioned, and the normally adverbial 'aujourd'hui' contrasts with the personification of 'le vierge, le vivace et le bel'. Furthermore, the mode is interrogative and the tense is future, contradicting the presentness of 'aujourd'hui'. 'Ce lac dur oublié' indicates that the past is lost to consciousness: the past is composed of forgotten *and* non-existent events ('des vols qui n'ont pas fui'), while the future has not yet become present. The reader is deprived of stable images and of a temporal reference point. Space becomes ambiguous and interacts with time, as the 'lac dur' is 'hanté' by the absent past of the 'transparent glacier des vols qui n'ont pas fui'. Again, 'glaciers' and 'vols' refuse to form a single, coherent image, while interacting to suggest the blocked temporal and dynamic potential of flowing and flying movements, linking the imprisonment of the 'unflown flights'[40] with that of the frozen landscape.

The second quatrain brings a measure of release from 'ce lac dur oublié' through the action of memory: 'Un cygne d'autrefois se souvient.' However, the subject of the memorizing which is taking place in the present tense is located in a bygone time ('un cygne d'autrefois'), displacing difference between present and past. Moreover, 'magnifique' and 'se délivre' are contradicted by 'sans espoir' and 'pour n'avoir pas chanté'. But the conjunction of 'resplendi' and 'ennui' in 'pour n'avoir pas chanté la région où vivre / Quand du stérile hiver a resplendi l'ennui' indicates that positive and negative attributes are not opposed: the monotony of 'ennui' is dazzling, and the swan's despair is magnificent. Visually, such paradoxical interactions do not add up to a coherent, realistic 'picture', but the variations on the theme of whiteness with its harsh, dazzling effect and its synaesthesic coldness create powerful sense impressions which link the swan with its surroundings and connect textual with imaginary space.

The colour white (unnamed so as to retain maximum suggestive potential) is from the outset an implied attribute of the swan and of the frozen landscape, and the links between the swan and 'aujourd'hui' associate whiteness with a luminous quality, reinforced by '*transparent* glacier' and '*resplendi* l'ennui'. ('Ennui' rhymes with 'lui', which also suggests 'luire'.) A possible reading of line 5 is that the 'c'est lui' of 'Un cygne d'autrefois se souvient que c'est lui' refers back to 'aujourd'hui' of line 1 as well as forwards to 'qui sans espoir', showing that the swan recalls his affinity with the light and the presence of 'aujourd'hui'. The suffusion of whiteness with luminosity evokes an immaterial quality which is heightened by the emotional resonances of overt or implied whiteness in 'Quand du stérile hiver a resplendi l'ennui', 'cette blanche agonie', 'l'horreur du sol' and 'songe froid de mépris'. Whiteness is free-floating, not exclusively attached to any particular object. Its ethereal quality is highlighted by the ambiguous temporality of the 'cygne' ('un cygne d'autrefois') and by the reference to the 'cygne' as a 'fantôme' in the last tercet.

The tercets open with a conflict between the swan and his surroundings: 'Tout son col secouera cette blanche agonie / Par l'espace infligée à l'oiseau qui le nie' (note use of future tense, distancing this action from the present). However, the swan cannot deny 'l'horreur du sol où le plumage est pris'. As suggested earlier in 'le glacier des vols qui n'ont pas fui', the swan and the ice are inseparably intertwined. There has been much debate as to whether the ending of the poem represents a failure or a triumph.[41] The point is rather that the swan becomes a site of intersecting contradictions, where magnificence and 'pur éclat' are unthinkable without 'exil inutile' and vice-versa, and where whiteness is *at once* agonizing coldness and magnificent brilliance. By combining the qualities of the white landscape and the luminous 'aujourd'hui', the 'cygne' becomes a 'Cygne/Signe', an irreducible nexus of interacting associations.

The homophony of 'Cygne/Signe' and the presence of 'signe' in the rhyme 'assigne/Cygne' draw the reader's attention to the parallels between the relationship of the swan to its surroundings with that of the poem to the page and of imaginary to textual space. The empty white frozen landscape, within which the 'vols' are a purely potential force, recalls the 'vide papier que la blancheur défend' ('Brise marine'), where writing is a latent presence. The violent action of 'déchirer' which will perhaps be performed by the bird's wing depends on a conflict (charged with aggressive and possibly sexual tensions) between 'aujourd'hui' and the 'lac dur', a conflict which is in fact denied as the 'aujourd'hui', the swan's flights and the 'glaciers' are seen to be equivalent. The swan's inner affinity with the white landscape enables him to become fully part of it: 'Fantôme qu'à ce lieu son pur éclat assigne / Il s'immobilise au songe froid de mépris.' This harmony between figure and surroundings is precisely what Mallarmé sought in the relationship between text and page, where the ideal poem, rather than violating/tearing the virginal whiteness of the page, would embody it, becoming itself a translation of silence: 'le poëme tu, aux blancs; seulement traduit, en une manière, par chaque pendentif' (*MOC*, p. 367). This silent white writing is evoked by the visible signifier of the 'Cygne', which is an imprint of black on white, but which also evokes an imaginary 'Signe/Cygne': the sinuous pattern of writing translates the silence and emptiness of the page by outlining an imaginary white figure on a white background.

The emphasis placed on the final image of 'Le vierge, le vivace' is typical of Mallarmé's techniques in his sonnets, where the last line often concentrates and refracts the series of 'reflets réciproques' evoked throughout the poem. Moreover, connections between textual and imaginary space emerge most strongly at the end, when imaginary space has already been evoked and can influence the way the reader perceives the text. It is interesting that in 'Le vierge, le vivace' (as in 'Ses purs ongles'), the final line evokes the image of a constellation, here the constellation named after King Cygnus, who was singing a lament for his loved one when he was transformed into a swan and flew into the stars.[42] 'Les Dieux antiques', a very free translation by Mallarmé of a book on mythology by George William Cox,[43] refers to stories which explain the names of constellations through the association of human figures with stars. Mallarmé points out that myths are often born from language itself, taking the form of stories told to explain apparent similarities between words with different meanings or to invent meanings for words or names whose meanings had been forgotten. In a note, he refers to the frequency with which these stories are connected with the annual and daily rhythms of the solar cycle, 'la lutte de la lumière et de l'ombre . . . La Tragédie de la Nature' (*MOC*, p. 1169). The occurrence of images of constellations in Mallarmé's poems at junctures which also foreground analogies between textual and imaginary space indicate that these poems can be seen as myths based on language, where language itself becomes an object of 'metamorphosis'.

SYNAESTHESIC SIGNS

'Ses purs ongles' ends on the image of the 'septuor', which evokes the seven stars of the constellation of the Great Bear and which is related to the myth of Callisto as recounted in 'Les Dieux antiques'. This sonnet has inspired such an extraordinary number of commentaries[44] that it cannot be discussed without retracing familiar tracks, notably in relation to the rhyme scheme and the mysterious 'ptyx'. However, it is an essential text to consider here because of the extent to which it focusses on the imaginary transformation of language. 'Ses purs ongles' invites its reader to perceive the beauty of language, its 'notion pure' which is a fictive creation of the words themselves.[45]

The first version of the sonnet (dated 1868: the final version was published in 1887) was entitled 'Sonnet allégorique de lui-même'. 'Lui-même' can be taken as evoking, not just this particular sonnet, but the sonnet form as such, whose unrivalled capacity for reflexivity and tight dramatic structure[46] make it the perfect instrument for transforming words into a network of 'reflets réciproques'. A vital feature of the Franco-Italian sonnet is its division into four separate parts, the major division occurring between the octet and the sestet, with further subdivisions into quatrains and tercets. This quaternary structure, with spaces between each section, creates a strong visual framework and also suggests the possibility of non-linear relationships between the component parts. The prominence of the rhyme scheme ('in the sonnet, it was rhyme more than any other feature that defined the form of the poem')[47] encourages perception of spatial as well as sequential relationships between lines. Moreover, whereas the quatrains often form an oppositional structure, the tercets tend towards synthesis, both because of their relative shortness and because the asymmetry of their trilineal units and the integration of the rhyme scheme bind them together into a single whole.

The sonnet form, then, has its own clearly defined dynamics, within the context of a highly ordered and stable structure, a paradox which greatly appealed to Mallarmé.[48] Moreover, its division into separate parts enables it to operate on different levels simultaneously, a feature which also attracted Mallarmé, who prided himself on having ordered his 'impressions étagées'[49] so perfectly that each element was immutable. Even individual letters, especially 'x' and 'o', play a significant role in the overall structure of the sonnet and contribute to its meaning, recalling Mallarmé's description of the 'livre' as an 'expansion totale de la lettre' (*MOC*, p. 380). Mallarmé is fascinated by the possibility of creating an infinite number of correspondences from a finite quantity of elements. This is the basis of languages, where the letters of the alphabet provide the foundation for all further combinations, of which the line of verse is the most perfect, integrated form: 'vingt-quatre lettres . . . sont, par le miracle de l'infinité, fixées en quelque langue . . . puis un sens pour leurs symétries, action, reflet, jusqu'à une transfiguration en le terme surnaturel, qu'est le vers' (*MOC*, p. 646).

Poetry is a perfecting of language, a 'complément supérieur' which 'rémunère le défaut des langues' (*MOC*, p. 364). Mallarmé saw the function of linguistics as complementing poetry. In about 1869, he planned to undertake extensive studies on linguistics, which he described as the 'fondement scientifique' of his Book.[50] But he also envisaged that poetry itself could incorporate this metalinguistic function. In a text which appears to allude to 'Un coup de Dés', Mallarmé refers to it as 'un poème critique',[51] and in an exceptional commentary on 'Ses pur ongles' in a letter to Cazalis, he explained that the poem had been extracted from 'une étude projetée sur *la Parole*'.[52] Although the notes for Mallarmé's study of linguistics are dated 1869 and there is no reference to the project in his correspondence before that year, his son-in-law, Dr Bonniot, situates the project 'vers les années 1865–1869' (*MOC*, p. 1629). Whether or not Mallarmé was referring to this precise project in his letter to Cazalis, there are striking parallels between the views of language expressed there and the poetics of 'Ses purs ongles'.

In the notes, Mallarmé declares that the task of poetic language is not to express beauty, but to show the capacity of
language itself to become beautiful: 'Dans le Langage poétique –
ne montrer que la visée du langage à devenir beau, et non à
exprimer mieux que tout, le Beau' (*MOC*, p. 853). In other
words, poetry does not aim to *evoke* beauty, but to effect an
aesthetic *transformation* of language. In the commentary on 'Ses
purs ongles', Mallarmé expresses the hope that the sonnet is
sufficiently poetic not to have a meaning, and that any meaning
which it does contain will be 'évoqué par un mirage interne des
mots mêmes'.[53] 'Mirage' emphasizes the visual quality of the
imaginary space which emerges from the words themselves, and
we shall see that it is a mirage which embodies the beauty and
perfection of language. This beauty is an attribute of the synaesthesic qualities of language and of the imaginary space which
they evoke. In the notes, Mallarmé pays particular attention to
the relationship between the phonetic and the graphical aspects
of language, which are destined to be joined together: 'les deux
manifestations du Langage, la Parole et l'Ecriture, destinées . . . à
se réunir toutes deux en l'Idée du Verbe' (*MOC*, p. 854). He
emphasizes that verse is both an oral and a written form and
refers to the pleasure of visual rhymes and the possibility of
combining phonetic similarities with graphical differences: 'le
plaisir de l'œil s'attardant parmi la parité des signes éteints (je
suppose l's du pluriel) et lui opposer une rime sur un son le même
au singulier' (*MOC*, p. 855). 'Ses purs ongles', too, plays simultaneously on the graphical and the phonetic aspects of rhyme.

Rhyme is a key element in this sonnet, both in terms of its
formal structure and of links between textual and imaginary
space. The rhyme scheme is very striking, partly because of the
number of exotic words in the rhyming position and the prominence of the mysterious letter 'x' (suggesting the unknown), and
also because the same rhyming sounds are used in the tercets, with
their genders reversed, and with 'ixe' replacing 'yx', thereby
creating a mirroring effect between octave and sestet and
drawing the reader's attention to the contrast between graphical
difference and acoustic similarity. The choice of 'rimes croisées'
rather than 'rimes embrassées' in the quatrains adds to the prismatic effect. Moreover, the poem's drama centres on the death of
light and the possibility of its recreation through reflection, which
is paralleled on a linguistic level by the death of meaning and the
possibility of recreating it in the form of 'reflets réciproques'
between words, of which rhyme is the privileged instrument.

Even more than in 'Le vierge, le vivace', paradoxes, ambiguities, contradictions and negations mean that visual impressions cannot crystallize into a coherent image: rather than forming pictures of known objects, the reader is invited to engage in imagining activity through the continuous making and unmaking of images. For instance, in the second line, syntactical and grammatical ambiguities create semantic slippages which produce illogical and unvisualizable equivalences between light and darkness. 'L'Angoisse' is associated with light through the 'purs ongles' of line 1[54] and the 'lampadophore' of line 2. However, its apposition to 'minuit' suggests that it can also be read as a personification of 'ce minuit', although grammatically, 'ce minuit' is more likely to be an adverbial phrase of time. The position of 'vespéral' in the next line also creates ambiguities. Its apposition to 'rêve', which is opposed to 'Phénix' ('Maint rêve vespéral brûlé par le Phénix') suggests that 'Phénix' emits bright light and heat which destroy (burn) 'maint rêve'. However, 'vespéral' could also qualify 'Phénix' (as in the first version of the sonnet), in which case 'rêve' can be identified with the 'Phénix', which burns itself out at dusk and is sustained through the night only by the 'purs ongles' of 'L'Angoisse, ce minuit'.[55]

From the last line of the first quatrain through to the end of the second quatrain, images of absence predominate. The suggestion that the 'rêve' might be preserved through the brightness of 'purs ongles' is countered by the absence of a 'cinéraire amphore' in which the ashes of 'maint rêve' could be gathered together and contained. Objects are evoked in strikingly negative terms: the 'cinéraire amphore' is absent, the 'salon' is empty, the 'ptyx' is 'aboli' and the 'Maître' too is absent, having gone to 'puiser des pleurs au Styx / Avec ce seul objet dont le Néant s'honore'. Not surprisingly, 'ce seul objet dont le Néant s'honore' (the 'ptyx') is a non-object, absent and meaningless: 'Aboli bibelot d'inanité sonore.' Paradoxically, the overwhelming sense of emptiness is not conveyed in abstract terms: it is the *sensation* of the Void which emerges through these shadowy, absent presences.[56] In fact, Mallarmé originally wrote this sonnet for a collection entitled *Sonnets et eaux-fortes*, which was to group together sonnets by contemporary poets and etchings by the most famous contemporary artists. He was fully aware that the poem was lacking in the 'plastic' qualities which would be pleasing to illustrators, but emphasized its suggestive evocations of black and white: 'il est peu "plastique", comme tu me le demandes, mais au moins est-il aussi "blanc et noir" que possible, et il me semble se prêter à une eau-forte pleine de Rêve et de Vide'.[57]

Although Mallarmé was not well disposed towards illustration, he was attracted to the contrast between black and white in etchings and lithographs, which could 'reflect' the image of writing on the page. In the case of 'Un coup de Dés', which was to have been illustrated by lithographs by Redon, he specifically requested a 'fond dessiné', so that the poem's pattern of black on white would contrast with the lithographs.[58] In both versions of the 'Sonnet en yx', the sky is dark, and the first version emphasizes the blackness of the 'Salon' and the darkness of the mirror's surface, implying that the etching (if the artist had followed the poet in this respect) would have had a dark background, contrasting with the white surface of the page. The chromatic inversion which could be performed by the etching is paralleled by the imaginary configuration of the bright 'septuor' – light on a dark background – which emerges at the end of the poem. In fact, as David Scott has pointed out, 'the form of the sonnet itself embodies the décor it evokes, rendering further illustration, in a sense, otiose'.[59]

In 'Ses purs ongles', imaginary space has strongly aesthetic connotations, and the perception of parallels between textual and imaginary space is the factor around which the whole sonnet revolves: centred on the rhyme scheme, these analogies permeate every level of the poem's semantic, spatial and phonetic structure. As in 'Le vierge, le vivace', it is essential to note that reflexivity remains indirect, at the level of suggestion, never reference. Although the imaginary space evoked is analogous to that of the text, the text never becomes explicitly self-referential, and imaginary space remains irreducible. The reflexive dimension of the imaginary intensifies as the poem proceeds, and the progressively inward focus of the imaginary gaze is paralleled in the increasing reflexivity of the reading process.

Each section of the poem on the page is associated with a different location in imaginary space. In the transition from the first to the second quatrain, the imaginary gaze is deflected from the night sky towards the inner space of the 'salon'. This movement towards the interior corresponds to an increasing sense of emptiness, and also to an increasing focus on language itself, notably in the form of the 'ptyx'. The journey towards the centre of the sonnet is also a journey towards the void and the emptiness of language. 'Le Néant' is named in the last line of the second quatrain and is figured graphically in the blank space at the centre of the sonnet, which contrasts with the darkness of 'Styx' and the blackness of writing. The figure of the 'Maître', who has gone to 'puiser des pleurs' and the images of death, darkness and the underworld recall the mood of 'Angoisse' of the first quatrain.

However, there is a slight change of tone here, hinging on the description of 'ptyx', first as an 'aboli bibelot d'inanité sonore', and then more positively as 'ce seul objet dont le Néant s'honore'.

This is not the place to recapitulate the fascinatingly diverse interpretations of 'ptyx'.[60] Mallarmé himself expressed the hope that 'ptyx' had no meaning, so that he could create its meaning through rhyme.[61] It is extremely ironic that commentators should have expended so much effort on finding a referent for a word whose very *raison d'être* is to have none. On the other hand, to characterize it as an em/pty signifier which has no meaning at all would be equally to miss the point. It can hardly be coincidental that 'ptyx' derives from the Greek root meaning 'fold' or 'double up',[62] a concept which Mallarmé associates with rhyme, and which strongly connotes reflexivity. The function of the 'ptyx' is not to signify but to perform, by prismatically reflecting the meanings projected onto and through it by other words, especially the words with which it rhymes. The 'ptyx' embodies at once the poverty and the richness of language: its meaninglessness and its capacity to resonate with infinite meanings. The 'inanité sonore' of the 'ptyx' is a necessary precondition for it to become the quintessential rhyme: hence its value to the 'Néant'.

Although the 'ptyx' as an imaginary object is a negative presence, without visual attributes, it rhymes with the flaming 'Phénix' on one side and the black 'Styx' on the other, thus becoming a focus for the conflict between light and darkness. It is therefore a point of transition, a site of dynamic exchange of sensations. (Interestingly, 'onyx', the first rhyming word in 'yx', is also visually ambiguous, since it normally appears black but reveals its colours when turned to the light.) Moreover, through its qualification as an 'Aboli bibelot d'inanité sonore', the 'ptyx' is indirectly connected with the other set of rhyming sounds running through the sonnet, since the letter 'o' figures prominently in these rhymes and in the line 'Ab*o*li bibel*o*t d'inanité s*o*n*o*re'. 'Aboli bibelot' onomatopoeically conveys incoherent babbling, while the round hollows of the 'o's graphically outline the empty resonance of the 'ptyx'. The letter 'x' (contained in 'ptyx') embodies in microcosm the prismatic, chiastic quality which is vital to the sonnet as a whole and which is enacted in its 'rimes croisées'. Its shape is also analogous to the sonnet's quaternary structure. The shape of the letter 'o' evokes nullity (it also indicates the zero of 'nul ptyx'), the circularity of the poem's structure, and the containing function of the absent objects. The 'x' further suggests the prismatic structure of the constellation, and the shape of the 'o' embodies the containing function of the mirror frame.[63]

This prominence of individual letters, which encapsulate textual and imaginary space in microcosm, recalls Mallarmé's description of the 'livre': 'Le livre, expansion totale de la lettre, doit d'elle tirer, directement, une mobilité et spacieux, par correspondances, instituer un jeu, on ne sait, qui confirme la fiction' (*MOC*, p. 380). It also recalls the Cabbala, where letters are accorded special significance. Mallarmé said of 'Ses purs ongles' that 'en se laissant aller à le murmurer plusieurs fois, on éprouve une sensation assez cabbalistique'.[64] In addition to the prominence of 'x' and 'o', the repetition of 's' sounds in the letter 's' itself, in 'c's, aspirated 't's and in 'x' creates a mysterious whispering sound, for instance in 'L'Angoi*ss*e, *ce* minuit' and 'de *sc*intill-a*t*ions *s*itôt le *s*eptuor'. In the notes referred to above, Mallarmé describes 's' as 'la lettre analytique: dissolvante et disséminante, par excellence' (*MOC*, p. 855), characteristics which accord with the destructive function he attributes to writing.[65] The letter 's' opens the sonnet[66] in the capital of 'Ses' and appears in the final image of the 'septuor'; it also opens the second quatrain and appears again as a capital letter in 'Styx', where it graphically suggests the meandering of the dark underground waters. Mallarmé associates curvature and darkness with writing, 'ce pli de sombre dentelle qui retient l'infini' (*MOC*, p. 370). Here, the absence of the 'Maître' and his descent to the Styx evoke the 'disparition élocutoire du poëte', whose suicidal act of writing necessitates his disappearance as a speaking subject.

The gold which appears at the beginning of the first tercet, mysteriously nominalized as 'un or', also has esoteric associations (the gold of the alchemists). In sensory terms, its most striking aspect is the autonomy of colour, whose freedom is emphasized by its rhyming position and its severance, through *enjambement*, from 'Agonise selon' at the beginning of the following line. Its brightness contrasts with the darkness and emptiness of the second tercet. Moreover, its position in imaginary space 'proche la croisée au nord vacante' and its textual adjacency to the octave suggest a connection with the first quatrain and reinforce the parallel between the octave and the window, the sestet and the mirror. In fact, the death agony of 'un or' can be seen as a replay of the burning out of the 'Phénix' in the first quatrain, with the crucial difference that here, the gleam of 'un or' is caught by (and may even be produced by) the décor of a frame, which turns out in the second tercet to be that of a mirror. The frame's motif of 'des licornes ruant du feu contre une nixe', where 'licornes' contains 'or' (light), indicates that the drama of the conflict of light and darkness is now being played out on a decorative, aesthetic level (which also has sexual connotations, with the male 'licornes' and the female 'nixe'), following the pattern ('selon le décor') of the figures on the mirror frame.

Moreover, the décor of the 'lic*or*nes' and the '*nixe*' contains the sonnet's rhyming sounds, indicating a parallel between the imaginary 'cadre' and the rhyming framework of the sonnet, especially since the rhymes of the octet are graphically 'mirrored' in those of the septet. The re-enactment of the solar drama in the mirror frame is modelled on the sonnet's rhymes, and the 'or' which emerges in imaginary space can be seen as a 'mirage interne des mots mêmes' which emanates from their 'reflets réciproques'. The 'mais' with which the first tercet begins clearly indicates an opposition to the quatrains: the décor of the mirror frame which creates a dynamic interaction between light and darkness, exuding the golden gleam of 'or', contrasts with the absence of the 'ptyx'. However, just as the experience of the void at the centre of the sonnet and the emptying of meaning enacted in the 'ptyx' were a necessary prelude to the re-emergence of light in a different form, here the 'nixe' must be destroyed before the 'scintillations' can emerge as pure reflections in the void enclosed by the frame: 'Elle, défunte nue dans le miroir, encor / Que, dans l'oubli fermé par le cadre, se fixe / De scintillations sitôt le septuor.'

One is reminded of Mallarmé's declaration: 'après avoir trouvé le Néant, j'ai trouvé le Beau'.[67] Beauty can only emerge from the void, and even then it remains hypothetical. The 'peut-être' of the first tercet already expressed doubt: here, the dependence of 'se fixe' on 'encor / Que' makes it a subjunctive form, and 'sitôt' indicates a possible, rather than an actual event. The *enjambements* at 'encor / Que' and 'se fixe / De scintillations' increase the tension: the reader's gaze is halted by the line ending, but pushed forward by syntax; at once transfixed by 'se fixe' and irresistibly catapulted into the next line to discover 'De scintillations sitôt le septuor'. (The use of the partitive article 'de' rather than the indefinite article 'des' renders the 'scintillations' more intangible.) Mallarmé associated light, and the term 'scintiller' in particular, with beauty and with his projected Book.[68] The 'septuor' here suggests a purely imaginary, hypothetical configuration, stellar and musical. At the same time, this glittering image is the culmination of the correspondences between textual and imaginary space throughout the sonnet and draws the reader's attention to this relationship of similarity and difference. Its reflection in the mirror creates fourteen points of light, like the fourteen rhymes of the sonnet, which, again like the constellation of the Great Bear,[69] are arranged in patterns of four and three.

The successive interiorization of spaces (from the night sky, to the 'salon', to the mirror) which is followed by the linking of the mirror with the 'external' space of the sky can be read as a metaphor for the way in which the reader is drawn into the inner depths of language, experiencing the hollowness at its centre, and is then shown its 'notion pure', its imaginary apotheosis, in the 'septuor'. The 'septuor' is an imaginary, poetic re-creation of the décor of 'minuit' suggested by the 'purs ongles' in the first quatrain: the poem has come full circle. The 'septuor' is both visual and musical, reflecting the aesthetic qualities of language which have been revealed through the sonnet's *rapprochement* of the graphical and the acoustic aspects of words, 'la Parole' and 'l'Ecriture'. The graphical and acoustic configuration of the self-reflecting sonnet itself evokes the imaginary luminous and sonorous 'septuor' which emerges inside the mirror. As is the case with the reflections in the mirror, the source of the sonnet's 'reflets réciproques' is internal, from its own 'cadre', rather than from 'external' reality.

In addition to its synaesthesic and prismatic qualities, the stellar septet invests textual space with an imaginary cosmic dimension. Interestingly, Mallarmé's comparisons of the alphabet with the zodiac and of writing with the stars are echoed in the book by Lévi recommended to him by Lefébure, which speaks of 'l'écriture des étoiles' and which refers to 'l'alphabet cabalistique' as 'le résumé de tout le ciel'.[70] The number of signs in the zodiac – twelve – was of particular interest to Mallarmé because of its correspondence to the number of syllables in the alexandrine, 'le numérateur divin de notre apothéose' (*MOC*, p. 333). He refers to 'une secrète direction confusément indiquée par l'orthographe et qui concourt mystérieusement au signe pur général qui doit marquer le vers' (*MOC*, p. 855), suggesting an occult correspondence between the shape of letters and the numerical structure of the verse, which he describes as a spiritual zodiac (*MOC*, p. 850). The seven of 'septuor' (note repetition of the 'pt' of 'ptyx'), which corresponds to the structure of the sonnet form, was also regarded as the magical number *par excellence* 'parce qu'il est composé du ternaire et du quaternaire', and 'les sept couleurs du prisme, les sept notes de la musique, correspondent aussi aux sept planètes des anciens'.[71]

The appearance of the 'septuor' in the empty space left by the disappearance of the nymph recalls the Greek myth of Callisto recounted in 'Les Dieux antiques', where it is compared with the Indian myth of the seven sages. The nymph Callisto, whose name means 'la plus belle' was the daughter of Arcas, 'le brillant' (note link between light and beauty). The etymological connection between Arcas and Arctos (bear) gave rise to the story that Callisto was transformed into a bear, and because the name of the constellation 'Arcturus' came from the same root as Arcas, it was said that these stars were inhabited by bears: hence the name of the Great and the Little Bear. In the Indian myth, the word meaning 'brilliant' which designated the constellation came from the same root as the word meaning sage, and so the constellation was said to be inhabited by the seven sages (*MOC*, pp. 1173 and 1243). In both myths, perceptions of reality are coloured by fictions created by language. In 'Ses purs ongles', the reader's perception of textual space itself is altered by the synaesthesic 'septuor', a 'mirage' similarly emanating from language, which transforms its ontological status, causing it to oscillate between the textual and the imaginary.

SPATIAL VERSE

'Un coup de Dés'[72] appears at first sight to be radically different from 'Ses purs ongles'. It was Mallarmé's most experimental poem, published in 1897, and it is sometimes seen as a prefiguration, or even as a part, of his 'Livre'.[73] The richness and complexity of this spatial text remain unrivalled, and its appearance is disconcerting even today. The words are scattered over the page, often with enormous blank spaces between them, and there is a striking variety of typefaces (eleven in all). With the exception of the initial title page (which forms part of the poem, and was to be printed on the same paper), Mallarmé uses the full spread of the double page, which is unusually large.[74] Despite these innovations, however, the fundamental preoccupation of 'Un coup de Dés', like that of 'Ses purs ongles', is the aesthetic transformation of language, here through the creation of a new genre, based on the principles of verse translated into a spatial form. To an even greater degree than in previous texts, language here acquires 'diagrammatic' qualities, with very close visual and structural connections between textual and imaginary space.

Mallarmé himself was fully aware of the shock 'Un coup de Dés' was bound to create. Valéry recounts that when Mallarmé showed him the text, he asked with pride: 'Ne trouvez-vous pas que c'est un acte de démence?' (*MOC*, p. 1582). Unfortunately for Mallarmé, this was indeed the view taken by printers, who refused to comply with his instructions (the verdict of the Didot publishing house was 'C'est un fou qui a écrit ça'),[75] and although the poem was published several times, it was not until the edition by Ronat and Papp in 1980 that it appeared in an authentic form, with full-size pages, correct typeface sizes and proper alignment between the sides of the double page.[76] The most immediately striking aspect of the text is what Mallarmé called in the preface its 'espacement de la lecture'. It is no longer just the words themselves, but the spaces between them, which determine how the text is read. The act of reading itself acquires unprecedented importance, since, like a musical score, the text dictates its own unique rhythms, which are realized only as the poem is 'performed' in reading. The tempo of reading is a direct consequence of the text's spatial disposition, and the rhythms of textual and imaginary space mirror one another, as the pattern of words on the page becomes a graphic reflection of the movements and outlines of objects in imaginary space. Imaginary movements of rising and falling are also closely connected with the rising and sinking motion of the page as it is turned.

According to Ronat, the 'discovery' of 'Un coup de Dés' in the new edition is also a discovery of its architecture, and specifically of the number twelve on which it is based. 'Le nombre DOUZE apparaît partout, sous la forme de ses diviseurs ou de ses multiples.'[77] It is in the typographical structure that Ronat finds the dominance of the number twelve to be most striking: 'la phrase-matrice UN COUP DE DES est composée en corps 60, le mot POEME de la première page est en corps 36 et le nom de Mallarmé, tout comme la séquence SI C'ETAIT LE NOMBRE . . . est en corps 24!'[78] There has been a great deal of controversy over the legitimacy of according such importance to numbers.[79] Given Mallarmé's obvious interest in number, there is nothing improbable in the importance of number *per se*, especially since it is a crucial element in the poem's imaginary drama. However, the prominence of numbers related to twelve in the typeface sizes is less surprising if one takes into account that the French system of typographical measurement is based on units of twelve points, the 'douze' or 'cicéro'. There is no doubt that Mallarmé was fascinated by typography and by newspaper layouts (he declared that typographical composition had almost acquired the status of a ritual: *MOC*, p. 380), and it is possible that he was acquainted with the technical aspects of typography.[80] His fascination with the number twelve would no doubt have whetted this interest, but the mode of composition of 'Un coup de Dés', Mallarmé's general comments on typography and his handwritten corrections on the proofs suggest that he was mainly preoccupied with its *visual* aspect.

Typography appealed to Mallarmé largely because of its

impersonal quality: 'le vers n'est très beau que dans un caractère impersonnel, c'est-à-dire typographique'. He preferred Roman script to italics, which were 'trop près de l'écriture' (*MOC*, p. 1340). Roman type is closer to engraving than to calligraphy: Mallarmé wrote to his publisher Deman: 'trouver un des beaux types romains qui soient et faire graver',[81] and he referred to the pages of 'Un coup de Dés' as 'au fond, des estampes'.[82] The monumental aspect of the Didot typeface in which the proofs are printed embodies these qualities. The poem was written on graph paper, allowing Mallarmé to 'compose' the blanks as well as the text: there is no indication that he specified type sizes other than by this visual means, and his handwritten corrections on the proofs are also concerned with visual questions of alignment and letter shape.[83] Arguably, then, the most important factor to take into account when analysing the typographical structure is the number and relative size of typefaces which present themselves to the eye, rather than their typographical sizes.[84] On this basis, eleven different sizes can be distinguished, five of which appear in italic and six in roman type (see diagram 1). In this way, Mallarmé translates the hierarchical structure of the sonnet into a more radical form. 'Pourquoi – un jet de grandeur, de pensée ou d'émoi, considérable, phrase poursuivie, en gros caractère . . . ne maintiendrait-il le lecteur en haleine . . . autour, menus, des groupes, secondairement d'après leur importance, explicatifs ou dérivés – un semis de fioritures' (*MOC*, p. 381).

The structure of 'Un coup de Dés' can be seen as a visual 'translation' of the principles of verse. In his preface to the poem, Mallarmé refers both to his desire to create a new genre and to his 'culte' of the 'ancien vers', insisting that the text is 'sans nouveauté qu'un espacement de la lecture'. The structuring role of the 'blancs' and of the page as a spatial unit takes over the rhythmic and structural function of the 'ancien vers'. Number is indeed central both to the structure of the text and to its imaginary drama: 'SI . . . C'ETAIT . . . LE NOMBRE . . . CE SERAIT . . . LE HASARD.' As Blanchot and others have pointed out: 'il y a dans "Un coup de Dés" une étroite correspondance entre l'autorité de la phrase centrale déclarant invincible le hasard et le renoncement à la forme la moins hasardeuse qui fût: l'antique vers'.[85] Certainly, Mallarmé was attracted to the impersonality of the 'vers' and its resistance to chance.[86] However, 'Un coup de Dés' can be seen as an attempt to create an even more impersonal, absolute form, exploiting to a hitherto unprecedented extent the full potential of poetic language, while at the same time recognizing the impossibility of achieving its ultimate aim.

1	# UN
2	## POEME
3	### *SI*
4	STEPHANE
5	QUAND
6	*COMME SI*
7	*Un*
8	que
9	*Une*
10	autrement
11	*issu*

1	## UN COUP DE DES // JAMAIS // N'ABOLIRA // LE HASARD
2	## POEME
3	### *SI* // *C'ETAIT* / *LE NOMBRE* / *CE SERAIT*
4	STEPHANE MALLARME
5	QUAND BIEN MEME LANCE DANS DES CIRCONSTANCES ETERNELLES / DU FOND D'UN NAUFRAGE // SOIT // LE MAITRE // EXISTAT-IL / COMMENCAT-IL ET CESSAT-IL / SE CHIFFRAT-IL / ILLUMINAT-IL // RIEN / N'AURA EU LIEU / QUE LE LIEU // EXCEPTE / PEUT-ETRE / UNE CONSTELLATION
6	*COMME SI* / *COMME SI*
7	*Un coup de Dés jamais n'abolira le hasard*
8	que / l'Abîme / blanchi / étale / furieux / sous une inclinaison [etc.]
9	*Une insinuation* / *simple* / *au silence* / *enroulée avec ironie [etc.]*
10	autrement qu'hallucination éparse d'agonie [etc.]
11	*issu stellaire [etc.]*

Note: Double // indicates text on different double pages.

Diagram 1. Mallarmé, 'Un coup de Dés', typographical structure.

The pages are the isomorphic units on which the structure of the poem is based, replacing the syllabic pattern of the line of verse. Moreover, the page is treated as a visual field: the 'blancs' create the rhythm, 'scanning' the movement of reading. 'L'avantage . . . de cette distance copiée qui mentalement sépare des groupes de mots ou les mots entre eux, semble d'accélérer tantôt

et de ralentir le mouvement, le scandant, selon une vision simul-
tanée de la Page: celle-ci prise pour unité comme l'est autre part
le Vers ou ligne parfaite' (preface). The analogy between page
and verse is reflected numerically: the text comprises six signa-
tures (sheets), folded into twelve double and twenty-four single
pages. Mallarmé himself numbered the pages 1–24, and the title
page should be treated as part of the poem. The central double
page, number 6, is like the 'caesura' in that it marks the centre of
the text, but it is also a 'pli' which both divides and joins: it must
be counted as part of both the first and the second 'half' of the
text in order to create two units of six.

The 'pli' along which the pages fold is especially prominent at
the centre of the text, whose symmetry is emphasized by the
typographical layout, but throughout the poem it divides and
joins the double pages, which form the shape of the letter 'v' and
which move like a bird's wings, comparable to the structure of
lines of verse linked by rhyme. 'Ainsi lancé de soi le principe qui
n'est – que le Vers! . . . les vers ne vont que par deux ou plusieurs,
en raison de leur accord final, soit la loi mystérieuse de la Rime
. . . un équilibre momantané et double à la façon du vol, identité
de deux fragments constitutifs remémorée extérieurement par une
parité dans la consonance' (*MOC*, p. 333). Whereas in verse, this
dynamism is imaginary, here it is realised visually and spatially in
the turning of the page, the 'aile de papier' (*MOC*, p. 374).
Mallarmé envisages that the rhythm of the 'Livre' would be
'impersonnel et vivant, jusque dans sa pagination' (*MOC*,
p. 663). The rhythmic function of the 'pli' is analogous to that of
the 'vers': 'le Vers' is the 'maître du livre' (*MOC*, p. 375), and 'les
plis perpétueront une marque, intacte, conviant à ouvrir, fermer
la feuille, selon le maître' (*MOC*, p. 381). At the same time, the
closed page is a virginal fold, which is violated in the act of
reading: 'le reploiement vierge du livre, encore, prête à un sacrifice dont saigna la tranche rouge des anciens tomes; l'introduction
d'une arme, ou coupe-papier, pour établir la prise de possession'
(*MOC*, p. 381).

If the pages embody the function of verse, the typography
embodies the function of prose as perceived by Mallarmé, which
'plays' with syntax: 'le vers par flèches jeté moins avec succession
que presque simultanément pour l'idée . . . diffère de la phrase ou
développement temporaire, dont la prose joue, le dissimulant,
selon mille tours' (*MOC*, p. 654). Both verse and prose subvert
the temporal structure of language, and their difference is prob-
lematized in a way similar to that between music and literature,
which Mallarmé discusses in 'La musique et les lettres' (*MOC*,

pp. 635–57). Barbara Johnson has analysed Mallarmé's use of the 'thyrse' image (composed of a straight line and an arabesque) as a figure for these relationships, holding that his reading of the Baudelairean 'thyrse'; involves deconstructing binary differences.[87] 'Un coup de Dés' cannot properly be characterized as either 'vers libre' or prose poetry: it is a new genre, based on the principles of verse but transgressing boundaries between verse and prose and showing, by its spatial composition, that poetry can exploit the visual, musical and performative potential of language, rivalling the Wagnerian *Gesamtkunstwerk*.

The poem's performative quality means that the visual space of the text which takes shape as one reads enacts the patterns and rhythms of objects and events evoked in imaginary space. Despite its length, 'Un coup de Dés' is not properly speaking a 'narrative' poem. Analogies and qualifications proliferate to the extent that imaginary space remains in a state of instability, where images and meanings are made and unmade with dizzying rapidity, and the typographical and syntactical structures invite a layered, 'spatial', rather than a chronological reading. However, since the text is *also* linear, there is constant interaction between potentially spatial and chronological modes of apprehension, creating a 'rythme total' (*MOC*, p. 367).

On the first double page, the words 'UN COUP DE DES' strike both the eye and the page. The shape, appearance and movement of the double page itself are linked with the image of the whitened 'Abîme' on double-page 3, which forms first the wings of a bird, then the sails and finally the hull of a boat, a womblike space from whose shadow the 'MAITRE' is engendered on double-page 4. The opening and turning of the page as one reads forms the 'v' shape of the wings of the 'Abîme' and also suggests the rocking movement of the ship and the rising and falling of the waves. This configuration also embodies the form of the letter 'v', evoking connections with the initial letter of 'vol', which appears on this page, and also with 'vers' and 'vierge' (both associated by Mallarmé with the 'pli' which their initial letter evokes). The 'ombre enfouie dans la profondeur par cette voile alternative' which is metamorphosed into the hull of a ship, from whence the 'MAITRE' will arise, is linked with the closure of the pages and the 'pli de sombre dentelle' (*MOC*, p. 370) of writing.

The dramas enacted here are erotically charged and revolve around the possibility of engendering the number and/or progeny. The 'MAITRE' is generated by the 'Abîme' in order to play the game (cast the dice) on its behalf, and the fact that the 'mer/Abîme' also aspires to rise upwards suggests that the dice throw is linked with the desire for ascent. This desire, together with the analogies we have observed between the 'Abîme' and the page, recalls the aspiration Mallarmé attributes to the page to become 'autre chose': 'ce semble que l'épars frémissement d'une page ne veuille sinon surseoir ou palpite d'impatience, à la possibilité d'autre chose' (*MOC*, p. 647). The refusal of the 'MAITRE' to 'jouer . . . la partie/au nom des flots' (double-page 4) leads to his shipwreck, and to a paradoxical interaction between death and birth, past and future, youth and old age. The 'vieillard', 'aïeul', 'ombre puérile' and 'ultérieur démon immémorial' on double-page 5 can all be seen as equivalent, which would make the 'MAITRE' father of himself: his union with the sea ('la mer/mère') is merely a 'fiançailles', and an illusory one at that.

On each double page, the disposition of the words enacts the drama which is taking place in imaginary space and which is performed in the movement of reading. This can apply to the position of objects (for instance the position of 'du fond d'un naufrage' at the bottom of double-page 2) to outlines (for instance the outline of the constellation on the last double page), to angles, movements and rhythms (the constant left–right downward diagonal of the text reflects the downward movement of the dice, the sinking of the ship, the slope of the wings, the movement of the waves, etc.), and also to the shape of individual letters, especially 's' and 'i', as we shall see below.

On double-page 3, the diagonal slope on the left-hand side reflects that of the 'Abîme'. The reader is also made aware of interactions between white/light and blackness/darkness. The rising movement of the 'Abîme' is connected with its whitening ('l'Abîme/blanchi'), darkening again after its fall in 'très à l'intérieur résume / l'ombre enfouie dans la profondeur par cette voile alternative'. This 'ombre' draws attention to the shadow enclosed in the interior depths of the fold in the page, which gradually opens out into the 'envergure' of a wingspan and then becomes 'la coque d'un bâtiment / penché de l'un ou de l'autre bord' just before one turns the page, a movement which enacts this 'listing' to one side. The typographical layout on double-page 4 enacts this hesitancy between 'l'un ou l'autre bord', since it is not always clear which side of the page should be read first, as in 'un / / envahit le chef' or 'un / naufrage cela'.[88] The blank space of the central margin is here clearly delineated by the text, which touches the margin eight times on either side. Reading straight across the page involves crossing the white gap of the margin, which becomes a progressively more significant space. Moreover, the long sweeps which the reading gaze must often make to follow the text increase awareness of the visual expanse of the page, and the uneven rhythms of reading also reflect the buffeting effect of wind and waves ('les vents', 'la tempête', 'flots', 'naufrage').

On double-page 4, the 'hésite' of 'hésite / cadavre par le bras' borders the margin: the text does not cross here and the reader halts and draws back, enacting the hesitation of the 'MAITRE'. On the following double page, the overwhelming blankness of the right hand side, broken only (and balanced) by the huge letters of 'N'ABOLIRA', invests the margin with even greater significance, as beyond it lies the void of an empty page. The sense of fear and hesitation has become stronger here, and it is linked with the potential sexual encounter between the 'aïeul' and the 'mer', an encounter which remains at the stage of 'Fiançailles', linking the failure to throw the dice with the failure to achieve this union. Since the 'MAITRE' can be the offspring of this union as well as its instrument, its fictitiousness calls his own existence into question. (Compare the sonnet 'Une dentelle s'abolit', which ends 'filial on *aurait pu* naître': emphasis mine.) Here, the word 'Fiançailles' advances right up to the borders of the 'pli' (to which it comes cloesr than does any other word on the page), but the reader's gaze is halted here, repulsed by this inviolate space and pulled right back to 'dont' on the far left-hand margin. The last word on the page, 'folie', initiates a fresh advance towards the central 'pli', but 'folie' suggests the folly of this approach.

Mallarmé's insistence on the exact size of the margin[89] shows that it is indeed a crucial space. Moreover, it figures prominently in the textual patterns of the sixth and central double page of the poem, which initiates the *'plume'* series. Here, the 'f' of 'Fiançailles' is capitalized, and Mallarmé makes corrections to this and to other 'f's in the text, asking that they should be more curved.[90] This has the effect of making them more 'feathery', and it is doubtless not coincidental that this section of the poem, from double-page 6 to double-page 8, written in italic script, centres on the image of a *'plume'*. The letter 'f', and especially double 'ff's, are prominent in this series. (Mallarmé also requests a more feathery 'f' on page 6.) The italic series begins with the words *'COMME SI'*, indicating that the actions which take place are analogous rather than subsequent to those which have already (or rather which have not already) taken place. The preceding series based on the 'MAITRE' and the 'COUP DE DES' itself hinged upon a conditional proposition ('QUAND BIEN

MEME'); '*COMME SI*' introduces a further qualification. Italic type is used to remarkably suggestive effect. We have seen that Mallarmé associates italics with writing. Pierre Duplan, discussing italics, points out that their obliqueness suggests a sliding motion, that they are associated with connotation rather than direct statement, that they evoke the tone of a confidential aside and/or citation, and that this 'espace rhétorique' is frequently a sexual one, since sexual references are frequently made obliquely. Moreover, they can connote enigma, secretiveness and a sense of fear, and also convey a brief, fleeting quality and a sense of dynamism.[91]

These features are all present in the imaginary space evoked in this series, which involves sexual innuendo, rapid movement, a sense of fear, and irony. Moreover, the disposition of the text around the central space of the margin enacts the '*insinuation* / / *simple* / *au silence* / / *enroulée avec ironie*' which '*voltige* / / *autour du gouffre* / *sans le joncher* / *ni fuir*'. In following the text, the reader's gaze constantly circles the margin, but the letters never mark it. The '*vierge indice*' indicates that the '*gouffre*' (like the margin) remains virginal, white and untouched, but that it contains a potential mark (or number). In order for this mark to become visible, virginity would have to be violated: hence the '*tourbillon d'hilarité et d'horreur*' which is associated with the circling movement and fear of penetration. The '*indice*' which might appear is related to the '*NOMBRE*' of the 'COUP DE DES' and to the 'ombre' which might have been engendered by the union of the 'MAITRE' and the 'Abîme'. What is at stake here (on one level at least) is the establishment of a principle of duality which would allow for the engendering of a third entity from the relationship between two distinct entities, for example the procreation of offspring from gendered beings or the creation of a stable pattern from the opposition of darkness/light or black/white. The 'COUP DE DES' would involve a process of division and of bringing together to make a total: in the throw, the dice would be separated, but the total score would be the product of both dice. (The task of the 'MAITRE', having thrown the dice, would be to 'en reployer la division'.)

It is not coincidental that the configuration '*si*' figures prominently on double-page 6, where it frames the chiastic pattern of the text on both sides, and where it also appears in '*in**si**nuation*', '**si***mple*' and '***si****lence*'. On double-page 8 it reappears in '*tor**si**on*', '**si***rène*', and occurs in typeface 3 in the word '**SI**', which belongs in the series '**SI** *C'ETAIT LE NOMBRE*', but which is the only word in the poem for which Mallarmé specially requested a particularly heavy type.[92] The graphical configuration '*si*' embodies the straight line and the arabesque of the 'thyrse', the figure which Mallarmé uses to problematize the duality of music and literature. Here, the questioning of duality focusses on the oppositions between black and white and between light and dark, which are necessary for a stable pattern to take shape. The failure to throw the dice, and the failure of the dice throw if it were to take place, are inseparable from the problem of difference, and its lack. The '*plume*' will remain '*solitaire*' and '*éperdue*' unless it can be joined by a '*toque de minuit*', whose blackness will provide a stable contrast, 'immobilizing' the feather: '*et immobilise / au velours chiffonné par un esclaffement sombre / cette blancheur rigide*'. However, black and white are also interchangeable here. The feather can be white on a black background or vice versa. The very letters on the page which embody the feathery form of the '*plume*' are black, and the '*prince amer de l'écueil*' who is the wearer of the '*toque*' is a Hamlet-like figure, whose '*plume*' was frequently represented as black.[93]

The '*velours chiffonné par un esclaffement **sombre***' suggests again the '*ombre*' image, whose associations with '*nombre*' are reinforced by the '*toque de minuit*', which evokes a '*coup/toc*' and the number twelve, or the alexandrine. The '*n/ombre*' is present in the '*pli*' of writing as well as in the virginal whiteness of the page, its '*vierge indice*'. The '*en foudre*' at the bottom of double-page 7 is connected with the events on the following page, with the feather's lightning-quick transition between light and darkness: '***SI** / la lucide et seigneurale aigrette / / de vertige / au front invisible / scintille / puis ombrage / une stature mignonne ténébreuse / / debout / en sa torsion de sirène.*' The relationship between the '*prince*' and the '*sirène*' parallels that between the 'MAITRE' and the 'Abîme', except that here there is the suggestion that an orgasmic climax has been reached (possibly occasioning the guilty '*expiatoire et pubère / muet / / rire*'), and that a result has taken place. The '*sirène*' (like the 'MAITRE') can be both a partner and an offspring of this act. Her '*stature mignonne ténébreuse*', with its '*torsion*', is graphically figured in the sinuous 's's on this page, while the heavy '***SI***' figures the apparent duality of the 'thyrse' and the 'idée', which Mallarmé associates with sinuosity and with the image of the 'sirène' (see *MOC*, p. 328 and p. 648). The prominence of 'u's in '*par d'impatientes sq**u**ames **u**ltimes / bif**u**rq**u**ées*' also indicates duality.

However, if it is the task of writing to 'fix' the 'sinueuses et mobiles variations de l'Idée' (*MOC*, p. 648), this task can only be accomplished in the context of stable difference, which is questioned here by the rapid interchange between light and darkness ('*scintille / puis ombrage*'), which also entails interchange between the male '*prince*' and the female '*sirène*'. With a blow of her phallic tail, the androgynous '*sirène*' destroys illusions of stable difference and identity, leading on the following page to the recognition of the illusory nature of identity and opposition and the impossibility of opposing '*LE NOMBRE*' to 'LE HASARD'. This page is the climax of the poem, bringing together six different typeface sequences (1, 3, 5, 9, 10 and 11) and completing the title phrase. The collapse of metaphysical opposition, sexual difference and dark–light contrast marks the end of desire and of the erection of the phallic 'plume', which is submerged by non-difference ('*Choit / la plume / rythmique suspens du sinistre / s'ensevelir / aux écumes originelles / naguères d'où sursauta son délire jusqu'à une cime / flétrie / par la neutralité identique du gouffre*'), leading to the victory, in huge letters, of 'LE HASARD'. The adjective '*flétrie*' which qualifies the '*plume*' and also the '*cime*' suggests softness, limpness and discoloration.

The penultimate double page affirms that 'RIEN . . . N'AURA EU LIEU . . . QUE LE LIEU', introducing the temporal setting of the future perfect within which the fictive exception of the last page can take place: 'EXCEPTE . . . PEUT-ETRE . . . UNE CONSTELLATION'. If nothing is identical to itself, then even the '*neutralité identique du gouffre*' is unstable: its dispersive action ('*inférieur clapotis quelconque comme pour disperser l'acte vide*') does not exclude the 'exception' of the dynamically forming constellation which emerges on the final page. By the same token, the constellation is not a real exception to 'LE HASARD' because it can be translated into the terms of the dice throw (the units of four and three stars of the 'Grande Ourse' multiply to make twelve, the total dice throw), and is already contaminated by 'LE HASARD'. The contours of the text on the last double page (especially the configuration on the bottom right) outline the constellation of the 'Grande Ourse', a configuration which would be formed by the diagonal alignment of dice showing three and four. It will be recalled that these numbers are significant in the composition of the sonnet form, and also of the alexandrine. The word 'vers' appears on this page, probably as a preposition, although its isolation suggests it could be read as a noun. 'Froide d'oubli et de désuétude' could also qualify the alexandrine, while 'veillant / doutant / roulant / brillant et méditant', like the phrase which runs through the poem in typefaces 3 and 1, '*SI C'ETAIT LE NOMBRE CE SERAIT* LE HASARD', is itself an alexandrine.

This clearly suggests that the 'ancien vers', and any form (like the poem 'Un coup de Dés' itself) which is based on the same principles is doomed to be subject to chance. The proliferation of analogy and structural symmetry means that everything is potentially different from itself: nothing is absolutely identical, and there is no 'unique Nombre qui ne peut pas / / être un autre'. Even the imaginary vision of the dark text as a bright constellation is merely another permutation in an infinitely reversible series. The constellation can constitute an 'exception' only on the basis of its pure fictionality, its impossibility. In a set of circumstances which can be posited only in a utopian future perfect, which always remains out of reach, the constellation might shine out as the perfect number: it allows a glimpse of a 'compte total en formation'.

The complex typographical structure of 'Un coup de Dés' means that the text can be read in many different strands, following different typeface series and syntactical sequences. However, it is dominated by a circular structure, even when one reads it in a linear fashion, where the last sentence ends on the words of the title phrase. The first three typeface series form an interlocking structure.

1. UN COUP DE DES / JAMAIS / N'ABOLIRA / LE HASARD
2. POEME
3. *SI* / *C'ETAIT* / *LE NOMBRE* / *CE SERAIT*

Series 3 can only be completed by a return to 'LE HASARD'. Interestingly, the first seven series (i.e. all the large typefaces, excluding 8/9 and 10/11) also combine to form a circular structure, where 1 and 7 reflect one another, with 'STEPHANE MALLARME' at the centre (see diagram 1). The series in typeface 5 is syntactically connected with typeface 1, suggesting that 'UN COUP DE DES' (typeface 1) can be the subject of 'QUAND BIEN MEME LANCE DANS DES CIRCON-STANCES ETERNELLES DU FOND D'UN NAUFRAGE', which continues with 'LE MAITRE / EXISTAT-IL / COM-MENCAT-IL ET CESSAT-IL / SE CHIFFRAT-IL / ILLUMINAT-IL / RIEN N'AURA EU LIEU / EXCEPTE PEUT-ETRE / UNE CONSTELLATION.' The '*NOMBRE*' series in typeface 3 is also syntactically connected with this series: '*SI* / *C'ETAIT LE NOMBRE* / *EXISTAT-IL*' etc. The 'Nombre' which appears on double-pages 4 and 9 is a metamorphosis of the 'ombre puérile' of double-page 5, and it is also the 'nom' of the 'MAITRE', and even of Stéphane Mallarmé himself. Looking at the typographical series listed in order of size, it emerges that 'UN

COUP DE DES', 'POEME', '*LE NOMBRE*', 'STEPHANE MALLARME' and 'LE MAITRE' can all be the subject of 'lancé': all are victims of 'le hasard', and all are subsumed in the imaginary constellation. This suggests that Mallarmé's desire for impersonality is connected with the wish to be subsumed in 'le vers', seen as 'le numérateur divin de notre apothéose' (*MOC*, p. 333), and which here appears in a new role, no longer simply syllabic, but 'le Vers, dispensateur, ordonnateur du jeu des pages, maître du livre' (*MOC*, p. 375). We saw above that the 'livre' embodied Mallarmé's ideal of reflexive, self-sufficient consciousness, and his notes for the 'Livre' contain the phrase 'm'identifier au livre'.[94]

'Un coup de Dés', then, recognizes the ubiquity of 'le hasard'. Even the transformation of the poem into a perfect rhythmic structure cannot counter this, since textual rhythm itself is predicated upon constant change, difference and division, which undermine stability and synthesis. However, the reader's experience of the text is also permeated with awareness of unfulfilled possibilities. The poem's 'notion pure', its encapsulation of universal, cosmic patterns through its fusion with the imaginary constellation, remains as a fictive (im)possibility: the page itself, which 'palpite d'impatience, à la possibilité d'autre chose' (*MOC*, p. 647) embodies the absence of a 'surface vacante et supérieure', in which the text inscribes the potential figure of 'un compte total en formation'.

CHAPTER 4

Putting the spectator in the picture: Kandinsky's pictorial world

For many years I have sought the possibility of letting the viewer 'stroll' *within the picture*, forcing him to become absorbed in the picture, forgetful of himself.[1]

A travers les moyens tangibles, nous découvrons les lois propres à l'art abstrait . . . Cette possibilité s'ouvre, si nous découvrons les tensions invisibles des éléments visibles . . . Ces tensions simples et primaires d'un élément à l'autre créent le *rythme*.[2]

INTRODUCTION

Turning now to the painting, we shall see how Kandinsky and Mondrian use the move away from depiction of objects, as Rimbaud and Mallarmé use the disruption of logical meanings, to evoke a space of 'sensory unreality' which is inseparable from the medium itself and yet cannot be fully identified with it, since it is also a product of the receiver's imagining activity. The pictorial colours and forms, like the poetic text, can be experienced as imaginary, while at the same time the activity of imagining is itself 'pictorial'. Whereas language needs to retain links with coded meanings in order to stimulate and reflect imagining activity, thereby transforming its own ontological status, painting, as we shall see, is more able to dispense with figurative and iconographical objects. These contrasts will be discussed further in chapter 6 below.

We saw in chapter 1 that Symbolism and *Jugendstil* were already tending strongly in the direction of abstraction. However, Kandinsky was the first artist to develop the potential of abstraction to the point of making it the basis of his work. This achievement is of far greater significance than the disputed timing of his first abstract watercolour, which bears the date of 1910,[3] or related controversies over who was really the first abstract artist. Discussing the reception of Kandinsky's paintings, Thomas

Messer points out that spectators tend to equate a lack of recognizable imagery with lack of meaning: 'the *recognizable* and the *meaningful* are all too often equated and confused'.[4] According to Vivien Barnett, the meanings of the pictorial elements are generated internally, 'first, within the composition of an individual work and, second, in relation to other works by Kandinsky', and it follows from this that 'meaning . . . is self-referential and hermetic within Kandinsky's art'.[5] It is indeed the case, as we shall see, that pictorial elements acquire meaning through these contexts, but the content of the picture does not consist in decipherable meanings, but is produced by the experience of the spectator while looking at the picture. Kandinsky's theoretical writings focus on, and invite the spectator to reflect on, this imginary dimension of pictorial space.

THEORY AND PRACTICE

Kandinsky's writings convey a vivid picture of the difficulties involved in making the transition to abstraction and also emphasize the crucial role of anti-materialist ideas in deciding him to take this step. Both Kandinsky and Mondrian make extensive use of theoretical writings in an attempt to encourage the sensitivity of spectators to the 'inner' effects of colour and form. In their late paintings, this reflexive function is increasingly integrated into the work itself through the inclusion of pseudo-figurative elements and also through skilful use of titles. Kandinsky distrusts excessively rational, analytical approaches to painting, and sees reflection on the pictorial medium as a means of explaining effects already experienced: 'Tendez votre oreille à la musique, ouvrez votre œil à la peinture. Et . . . ne pensez pas! Examinez-vous, si vous voulez, *après* avoir *entendu* et *après* avoir *vu*.'[6] Many criticisms have been levelled at Kandinsky's (and Mondrian's) theories: they are often seen as dogmatic and reactionary, redolent of an outdated 'subjective idealism',[7] and irrelevant to the radical innovations of the paintings. 'Si la pratique picturale est à l'avant-garde au début du XXe siècle, les théories et l'enseignement qu'elle produit reposent . . . sur un champ idéologique qui date de la fin du XVIIIe siècle.'[8] At the same time, painters' theoretical writings can be seen as pretexts for the paintings, which are merely illustrations, dependent for their meaning on theoretical discourse.[9]

It is undoubtedly the case that idealist presuppositions underlie much of Kandinsky's theory and that abstract painting, especially in its early stages, has difficulty in functioning independently of verbal language. Some of his statements point to an essentialist view of art as a transparent mediator of universal reality and/or subjective experience.[10] For instance, he affirms that 'form is . . . the expression of an inner content' (*KCWA*, p. 165) and that 'every work of art . . . produces in every man without exception a vibration that is at bottom identical to that of the artist' (*KCWA*, p. 258). This assertion conflicts with my view of the relationship between the medium and imagining activity as creating a content which does not have an *a priori*, independent existence. Moreover, many of Kandinsky's pronouncements about the effects of colours and forms attribute universal validity to associations which are clearly subjective and/or culturally determined. However, as we shall see below, Kandinsky's ideas are far more complex than such selective citation would suggest.

The fact that they emanate from the artist does not of course mean that Kandinsky's writings can be treated as 'keys' to his work. Kandinsky himself recognized that 'the artist can never grasp or fully recognize his own goal' (*KCWA*, p. 399). However, there are many reasons for taking the writings into account here. They place the pictures firmly in the context of ontological transformation in which we have discussed the poetry of Rimbaud and Mallarmé. Kandinsky was acutely aware that abstract painting demanded a new kind of response and felt that the public needed to be educated in this respect. His writings are aimed in large part at inspiring in spectators an attitude conducive to appreciation of his paintings: they therefore provide a valuable insight into Kandinsky's view of the ideal spectator. Moreover, far from being irrelevant to the radical innovations of his pictorial practice, the ideas expressed in Kandinsky's writings concerning the impact of the pictorial medium on consciousness are closely related to his techniques. His views are challenging and controversial in respects which have not as yet been fully acknowledged, largely because they undermine accepted norms of art historical discourse.

Felix Thürlemann has courageously confronted the 'intentional fallacy' problem and convincingly demonstrated the value of Kandinsky's commentaries on his own paintings as interpretative tools, while also treating the commentaries themselves as objects of criticism. He argues for their value in the absence of a critical discourse sufficiently developed to deal with the production of meaning through abstract form and colour.[11] He has also commented perceptively on the metapictorial role of figurative elements in the paintings of the Paris period (see below, p. 151), and I shall examine in this light the role played by iconographical references and figurative connotations in the Munich and Bauhaus paintings. Thürlemann, however, focusses mainly on specific commentaries by Kandinsky, whereas arguably the most important aspect of these commentaries is their methodology, which needs to be discussed within the wider context of Kandinsky's theories as a whole.

Kandinsky's principle of interpreting paintings in terms of their effects on the spectator is of greater interest than his attempts to quantify these effects in discursive language. His insistence that the content of the picture does not consist in the objects represented, but in the effects of the pictorial elements ('these contents are indeed what the spectator *lives*, or *feels*, while under the effect of the *form and colour combinations* of the picture', *KCWA*, p. 402) runs directly counter to the tendency among art critics to 'explain' the pictures by identification of iconographical sources. He is adamant that spectators should not equate the content of the picture with the objects it represents. 'It is common enough for the spectator who sees the object to imagine he sees the painting. He recognizes a horse, a vase, a violin, or a pipe, but may easily let the purely pictorial content escape him' (*KCWA*, p. 827). It is possible to see the object and the picture at the same time, but not all spectators have this facility, which 'springs from innate feeling and from practice' (*KCWA*, p. 827). Kandinsky points out that the connotations of objects can interfere with the effects of colour.

The colour white 'in isolation' conjures up an emotion, an 'inner sound'. So do the horse and the goose. But the last two emotions are totally different. White cloud. White glove. White fruit dish. White butterfly. White tooth. White wall. White stone. You can see that the colour white in all these cases is an element of secondary importance. For the painter it can be a major element, as a colour, but in all those cases it is itself coloured by the 'inner sound' of the object. (*KCWA*, p. 767)

The absence of recognizable objects, then, should encourage the spectator to pay more attention to the painting itself. The liberation from figurative objects is also a liberation from narrative and from 'literary' painting. 'The content . . . is not a literary narrative . . . but the sum of the emotions aroused by *purely pictorial* means' (*KCWA*, pp. 770–1).

When Kandinsky analyses a picture, he is less interested in its sources than in its goals – the dissolution of the object, and the subsequent effects of the pictorial elements on the spectator (who can be the painter himself). For instance, describing an egg-shaped form in *Picture with White Edge*, he says that 'following the edge with one's eye, one experiences an inner sensation like a succession of waves' (*KCWA*, p. 390). It is significant that Kandinsky frequently makes use of analogies in his commentaries, which is doubtless one of the reasons why they are felt to be so unsatisfactory. Roethel remarks that 'none of the statements that he made about his own works gives any interpretation of their meaning: his comments add to their mysteries rather than reveal them'.[12] However, to ask that Kandinsky's commentaries provide iconographical sources or conceptual interpretations of the paintings' meanings is completely to misunderstand his project of focussing the attention of the spectator on the imaginary dimension of colours and forms, which is better expressed through imagery than in analytical, discursive language.

Recognizable objects, which are easily nameable, provide a ready-made bridge between image and language. Indirectly, Kandinsky's work is in fact a defiance of the power of language to define, categorize and immobilize meaning: it is a refusal to 'name', comparable to Mallarmé's replacement of 'naming' by 'suggestion'. His recourse to figurative language to describe the effects of his paintings is acceptable if one is convinced by his argument that the effects which his pictures create are resistant to logical linguistic analysis. Kandinsky accused art critics of being too cerebral:

Tout ce que je connais d'écrit surtout sur la peinture moderne est assez loin de la perfection. Le manque d'"œil", c'est-à-dire de la capacité primordiale de voir la peinture, est en général la cause de cette imperfection. Le cerveau est une invention bienheureuse mais malheureux sont ceux qui s'imaginent que le cerveau tout seul est suffisant pour 'entrer' dans l'art et spécialement *dans* la peinture.[13]

Both Kandinsky and Mondrian wished to avoid the limitations of figurative representation without reducing the picture to a purely visual object. Their solution would be to use the suggestive power of colour and form, acting independently of figurative objects, to stimulate the imagination of the spectator so that the picture becomes the site of an imaginary space which cannot be reduced to purely visual elements. In Kandinsky, imagining activity comes into play where the pictorial medium subverts conceptual definition (for example by not representing nameable objects) and invites the spectator to 'empathize' with the pictorial elements and to imaginatively 'enter' pictorial space, which is experienced as rhythmic and as evocative of associations, sensations and emotions which cannot be translated into concepts or described in exclusively visual terms. This interpenetration of pictorial and imaginary rhythms creates an iconic dimension in the Peircean sense of 'Firstness', which is dependent, not on resemblance to figurative objects, but on the identification of the spectator's consciousness with the pictorial elements. At the same time, a basis for more general, abstract signification is provided by 'symbolic' elements. In his Bauhaus period, Kandinsky's desire to use the pictorial medium as a 'language', where individual elements had their own general characteristics which could be described in terms of 'rules', led him to attempt to codify and verbalize these tendencies. Unlike verbal language, however, even the most general meanings were associated with pictorial elements on the grounds of characteristics inherent in the forms and colours themselves. Later, Kandinsky would absorb this metapictorial function into the pictorial medium itself.

Kandinsky always maintained that practice preceded theory. In 1935, he wrote to Werner Drewes that he used to analyse individual parts of his 'compositions' from the point of view of draughtsmanship and painting ('zeichnerisch und malerisch'), but always 'post factum' and never 'ad factum'. He continues: 'I was pleased when I discovered little "formulas" by these means, but I didn't want to and couldn't begin with "formulas."'[14] During his Bauhaus period, he developed a very positivist approach, believing that 'pictorial theory had set foot on a scientific path in order to lead to precise instruction' (*KCWA*, p. 852). He continued: 'Theory will have to 1. Establish a well-ordered vocabulary of all the words that are now scattered and out of orbit. 2. Found a grammar that will contain rules of construction. Plastic elements will be recognized and defined in the same way as words in language. As in grammar, laws of construction will be established. In painting, the treatise on composition corresponds to grammar' (*KCWA*, p. 152). As early as 1904, he had affirmed that 'If destiny will grant me enough time I shall discover a new international language which will endure forever and which will constantly enrich itself. And it will not be called Esperanto. Its name will be *Malerei* [painting].'[15] These aims are interestingly close to recent attempts to establish a semiotic framework for the analysis of visual images, frequently based on linguistic models.[16] It should be noted, however, that Kandinsky is speaking here of a basic structure which the painter could subsequently manipulate in the course of composition, much as a poet can manipulate the rules of grammar.[17] Moreover, even in his most positivist phase, his main interest is in analysing the effect of pictorial elements on the spectator: experience always precedes analysis.

During most of his career, Kandinsky held that pictorial content was indefinable in conceptual, linguistic terms. In *On the*

Spiritual in Art, where he associates colours with certain moods, he qualifies these associations by pointing out that the effects of the visual image are indescribable in language. 'It must be continually emphasized that expressions such as "sad", "happy" etc. are extremely clumsy and can only serve as pointers to the delicate, incorporeal vibrations of the spirit' (*KCWA*, p. 201). In *Point and Line to Plane*, he argues that the pictorial elements 'create their own "language", unattainable in words' (*KCWA*, p. 636). Here he also relativizes the values he had attributed to black and white in *On the Spiritual in Art* (1912) by acknowledging their cultural basis (*KCWA*, p. 594). Ultimately, he also gave up on his hope that one day the laws of painting could be formulated in mathematical terms. In 1943 he wrote that while he still believed in the existence of laws underlying 'l'exactitude de la forme réalisatrice du contenu pictural', they were unknowable: 'nous ne les connaissons pas, et, je crois, ne les connaîtrons jamais'.[18] He also decided that it was impossible to formulate rules for evaluating the quality of a work:

Si on est d'accord sur la qualité d'une œuvre il doit y avoir quelque chose de 'positif', d'objectif au fond de cette affirmation. J'ai pensé aux temps anciens qu'on découvrirait à la fin des fins une ou deux formules exprimées en chiffres qui seraient les dernières et définitives preuves de la 'qualité'. Un tout petit changement, presque invisible, d'une seule couleur, donne d'un seul coup à l'œuvre une irreprochabilité illimitée. Il faudrait peut-être avoir des moyens de mesures . . . sans fin pour pouvoir calculer en chiffres toutes les relations et arriver ainsi à une formule.[19]

PICTORIAL AND IMAGINARY SPACE

The crucial question for the pioneers of abstract painting – and one which has continued to preoccupy critics – is the ontological status of pictorial space. In order to create 'imaginary' space, painting must evoke an absent dimension which is connected with, but not fully present in, the forms and colours perceived in the picture. In figurative painting, this 'absence' is created primarily by the illusory space which the painting represents, which is not identical to its material surface. However, by allowing the spectator access to recognizable objects, which can be confused with the 'content' of the picture, figurative painting enables him/her to react to the picture on a conceptual level, without responding to the non-figurative pictorial elements. On the other hand, the destruction of the illusory space of figurative painting could seem to reduce the picture to a material object. 'La présence de la chose figurée étant supprimée dans le tableau non-figuratif, que peut-il rester en lui, pense-t-on, sinon le tableau lui-même . . . prendre la couleur uniquement dans son existence "matérielle" ou, plus précisément, dans sa présence immédiate . . . serait prendre le tableau lui-même comme une simple surface peinte.'[20] We shall see that Mondrian's solution to this problem is similar to Kandinsky's in important respects, and that both are radically opposed to the modernist conception of pictorial space as purely optical.

Kandinsky's emphasis on the absorption of the subject into the picture, the forgetfulness of self (see *KCWA*, pp. 364–5) and the 'living' nature of the contemplated object has much in common with the theories of Theodor Lipps. His description in *Reminiscences* of his relationship to objects and especially to colours closely parallels Lipps' account of empathy, where the subject feels at one with the object, and the object (for example colour) is experienced as a living being (*AS* 1, p. 441). The concept of animation of matter is crucial to Kandinsky's aesthetics. His decision to move into abstract art was influenced by his discovery of this 'internal' dimension of matter and of colours and forms. 'Everything "dead" trembled. Everything showed me its face, its innermost being, its secret soul . . . likewise, every still and every moving point (= line) became for me just as alive and revealed to me its soul. This was enough for me to "comprehend", with my entire being and with all my senses, the possibility and existence of that art which today is called "abstract" as opposed to "objective"' (*KCWA*, p. 361). In his paintings, Kandinsky did not aim at representing external appearances, but at creating 'pictures that as *purely pictorial objects* have their own independent, intense life' (*KCWA*, p. 387). A successful picture is one which 'vibrates', which possesses a 'permanently living, immeasurably sensitive quality' (*KCWA*, p. 387). 'The creation of a work is the creation of a world' (*KCWA*, p. 373), or, in the more pithy German formula: 'Werkschöpfung ist Weltschöpfung'. Animation is inseparable from dynamism: 'movement is life, life is movement' (*KCWA*, p. 101).

In *On the Spiritual in Art*, Kandinsky explains that he is opposed to the reduction of space to the material surface of the canvas which can result from the 'turn away from the representational' (*KCWA*, p. 194). In *Point and Line to Plane*, he explicitly associates an over-emphasis on the material surface of the canvas with materialist values (*KCWA*, p. 670). He also rejects the Cubist construction of an 'ideal plane' in front of the material surface of the canvas, advocating instead a 'pictorial extension of space' which would both retain the surface of the canvas and create a three-dimensional ideal surface which would be extended in several directions through linear, formal and chromatic composition:

> The very thinness or thickness of a line, the positioning of the form upon the surface, and the superimposition of one form upon another provide different examples of the linear extension of space. Similar possibilities are offered by the correct use of colour, which can recede or advance, strive forward or backward, and turn the picture into a being hovering in mid-air. (*KCWA*, p. 195)

He goes on to explain in *Point and Line to Plane* that 'the way in which the formal elements advance and recede extends the PP [picture plane] forward (toward the spectators) and backward into depth (away from the spectator) so that the PP is pulled in both directions like an accordion', adding that 'colour elements possess this power in extreme measure' (*KCWA*, p. 648). The picture plane frequently seems to expand in many directions, surrounding the spectator, who is drawn *inside* pictorial space. 'Movement' along the surface of the picture plane is combined with recession into depth and movement towards the spectator.

In this way, the spectator is drawn into a space which operates differently both from a two-dimensional material surface and from conventional perspectival space, itself modelled on experience of 'material' space. 'The firm (material) placing of the elements upon a firm, more or less solid and to all appearances tangible PP and the contrasting "floating" of these elements having no material weight in an indefinable (non-material) space are fundamentally different, diametrically opposed phenomena' (*KCWA*, p. 670). The spectator experiences a 'transformation of the material surface', which is 'dematerialized' (*KCWA*, p. 761). Kandinsky emphasizes that in order to experience the 'floating sensations' produced by this treatment of the picture plane, which make it possible to free oneself 'from the pictorial surface in order to perceive indefinable space', the spectator must be able to see in the right way (*KCWA*, p. 671). Ideally, he should be able to experience the interplay between material and indefinable space.

Pictorial 'objects' are not subject to normal gravitational laws, but 'float' in space and frequently disperse in several directions, drawn by different centres of attraction. The sense of weightlessness carries cosmic connotations: 'Tendance vers une dématérialisation, abolition de la pesanteur, désir de s'éloigner du terrestre, découverte de l'univers' (*CB*, p. 179). Moreover, this transformation of the material surface means highlighting the temporal dimension of perception. 'Illusionistic depth . . . demands a certain, albeit immeasurable amount of time in order to follow those formal elements that extend into depth. Therefore, the transformation of the material PP into an indefinable space affords the opportunity of extending the dimension of time' (*KCWA*, p. 671). Kandinsky associates the importance of time in his painting with his move into abstraction: 'When I went over to abstract art definitively, the element of time in painting became indisputably clear to me, and I have employed it ever since' (*KCWA*, p. 550). Pictorial space is experienced as temporal through a structure which reveals itself 'only in the course of *time* to the engrossed, attentive viewer' (*KCWA*, p. 366), and through the 'tensions' of forms and colours. 'Tensions' are invisible properties of visible colours and forms, their inner 'forces' or capacity for movement. The task of pictorial composition is to juxtapose the pictorial elements so as to activate this potential. 'Les tensions inhérentes des éléments sont des forces statiques, qui attendent des rencontres pour devenir actives = dynamiques' (*CB*, p. 226). The orchestration of these encounters constitutes rhythm, which is 'la loi absolue de la composition' (*CB*, p. 76).

The transformation of pictorial space in Kandinsky's work must not be confused with the 'flatness' frequently associated with modernist painting, which, according to Greenberg, permits illusion – since any mark on a pictorial surface 'destroys its virtual flatness' – but an illusion 'of a strictly pictorial, strictly optical' kind. According to Greenberg, 'whereas the Old Masters created an illusion of space into which one could imagine oneself walking, the illusion created by a Modernist is one into which one can only look, can travel only with the eye.'[21] The reduction of pictorial space to superficial optical effects is in direct opposition to Kandinsky's desire to create a pictorial space within which the spectator can imaginatively live and move. This aim was inspired by his experience of highly ornamented peasant houses while travelling in the province of Vologda. 'I shall never forget the great wooden houses covered with carvings. In these magical houses I experienced something I have never encountered again since. They taught me to move *within the picture*, to live in the picture.' He describes the brightly coloured ornaments and the icon corner with its glowing lamp, and continues: 'I felt surrounded by painting, into which I had thus penetrated. The same feeling had previously lain dormant within me, quite unconsciously, when I had been in the Moscow churches, and especially in the main cathedral of the Kremlin.' Kandinsky wished to recreate this effect in his painting, by 'letting the viewer "stroll" *within the picture*, forcing him to become absorbed in the picture, forgetful of himself'. Moreover, the pictures inspired by this experience were 'so strongly painted that the object within them became dissolved' (*KCWA*, p. 369). This non-figurative imaginary space is radically different from figurative space: it is not simply an extension of the real space in which the spectator lives, but opens up a world of 'sensual unreality'[22] outside of known time and space. 'Demandez-vouz, si vous voulez, si cette œuvre vous a fait promener dans un monde inconnu de vous auparavant. Si oui, que voulez-vous encore?'[23]

IMAGINATION AND THE PICTORIAL MEDIUM

It was Kandinsky's fascination with colour, which he came to see as significant in its own right, which provided the immediate impetus for his move to abstraction. In *Reminiscences*, he recounts that Wagner's music awakened synaesthesic visions of colour existing as independently of objects as musical tones. In Rembrandt, he experienced 'the superhuman power of colour in its own right' (*KCWA*, p. 366), and on seeing one of Monet's 'Haystack' paintings, in which he was unable to recognize the object, he was overwhelmed by 'the unexpected power of the palette' which showed that 'objects were discredited as an essential element within the picture' (*KCWA*, p. 363). One evening he was startled by the sight of one of his own pictures, which was turned on its side so that he could not discern the object, but which appeared 'indescribably beautiful . . . pervaded by an inner glow' (*KCWA*, pp. 363–9). The same painting seen by daylight, with clearly discernible objects, was far less beautiful, leading Kandinsky to the conclusion that objects harmed his pictures. The effect of the object could interfere with that of the colour, reducing its impact (*KCWA*, pp. 766–7).

The evocations in 'Reminiscences' of the sensuous delight and the emotional resonances of colour are perhaps the most remarkable passages in Kandinsky's writing. The narrative opens: 'The first colours to make a powerful impression on me were light juicy green, white, carmine red, black, and yellow ochre. These memories go as far back as the age of three' (*KCWA*, p. 357). He recalls squeezing colours from tubes at the age of thirteen or fourteen: 'One squeeze of the fingers, and out came these strange beings, one after the other, which one calls colours – exultant, solemn, brooding, dreamy, self-absorbed, deeply serious, with roguish exuberance, with a sigh of release, with a deep sound of mourning, with defiant power and resistance, with submissive suppleness and devotion, with obstinate self-control, with sensitive, precarious "balance"' (*KCWA*, p. 372). Here, ready to play their roles, are the actors of Kandinsky's pictorial 'dramas'. Moreover, Kandinsky recognizes that to a certain extent, these pictorial 'actors' dictate their own roles: the palette is itself a source of inspiration, where the artist is open to the effects of chance. 'And I for my part owe much to chance: it has taught me more than any teacher or master . . . the palette . . . is itself a "work", more beautiful indeed than many a work' (*KCWA*, p. 372). In connection with pictorial composition Kandinsky frequently uses the term 'inner necessity' which implies that the artist is compelled to produce an image in a certain form: 'I do not choose form consciously, it chooses itself within me' (*KCWA*, p. 740).

Kandinsky attributes an active role to the medium in stimulating the compositional process. Sensation stimulates imagination: Kandinsky recounts that he 'derived spiritual experiences from the sensations of colours on the palette' (*KCWA*, p. 373). Although the word 'imagination' came to be used less frequently towards the end of the nineteenth century and in the early twentieth century, as August Wiedmann points out: 'the creative, mediating functions once attributed to this "queen of faculties" remained. They were simply transferred by the Expressionists to "the self, the soul, the spirit." '[24] Kandinsky is famous for his use of the term 'Geist', as in *Das Geistige in der Kunst* (*The Spiritual in Art*). He also uses the term 'Phantasie'. Discussing theatre, he affirms the importance of leaving 'a certain free space, which should separate the work of art from the ultimate degree of expression', a 'space for the operation of fantasy' which allows the imagination ('Phantasie') of the spectator to continue creating the work. 'The "fantasy" of the receiving subject . . . "continues to exert its creative activity" upon the work of art [am Werke weiter schafft]' (*KCWA*, p. 258). As pointed out in chapter 1, Kandinsky (like Mallarmé) greatly admired Maeterlinck, and was particularly attracted to this aspect of his theatre: he praises Maeterlinck's 'tendency to arouse the imagination of his audience' (*KCWA*, p. 146). He maintained that this technique would 'provide a necessary transition from the material to the spiritual' (*KCWA*, p. 146).

THE PAINTINGS

Kandinsky's work is usually divided into three periods, corresponding to his residence in Munich (1896–1921), at the Bauhaus (Weimar, 1922–4; Dessau, 1925–31; Berlin, 1932–3) and Paris (1933–44). Not surprisingly, these periods do not delineate homo-

Figure 1. Wassily Kandinsky, *Composition IV*, 1911; oil on canvas, 159.5 × 250.5 cm.

geneous styles. The first in particular is extremely varied, influenced by Symbolism, *Jugendstil*[25] and Neo-Impressionism, then by Fauvism: the Fauvist style merges into the famous semi-abstract and abstract lyrical paintings of *c.* 1909–14, followed by the rather mysterious stylistic fluctuations of 1915–17, coinciding with Kandinsky's visits to Sweden and Russia.[26] The work dating from the late twenties, a period when he held important offices in the art world of Post-Revolutionary Russia, already shows signs of the hardening of form which would characterize his Bauhaus paintings, and was probably influenced by contemporary developments in Russian art. The Bauhaus work is predominantly geometrical: the Parisian paintings reintroduce more organic forms, and also mark a return to the decorative detail of his early years as a painter.

The principal paintings in which Kandinsky forged his new 'language' of abstraction, his *Compositions*[27], are not simply spontaneous exercises in free colour composition, but are methodically worked out and derived from largely Biblical iconography. The significance of apocalyptic imagery in Kandinsky's semi-abstract paintings is not that it provides a key for their decipherment, but that it points to the *function* of abstraction itself, which was to herald the release from an old, corrupt world, and the birth of a new, purified one. The progression towards abstraction was not just a movement away from material reality, it was also a move *towards* a new vision of reality. This is why images of Judgement Day, the Deluge and the Resurrection abound in Kandinsky's pre-war paintings. (Kandinsky's first painting with an explicitly apocalyptic motif is *The Last Judgement*, 1910.)[28] Kandinsky's pre-war apocalyptical paintings connect destruction and regeneration on the thematic level with similar events in the process of painting itself, where the figurative (material) content is destroyed in order to create a new, purified (psychophysical) content: hence the emotionally charged character of these paintings.

Composition IV, 1911 (*RB* colour plate 383, see figure 1), marks a crucial phase in Kandinsky's development, containing at once figurative, iconographical and abstract elements. The primary 'content' of this semi-abstract painting consists in the spectator's response to the pictorial elements of colour and form rather than in a discursive meaning which can be explained in figurative or iconographical terms, but iconographical motifs play a role in the reflexivity of this response. *Composition IV* is one of the paintings on which Kandinsky himself provided a commentary (see *KCWA*, pp. 383–4), the existence of which further complicates critical

approaches to the work. In terms of conventional art historical
analysis (whose method is, precisely, 'historical', involving identification of sources), Kandinsky's commentary in fact contributes
nothing at all. This explains the otherwise surprising comment by
Peter Vergo that 'Kandinsky . . . says nothing in his essay on
Composition IV about the meaning of the picture'.[29] It is in connection with the same commentary that Roethel complained of
Kandinsky's lack of clarity in commenting on his own painting.
These criticisms would be nonsensical were 'meaning' not being
interpreted in a very restricted sense. While Kandinsky does not
indicate the sources of the painting or his intentions in painting it,
he does provide clarifications for the spectator who is prepared to
accept that the content is 'what the spectator *lives*, or *feels*, while
under the effect of the *form and colour* combinations of the picture'
(*KCWA*, p. 482). His commentary ascribes to the pictorial
elements of form and colour qualities which result from the
spectator's imagining activity, for example, static configurations
are described as if they were moving, and colours are described as
'light-cold-sweet'.

The iconographical approach, epitomized by the work of
Washton Long,[30] is useful in providing keys to Kandinsky's
sources, but its scope is limited. Both Jean-Marie Floch and Felix
Thürlemann, in their analyses of *Composition IV*,[31] address the
question of Kandinsky's creation of a new pictorial 'language'
which exceeds figurative and iconographical frameworks. Thürlemann furnishes an impressive demonstration that 'the detour
via iconographical comparisons is not necessary to comprehension of the 1911 painting'.[32] (As he points out, a great deal of
Floch's analysis is in fact iconography couched in semiotic terms.)
He begins by dividing the painting into sections, and notes the
contrast between long, straight, unbroken lines in the lower right
and shorter, bent, intersecting lines in the upper left. On the left
of the picture, he notes two different 'colour syntagms' – the
disordered mixed colours in the coloured patch on the left of the
picture, and the differentiated, ordered configuration of colours
in the 'rainbow'. Spatially, each of these colour syntagms is
aligned with one of the clusters of black lines (the 'horsemen'): the
relationship of opposition between the colour syntagms in turn
encourages us to see the relationship between the linear clusters as
one of confrontation, where the greater height of the linear cluster
on the right indicates its dominance. Since the right-hand side is
associated with order and the left with confusion, this relationship
indicates the dominance of order.

The left side of the picture thus becomes a microcosm of the painting as a whole, where conflict dominates on the left and harmony on the right. The similarities and contrasts between the 'sun'/'rainbow' configuration on the lower left and the sunlike image in the upper right corner also elucidate the relationship between the two sides of the picture. On the left, the 'sun' does not have a coloured aura: the source of light is separated from the manifestation of colour in the 'rainbow'. In the image on the upper right, however, the two are integrated: the colours of the rainbow are found in the 'sun's' aura. Moreover, by contrast with the colours of the 'rainbow' in the lower left, which are delineated in bands, the colours here are expansive and blend with one another. The left suggests conflict and potential order, while the right shows the realization of harmony in the form of 'expanded' coloured light.

This approach to *Composition IV* is a radical departure from critical norms, notably in its refusal to rely on iconographical sources and its emphasis on the picture as a self-contained unit. In this, Thürlemann follows Kandinsky's commentary (*KCWA*, pp. 383–4), taking his cue for a 'syntagmatic' analysis of pictorial structure from Kandinsky's emphasis on contrasting pictorial elements. However, Thürlemann himself points out that he has concentrated here on syntagmatic structure at the expense of other aspects discussed by Kandinsky, namely the 'physiognomical meaning of colours and forms'[33] and the sensory effects of spatiality and temporality. These aspects are rather more complex and arguably cannot be dealt with satisfactorily within the confines of Thürlemann's chosen framework of Greimasian semiotics. Thürlemann notes, however, that Kandinsky's metaphorical descriptions can be a means of reintroducing the natural world into abstract works. Discussing Kandinsky's commentary on *Picture with the White Edge* (*KCWA*, pp. 389–91), he remarks that it can be read as a narrative which tells 'the story of the forward movement of a self-metamorphosing actor ("white wave")'[34] and points out that the movement attributed by Kandinsky to the pictorial elements in fact involves a 'subject' who is at once pragmatic (performing the movement) and cognitive (interpreting it).

In addition to the overall compositional structure of *Composition IV*, (notably the pattern of left–right contrasts), linear and chromatic elements play an important role in stimulating imagining activity, while vestigial figurative and iconographical elements contribute to creating a 'metaphorical', reflexive dimension. In *Point and Line to Plane* (*KCWA*, p. 684), Kandinsky reproduced a diagram of the linear structure of *Composition IV*, described as 'vertical–diagonal ascent', which illustrates the principal 'lines of force' of the composition.[35] The vertical lines down the centre function as a fulcrum for the contours of the compositional structure as a whole, which form a roughly diamond shape. Diagonal vectors are suggested from the bottom of the vertical line at the centre on the right, along the reclining figures to the edge of the escarpment on the right and from there to the top of the vertical line right of centre. On the other side, this outline is balanced by the right–left diagonal of the 'escarpment' at the bottom, which joins the back of the horseman in the centre and from there extends to the tip of the vertical line left of centre. The entire 'diamond' is not visible, since the edges are intersected by the corners of the canvas. This diamond framework creates a sense of mobility.

On the left, ascending movement is blocked by the conflict between the arcs which are pointing in opposite and conflicting directions. On the right, however, ascending movement dominates. An imaginary diagonal line linking the 'heads' of the reclining figures on the right to the top of the vertical line right of centre creates a triangular structure of which the vertical line constitutes the base, and suggests a 'rising movement' in the reclining figures. The heads of the standing figures, which appear half way between the heads of the reclining figures and the top of the vertical line, also act as a point of attraction. The overall sense of movement in the picture leading upwards and towards the right is heightened by the attractive power of the startling depths of blue in the 'mountain'. The 'mountain' itself slopes towards the upper right, where its blue deepens dramatically, and leads the spectator's eye in the direction of the 'standing pair', whose vertical position in turn increases the suggestion of rising movement in the reclining couple on the lower right. The suggestion that the apex of the configuration of the standing figures forms a 'sun' motif is reinforced by the pale area, like a shaft of light, which emanates from it and extends towards the tip of the mountain.

The chromatic composition is based on contrasts, principally between the large expanse of blue in the mountain and of yellow in the escarpment. Optically, these colours contrast in that blue appears to recede, while yellow appears to advance. (Although they are not in fact complementary colours, Kandinsky, following Goethe, regarded blue and yellow as the principal pair of chromatic opposites, deliberately privileging the 'inner', 'emotional' effect of this opposition over that of red and green as complementary colours. See *KCWA*, pp. 178 and 184.) However, Kandinsky uses colour composition in order to moderate this opposition. Significantly, the moderation is more marked on the right than the left. There is a very noticeable difference between the temperatures of the yellows on the right and on the left, where they are much warmer, thereby contrasting more strongly with the blue. Moreover, the striking presence of reddish-purple, which modulates the opposition between blue and yellow in the sun motif in the top right-hand corner, in a small area between the escarpment and the mountain, and in the bottom right-hand corner, where the edges of the colours melt into each other, further affects the contrast between blue and yellow. In accordance with the phenomenon of simultaneous contrast,[36] both the blue and the yellow are tinged with the greenish after-image of the reddish purple, thereby toning down their opposition by making the yellow seem colder and the blue warmer and brighter.[37] In the bottom right, the reddish purple colour has been 'dragged' over the yellow, which appears from underneath, as does the blue in some places. Some blue is also superimposed on the yellow, creating a strong sense of interaction between these colours. Although the colours in the top right are not applied in this way, they also blend with each other in a manner which contrasts with the separate application of colours on the left side of the painting.

In this way, Kandinsky uses the positive emotional connotations of ascending movement and of chromatic harmony to invest the right side of the picture with cheerful associations. Moreover, colours on this side are more free-flowing, and harmonious lines contrast with the aggressive, spiky lines on the left.[38] Colours and forms thus acquire imaginary values which transcend the purely visual. In addition, pictorial space is 'dematerialized'. The striking dissociation of colour and contour creates a sense of disembodiment. Line is used independently of contour, and blurred colours often overrun contours, contrasting with their angular lines. This effect can be seen most clearly in the silhouetted castle shape on the top of the mountain, through which the colours of the sky are seen. These colours are fluid and mobile, and the large pale expanses undermine the solidity of material forms, suggesting a light airy space and emphasizing the hollowness of the silhouetted figures. Moreover, Kandinsky orchestrates advancing and receding colours to create ambiguous spatial effects. For instance, the mountain is positioned in front of the yellow escarpment, contradicting the advancing movement of yellow and the receding movement of blue: the advance of yellow is also held in check by the lines of the couple which pass in front of both the mountain and the escarpment, and, on the left, the yellow 'sun' is positioned behind the blue mountain. The mysterious, unreal quality created by the large white expanses and by the dissociation of colour from line, where forms appear hollow and colours float freely, is reinforced by these ambiguities, challenging the spectator's sense of reality and inviting active imaginative involvement with the 'otherness' of pictorial space. The large size of the canvas is a crucial factor in creating this effect.

Iconographically, the imagery in *Composition IV* is linked with Biblical themes. The standing figures can be identified as saints;[39] and the couple on the lower right is linked with the 'Garden of Love' theme[40] and resurrection.[41] The rainbow, the horseman[42] and the heavenly city on the hill are images from the Apocalypse.[43] The horseman motif is also linked with the image of St George killing the dragon, which symbolized for Kandinsky the triumph of spiritual over material values. The rider/horse motif played an increasingly significant role in Kandinsky's painting: from the fairytale image of a knight accompanied by a lady or riding to a castle, to St George killing the dragon, to the riders of the Apocalypse and the lyrical abstractions of paintings like the 'Arab' series of 1911. By 1911, the form of the horse and its rider had been abstracted to schematic outlines, as in *Composition IV*. The rider as a champion of spiritual values can be linked with the artist as the defender of 'the spiritual in art' (as in the image which appeared on the front of the *Blue Rider* almanac),[44] and Kandinsky compared the creative process with riding, where the horse is like the artist's talent and the rider like the artist who guides it (*KCWA*, p. 370). The painting was originally subtitled *Battle*, and Kandinsky said in a letter that it originated in a charge of cossacks through the streets of Moscow in the 1905 Revolution.[45] There is a close relationship between the painting entitled *Cossacks* (1910–11) and *Composition IV*. It has been suggested that the 'battle' in question is a spiritual one[46] and the fact that Kandinsky makes no references to the context in his commentary indicates that it is not intended to represent a particular 'battle'.

This contextual information can be used, not to supplant the content created by the impact of form and colour, but to enhance it. There is a close correlation between the expressive impact of the pictorial elements and their iconographical associations. On the left, the championing of spiritual values indicated by the horseman emerging from the blue mountain and the heavenly city lends added resonance to the aggressive linear conflict. On the right, the associations with saintliness and resurrection

reinforce the effects of chromatic harmony and ascending movement. The victory of spiritual values is suggested by the dominance of the horseman emerging from the right, and by the
harmonious potential of the rainbow and the sun. The tendency
to read pictures from left to right, and the directing of the
spectator's gaze upward to the top-right corner emphasize the
dominance of the positive side of the picture, indicating the
triumph of spiritual values. Although Kandinsky's own commentary does not refer to these contexts, he stated in a lecture given in
1914 that in his semi-abstract pictures he had not yet learned to
create purely pictorial meaning and was obliged to use objects as
a 'bridge' (*KCWA*, p. 395). In *Composition IV*, the iconographical
contexts enhance the suggestive potential of the pictorial elements
and provide a reflexive perspective on the imaginary transformation of pictorial space. The images of destruction and
regeneration are paralleled in the pictorial process itself: the birth
of a new, dematerialized pictorial space in *Composition IV* corresponds to the birth of a new heaven and a new earth witnessed in
the Apocalypse.

However, the general trend of critical response to the semi-
abstract pictures leaves no doubt that the presence of iconographical motifs encourages the spectator to 'translate' the
content into discursive terms, rather than experiencing it at the
level of the 'effect of the form and colour combinations of the
picture' (*KCWA*, p. 402).[47] Aware of this problem, Kandinsky
gradually eliminated even veiled objects and iconographical
images. By the time he painted *Composition VIII* (1923, *RB*, colour
plate 701, see figure 2), his 'vocabulary' had come to consist of
abstract colours and forms. *Composition VIII* is one of Kandinsky's
most remarkable paintings. Like *Composition IV*, it is a large
canvas (140 × 201 cm.), in a landscape format. According to
Roethel, 'there appears to be no logic in the imagery; the com-
ponents do not "respond" to each other; no organic continuity is
evident and no psychological associations are evoked'.[48] In fact,
however, the imagery is logically constructed so as to maximize
contrasts, and the spectator is invited to engage with the dynamics of pictorial space, whose imaginary dimension is intensified
through its 'cosmic' connotations.

Implied movement of colours and forms creates patterns of
dynamism which expand the picture plane in many directions.
The fact that movement is suggested in several directions at once
and the absence of a single gravitational centre acting as a
fulcrum make it impossible to hold the picture together in a single,
all-encompassing gaze: the spectator is required to experience

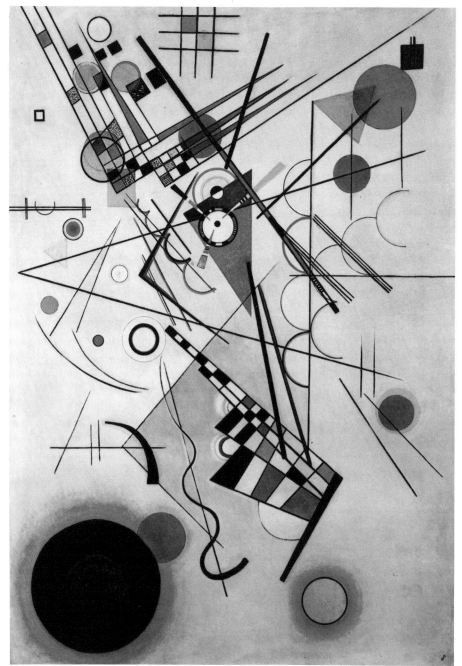

Figure 2. Wassily Kandinsky, *Composition VIII*, July 1923; oil on canvas, 140 × 201 cm.

the pictorial rhythms in time, through sequential scanning movements. The dynamism suggested by lines converging in angles (especially acute angles) contrasts with the more restful form of the circle, whose brevity and concentration can even diminish to that of a point. As well as the dynamics operating along the two-dimensional plane, there is also movement into depth and towards the spectator, who is deprived of a privileged viewpoint from outside the picture and is drawn into active imaginative involvement with pictorial space. Kandinsky makes extensive use of overlapping of various kinds to create an impression of depth. Where superimposition contradicts the natural tendency of colours to advance or recede, this results in spatial ambiguity and dynamism, since the forms cannot be held in a stable position on a single plane.

Several centres of dramatic interest can be discerned: the large and complex circular form in the top left-hand corner, in the direction of which the checkerboard form with two acute angles on the right-hand side of the picture is pointing; the circle enclosed in a triangle slightly right of centre, into which many angular forms are directed, and the pink rectangle overlaid by a checkerboard form in the upper right-hand corner. The large circle in the upper left immediately attracts the eye, owing to its size and its striking black ring, which combine to create a sense of great heaviness, contrasting with its position at the top of the picture. The second centre, while not so immediately striking as the heavy circle, is none the less perhaps the most dramatic point in the picture, suggesting a high level of excitement created by an accumulation of contrasting tensions, the focus of which is the black point in the middle of the white circle. The triangle, with its outwardly pointing acute angles, contrasts with the white circular area inside it, which in turn contains a more extreme form of the circle, a point, towards which three red-tipped, elongated angular forms penetrate inwards, forming a counterpoint to the eccentric angles of the triangle and piercing the thick circumference of the circle, extending through the white space, and almost touching the black point at the centre. Suspense is maximized by the strongly compelling centripetal movement created by the dynamism of the elongated forms (which taper into extremely acute angles), the attractive force of the central black point which pulls them into depth, and the arrest of this movement just short of its goal, a contrast which at once heightens tension and maintains it indefinitely.

Another centre of attention is the pink rectangle in the top right-hand corner. This rectangle acts as a magnet for many lines in the upper part of the picture which point in its direction and provide a counterpoint of cumulative smaller movements to the strong right–left thrust of the double-angled checkerboard form which passes in front of it. At the same time, angular forms pointing upwards (notably the pale pink acute angular form right of centre, the thick black and green acute angle inside it, and the blue obtuse angular form to its left) and downwards (notably the complex checkerboard form right of the yellow circle on the lower left) add to the counterpoint of contrasting movements, which is further complicated by the dynamics of colour, which are particularly striking in the circular forms. In the angular forms, movement across the plane and into depth is suggested through the direction in which the angles are pointing.

The emphasis on contrasts encourages the spectator to experience the relationships between pictorial elements as 'dramatic'. The most striking example is that of the elongated angular forms piercing the circle enclosed in the triangle (two of the three clearly pass through – under and over – the circumference) and stopping just short of the black point in the centre. The red tapering forms are static, but their acute angles, and the fact that they are all pointing towards the same object (the black point) invite the spectator to perceive them as directional and dynamic. This movement evokes aggression and desire, and creates a sense of excitement and suspense. The circular forms, by contrast, are self-contained, but their coloration can suggest movement, especially towards and away from the spectator. Moreover, in the case of the small red circle in the upper left, the appearance of an expansive yellow aura to its lower right suggests movement in this direction and creates a link with the other two circles in this part of the picture, one of which is yellow and one of which has a yellow aura. The eye connects this 'triangle' of circles because of their formal similarity, because they all have yellow in common, and because together they form a 'triangle' of the primary colours. At the same time, the contrast between the lower circles is intensely striking. In the circle on the left, the bright yellow centre pulsates intensely, its expansive tendencies held in check by the black contour and heightened by juxtaposition with a blue and violet aura. The blue circle lower down is superimposed on a pale pink one, which in turn is surrounded by a yellow aura, where the frontal position of the blue contradicts its tendency to recede, and the reverse for the yellow. An alternative reading would be to see the blue circle as an opening into depth: Poling describes it as 'presque un trou'.[49]

These effects of spatial ambiguity are not confined to particular

configurations, but affect the picture plane as a whole, where a
stable background or base line is lacking. The picture plane itself
varies in hue and saturation: the lower left-hand side about
two-thirds of the way across and up as far as the blue obtuse angle
has a bluish tinge; the rest tends towards yellow. These chromatic
fluctuations suggest changes in depth and luminosity, approxi-
mating atmospheric effects, and create advancing and receding
movements, so that the whole of pictorial space appears to
'vibrate'. Moreover, there is no clear distinction between solid
forms and background space. The blue obtuse angle and the pale
pink acute angle already remarked on form the tips of planes
whose open-ended bases merge with the picture plane, but which
acquire density through their distinctive coloration. The space
enclosed by the acute angle which culminates at the top of the
picture becomes tinged with pink below the base of the large
brown and green triangle. As it passes over the triangle, its
superimposition causes a chromatic change in the triangle, indicating that it has acquired density (the circle and its surround
remain white, suggesting that they are positioned in front of the
triangle). The blue angular form on the left varies in saturation:
whereas the base is open-ended and chromatically indistinguish-
able from the picture plane, its density increases towards the top.

The overlapping effects which indicate depth sometimes
appear illogical and contradictory. The pink angular form brings
about a change in the hue of the triangle as it passes over it, but
leaves the blue angular form unaffected at their point of intersection. This could be explained if the blue form were in front, but in
this case one would expect a chromatic change in the left tip of the
brown triangle, which it intersects. Near its summit, the pink
form also overlaps the left tip of the yellow triangle without
producing any colour change. In the third centre referred to in
the upper right, it is not clear why the yellow circle which appears
in front of an orange-brown one should turn the latter to green;
why the checkerboard's apparently colourless squares, superimposed on the pink square, should turn it such a dark colour, or
why a mottled black square in the checkerboard form which is
partially superimposed on the blue circle with the yellow surround in the upper right should become transparent.

The spatial organization of *Composition VIII* thus operates very
differently from that of 'real' space. No single set of co-ordinates
can account for the picture as a whole: the spectator is therefore
encouraged to perceive it sequentially, in parts, and spatial
relationships are often ambiguous. Moreover, pictorial space is
subject to change in time, in the act of looking. Through the

imaginative involvement of the spectator, which activates the tensions inherent in the pictorial elements, the static surface of the canvas is experienced as a network of intersecting rhythms. It is noticeable that the lower half of the canvas is emptier than the top half: this accentuates the difference from 'real' space, where heavy shapes would 'sink' to the bottom, while here they seem to 'float'. This picture is a remarkable example of Kandinsky's creation of 'un monde autre' (*CB*, p. 176), which embodies the 'tendance vers une dématérialisation, abolition de la pesanteur, désir de s'éloigner du terrestre' (*CB*, p. 179). The circles and their auras evoke 'cosmic' connotations, which are enhanced by the atmospheric effects and the sense of weightlessness produced by the suspension of forms in empty space, and especially by the positioning of the large, 'heavy' black circle at the top of the canvas. These connotations invite the spectator to reflect on the analogy between pictorial and cosmic rhythms. 'Le principe premier et primordial est le rythme . . . Il est donc naturel que toute création humaine . . . participe de la même pulsation cos-mique' (*CB*, p. 235).

In *Composition IV*, the reflexive level of imagining activity necessitated knowledge of iconographical contexts outside the picture. Here, this level is more self-contained: the cosmic conno-tations of the circular images draw the spectator's attention to the creation of a 'world' within painting itself. (According to Kan-dinsky, 'in every true work of art, a new *world* is created that has never existed': *KCWA*, p. 832.) The circle is without doubt the most prevalent form in the paintings of the 1920s (see, for instance, *Circles within a Circle*, 1923 (*RB*, plate 702) and *Several Circles*, 1926 (*RB*, colour plate 767, see figure 3). Kandinsky agreed that the circle was 'a link with the cosmic',[50] though he maintained that the main reason for his attraction to this form was his 'extreme sensitivity to the inner force of the circle in all its countless variations' (*KCWA*, p. 740). He saw in the circle 'the synthesis of the greatest oppositions. It combines the concentric and the excentric in a single form, and in balance.'[51] It is interesting that he compares the importance of the circle in his work with that of the horse,[52] which also has metapictorial significance as an image of the creative process.

Although a knowledge of Kandinsky's writings is not necessary in order to experience the imaginary dimension of pictorial space in *Composition VIII*, theory and practice are closely connected in the Bauhaus period, and many of the effects created in *Composition VIII* are discussed in the writings, for example the contrast between curved and straight lines, triangles and circles, floating

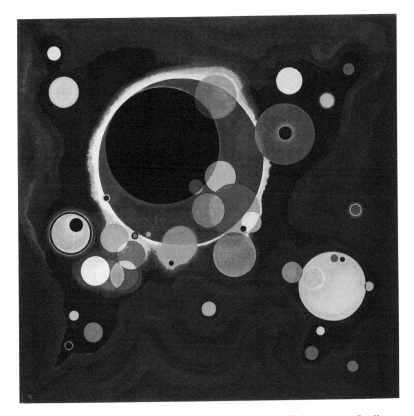

Figure 3. Wassily Kandinsky, *Several Circles*, January–February 1926; oil on canvas, 140.3 × 140.7 cm.

effects, and the dematerialization of pictorial space. In the Bauhaus writings, Kandinsky refers to the role of cultural differences in contributing towards distinctions between symbolic values attached to colours, but he none the less believes that there are similarities based on reactions to properties intrinsic to the colours (*KCWA*, p. 594). At this time, Kandinsky hoped that theoretical analysis would one day be able to provide 'rules' of pictorial composition. Gradually, however, he became more sceptical about the power of verbal language to account for the infinite subtleties of the pictorial medium, and he finally concluded that the laws of painting were unknowable. In his Paris period, he devoted his attention to exploring the enigma of the pictorial medium within painting itself, paying unprecedented attention to unusual chromatic nuances and to tiny decorative detail.

The latter is reminiscent in some respects of Kandinsky's very early work, especially his drawings, his costume designs and his paintings on furniture.[53] He is also increasingly fascinated by analogies between works of art and living organisms. Discussing the history of abstract art, he views its development as parallel to that of natural organisms, and considers its future to be the creation of increasingly complex 'art-organisms' (*KCWA*, p. 628). In the Bauhaus period, he had made extensive use of pictures of natural phenomena to illustrate the parallels between nature and art, and in the 1930s, the influence of biological images becomes central to his work.[54] Towards the end of the Bauhaus period, the forms in his painting had begun to loosen and to acquire organic connotations. (See, for instance, *Hovering Pressure*, 1931, *RB*, plate 1009.) In the Paris paintings, the rigid geometrical shapes of the Bauhaus increasingly give way to more fluid forms, both biomorphic and decorative.[55] (See, for instance, *Monde bleu*, 1934, *RB*, colour plate 1039.) Sometimes, geometrical and 'free' forms are juxtaposed (see *Rigide et courbé*, 1935, *RB*, plate 1063).

In many of the late Bauhaus and the Paris paintings, the titles invite anthropomorphic associations. For instance, *Calmed* (1930); *Dreamy* (1932); *Defiant* (1933); *Cool Distance* (1932); *Gloomy Situation* (1933); *Relations* (1934);[56] *Tension tranquille* (1935); *L'Ensemble chaud* (1939); *Unanimité* (1939); *Modération* (1940); *Thème joyeux* (1942); *Tensions délicates* (1942); *Accord* (1943); *Epanouissement* (1943); *Inquiétude* (1943); *Isolation* (1944); *Elan tempéré* (1944). The pictorial motifs increasingly come to appear as living creatures which are constructs of the medium itself, purely pictorial 'beings'. In some paintings, the relationships between the figures can be seen as analogous to human relationships, for example *Gloomy Situation*,[57] *Entre-deux* (1934) (*RB*, plate 1038), and *Accord réciproque*, 1942 (*RB*, colour plate 1125). In others, decorative and/or biomorphic pictorial figures appear to exist independently of one another, and of the spectator, in an autonomous, self-contained space, as in *Chacun pour soi*, 1935 (*RB*, colour plate 1035). In 1938, Kandinsky declared that 'abstract or non-figurative or non-objective art' should in fact be called 'concrete' (*KCWA*, p. 830), because the work of art creates an alternative world which exists alongside the 'real' world (*KCWA*, p. 832). The Paris paintings have attracted both less commentary and more criticism than either the Munich or the Bauhaus paintings. This reaction may be due to their enigmatic and whimsical qualities: it is sometimes felt that these paintings are too 'light', that they lack the exuberance of the Munich period and the 'gravitas' of the Bauhaus canvases. However, it is in these canvases that Kandinsky succeeded most fully in achieving his aim of

Figure 4. Wassily Kandinsky, *Accord réciproque*, 1942; oil and enamel on canvas, 114 × 146 cm.

painting pictures which could be described as 'purely pictorial fairytales' (*KCWA*, p. 782), where the pictorial elements appear to create their own 'world'.

In *Accord réciproque*, 1942 (*RB*, colour plate 1125, see figure 4), the two figures to either side of the centre possess anthropomorphic qualities while retaining their purely pictorial character. The figure on the left is somewhat larger and more angular: its predominant colour is red. The figure on the right is slighter and contains curved and crescent forms: its predominant colour is blue. The figure on the left leans forward slightly, as if to make an advance. This 'couple' could be seen as a male–female pair, 'personifying' contrasting pictorial tensions, and one is invited to read sexual and psychological associations into their 'accord'. At the same time, the title evokes musical associations which are strongly borne out in the imagery, which suggests a musical score and instruments on the left. The figures themselves can be seen as personifications of musical qualities, and even as strange musical

Figure 5. Wassily Kandinsky, *Courbe dominante*, April 1936; oil on canvas, 129.4 × 194.2 cm.

Figure 6. Wassily Kandinsky, *Actions variées*, August–September 1941; oil and enamel on canvas, 89.2 × 116.1 cm.

instruments with complicated appendages. In addition to these biomorphic and musical associations, the large figures also evoke analogies with musical sounds. A black 'ledge' protruding from the form on the right supports two small figures from which a cluster of tiny forms is launched upwards. The clusters of 'floating' geometrical and decorative forms suggest various sounds, ranging from the 'loud' red circle to the delicate cluster of 'small' sounds on the upper left. The varying sizes of the shapes floating in the central space indicate different degrees of distance, creating a sense of depth. The partitioning of the canvas into panels creates a triptych effect, where the main pictorial figures, which extend into the centre from the side panels, appear to be positioned in front of the central space, which recedes into the distance. Various 'stories' can be constructed around the identities and actions of these delicately nuanced pictorial figures, but, like the sounds evoked by the pseudo-musical notes in the 'score' on the left, their identity is purely speculative and imaginary.

In most of the Paris pictures, the coloration of the space within which the pictorial elements are poised is subject to subtle fluctuations, which create delicate atmospheric effects. Moreover, a hitherto little explored but crucial feature of these canvases is the introduction of new articulations of the picture plane, which have significant consequences for the relationship between pictorial space and imagining activity. Spatial ambiguity can be created by the articulation within one painting of planar forms which appear to obey different spatial logics. In *Courbe dominante*, 1936 (*RB*, colour plate 1069, see figure 5), which Kandinsky considered to be one of his most important works, the complex interaction of different planes means that the picture consists of distinct but intersecting 'spaces'. The flowing form which gives the picture its name and other similar forms create a curving space which contrasts with the concertina-like structure of the 'steps' on the lower right. In *Actions variées*, 1941 (*RB*, colour plate 1121, see figure 6), two rectangular panels and a large, irregularly shaped blue opening on the left introduce spaces whose location is ambiguous, interacting with, yet also existing independently of, the main picture space. In some cases, overlapping effects create a sense of different layers, for example the violet circle to the lower right of the beige panel at the top, and the yellow 'overhang' in front of the panel on the left. The edges of the irregularly shaped blue opening on the left and its dark colour create the effect of a 'hole' within pictorial space, giving the spectator a glimpse into 'deeper' space: it is not clear how its biomorphic insert is situated

Figure 7. Wassily Kandinsky, *L'Accent rouge*, June 1943; oil on board mounted on panel, 41.8 × 57.9 cm.

in relation to these locations. Moreover, space is rendered indefinable by the atmospheric fluctuations of the blue 'medium', in
which the forms appear to float.

A particularly striking aspect of the new treatment of pictorial
space is segmentation, the simplest form of which is where the
whole canvas is divided into grids or panels: see, for instance,
Chacun pour soi, Bagatelles douces, 1937 (*RB*, colour plate 1077);
Trente, 1937 (*RB*, plate 1074); *Parties diverses*, 1940 (*RB*, plate
1110); *Sept*, 1943 (*RB*, plate 1151) and *L'Accent rouge*, 1943 (*RB*,
colour plate 1159, see figure 7). Segmentation has the effect of
encouraging the spectator to perceive the picture sequentially
and of focussing attention on tensions between analysis and synthesis in the pictorial structure, as implied by the titles *Division-
unité* (1934 and 1943). (This preoccupation with the division and
unity of pictorial space compares interestingly with similar concerns in Mondrian.) Even where there are no obvious panels or
inserts as such, the decorative motifs themselves can function as
subdivisions of the pictorial figures, which split into infinitesimal

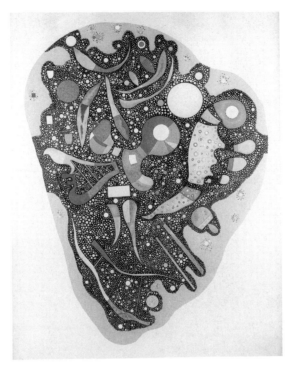

Figure 8. Wassily Kandinsky, *Ensemble multicolore, (Entassement réglé)*,
1938; oil and enamel on canvas, 116 × 89 cm.

parts (see, for instance, *Bleu de ciel*, 1943; *RB*, colour plate 1111).
It is interesting in this respect to compare *Composition VIII* with
Ensemble multicolore 1938 (*RB*, colour plate 1088, see figure 8). The
circular forms in *Ensemble multicolore* have quite a different effect:
the blue insert, which in turn encases a black space, and the
profusion of decorative and geometrical forms inside suggest a
glimpse, not of an infinitely large, cosmic space, but of an
infinitely small, organic space, which is *also* infinitely large in its
limitless detail. This creates the impression that the pictorial
elements themselves can expand indefinitely, depending on the
spectator's capacity to perceive ever smaller details and finer
nuances. The possibility of infinite subdivisions, with no stable
endpoint, opens up the imaginary within the visual. Similarly, in
Parties diverses, the separate but sometimes interconnecting spaces,
filled with unfamiliar forms, evoke the sense of independent
lifeworlds which are radically different from the human. Some
shapes are amoebalike, others more decorative. The spectator
has the impression of looking into a microscope, seeing details

Figure 9. Wassily Kandinsky, *Fragments*, May 1943; oil and gouache on board, 41.9 × 57.7 cm.

Figure 10. Wassily Kandinsky, *Succession*, 1935; oil on canvas, 78.7 × 99 cm.

which would normally be invisible. Whereas in a painting like *Composition VIII*, one is exposed to familiar sensations of move-ment, weight, lightness, etc., spatial laws here seem unrelated to human time: time itself appears to be spatialized and 'frozen', it is not clear whether momentarily or eternally.

This 'frozen' space is still dynamic in that it cannot be grasped in one, but keeps subdividing into different parts. Moreover, the insertion of 'panels' which themselves contain pictorial motifs, as in *Actions variées, L'Accent rouge, Composition IX*, 1936 (*RB*, colour plate 1064) and *Courbe dominante*, 1936, suggests the presence of 'pictures within pictures' (Kandinsky entitled a painting of 1929 which uses this technique *Picture within a Picture*) and introduces a reflexive dimension whereby the relationship of the insert(s) to the larger picture can be seen as analogous to that between the painting and reality and between imaginary and pictorial space. The existence of the insert within the painting undermines the 'reality' of pictorial space, just as the existence of the painting within the real world undermines it by providing a counter-reality. This effect is accentuated where the insert provides an opening onto a space 'beyond', as is the case with the motif on the left in *Actions variées*. The separateness of the panels also suggests the separateness of pictorial space and the space of the spectator. In many of these paintings there is no sense of 'deep' space which could draw the spectator in. These self-absorbed paintings evoke 'other' worlds, languages, beings and spaces, which make no concessions to external reality, and require a willingness on the part of the spectator to explore their 'otherness'. Moreover, the rectangular inserts often contain motifs which evoke inscriptions, suggesting metapictorial commentary and inviting the spectator to reflect on the relationship between imagining activity and pictorial space. In *Courbe dominante*, as in many other paintings, the 'panel' in the upper left contains motifs which are similar to forms elsewhere in the picture, and which Barnett refers to as 'signs'.[58] This 'signlike' aspect is a crucial feature of the pictorial forms in the Paris paintings.

The style of the paintings of this period has evoked comparisons with Asian and Chinese art.[59] It is impossible and unnecessary to isolate a single source for this eclectic imagery, but it would seem likely that Egyptian art played a significant role, especially since segmentation and hieroglyphlike figures become prominent in Kandinsky's work after his visit to Egypt in 1931, although he had already begun to experiment with these techniques earlier (see, for instance, *Levels*, 1929; *RB*, colour plate 896). When the 'signlike' pictorial figures are placed in rectangular panels (as in

Figure 11. Wassily Kandinsky, *Crépuscule*, June
1943; oil on board, 41.8 × 57.6 cm.

Courbe dominante or *Actions variées*), or arranged along lines, as in
Fragments, 1943 (*RB*, plate 1155, see figure 9) and *Succession*, 1935
(*RB*, plate 1055, see figure 10), where they encourage the spectator to 'read' the picture from left to right, they evoke analogies
with writing. (Some of the black/white images, notably in *Trente*,
are also evocative of Taoist calligraphy.) The spatial organization
of these paintings is similar to Egyptian pictures containing bands
of hieroglyphs. The pictographic nature of hieroglyphic characters situates them ambiguously between figurative images and
abstract signs, which is precisely the ambiguity which Kandinsky
is exploring in these paintings. In *Succession*, however, the gaily
coloured, biomorphic forms are very different from Egyptian
hieroglyphs. The linear arrangement and the shapes here evoke
musical symbols, a form which interested Kandinsky, and which
plays a significant role in the Paris paintings. (See, for instance,
Stabilité animée, 1937; *RB*, plate 1084, and *Accord réciproque*.) This
analogy with musical signs introduces a synaesthesic dimension.
    The tone of the Parisian paintings ranges from the mysterious

and magical to the whimsical and playful. The mysteriousness of the pictorial 'signs' is in several cases enhanced by the positioning of light figures on a dark background, which can make them appear to 'float' and creates luminous effects. Kandinsky exploits the contrastive potential of dark grounds in many of his gouaches and oils on board of this period to create an 'other-worldly' quality: see, for instance, *Figure blanche* (*RB*, plate 1142). In *Crépuscule*, 1943 (*RB*, colour plate 1157, see figure 11), a dark-brown backdrop offsets the insert, which evokes a hidden source of light, irradiating the canvas and making the colours appear translucent and ethereal. In *Fragments*, the pictorial signs are inscribed on dark panels which are in turn set in a mosaiclike background, suggesting 'fragments' of mural inscriptions and evoking lost civilizations. In some paintings, these indecipherable pseudo-signs and symbols evoke silence and death. Elsewhere, by contrast, the pictorial figures take on a playful, humorous aspect. In *Bleu de ciel*, for instance, the figure in the top-left corner looks remarkably like a rocking horse, merrily drawing our attention to the games being played with our imagination by the multi-coloured inhabitants of this pictorial 'fairytale'. The paintings of this period frequently show figures which are involved in activities of perching, balancing, etc., and which have the effect of drawing our attention to Kandinsky's exploration of the relationship between dynamism and stasis. See, for instance, *Stabilité animée*, *Petits accents*, 1940 (*RB*, plate 1108), *Parties diverses*, and *Balancement*, 1942 (*RB*, plate 1124).

In *Stabilité animée*, two figures analogous to sealions balancing balls, one in a stable and one in an unstable position, highlight the contrast between 'stability' and 'animation' embodied in the opposition between stable and unstable forms. Thürlemann has argued that here, 'le discours figuratif . . . joue le rôle d'un commentaire, d'un méta-discours explicatif au service de la dimension abstraite'.[60] Indeed, it appears to be the case that the more Kandinsky's confidence in the possibility of creating a purely pictorial world increases, the more he feels at liberty to introduce 'figurative' associations which can provide a reflexive perspective on the pictorial elements. However, as with the pictorial 'signs', which suggest the inscription of 'commentaries' within the paintings themselves, these are not of course truly figurative forms, but *pseudo*-figures, constructs of the pictorial elements which resemble organic forms without being reducible to precise objects. Any figurative connotations ascribed to them are imagined by the spectator, and their resemblance to living organisms introduces a 'metaphorical' dimension which itself draws the spectator's attention to the capacity of imagination to 'animate' the pictorial elements. Moreover, the function of the pictorial 'signs' is to *resemble* signs, but without in fact belonging to any code system: in this way, they signal their own inscrutability and 'tease' the spectator. Some of the paintings also contain motifs which look like esoteric symbols (for example *La Flèche*, 1943: *RB* colour plate 1148), but which are similarly indecipherable. Whereas the vestigial iconography of the semi-abstract Munich paintings and the cosmic connotations of the Bauhaus paintings introduce a reflexive level which invests pictorial space with spiritual and metaphysical implications, here the pseudo-figures and signs focus the spectator's attention on the animating capacity of imagination itself and on the irreducible enigma of the imaginary dimension of the pictorial elements.

The Paris paintings, then, construct from the pictorial elements figures which are at once analogous to and different from real 'beings' and 'objects'. The tales told by these figures are imagined by the spectator while under their spell: they cannot be spoken for by iconographical or theoretical discourses. The polyvalence of these pictures defies discursive analysis, and their reflexivity, where the very elements which excite imagining activity themselves invite reflection on this process, integrates imagination and reflection to an unprecedented degree and invites the spectator to experience the figures as characters in 'purely pictorial fairytales'.

CHAPTER 5

Between the lines: form and transformation in Mondrian

Non-figurative art is created by establishing *a dynamic rhythm of determinate mutual relations* which *excludes the formation of any particular form.*

(*MCWA*, p. 295)

I think that the destructive element is too much neglected in art.[1]

PRACTICE AND THEORY

Mondrian came to abstract painting later than Kandinsky: from 1911, under the influence of Cubism, he began 'abstracting' from nature, but it was not until 1917 that he began to paint independently of natural appearances. The path which led to this development, and the subsequent transformations in his method, are carefully plotted, each painting representing a new stage in what could almost be seen as a vast pictorial experiment, lasting a lifetime. In fact, Mondrian saw his Neo-Plastic painting as a stage in the process of transforming the environment, and his studio as a 'laboratory' in which the environment of the future was researched.[2] Painting was considered as 'a preparation for a future architecture' (*MCWA*, p. 340). In a distant future, art would be superseded: ultimately, 'we will no longer have the need of sculptures and pictures, for we will live in realized art' (*MCWA*, p. 344). Mondrian's ideal environment, for which his painting provided the model, was one where the accidental and the particular – notably specific objects and the artist as an individual – would be replaced by the 'universal'. This was not the universal of abstract thought, of philosophy, but one where concrete entities would be experienced in terms of mutually constructive and destructive relationships.

There are striking parallels between Mondrian's aim of 'transforming' the environment according to Neo-Plastic principles and Mallarmé's project of 'replacing' the universe with the

'Livre'. These parallels show how the fundamental principles of Symbolist aesthetics – as opposed to the much more superficial issue of Symbolist iconography, traces of which can be seen in Mondrian's early work – are projected into and extended through the aesthetics of abstraction. Mallarmé's desire to transpose reality into relationships, where words themselves become both instruments and objects of ontological transformation, is similar to Mondrian's desire to realize an art of 'pure relationships' (*MCWA*, p. 294) which would ultimately transform and absorb the whole of reality. Severini noted the connection between Mallarmean poetics and Neo-Plastic aesthetics when he declared in the pages of *De Stijl* in 1919: 'Now, for the first time, we have a plastic art that achieves the same relations as the work of Mallarmé.'[3]

Michel Seuphor reports that the only flower he ever saw in Mondrian's studio was an artificial tulip whose leaf was painted white, to banish the green which reminded him too much of nature.[4] This brings to mind Mallarmé's description of the ideal flower as 'l'absente de tous bouquets' (*MOC*, p. 368), and these very words are cited by Michel Butor with reference to Mondrian's tulip.[5] Mondrian did in fact paint flowers, both as a young painter and later when he badly needed money. Looking back on his early flower paintings, he emphasizes his interest in structure. 'I enjoyed painting flowers, not bouquets, but a single flower at a time, in order that I might better express its plastic structure' (*MCWA*, p. 338). Mondrian's aim of depicting reality in terms of underlying structure rather than of outer appearances or particular details again brings Mallarmé to mind. 'Cette visée, je la dis Transposition – Structure, une autre' (*MOC*, p. 366): the wager of the 'Livre' was to embody 'l'hymne, harmonie et joie, comme pur ensemble groupé . . . des relations entre tout' (p. 378). Mondrian declared that: 'all things are a part of the whole: each part obtains its visual value from the whole and the whole from its parts. Everything is expressed through *relationship*. Colour can exist only through *other* colours, dimension through *other* dimensions, position through *other* positions that oppose them. That is why I regard relationship as *the principal thing*' (*MCWA*, p. 86).

As with Kandinsky, there is a tendency among art critics to dismiss Mondrian's writings and to separate a pictorial practice seen as revolutionary from a theory seen as retrograde. According to David Craven, '[Mondrian's] acceptance of science and technology was progressive, his theoretical premises were reactionary – ontologically though not socially – and their visual results were revolutionary'.[6] We saw that in Kandinsky, despite their idealist elements, the theoretical writings constitute a powerful challenge to the predominance of iconographical analysis in conventional art historical criticism, while at the same time contradicting modernist conceptions of the space of abstract painting as a 'strictly pictorial, strictly optical' kind, into which 'one can travel only with the eye'.[7] As with Kandinsky, Mondrian's theories are in fact intimately related to his pictorial innovations. However, criticisms of his writings as excessively naïve, dogmatic and repetitive, are all too often justified. Moreover, unlike Kandinsky, who acknowledges both the inability of the artist fully to grasp his own project and the incapacity of words to describe the subtlety of pictorial processes and their effects on the spectator, Mondrian believes that the modern artist can and must become fully conscious of his own work. His great emphasis on binary divisions and revelation of pre-existing truths sets his writings in a firmly metaphysical framework.

Furthermore, this framework is hierarchical, and Mondrian consistently associates the feminine principle with the negative pole of the 'individual' and the 'natural', which it is the task of Neo-Plasticism to overcome. Unlike many other critics, the Marxist critic Harold Rosenberg believes that Mondrian's writings play an important role in replacing the painting in the context of radical avant-garde politics.[8] However, although we shall see in the next chapter that Mondrian's ideas on society are innovative and have a strongly utopian flavour, the 'universal' towards which he aims in both art and life is in fact partial. Mark Cheetham writes that Mondrian has 'established a masculinist frame for abstract painting',[9] and indeed Mondrian associates abstraction itself with the male principle and representation with the female (see *MCWA*, p. 69). Moreover, this framework is not simply confined to iconography but concerns Mondrian's pictorial structure itself, where the vertical is associated with the 'male' and the horizontal with the 'female' (see chapter 1 above, p. 37). However, Mondrian's associations of this sort, like Kandinsky's linking of colours with particular emotions and sensations, are clearly not universal but subjective, and the spectator can therefore project his/her own associations onto the colours and forms in a way which would not be possible with highly gendered iconography (for example Symbolist *femme fatale* images). Moreover, Mondrian's practice arguably moves ahead of his theory, and we shall see that his late, New York works indicate an affirmation of difference and change which implicitly undermines many of his theoretical presuppositions.

The prominent role attributed by Mondrian to his writings again raises the question of the reliance of the paintings on verbal language. Like Kandinsky, Mondrian claimed that his theories were derived from his paintings, not vice versa. 'It is logical for the artist, *after creating* the new art, to try to become *conscious* of it' (*MCWA*, p. 40). Seuphor points out that the ideas which formed the basis of Mondrian's essays later published in *De Stijl* were jotted down in notebooks while he was working on his famous sea paintings (which developed into the 'plus-minus' series) in Domburg in 1914.[10] This suggests a dynamic interaction between pictorial practice and theory, where new thoughts are inspired by the pictorial process itself. Ideas do not programme pictorial practice: they arise out of it. In around 1919, Mondrian wrote to van Doesburg: 'Today I looked at my work and was so struck by its lucidity that I wrote another article.'[11] Near the end of his life, when he was working on his final completed painting, *Broadway Boogie-Woogie*, Mondrian's painter friend Charmion von Wiegand, who was watching his radical innovations, exclaimed in shock and amazement: 'But Mondrian, it's against the theory!' Whereupon Mondrian replied: 'But it works. You must remember, Charmion, that the paintings come first and the theory comes from the paintings.'[12] Also like Kandinsky, Mondrian was aware that his paintings could not 'work' without the spectator's active involvement, and his writings were designed to encourage this. He cites Kandinsky: 'Si une expression froide et décorative résulte du tableau néoplasticien, la faute en est à l'artiste et non à la plastique néoplasticienne. Toutefois, l'expression d'un tableau dépend aussi de l'observateur. Et en ceci Kandinsky a bien remarqué que le "froid" peut devenir "chaud" (tout comme le "chaud" peut devenir "froid").'[13]

In Mondrian's later writings there is a clear move, which is consonant with changes in his pictorial practice, towards greater emphasis on the relative and dynamic at the expense of the absolute and constant. Just as Mallarmé in 'Un coup de Dés' takes the principle of analogy right up to and beyond the limits of its own coherence, in his 'Boogie-Woogie' paintings, Mondrian explores in visual terms the paradoxes at the heart of his 'classical' Neo-Plastic theory. However, although the move towards greater dynamism is reflected in his theoretical writings, Mondrian himself does not recognize the extent to which this development both undermines his aesthetic principles as previously expressed and was implied by them from the outset. The paradoxes which come to light in pictorial terms are not fully verbalized. Possibly, had he lived longer after painting the 'Boogie-Woogie' pictures,

Mondrian would have confronted these issues in his writings, but his unfailing confidence in the evolutionary force of his pictorial ideas and their growing realization in the environment and his continuing belief in the existence of a higher power[14] suggest that he would have been unwilling to verbalize the subversive implications of the 'peinture critique' of his late work.

PICTORIAL AND IMAGINARY SPACE

The crucial issue for Mondrian's aesthetic, as for Kandinsky's, is the ontological status of pictorial space. Art historical discourses which do not address the question of the imaginary dimension of pictorial space are unable to engage with the intersection of formal and ontological issues in Mondrian's painting. Greenberg's classically modernist account of pictorial space, which we have contested in the case of Kandinsky, was in fact formulated with respect to Mondrian. 'The first mark made on a surface destroys its virtual flatness, and the configurations of a Mondrian still suggest a kind of illusion of a third dimension. Only now it is a strictly pictorial, strictly optical third dimension.'[15] This view of modernist painting was further developed by Fried in his distinction between the 'objecthood' of literalist art (exemplified in Minimalism), which he characterizes as 'theatrical' and as 'the condition of non-art', and modernist painting which by contrast suspends objecthood, renders substance optical and is 'anti-theatrical'. Sculpture can achieve the latter effect by emphasizing its 'syntactical' qualities, as in the work of Anthony Caro, where 'the mutual inflection of one element by another, rather than the identity of each, is what is crucial'.[16]

It is easy to understand how – especially in the early New York paintings – Greenberg could have seen in Mondrian's work a three-dimensional quality of a purely optical, pictorial kind, and how Mondrian's art of pure relationships could be described as 'syntactical' in the sense of Fried's description of Caro. His painting might therefore seem to map comfortably onto classical modernist models of pictorial space. However, Bois points out that for Mondrian himself, the effect of optical three-dimensionality created by marking the canvas was not a positive feature, but rather a problem for which he sought radical solutions in his New York paintings. He also points out that Greenberg had previously espoused a different view of Mondrian's pictures, which emphasized their physical presence and their 'quality of inscribed objects in the real space of the room'.[17] Bois himself goes so far as to say that Mondrian is 'seeking the sculptural in painting: he tries to give his works, which are autonomous entities, the literal quality of an object which will render them optically impenetrable'.[18] He cites G. L. K. Morris, whose position is close to early Greenberg. '[Mondrian's pictures] remain the strongest examples yet conceived of painting projected as sculpture . . . Mondrian gives us a thing in itself, – and here we have something entirely new, a fragment of the modern world, concise, compact and complete'.[19]

On this view, Mondrian's painting belongs more in Fried's category of (literalist) 'objecthood' than in that of (modernist) 'art'. In fact, it shares features of both, but is reducible to neither. There is ample evidence that Mondrian himself wished his paintings to be perceived in 'real' rather than simply 'optical' space. Already by 1916 he had replaced the frame with a thin strip of wood which he set flush with the surface of the painting, and beginning with his diamond compositions in 1918 he set the framing strip back from the surface. He explained the reasons for this innovation:

So far as I know, I was the first to bring the painting forward from the frame, rather than set it within the frame. I had noted that a picture without a frame works better than a framed one and that the framing causes sensations of three dimensions. It gives an illusion of depth, so I took a frame of plain wood and mounted my picture on it. In this way I brought it to a more real existence.[20]

He declared: 'Moving the picture into our surroundings, by giving it real existence, has been my ideal ever since I came to abstract painting' (*MCWA*, p. 354). He also wrote that he admired Harry Holtzman's work because there 'we see the "picture" still more from the wall brought into surrounding space. In this way, the painting "annihile" [annihilates] literally the volume and becomes more real.'[21] Moreover, although from reproductions, one might imagine that Mondrian's paintings are perfectly regular, with smooth glossy surfaces, this is not in fact the case: there are irregularities, and the trace of the brush is frequently to be seen.

However, Mondrian believed that painting should not express space, but should 'determine' (structure) it. 'The action of plastic art is not space-expression but space-determination' (*MCWA*, p. 348). Both painting and sculpture should destroy naturalistic space. 'In painting, the empty canvas is an expression of naturalistic space . . . In sculpture, the statue as a whole is a filled-up naturalistic space-expression . . . Both *expressions have to be destroyed* in order to reach abstract expression . . . consequently, not the construction of space (form), but the destruction of it is what abstract art requires' (*MCWA*, p. 385). Noam Gabo reported that Mondrian was:

against space. Once he was showing me a painting . . . 'My goodness!' I said, 'Are you still painting that one?' I had seen it much earlier. 'The white is not flat enough', he said. He thought there was still too much space in the white, and he denied any variations of colour. His ideas were very clear. He thought a painting must be flat, and that colour should not show any indication of space.[22]

Mondrian's paintings are in fact projected into three-dimensional space while at the same time negating it: like good Christians, they are destined to be 'in' the world but not 'of' it. They are positioned in 'real' space, not by partaking of volume, but by denying it, hence becoming, in Mondrian's terms, 'more real'. The negation of volume, as we shall see, takes place through oppositional structures, thus bringing Mondrian's painting close to Fried's model of 'syntactical' modernist sculpture, which he opposes to the 'theatricality' of literalist painting. The 'syntactical' quality ascribed by Fried to Caro's sculpture, which resists being seen in terms of objecthood through 'the mutual inflection of one element by another, rather than the identity of each'[23] is in fact very close to Mondrian's pictorial aesthetic. At the same time, however, Mondrian's painting also partakes of 'theatrical' qualities in that it is concerned with the actual circumstances in which the beholder encounters the work and in that 'the total space is hopefully altered in certain desired ways by the presence of the object'.[24]

The painting can be experienced, not simply as a visual pattern, but as a dynamic process of construction and destruction, of limitation and expansion which negates naturalistic space by destroying particular forms, liberating imagination from their constraints. Unlike naturalistic space, it is in harmony with the rhythms of consciousness. 'Man . . . opposes his rhythm to nature's rhythm and creates his *own environment* – in opposition to nature' (*MCWA*, p. 219). It has often been remarked of Mondrian's paintings from 1917 onwards that they frequently appear to extend beyond the frame. Whereas in Kandinsky, the spectator is encouraged to experience imaginary space by imaginatively projecting him/herself *inside* the picture, in Mondrian's paintings from 1917 onwards, the spectator is invited imaginatively to 'project' pictorial space itself beyond the confines of the picture frame. By leading the spectator's gaze 'into' the surrounding space of the room, these paintings radically reverse the effect of perspectival space, where the picture functions as a 'window' through which the spectator is invited to look 'out'. Because the painting itself has abolished 'naturalistic' space through its forms, proportions, colours and dimensions, it provides a model for the transformation of the environment, thereby affecting the spectator's perception, not just of the picture, but of its relation to its surroundings. Indeed, Mondrian organized his studio space according to the aesthetic principles established in his paintings. He declared that: 'It will be possible for the Abstract-Real "painting" to disappear as soon as we can bring its beauty to equal expression through the colour articulation of the room' (*MCWA*, p. 112). In this way, the 'mind-matter duality' would be reconciled (*MCWA*, p. 30). According to Mondrian, 'harmony is necessary for happiness: harmony between the outward and the inward' (*MCWA*, p. 108).

This raises the question of the extent to which the term 'imaginary' can be used in the context of Mondrian's own conception of his work. Mondrian himself did not use the term imagination, except in a derogatory sense, because he associated imagination with the fantastic, which was opposed to the real and the true. He declared that 'it is illogical to attempt to experience reality through fantastic feelings . . . there is no need for art to create a reality of imagination . . . Art should . . . follow . . . only those intuitions relating to true reality' (*MCWA*, p. 341). There is no room for fantasy in aesthetic contemplation: 'Only in the moment of aesthetic contemplation . . . do we cease to *fantasize*. Then we are open to the revelation of truth; we see pure beauty!' (*MCWA*, p. 95). Fantasy is opposed to truth: 'All fantasy is false' (*MCWA*, p. 364). Truth for Mondrian means the universal and objective as opposed to the individual and subjective, with which he associates fantasy and imagination. It is the task of the artist to reveal the universal, the pure relationships which lie hidden behind natural appearances. Pure art is 'a direct plastic expression of the universal' (*MCWA*, p. 42).

The artist obtains knowledge of the universal through what Mondrian calls 'intuition' ('intuitie'), which is the creative force: 'Art is created through intuition' (*MCWA*, p. 328). Intuition is defined as 'the universal consciousness' which is 'the wellspring of all the arts' (*MCWA*, p. 30). It enables the artist to perceive the universal behind appearances ('intuition discerns the plastic laws veiled in nature's aspect': *MCWA*, p. 350) and inspires the desire to recreate the environment in accordance with this vision. It is associated with the objective as opposed to the subjective. 'Abstract art is not the expression of man's predominantly subjective vision. It is the expression of man's objective vision realized by intuition' (*MCWA*, p. 371). The aim of intuition is to bring about 'the unification of man with the universe' (*MCWA*, p. 345). It is 'self-denying, self-destructive, expansion' (*MCWA*, p. 382), and it unites sensibility and intelligence.

Mondrian places great emphasis on the creative interaction between reason and feeling in intuition. 'Intuition enlightens and so links up with pure thought. They together become an intelligence which is not simply of the brain, which does not calculate, but feels and thinks. Which is creative both in art and life . . . those who do not understand this intelligence regard abstract art as a purely intellectual product' (*MCWA*, p. 293). Intuition is in the process of evolving towards ever greater self-awareness: 'art . . . shows that in the course of progress, intuition becomes more and more conscious' (*MCWA*, p. 293). Intuition which has reached the point of self-awareness can overcome the individual and reach the universal. 'Only *conscious* man can mirror the universal: he can *consciously* become one with the universal and so can *consciously transcend* the individual' (*MCWA*, p. 80). Modernity is characterized by 'the autonomous life of the human spirit becoming conscious' (*MCWA*, p. 28). This emphasis on self-consciousness justifies the artist's theoretical activity.

'Intuition' is the term in Mondrian's writings which corresponds most closely to 'imagination' as it has been used here, although not in terms of its rejection of fantasy and its claims to universal truth. Mondrian's description of intuition as self-negating and his desire to eliminate the individual and particular in favour of the universal and objective recalls Mallarmé's view that 'l'œuvre pure implique la disparition élocutoire du poëte' (*MOC*, p. 366). Mondrian, like Mallarmé, saw the pre-given existence of the natural world as an obstacle to be overcome: natural reality, which is contingent and limited, must be destroyed through the dynamism of oppositional relations. Mallarmé hoped that the aesthetic ordering of the 'vers' and the 'Livre' would eliminate the contingency of real existence. He believed that he himself had become 'impersonnel . . . une aptitude qu'a l'Univers spirituel à se voir et à se développer, à travers ce qui fut moi'.[25] Mondrian declared that: 'In order to understand the true meaning of Abstract Art, we have to conceive us [ourselves] as an reflex [reflection] of reality. This means we have to see us as a mirror in which reality reflects itself' (*MCWA*, p. 367).[26] However, the insights provided by Mondrian's 'intuition' are held to give access to absolute truth, to 'reality'. Mondrian declares that 'there is no question of creation, for *all is created*' (*MCWA*, p. 367): the artist has simply to discover the transcendental reality

which lies behind appearances, and pictorial space is the privileged site where 'the plastic laws veiled in nature's aspect'
(*MCWA*, p. 350) are revealed. For Mondrian, reflexivity means
both artist and spectator becoming aware of the process of transformation of the particular into the universal, whereas for Mallarmé, as we have seen, it involves a *critique* of this process and the
recognition of its fictiveness.

'Intuition', then, does not map exactly onto the concept of
imagination as we have defined it here: it is similar in terms of its
grasping of relations rather than particulars, its creation of interaction between consciousness and its surroundings, and its
capacity for self-negation and self-awareness, but not in terms of
its supposed access to a reality preceding and transcending
external appearances and the medium itself. The 'imaginary'
dimension of Mondrian's paintings is a product of the relationship between the picture and the imagining activity of the spectator: rather than reflecting an *a priori* truth, it is generated by this
interaction itself. Moreover, the projective function of Mondrian's painting, which invites the spectator to envisage the
transformation of the environment, is imaginary in a fictive,
utopian sense, but this dimension was not recognized by Mondrian. For him, intuition is 'absolutely true and actual' (to use
Hegel's terms).[27] He sees the virtual, projective dimension of his
painting as an enterprise to be realized rather than as mere
speculation. Having referred to 'the earthly paradise', he maintained in 1919/20: 'What I have spoken of is to some degree quite
attainable . . . don't regard it simply as a daydream' (*MCWA*,
p. 120). In 1926 he declared that 'the creation of a sort of Eden is
not impossible if there is the will' (*MCWA*, p. 211). Mondrian
increasingly recognized that in the present, his project could be
achieved only 'within the limits of the plastic means' (*MCWA*,
p. 342), and that fuller realization could take place only in a
distant future, but he never analysed the implications of this
'deferral'.

MONDRIAN'S EARLY WORK

Mondrian developed the distinctive style of painting which is
called Neo-Plasticism (a bad translation of the Dutch, 'nieuwe
beelding'),[28] whose principles he was already elaborating in 1914
and which he explained in his articles in the magazine *De Stijl*
between 1917 and 1927. He emphasized that he found the road to
abstraction alone. 'After several years, my work unconsciously
began to deviate more and more from the natural aspects of

reality. Experience was my only teacher; I knew little of the modern art movement. When I first saw the works of the Impressionists, van Gogh, van Dongen, and Fauves, I admired it. But I had to seek the true way alone' (*MCWA*, p. 338). In fact, his new method evolved directly out of his experiments with Cubism, and although his aims were very different from those of the Cubists, he freely recognized the importance of Cubism for the development of his work, referring to it later as 'sublime' (*MCWA*, p. 297). In 1914 he wrote: 'I was influenced by Picasso's work, which I *greatly* admire.'[29] However, Mondrian soon came to the conclusion that Cubism did not go far enough in exploring the consequences of its own discoveries. Ultimately, he evolved a method which was highly personal and which was linked with his philosophical ideas.

The Dutch art world when Mondrian was a young artist (he enrolled in the Amsterdam State Academy in 1892 at the age of twenty) was a predominantly conservative, inward looking one, with little influx of foreign art. It was not until about 1905 that the work of van Gogh (which was exhibited on an unprecedented scale in Amsterdam that year) and of the Impressionists and Neo-Impressionists began to have a significant influence. The work of the Dutch Symbolists, notably Jan Toorop and Thorn-Prikker, which incorporated elements of Art Nouveau, was considered marginal to the mainstream Dutch landscape tradition. However, already before the end of the century, new art critical discourses, with a specifically Dutch slant, had begun to emerge.[30] In 1907, an exhibition in Amsterdam contained Fauvist works by Kees van Dongen, Otto van Rees, Jan Sluyters (whom Mondrian had met several years earlier), and others. In 1909, Holland acquired an avant-garde art journal, *De Kunst*. Mondrian welcomed these new developments. Jan Toorop's introduction of a Neo-Divisionist brushstroke influenced his work, and he wrote in 1909 that 'paint should be applied in pure colours set next to each other in a pointillist or diffuse manner'.[31] In 1909, Mondrian's painting was exhibited alongside Fauvist canvases by Jan Sluyters. He also met Jan Toorop that year, and in 1910, together with art critic Conrad Kickert and fellow painters Jan Sluyters and Jan Toorop he founded the 'Circle of Modern Art'. By this time, he had probably already seen Cubist works, at least in reproduction, and the following year the Circle held its first exhibition, which included works by Cézanne, Braque, Picasso and Derain. In early 1912 he moved to Paris, where he remained until 1914, and where he would return to live and work in 1919.

Despite his interest in pictorial innovations prior to Cubism, Mondrian later expressed his suspicion of the 'decorative' element involved in the flattening of perspective and the use of broad outlines and intense colour.[32] In 1914, he wrote that in his earlier works, 'I sought monumentalism, and tried to achieve abstraction by converting natural colours into a few exaggerated colours. Later, though, I became convinced that this work was too external and, although good of its kind, perhaps not "constructed" enough.'[33] Mondrian differs from Kandinsky in privileging experimentation with form over chromatic innovations, but this rejection of the 'external' brings to mind Kandinsky's insistence on 'internal necessity'. Kandinsky's writings and the *Blue Rider* almanac were influential in Dutch artistic circles before the First World War, as can be seen from van Doesburg's articles in *De Stijl* from 1912,[34] and Mondrian also refers to Kandinsky in his writings.

Mondrian's early work is quite fascinating in its own right and merits more detailed attention than it has received hitherto.[35] A particularly interesting aspect is the prominence of preoccupations such as the search for structure and the imparting of a spiritual dimension to the purely pictorial elements of line and colour, which would be central to his later painting. At the same time, we can also see characteristics which might have led him into abstraction along a different path. In the truly extraordinary series of 'dune' paintings executed between 1909–10,[36] the whole canvas is treated as a colour field, exploiting contrasts of expansion and recession, straight and irregular edges, and the monumental, contemplative qualities of these paintings invite comparison with a late Rothko.[37] The early works in which Mondrian explores compositional problems such as expansion and limitation far outstrip in pictorial interest works which are more concerned with non-naturalistic use of colour, such as *Zeeland Farmer*, 1910 (*O* 241, *S* 234).

The same is true of the paintings which could be described as Symbolist, although, as Welsh points out, they have little to do with the heavily Art Nouveau influenced style of the Dutch Symbolists and are more closely related to Mondrian's readings in Theosophy. The most famous painting of this type is *Evolution (Triptych)*, 1910–11 (*O* colour plate XXIII, *S* 324, see figure 12), which Champa has unkindly though understandably described as 'that great disaster of quality and theosophical notation'.[38] The canvas is unusually large: 183 × 87.5 cm. for the central panel and 178 × 87.5 cm. for the side panels. The size of the central panel indicates its importance, and Mondrian intended it to be

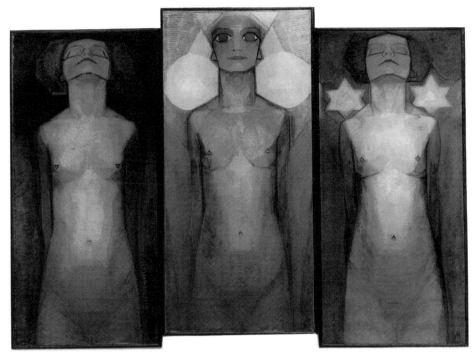

Figure 12. Piet Mondrian, *Evolution (Triptych)*, 1910/11; oil on canvas, 178 × 87.5, 183 × 87.5, 178 × 87.5 cm.

hung slightly higher than the side panels. Also, it represents the culmination of the process of 'evolution' towards greater spiritual enlightenment. This progression is indicated by the shift from the red colour of the forms above the shoulders of the woman on the left (probably a schematic representation of the passion flowers which appear in this position in *Passion Flower*, 1908: *O* 197, *S* 62) to the greater prominence of yellow in the right and the centre; by progressive geometrization of forms and straightening of lines; by the transition from downward pointing triangles in the nipples and navel on the left to upward-pointing triangles in the centre, and, above all, by the progression from closed eyes to the open-eyed stare of the central figure, indicating enlightenment. The woman here has taken on strongly androgynous qualities, consonant with the view, prevalent among Theosophists and Symbolists, that the androgyne represented the highest stage in human evolution. Welsh has examined the connections between the geometrical forms of *Evolution (Triptych)* and Theosophical symbolism.[39]

If the influence of Theosophy had been limited to this kind of formal symbolism, its effect on Mondrian's work would have been largely detrimental. However, although he was attracted to Theosophy's investigation of hidden structures and its 'mystical mathematics', he soon came to see its pictorial equivalent in terms of the dynamics of pictorial composition, rather than in the conventional symbolism of specific forms. 'To the shape of the cross . . . we readily attach a particular, rather *literary* idea. The cross form, however, is constantly destroyed in the New Plastic' (*MCWA*, p. 99). We saw in chapter 1 above that Mondrian was also interested in other attempts to establish connections between matter and consciousness and to discover the basis for a universal pictorial 'language'. However, his use of philosophy is pragmatic and eclectic, since his mode of discovering new ideas is primarily pictorial. He is in fact on record as having said: 'I do not want *pictures*, I just want to find things out.'[40] Indeed, as we shall see below, the insights of Mondrian's pictorial practice were consistently ahead of his theory. His exploration of the possibilities of the pictorial medium led him to develop a mode of signifying which, like the Peircean 'diagram', enables the spectator to make new discoveries derived directly from the construction of the painting itself.

TO *DE STIJL* AND BEYOND

Mondrian's pictorial practice and his theory are very closely linked, and the remainder of this chapter will examine them together.[41] His theory of the 'universal', which necessitates the overcoming of the 'particular', corresponds exactly to his search for pictorial relationships which negate particular forms. In 1908, Mondrian began a series of paintings on the theme of a single tree. Tracing the development of this particular series will take us right up to his Cubist phase, from whence he moved into the 'plus and minus' paintings of 1914 to 1916, followed by the compositions with coloured planes of 1917, influenced by Bart van der Leck. This was the final stage before he joined up the free floating rectangles in the grids which formed the basis of his classical Neo-Plastic style. In 1917, the first issue of the magazine *De Stijl* appeared. The moving spirit behind the magazine and the group of painters and architects based around it was Theo van Doesburg, but Mondrian was the theoretical leader and was recognized as 'the father of Neo-Plasticism', the style of painting which he evolved after his break with Cubism in 1913 to 1914. In 1925, he resigned from the group owing to the famous disagreement with van Doesburg over the latter's infringement of Neo-Plastic

Figure 13. Piet Mondrian, *The Red Tree*, 1908; oil on canvas, 70 × 99 cm.

Figure 14. Piet Mondrian, *The Blue Tree*, 1908/09?; tempera on board, 75.5 × 99.5 cm.

principles by using diagonal lines in his paintings. Mondrian himself continued to elaborate and modify the principles of Neo-Plasticism right up to his death in 1944.

In addition to the interaction between the vertical axis of the tree trunk and the horizontal axis of the horizon line, the tree motif was of special interest to Mondrian because of the way in which the branches stretch out into surrounding space. It is this aspect which Mondrian explores in his 'Tree' series, which brings about a progressive integration of form and space, where form fragments and ultimately restructures pictorial space as a configuration of intersecting planes, from which the 'object' can no longer be distinguished. The gradual elimination of the object is a logical consequence of this progressive integration. The beginnings of this transformation can be observed in *The Red Tree*, 1908 (*O* colour plate XXVIII–XXIX, *S* 283, see figure 13). The dramatic quality of this picture is due both to the strong contrast of red and blue and to the dynamically twisting forms of the tree itself, which reach outwards into space and downwards towards the earth, as if in an attempt to create an organic unity between form and space, earth and sky. The tree in fact envelops most of the canvas. At the same time, the contrast between red and blue, where blue is used mainly for space and red for the tree and the earth, highlights their separation. Moreover, Mondrian believed that lack of equilibrium between the vertical and the horizontal, where one predominated over the other, was 'tragic', and here we can see a clear dominance of the horizontal over the vertical owing to the format of the picture and the position of the tree.

The 'tree' theme is further developed in several pictures of 1909–10. In *Tree*, 1909–10 (*O* 223, *S* 285) and *The Blue Tree, c.* 1908–9 (*O* colour plate XXVI, *S* 284, see figure 14), the background space is very strongly painted, with large juxtaposed brushstrokes which emphasize the continuity of figure and ground. There are also geometrizing tendencies in the treatment of the tree itself. In the latter painting, the 'background' space within the tree's radius is delineated in brushstrokes which follow the sweep of the branches, and curving lines trace a semi-circular form around the tilting triangular shape of the tree. A line even connects the end of a branch on the lower left with the trunk of the tree, creating a circular effect. There is a strong sense of conflicting forces here, where the contour lines appear to 'enclose' the tree, gathering up its energy in itself and also, following the vectors of its branches, pulling it downwards towards the earth. This centripetal movement could be said to be reinforced by the diagonal direction of the brushstrokes depicting the 'sky', and

Figure 15. Piet Mondrian, *Horizontal Tree*, 1911–12; oil on canvas, 65 × 81 cm.

Figure 16. Piet Mondrian, *Grey Tree*, 1912; oil on canvas, 78.5 × 107.5 cm.

also the bristling lines forming part of the structure of the tree itself. However, these strokes and lines can also be seen as being directed outwards, away from the tree, creating a tension between centripetal and centrifugal forces, and between the tree and surrounding space. The interaction between figure and ground is emphasized by the fact that both the tree and the earth are overpainted in parts by blue.

Given Mondrian's preoccupations at this time, it is not surprising that he was excited to discover the work of the Cubists, in particular their use of 'passages', where contours are broken and forms seem to merge with space. See, for instance, the two versions of *Still Life with Ginger Pot*, 1911–12 (*O* colour plate xxiv, *S* 36) and 1912 (*O* colour plate xxv, *S* 366), where the latter shows strongly Cubist tendencies. However, Mondrian uses Cubist techniques to his own distinctive ends, which are not to portray the object *qua* object, but rather to analyse its hidden structure. His aim was to find a compositional structure which would avoid 'limiting form', which is '*descriptive*' (*MCWA*, p. 343). In the later 'tree' paintings, dating from 1911–12 (*Horizontal Tree*, 1911–12, *O* 248, *S* 368, see figure 15; *Grey Tree*, 1912, *O* plate xxvii, *S* 335, see figure 16, and *Flowering Apple Tree*, 1912, *O* colour plate xxx, *S* 345, see figure 17), we see an increased tendency to integrate form and space, using techniques influenced by Cubism.

In *Horizontal Tree*, the structure of the tree itself is rendered in intersecting arcs, which cut through each other and the surrounding space, which takes on a crystalline, refracted quality. Because the arcs are open, they frame space without delimiting it, and form planes which integrate figure and ground. ('It is clear that the open form is less limiting than the closed form': *MCWA*, p. 346.) Not only this, but there is a marked movement towards symmetry: here, the overall contour of the tree is straighter than in previous versions, tending towards a 'T' structure. The horizontal still dominates the vertical, and the branches still curve downward towards the ground, but this lack of balance is partially offset by the faint outline of a large circle at the centre of the composition and by the presence of vertical and horizontal lines intersecting at right angles. In *Grey Tree*, there is a greater sense of equilibrium, created partly by the balance of upward and downward facing arcs. Movement towards the edges of the canvas is suggested by the lateral extension of the branches, and ascending movement is indicated by the convergence of two arcs in a point in the top centre of the picture. At the same time, the arcs at the top can be seen as curving inwards towards the tree, thereby creating a balance between centripetal and centrifugal movement. Later,

Figure 17. Piet Mondrian, *Flowering Apple Tree*, 1912; oil on canvas, 78 × 106 cm.

in the harmonious composition of *Flowering Apple Tree*, the tension of the tree trunk and branches, struggling to integrate with surrounding space, has been resolved. The tree is released from its contingent, separate, individual existence and dissolved into a network of intersecting curvilinear planes, whose delicate hues evoke the 'flowering' of the title. The curving lines create a dynamism which is offset by the equilibrium of curve and countercurve.

In the paintings between 1912 and 1914, the curved line is gradually straightened (Mondrian saw the curve as too close to nature) and the object becomes less and less visible, sometimes also disappearing from the title, which is simplified to *Composition*. For instance, *Composition 6*, 1914 (*O* colour plate xxxix, *S* 431), contains only residual curves. The arrangement of the composition in an ovoid space in many of these pictures has been linked with Cubist techniques (though Mondrian differs in his use of clear boundaries) and also with the androgyne myth.[42] The breaking down of the object which we see taking place here is not an end in itself, but a means of achieving the integration of form and space and revealing the universal behind the particular. As Tomassoni writes:

Mondrian was not interested in the specific aims of the Cubist style, such as multiple perspective, the breaking down and reconstruction of objects, spatial condensation, and the multiple representation of the same object simultaneously . . . his fundamental concern was to liberate form from any particular definition, to purify vision from the contingent, and to isolate the object from the instability of phenomena by assigning it to a higher order.[43]

While he praises the Cubists for breaking 'the closed line, the contour that delimits particular form', Mondrian also maintains that 'Cubism loses unity by following the fragmented character of natural appearances. For objects remain objects, despite their fragmentation' (*MCWA*, p. 64). According to Mondrian, Cubism did not go far enough. 'Gradually I became aware that Cubism did not accept the logical consequence of its own discoveries; it was not developing abstraction toward its ultimate goal, the expression of pure reality . . . particularities of form and colour . . . obscure *pure reality*' (*MCWA*, p. 338). At this time, Mondrian, 'impressed by the vastness of nature', was 'trying to express its expansion, rest and unity' (*MCWA*, p. 339). His solution to this problem can be seen in the 1914 *Sea* and *Pier and Ocean* series. Here, the straight lines which had hitherto been joined together to form rectangular planes begin to separate and appear singly or in the form of vertical–horizontal intersections (hence the name 'plus–minus' which has been given to these compositions). In this way, not only is any suggestion of volume avoided, but no individual planes are created, and the spectator is invited to experience the 'object' through its plastic rhythms. In *Composition 10, Pier and Ocean*, 1915 (*O* 289, *S* 415), the predominance of vertical lines at the bottom centre (the 'pier') leads the spectator's eye upwards and outwards into the 'sea', where the more extended horizontal lines and the larger areas of empty space suggest the movement of waves breaking away from the pier, while the greater compactness at the top suggests recession into the distance. (In a study for this picture (*O* 289³), the diagonal lines clearly indicate the movement of waves breaking away from the pier.) The fact that the frame crops the picture at the top and bottom increases the sense of vertical extension: a larger area is cropped at the top, accentuating the impression of movement towards the top of the canvas.

Writing later of this period, Mondrian observed that 'vertical and horizontal lines are the expression of two opposing forces . . . I recognized that the equilibrium of any particular aspect of nature rests on the equivalence of its opposites' (*MCWA*, p. 339). The crossing lines themselves form larger configurations, which prevent them being seen as individual forms. 'Even the most perfect, the most general geometrical form expresses something specific. To destroy this limitation (or individuality) of expression as far as possible is the task of art, and constitutes the essential of all style' (*MCWA*, p. 52). However, the elimination of planes meant that space once again appeared as a background. In 1916, Mondrian met the painter van der Leck, whose technique of painting rectangles in pure colours encouraged him to experiment with compositions using flat planes. (See, for instance, *Composition in Blue B*, 1917; *O* 297, *S* 433 and *Composition No. 3 with Colour Planes*, 1917; *O* colour plate XLI, *S* 428.) These planes do not represent anything: they create rhythmic relationships, and the 'cutting' action of the edges of the canvas, which intersect the rectangles, suggests that they extend beyond its confines. However, this technique left unsolved the problem of the distinction between figure and ground, since the rectangular blocks often appeared to 'float' in front of the ground. Also, the rectangles could still be perceived as individual, particular forms.

It was then that Mondrian had the idea of joining up the rectangles into the grids which were to form the basis of compositional structures throughout the remainder of his career. Apart from a short period in 1918–19, he did not use mathematical calculations in composing these grids, but relied on intuition.[44] He began by using irregular grids but found them too disorderly and moved to a regular format in the diamond composition of 1918, *Lozenge with Grey Lines* (*O* 305, *S* 445), which, when viewed in the original, is a highly dynamic picture, with lines of differing thicknesses which create 'popping' effects. Mondrian disagreed with van Doesburg's criticism that the regular format created too much repetition, but changed his mind when he saw a black and white reproduction of one of his lozenge paintings in *De Stijl*, which reduced the different colours of the planes in the original to the same grey tone and made the picture appear too uniform. This encouraged him to experiment again with more irregular grids, and to use stronger colours, contrasting with his earlier use of pastel shades. In his late 1919 and early 1920 compositions, he seeks to combine the advantages of the regular and irregular grid forms: by simplifying the structure, he emphasizes the coherence of the rectangular form, but he also makes it difficult for the spectator to perceive any rectangle in isolation, as the lines constantly divide large rectangles into smaller ones and lead out of one rectangle into another. (See, for instance, *Composition with Grey, Red, Yellow and Blue*, 1920: *O* 316, *S* 449.)

In these compositions, Mondrian explores the simultaneously analytical and constructive function of the line, which 'separates and unites at the same time'.[45] The rectangles are 'open' forms in the sense that they are not self-sufficient, but open out onto other rectangles. Here, not only horizontal and vertical lines, but also limitation and expansion are opposed to and balance one another. The grid form suggests both closure, as a 'mapping of the space inside the frame onto itself'[46] and openness, as a potentially centrifugal, expanding structure. (As in the earlier paintings, the edges perform a 'cutting' function.) The repetition of right angles and of rectangular planes, which are the regular elements in the composition, is offset by differences in proportion and colour. From 1920, the colour composition takes on more importance in its own right, as the colours become more saturated and almost entirely primary, and constitute a 'counterpoint' to the formal composition. Bart van der Leck was already juxtaposing unmixed primary colours in 1916, but Mondrian, with his concern for equilibrium, felt the need to mix the primary colours with white in order to balance their tonal values. Now, however, he was discovering a new kind of equilibrium, which was based on equivalence of opposites rather than on symmetry. 'Abstract-real plastic has to transform symmetry into equilibrium, which it does by continuous opposition of proportion and position; by plastically expressing *relationships* which change each opposite into the other' (*MCWA*, p. 40). This 'opposition of proportion and position', where changes in proportion and colour are opposed to constancy of position in the right angle, is the basis of the Neo-Plastic 'language' which Mondrian continues to refine and perfect in his classical Neo-Plastic paintings of the twenties.

Mondrian later described how in these pictures 'space became white, black or grey; form became red, blue or yellow . . . It was evident that rectangles, like all particular forms, obtrude themselves and must be neutralized through the composition. In fact, rectangles are never an aim in themselves but a logical consequence of their determining lines, which are continuous in space; they appear spontaneously through the crossing of horizontal and vertical lines' (*MCWA*, p. 339). An example of how line is used to create intersections over the whole surface of the composition can be seen in *Composition with Red, Yellow and Blue*, 1921 (*O* 325, *S* 455, see figure 18), reproduced here in diagrammatic form (see diagram 2). Champa has criticized the 'lack of pictorial animation' in this picture, arguing that its tension is due simply to quantitative impacting and that the black lines fail to dynamize the interchange between the white and the colour

Figure 18. Piet Mondrian, *Composition with Red, Yellow and Blue*, 1921; oil on canvas, 80 × 50 cm.

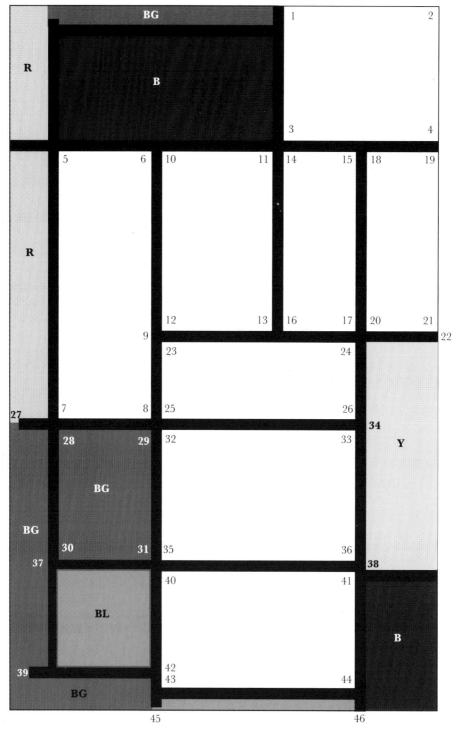

Key: B = Black, BL = Blue, BG = Blue Grey, R = Red, Y = Yellow

Diagram 2. Mondrian, *Composition with Red, Yellow and Blue*, 1921.

rectangles and can too easily be read as 'imposed drawing, rather than plane connection'.[47] It is true that here Mondrian has not fully mastered balancing the interaction between areas of colour and non-colour (as he calls white, black and grey), and the use of bluish whites (in the rectangles 1–3–4–2, 5–7–8–6, 18–20–21–19 and 40–43–44–41: see diagram 2) and of blue-grey in the lower left-hand corner and base and in the rectangle 28–30–31–29 creates an air of uncertainty which is not present in the compositions based on pure primary colours and non-colours. However, what is exciting here is the way in which the spectator's attempts to perceive a rectangular form as a whole or to establish a single set of co-ordinates which could hold the image in a stable framework are constantly thwarted by subdivisions and passages created by the lines.

The long 'corridor' which starts at the base from points 45 and 46 and extends up to 10 and 15 at the top invites perception of the lines 45–10 and 46–15 as boundaries. However, these boundary lines are intersected by horizontals twice on the left and once on the right. The most 'active' lines here are 27–34, which cuts right across the rectangle 23–35–36–24, and 9–22, which cuts through the rectangle 10–25–26–15, both of which, if they had remained 'intact', could have functioned as stable focal points for the composition. (The effect of 37–38 is less dramatic, since rectangle 40–43–44–41 is already distinguished by a slight difference in hue.) Moreover, the horizontal line 9–22 itself forms the base of three further rectangles. A left–right directionality is created by the fact that the vertical 11–13 is positioned right of centre of the rectangle 10–12–17–15, creating an asymmetrical effect which is in turn balanced by the rectangle 14–16–21–19. This rectangle is further subdivided, creating an unresolvable tension between movement towards the inside and towards the outside of the picture. The rectangle 10–12–17–15 cannot function as a stable focal point, because it is destabilized by 14–16–21–19, but 14–16–21–19 is itself destabilized by the fact that 14–16–17–15 (which is white) is part of 10–25–26–15. It thereby directs the viewer's gaze into and down the central 'corridor', whereas 18–20–21–19, which is both open and bluish white, like 1–3–4–2 above it, directs the viewer's gaze out of the picture. The predominating direction of this outward movement is upwards and to the right, accentuated by the fact that the three lines in the lower left stop short of the edge (especially the line 39–42), directing the spectator's gaze inwards and upwards. In this way, centripetal movement on the lower left is countered by centrifugal movement on the upper right, and the self-reflexive grid becomes expansive.

Colour and line work together here to create dynamic effects, and it is not true to say, as Champa does, that drawing fails to activate interchange between white and coloured rectangles and that it is 'superimposed'.

The main changes which take place from now on right up to 1932, when Mondrian introduces the double line for the first time, are reduction of means of expression, increased interplay between the internal compositional structure and the cutting edges of the 'frame' (i.e. the boundaries of the picture), and the creation of invisible diagonal axes. The shift towards greater economy and equilibrium, which coincides with increased emphasis on a square or near-square format, can clearly be seen from 1922 onwards. Mondrian said: 'In my paintings after 1922 I feel I approached the concrete structure I regard as necessary' (*MCWA*, p. 356). In retrospect, he judged his earlier rectangular compositions to be too vague and unstructured. The clearest and most succinct account of the principles of the Neo-Plastic 'language' is found in an article by Mondrian published in *De Stijl* in 1927, entitled 'The Plastic Means'.

The plastic means must be the plane or the rectangular prism in primary colour (red, blue, yellow) and non-colour (white, black, grey) . . . The equivalence of the plastic means is necessary. Although differing in dimension and colour, they must nevertheless have the same value. Equilibrium generally requires a large area of non-colour and a smaller area of colour or volume . . . Constant equilibrium is achieved through the relationship of position . . . Equilibrium neutralizes and annihilates the plastic means and is achieved through the relationships of proportion in which they are placed and which creates the living rhythm.[48]

Repetition of the stable perpendicular is offset by the differences of colour and dimension. The function of pictorial composition is to abolish the particularity of the plastic means through relationships of opposition and equivalence. This principle operates at two levels in the Neo-Plastic structure: overall equivalence between the stable (unchanging) and the dynamic (changing) levels of the composition (repetition of the right angle and variations in colour and dimension), and equivalence at the dynamic level itself between different colours and dimensions through the balance of small areas of colour and large areas of non-colour. The 'equivalence of opposites' (*MCWA*, p. 53) creates equilibrium, which reveals the 'universal'. The paradox which will later emerge is that this equilibrium is itself dynamic, and that the 'universal' is inseparable from the principles of movement and change embodied in the rhythmic element of the composition, which was originally seen as relative and subjective (*MCWA*, p. 64).

In the course of the 1920s, Mondrian decreases the number of rectangles, which therefore become larger, and strengthens their colours. From 1922, he experiments with ever larger white rectangles, which are balanced by much smaller rectangles in strong, pure colours. Here, the 'constant equilibrium' of the right angle is balanced by the 'dynamic equilibrium' created by the relationship between different sized rectangles, where large areas of 'non-colour' are balanced by small coloured rectangles. We noted above that in *Composition with Red, Yellow and Blue*, 1921, the intersection of certain rectangles by the frame created the impression that the composition extended beyond its confines. There, however, the segmentation of pictorial space into small units meant that the internal compositional structure was dominated by the external frame. The enlargement of the rectangles, and especially the presence of very large, dominant white rectangles establishes a greater balance, and also a tension, between the 'internal' composition and the 'external' frame. In fact, the lines of the frame and its format are themselves increasingly active parts of the composition. Sometimes the edges of the large white internal rectangle are cut by the frame, and sometimes they are intact, but in both cases, the off-centre position of the rectangle creates an asymmetry which contrasts strongly with the regular format of the frame. The tension between symmetry and asymmetry, where the strength of one closely matches the other, creates an oscillating effect which results in perception of neither symmetry nor asymmetry, but the relationship between them.

Champa has described the 'worked area' (the lines and coloured rectangles) between the interior white rectangle and the exterior frame which is a prominent feature of the 1921–3 canvases as 'a kind of painted frame existing between the true framing edge of the picture and the black line frame that encloses the unworked, white, inside motifs'.[49] (See, for instance, *Composition II*, 1922: O 348, see figure 19.) This points to the role of the large internal white rectangles as images of paintings. The rectangles divide and subdivide the picture plane, enabling pictorial space to be experienced as pure relationships, rather than as a pattern of fixed, particular forms. In this way, they do not 'reflect' *actual* pictures, but rather suggest their ideal function, which would be to act as space dividers, to the point, as we have seen above, of actually becoming integrated with the environment. Mondrian even claims that 'a picture functions just as well or even better with its face to the wall, for then it appears as a "plane" and as part of the architectural construction' (*MCWA*, p. 389). The reflexive dimension of these paintings, far from

Figure 19. Piet Mondrian, *Composition II*, 1922; oil on canvas, 55.6 × 53.4 cm.

making them 'self-referential' and tautological, means that they actively redefine the relationship between the picture and its surroundings. In presenting a model of ideal space, the picture also functions as a critique of real space and invites the spectator to become aware of his/her position between them and to reflect on their relative degree of 'harmony between the inward and the outward' (*MCWA*, p. 108).

Mondrian's insistence that only vertical and horizontal lines could be used in Neo-Plastic compositions means that the linear framework of these paintings corresponds to the structure of the room in which they are placed. Writing about the large internal rectangles in the 1920s paintings, Michel Butor has suggested that 'ce carré intérieur c'est le tableau lui-même, blanc vide, pure ouverture', and that it can also be seen as a 'chambre dans la chambre', the model of a 'chambre future'.[50] It is important to realize, however, that the 'model', for Mondrian, is not in fact the 'blanc vide' embodied in the large white rectangles, but the active and structured *division* of space which is brought about by the pictorial tensions between symmetry and asymmetry. The sense of emptiness, space and silence evoked by the large white rectangles is not what Mondrian wishes to express. 'Empty space is unbearable . . . Plastic art is not the expression of space but of life in space' (*MCWA*, p. 356). Perhaps as a response to this danger, in the late 1920s, Mondrian will move to a more actively divided compositional structure.

The remarkable sense of interaction between the internal composition and the framing edges which Mondrian developed in the 1920s may well be connected with his experiments with diamond compositions,[51] which began with a series in 1918, followed by an isolated example in 1921 and by another series in 1925. (He returned to this format in 1930, 1931, 1933, and of course in his famous final painting, *Victory Boogie-Woogie*.) The diamond compositions are a fascinating feature of Mondrian's work. Their appearance can be linked with several contexts: the diamond-shaped escutcheons which hang in Dutch churches and which can be seen in many paintings of Dutch church interiors,[52] van Doesburg's use of a diamond format in his designs for stained-glass windows of 1917,[53] and van Doesburg's break with Neo-Plasticism in 1924 to found Elementarism, which introduced diagonal lines into the composition.[54] The first diamond composition using an irregular grid is in 1921 (see *Composition in a Square*, 1921, *O* 336), and the effect of the 'cutting edges' is even more dramatic here than in the rectangular compositions of the same period, because of the contrast between the perpendicular lines of the composition and the diagonal lines of the edges. This effect is further developed in the remarkable 'contrapuntal' compositions of the later diamonds.

A letter written by Mondrian to van Doesburg in 1919 indicates that the diamond compositions indeed heightened his awareness of the contrapuntal relationship between the composition and the frame. 'I hang several pieces now like *this*: ◇, in order that the composition becomes like this +; whereas in this way □ the composition is like this ×.'[55] Paradoxically, the diamond format places increased emphasis on the horizontal/vertical axes of the composition and in fact allows longer horizontal and vertical lines.[56] Moreover, it is most interesting that Mondrian refers in this letter to the diagonal impetus of the *rectangular* composition. As noted above, emphasis on the invisible diagonal axis is one of the most remarkable features of the paintings of the late twenties and carries through into the early thirties.

The diagonal axis is invisibly inscribed by the strategic positioning of the pointing edges of internal rectangles, an effect which is reinforced by the alignment of the pointing edge with a corner of the frame, as in *Composition with Red, Yellow and Blue*, 1928 (*O* 381, *S* 534), where there is a very clear diagonal axis running between the lower left and the upper right. The direction in which the eye follows the axis depends mainly on the positioning of the larger rectangle, towards which the eye is drawn. This is particularly true if the large rectangle is white, as in *Composition*, 1929 (*O*, 387, *S* 541, see figure 20), where the combination of a very strong diagonal impulse towards the upper right and the positioning here of a large white rectangle emphasizes its potential integration with the surrounding space, but the composition is also held firmly in place by the strong black lines and the unflinchingly stable rectangles of unadulterated red and black.

A noticeable feature of this painting is the uneven thickness of the black lines: the first horizontal line from the top is clearly much thicker than the others. This was not in itself a new development, but from now on, the lines were to play an increasingly active role in the composition. In *Composition with Red, Black and White*, 1931 (*O* colour plate LIV, *S* 561), they 'dig into' the ground, 'dematerializing' the planes by pushing them forwards, making them 'float' slightly in front of the lines. Then, in *Composition B with Grey and Yellow*, 1931 (*O* 407, *S* 368), Mondrian introduces the double line for the first time. From now on, right up to 1941, after his arrival in New York in 1940, black lines will be the dominant element of the composition. His motives are clear. 'In order to abolish the manifestation of planes as rectangles, I reduced my colour and accentuated the limiting lines, crossing them over the other. Thus, the planes were not only cut and divided, but their relationships became more active' (*MCWA*, p. 340). This description gives the impression that the new development results in greater liberation. However, the proliferation of black lines can also create an oppressive effect, a characteristic which has been linked with the atmosphere created by the threat of war. Interestingly, the vertical format dominates in many of these canvases, which, for Mondrian, is associated with the 'tragic'. This format increases the sense of constriction, an effect which is also created by the crossing over of the lines in front of coloured rectangles, which are pushed back 'behind bars', as in the rectangles in the upper left of *Abstract Composition*, 1939 (*O* 445) and *Rhythm of Black Lines*, 1935–42 (*O* 449, *S* 396). Coloured rectangles which are not overlaid with lines are small

Figure 20. Piet Mondrian, *Composition*, 1929; oil on canvas, 52 × 52 cm.

and create the impression that they are 'trapped' between the lines, like the yellow rectangle to the right of *Rhythm of Black Lines*. Writing about *Composition 1936–42* (*O* 450, *S* 586, see figure 21), Butor speaks of 'une impression de grille derrière laquelle le petit carré bleu est comme prisonnier'.[57]

The oppressive quality of the lines is accentuated by emphasis on centripetal movement, such as in *Composition 1936–42*, where the lines 'crowd' towards the centre. Despite this oppressive quality, however, it is very noticeable in these paintings that Mondrian has moved towards increased emphasis on rhythm.[58] The complexity of the patterns in *Rhythm of Black Lines*, *Composition 1936–42* and *Composition II with Red, Yellow and Blue*, 1939–42 (*O* colour plate LXI, *S* 608, see figure 22) makes focussing difficult: if one does maintain a fixed focus, the lines themselves appear to expand and dilate, taking on almost organic qualities, and optical flickers appear at the intersections. A group of these paintings, including the three just referred to, were begun in Europe and finished in New York, where Mondrian arrived in

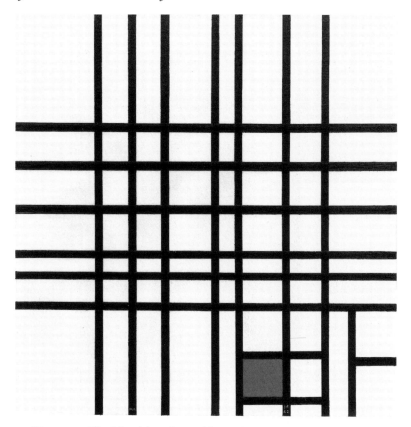

Figure 21. Piet Mondrian, *Composition 1936–42*, 1936–42; oil on canvas, 62.6 × 60.3 cm.

1940. A remarkable feature of several of the paintings to which Mondrian put the finishing touches in New York is the addition of small strips of free-standing colour. (See, for instance, *Composition II with Red, Yellow and Blue*, to which Mondrian has added a blue and a red strip, and *Place de la Concorde*, 1938–43, *O* 462, *S* 602, to which several strips have been added.) In *Composition II with Red, Yellow and Blue*, the restlessness of the irregularly placed bands of vertical and horizontal lines takes on a lighter mood through the presence of brightly coloured yellow and red rectangles and through the addition of a blue strip on the left and a small red one on the right. Moreover, the dominance of the vertical pattern is offset by increased numbers of horizontal lines.

The most startling transformation, however, was that of the black lines themselves. In *New York*, 1941–2 (*O* colour plate LXII, *S* 616), coloured lines make their appearance alongside black

Figure 22. Piet Mondrian, *Composition II with Red, Yellow and Blue*, 1939–42; oil on canvas, 72 × 69 cm.

ones, and in *New York City I*, 1942 (*O* 458, *S* 619, see figure 23), the black lines have completely disappeared and have been replaced by coloured ones. The effect here is one of tremendous brightness (caused by the predominance of yellow lines) and dynamism (caused by uneven spacing and intersections). Neither horizontal nor vertical axes predominate. The dynamics of perception are transferred onto the lines themselves, which appear to move as the spectator perceives them in different configurations. The uneven spacing of the lines makes it difficult to focus and creates a 'swinging' rhythm as one's gaze shifts from one chromatic con- figuration to another, while a 'staccato' effect is created by the irregular intersections. The varying distances between intersec- tions on both vertical and horizontal axes encourage different speeds of perception. The eye moves quickly along unbroken stretches of line, but this movement is halted and becomes more

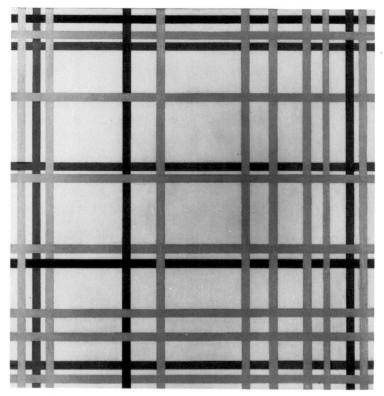

Figure 23. Piet Mondrian, *New York City I*, 1942; oil on canvas,
119.3 × 114.2 cm.

'jerky' owing to the interruptions caused by horizontals crossing
verticals and vice versa. These intersections create interactions
between horizontal and vertical axes. The crowding of lines on
the right side of the picture and the positioning of larger rectangles on the left cause movement towards the left, which is
halted by the positioning of three vertical lines down the left side
of the canvas, which in turn intersect with horizontals leading
inward to the larger rectangles. At the same time, the fact that the
lines run to the edge of the canvas suggests their possible extension
beyond, maintaining the tension between 'inner' and 'outer'
movement which we have seen earlier.

The introduction of coloured lines changes the spatial effect of
linear intersections. The final appearance of the painted canvas is
directly related to Mondrian's compositional technique, which
now involves the use of coloured tapes, which he placed over the
canvas and moved about until he found the best arrangement.[59]
The weaving of the lines under and over one another increases the

The weaving of the lines under and over one another increases the sense of dynamism and also introduces the sense of spatial ambiguity which we discussed at the beginning of this chapter. The passing of lines 'behind' or 'in front' of one another is in fact more a thickness than a depth, which does not extend in space but consists simply of the texture of the lines which pass behind or in front of one another, but it may seem to imply depth. Charmion von Wiegand recounts that Mondrian, while recognizing the difficulties involved, aimed at maintaining the surface plane. 'I asked him if using the coloured lines was not more difficult because the varied intensity of red, blue and yellow does not maintain the surface planes as easily as the black lines. He was aware of that but confident of finding proper solutions.'[60] In *New York City I*, yellow lines generally pass in front and blue and red behind, but this order is sometimes reversed, so that the spatial relationships appear to change as one's gaze moves through the picture. However, the predominance of yellow, which has a tendency to advance towards the spectator, and the fact that almost all the yellow lines pass in front of the others, mean that despite the weaving process, Mondrian has not altogether succeeded in retaining the surface plane. This problem will be solved in his radically innovatory compositions, *Broadway Boogie-Woogie* and *Victory Boogie-Woogie*.

Mondrian later described the last phase of his work. 'I came to the destruction of volume by the use of the plane. This I accomplished by means of lines cutting the planes. But still the plane remained too intact. So I came to making only lines and brought the colour within the lines. Now the only problem was to destroy these lines also through mutual oppositions' (*MCWA*, p. 357). On one level, Mondrian's aim as expressed here was the same as it had always been: the destruction of the particular in order to express the universal. However, his New York paintings, especially the 'Boogie-Woogie' pictures, appear more dynamic than his previous work. According to Mondrian himself, his work was a progression towards an aim which had always been present, even if not fully achieved. In 1943 he wrote: 'Many appreciate in my former work just what I did not want to express, but which was produced by an incapacity to express what I wanted to express – dynamic movement in equilibrium' (*MCWA*, p. 357). Arguably, however, he only discovered the value of dynamic movement as a result of his own pictorial experimentation and also through the influence of jazz and of the urban environment, especially New York.

Mondrian had begun by establishing a distinction between

rhythm in nature, which he characterized in terms of repetition, and rhythm in Neo-Plasticism, consisting of differences of colour and proportion which were rendered 'equivalent' by the pictorial composition. Neo-Plastic rhythm is superior to natural rhythm, but it is still inferior to the 'universal'. 'The new plastic is dualistic through its composition. Through its exact plastic of cosmic relationship it is a direct expression of the universal; through its rhythm, through its material reality, it is an expression of the subjective, of the individual' (*MCWA*, p. 31). Rhythm is subject to change, as opposed to the 'immutable' position of the right angle (*MCWA*, p. 86), which expresses the universal. Later, however, Mondrian began to see rhythm itself in more positive terms: rhythm is associated with openness and freedom, as opposed to the limitation of particular form. Interestingly, this positive concept of rhythm was influenced by jazz, and emerged strongly for the first time in 1927 in an article on 'Jazz and Neo-Plastic' (*MCWA*, pp. 217–22). This article also seems to have been inspired by Mondrian's work on his studio interior.[61] Mondrian was a great enthusiast of jazz and jazz dancing, and he saw jazz as an ally of Neo-Plasticism in transforming the environment. 'Jazz and Neo-Plasticism are already creating an environment in which art and philosophy resolve into rhythm that has no form and is therefore "open"' (*MCWA*, p. 221). The bar, where jazz is played, is seen as an ideal environment. 'In the bar . . . everything is subsumed by rhythm. There is no emptiness, no boredom: rhythm fills everything without creating new oppression – it does not become form' (*MCWA*, pp. 221–2).

Whereas previously, Mondrian had believed that 'the pure relationships of position' (i.e. the right angle) could themselves express the universal 'without resulting in forms' (*MCWA*, p. 29), he learned through pictorial experience that this was not the case, as the 'constancy' of the right angle itself created symmetry. 'The relationship of position – the right angle – is constant. Through opposition, the relationships of dimension vary continually so that all symmetry can be destroyed. Precisely through these variable relationships in Neo-Plastic composition, the static character of the constant relationship can be annihilated and the work can be dynamic and fully human' (*MCWA*, p. 305). Paradoxically, it is in fact the changing elements of the composition which are the most essential in destroying the particular: 'As regards the relations of dimension, they must be varied in order to avoid repetition . . . it is precisely they that are most appropriate for the destruction of the static equilibrium of all form' (*MCWA*, p. 294).

By the time Mondrian wrote these articles (1936 and 1938), he had already painted his dynamic 'linear' pictures of the 1930s. Interestingly, here it is the crossing of the lines at irregular intervals which creates the strongly rhythmic effect, so that the right angle itself becomes a locus of dynamism. This indicates precisely the radical shift in Mondrian's Neo-Plastic aesthetic: constant equilibrium, or the universal, has itself been transmuted into the principle of change and transformation. Many years earlier, Mondrian had written: '*Deep within the mutable is the immutable . . . universal beauty*' (*MCWA*, p. 104): later he discovered that the opposite was also true, and proclaimed that 'universal beauty' arises from 'dynamic rhythm' (*MCWA*, p. 289). This development is in fact a logical consequence of his long held belief that opposites are reversible, and its implications are fully explored in pictorial terms. His theory follows the painting through in discussing the positive role now ascribed to rhythm, but does not critically examine the relationship between this position and his previously held views.

It is unlikely that Mondrian would have reached this radical conclusion had it not been for the combined influence of jazz and the 'metropolis'. Mondrian believed that the origin of all art was in '*the reciprocal interaction of the individual and the environment*' (*MCWA*, p. 327), and at no time was the influence of the environment stronger than on his arrival in New York. Already in 1918/19 he had proclaimed the importance of the life of the metropolis for abstract art: 'Abstract-Real painting developed under the influence of the completely modern cultural life of the metropolis' (*MCWA*, p. 59). In his 1927 article on jazz, he had also discussed 'the open rhythm that pervades the great city' to which 'all manner of construction, lighting, and advertisements contribute' (*MCWA*, p. 221). In 1942/3 he declared: 'The metropolis . . . produced Abstract Art: the establishment of the splendor of dynamic movement' (*MCWA*, p. 348). New York realized his dreams to an unprecedented extent: he loved the flashing neon lights and activity of Broadway: he visited jazz cafés with friends, and was especially attracted to Boogie-Woogie, with which he compared his Neo-Plastic aesthetic. 'True Boogie-Woogie I conceive as homogeneous in intention with mine in painting: destruction of melody, which is the equivalent of destruction of natural appearance, and construction through the continuous opposition of pure means – dynamic rhythm' (*MCWA*, p. 357).[62]

It is not surprising that these experiences influenced his painting. Von Wiegand recounts that Mondrian was 'terrifically impressed by the dynamism he found in New York and wanted to

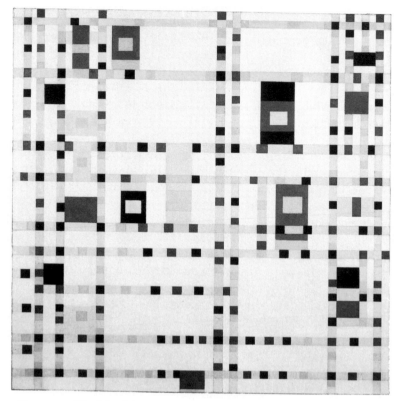

Figure 24. Piet Mondrian, *Broadway Boogie-Woogie*, 1942–3; oil on canvas,
127 × 127 cm.

make his paintings more dynamic. They were too classically balanced once he looked at them with American eyes.'[63] Mondrian's titles of this period draw the spectator's attention to the painting's function as a 'diagram' of the imaginary rhythmic space of which it constitutes a model, but which is already taking shape in the environment. The titles *Broadway Boogie-Woogie* and *Victory Boogie-Woogie* are in themselves metaphorical, the former suggesting synaesthesia of urban and musical rhythms, and the latter evoking the sense of triumph produced by the rhythmic transformation of space.

In *Broadway Boogie-Woogie*, 1942–3 (*O* colour plate LXII, *S* 624, see figure 24) and *Victory Boogie-Woogie*, 1943–4 (*O* colour plate LXIV, *S* 626, see figure 25), the innovations of previous paintings have been taken much further. Both paintings are at once incredibly fragmented and extremely tightly structured, creating rhythmic spaces where freedom and vitality coincide with perfectly constructed order. A radical innovation in *Broadway Boogie-*

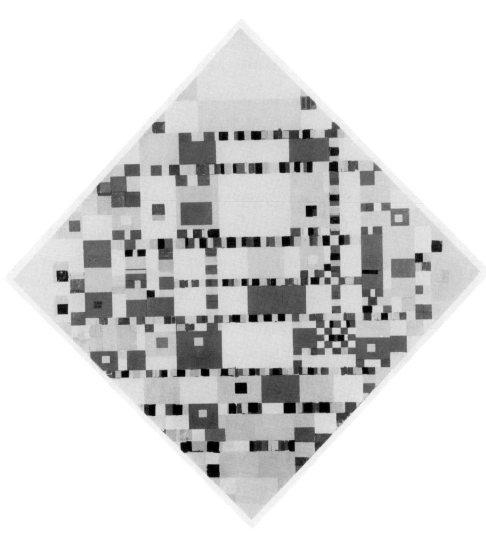

Figure 25. Piet Mondrian, *Victory Boogie-Woogie*, 1943–4; oil and collage on canvas, diag. 177.5 cm.

Woogie is the introduction of rectangles within rectangles and the fragmentation of lines into tiny coloured cubes. In some places, the sides of the rectangles directly adjoin the surrounding lines, from which they are separated by chromatic contrasts, while in other places the rectangles merge completely with the 'lines', undermining the distinction between structural and chromatic elements. Moreover, instead of being determined by the linear framework, the coloured rectangles are now unevenly distributed in the non-coloured spaces and are not always aligned with the edges of the colour cubes within the lines, thereby creating 'syncopated' rhythms. In comparison with *New York City I*, the spectator's progress through *Broadway Boogie-Woogie* is far more uneven: the staccato effect created by linear intersections now occurs almost constantly, even without intersections, because of the fragmentation of the lines into cubes. Apart from a few short sections of yellow line near the top, there are no lines one can follow without constant 'interruptions'. Again with the exception of three instances involving yellow lines near the top, linear crossings involve colour changes which do not privilege one line over the other, creating true intersections and maintaining a perfectly flat plane. These intersections create colour changes at the right angle (even where both lines were previously the same colour), emphasizing its new status as a locus of change and transformation.

Victory Boogie-Woogie, which remained unfinished after Mondrian's death, although he had declared that 'now I have only to paint it',[64] shows him taking the destructive process even further. The fact that pieces of coloured paper remain stuck to the canvas heightens its aura of fragmentation and ordered chaos. It seems fitting that Mondrian's last composition should have been in the diamond format, which was such a crucial source of pictorial innovation. Indeed, this picture has already moved on considerably from its predecessor. Linear structure is now barely discernible, and the processes of construction and destruction seem infinitely reversible as rectangles fragment into tiny cubes and cubes form rectangular and linear configurations which are in turn broken up. The areas of non-colour which in *Broadway Boogie-Woogie* still constituted empty spaces between the intersecting lines and rectangles are now themselves absorbed into the overall asymmetrical structure, which fully integrates figure and ground. Moreover, whereas in *Broadway Boogie-Woogie*, the rectangular 'blocks' between the lines were predominantly vertical, in *Victory Boogie-Woogie*, there is a balance of vertical and horizontal elements. Much of the 'jubilance' of this picture is created by its colours, which are extraordinarily pure and bright, while the presence of large spaces of 'non-colour' prevents any sense of saturation or overcrowding. The bright cubes of the primary colours, which appear to 'flash' at the viewer, and the fragmentary, rhythmic, asymmetrical composition create a raw, visceral quality unprecedented in Mondrian's work.

There is an even greater degree of unevenness and asymmetry than in *Broadway Boogie-Woogie*. The viewer's attempts to find a 'path' through the painting are constantly defeated: the entire surface 'pulsates' as the eye is drawn at varying speeds and in continually changing directions. A strong sense of time is created by the differing 'lengths' of the coloured strips. A small number of basic elements are combined in seemingly infinite ways: all that remains 'constant' are the basic colours and rectangular forms, but repetition is subject to such variation that constancy itself cannot be separated from change, just as construction interacts with destruction and limitation with expansion. There appears to be no pre-established pattern or hierarchy of elements, and yet it is the perfection of order which creates this sense of liberation. Mondrian utilizes the potential of the diamond format to create a sense of instability, and also to suggest the 'cropping' of the picture's field from a wider space, indicating the possibility of a completed rectangle outside the boundaries of the picture. Not only are the corners emptier, but the top is much 'lighter' than the bottom, leading the spectator's eye upwards and outwards.

It has often been observed that the grid formats of the 'Boogie-Woogie' paintings are similar to the layout of New York streets seen from above, and comparisons have been made with street intersections, traffic lights and flashing neon lights, as well as with jazz. J. J. Sweeney describes the beat/off-beat rhythm of the *Boogie-Woogies*': 'The eye is led from one group of colour notes to another at varying speeds; at the same time contrasted with this endless change in the minor motives we have a constant repetition of the right angle theme like a persistent bass chord sounding through a sprinkle of running arpeggios and grace notes from the treble.'[65] Judged by comparison with Mondrian's earlier, classical work, the 'Boogie-Woogie' paintings have been seen as expressing 'sublime desperation'.[66] Arguably, however, the title *Victory Boogie-Woogie* does indeed indicate a victory. The *Boogie-Woogies* celebrate, not only the transformation of pictorial space through dynamic equilibrium, but also the appearance of this dynamic equilibrium in the rhythms of modern life. Instead of the 'universal' hidden behind appearances, Mondrian now sees 'the real content of art' as 'the expression of pure vitality which reality reveals through the manifestation of dynamic movement' (*MCWA*, p. 348). These changes in the environment increased Mondrian's confidence in the possibility of transforming the world in accordance with Neo-Plastic vision, and *Victory Boogie-Woogie* jubilantly proclaims the possibility of transposing material reality by '*excluding the formation of any particular form*' through a '*dynamic rhythm of determinate mutual relations*' (*MCWA*, p. 295).

The radically different appearance of the 'Boogie-Woogie' paintings bears testimony to Mondrian's discovery, by pictorial means, of the implications of the reversibility of binary oppositions, where the principle of constancy can no longer be separated from that of change. The rhythms of pictorial composition transform space, fragmenting its surface into infinite relationships. The medium itself 'takes the initiative' in an endless process of destruction and construction which indefinitely repeats itself in different ways and defies synthesis. On one level, this can be seen as a re-emergence of the 'particular', owing to the impossibility of a synthesis where particulars are subsumed into a whole. As in the sublime, the imagination is overwhelmed by the seeming infinity of these processes, yet they also function as 'negative presentations' of what lies beyond the scope of imagination, which is made aware of its own limits. These paintings can be perceived as sites of a utopian imaginary space, as fragments of what will one day be a rhythmic whole, in a future when the environment will be transformed in accordance with pictorial 'laws', and 'we will no longer have the need of pictures and sculpture, for we will live in realized art' (*MCWA*, p. 344).

CHAPTER 6

Universal exceptions: sites of imaginary space

La Littérature existe et, si l'on veut, seule, à l'exception de
tout.   (Mallarmé, *MOC*, p. 656)

When the universal dominates, it will permeate life, so that
art . . . will decay, and a new life . . . will replace art.
                                                   (Mondrian, *MCWA*, p. 42)

In the poems and paintings which we have examined here, the
poetic/pictorial medium itself is a starting point for constructing
and exploring imaginary spaces whose content cannot be translated into abstract conceptual terms separate from the medium.
The receiver's imagination is stimulated to exceed logical and
empirical boundaries, projecting an imaginary space which is
indefinable, and which transforms the medium itself, like the
Kantian aesthetical idea, into a site of 'negative presentation'. At
the same time, there are very close connections, of a predominantly rhythmic nature, between imagining activity and textual/
pictorial space. These rhythmic relationships, where imagination
actively participates in and transforms experience of the sensory
presence of the medium, can function as a model for the ideal
relationship between consciousness and the environment as a
whole. In this way, textual/pictorial spaces become sites of
imaginary space with utopian implications, both aesthetic and
social.

PERFECTING SIGNS

We saw in chapter 1 above that Peirce maintains that 'the most
perfect of signs are those in which the iconic, indicative, and
symbolic characters are blended as equally as possible' (IV.448),
and also that he cites the 'diagram'[1] as an example of a sign
which, though mainly iconic, also contains symbolic and indexical characteristics. The diagram is symbolic in that it enables us
to create abstractions. It is indexical by virtue of having an
'individual existence connected with the individual object'

(IV.531). It is also 'an icon of the forms of relations in the constitution of its object' (IV.531). In the poetry and the painting we have discussed here, we have observed 'diagrammatic' modes of signifying which combine the Peircean categories of 'Firstness', 'Secondness' and 'Thirdness'. Here, the 'objects' constructed by the receiver's imagining activity defy description in logical terms abstracted from the 'forms of relations' embodied in the medium. The rhythmic properties which the receiver activates in the medium, and which link textual/pictorial and imaginary space, are an 'iconic' characteristic, but they also suggest virtual, intangible qualities, such as dynamism and infinity, which invite the receiver to 'generalize' and 'create abstractions'. As we have seen, metadiscursive elements perform an 'indexical' function in drawing the receiver's attention to the relationship between textual/pictorial and imaginary space. Moreover, in focussing on the irreducible 'otherness' of the text/picture, the receiver also becomes more aware of the particular, individual features of its medium (an indexical characteristic).

In Rimbaud and Mallarmé, disruption of discursive meaning and evocation of indefinable imaginary spaces are combined with enhancement of the spatial and visual resources of language, enabling imaginary space to be 'reflected' in the text. This mode of signifying causes language to become more 'iconic'. In the painting of Kandinsky and Mondrian, disruption of figurative representation is connected with the aim of creating an autonomous pictorial 'language', where forms and colours function as purely relational entities and operate according to their own 'rules', a feature associated with symbols. Paradoxically, this apparently increased autonomy of the pictorial 'language' can lead to increased reliance on verbal language, since the pictorial rules and the principles underlying them can be formulated only in the words of theoretical texts, whose function can be compared with that of dictionaries or grammars. As we have seen, however, unlike verbal language, the 'rules' of pictorial 'language' are directly derived from properties of the forms and colours themselves. Moreover, in the late works of both painters, the metapictorial dimension is more closely integrated into the paintings, through allusions to the external world which have the status of analogies rather than of representations, and which can function as visual 'metaphors' or personifications of the pictorial elements.

These metapictorial elements, like the metapoetical aspects of the poetry of Rimbaud and Mallarmé, combine iconic and indexical functions by accentuating the links between pictorial and imaginary space, while at the same time drawing the receiver's attention to this relationship. The role played by titles here inevitably increases the involvement of the verbal medium in painting. The resulting reflexivity, where the relationship between imaginary space and the medium itself becomes the object of imagining activity, introduces an element of 'Thirdness' or representation. Experiencing textual or pictorial space as 'imaginary' involves a transference of subjectivity from the receiver to the textual/pictorial medium: the 'je' thereby becomes inseparable from the object of its own critical reflection, in which it experiences itself as 'autre'. Imagining activity is differed/deferred from itself through this reflexive interaction with the medium, which cannot be definitively 'aufgehoben' into imaginary space. The text/picture becomes a 'site' of imaginary space, not by being absorbed into imagining consciousness, but by becoming ontologically undecidable.

Peirce emphasizes the diagram's capacity for epistemological innovation deriving from its form. Although symbols allow us to create abstractions, because they are based on pre-existing habits or conventions, they do not enable us to add to our knowledge (IV.531). The icon, in the form of the diagram, on the other hand, can furnish us with knowledge, in that 'by observation of it other truths concerning its object can be discovered than those determining its construction' (II.279). Diagrams 'show relations between elements which before seemed to have no necessary connection' (I.383); they therefore have the 'capacity of revealing unexpected truth' (II.279). Through diagrams, it is possible to infer ideas not contained in the data (I.383). Peirce's account of diagrams as repositories of 'unexpected truths' is similar to Kant's 'aesthetical idea', which 'discloses a new rule that could not have been inferred from any preceding principles or examples' (*CJ*, p. 161/180), and can be related to the concept of the art work as innovatory and as orientating the receiver towards the realm of the potential rather than the actual.[2]

We saw that Kant's 'aesthetical idea' was prefigured in Baumgarten's discussion of 'extensive clarity', where aesthetic truth, which is sensory, surpasses conceptual truth. Aesthetical ideas and symbols stimulate imagination to exceed conceptual knowledge and to experience the unknowable as a negative dimension of the sensible. As in the Peircean diagram, in the Kantian symbol, which 'aesthetically enlarges the concept itself in an unbounded fashion', (*CJ*, p. 158/177), the representation initiates thought rather than vice versa. This is not conceptual thought, but the self-subverting activity of imagining, stimulated by excessive/ungraspable objects, which transgresses the boundaries of verbal definitions and concepts and experiences the indefinable 'rational idea' as an unpresentable dimension of the symbol/aesthetical idea itself. Similarly, Rimbaud, Mallarmé, Kandinsky and Mondrian, albeit in very diverse ways, seek to transgress the boundaries of conceptual, codified thought and to make new breakthroughs through exploration of the imaginary dimension of sensation and of the poetic and pictorial mediums themselves.

For Rimbaud, the state of 'voyance' and knowledge of the unknown can be reached only through a 'dérèglement de *tous les sens*' (*RO*, p. 346), involving radical sensory and semantic disruption, through which poetry becomes a 'hallucination des mots' ('Délires II', 'Alchimie du verbe'). For Mallarmé, even the void, which is the key to beauty, must be experienced as a sensation.[3] He declared that 'il faut penser de tout son corps' and described how he used this method in writing poetry.[4] In the act of writing, the poet should '[céder] l'initiative aux mots' (*MOC*, p. 366). Mallarmé told Degas: 'ce n'est point avec des idées que l'on fait des vers . . . C'est avec des mots'.[5] Kandinsky says that he 'thinks' pictorially: 'I only get ideas that can be expressed pictorially, and do not permit description in words' (*KCWA*, p. 378). For Mondrian, painting itself becomes a way of 'finding things out', which takes the place of abstract thought. He declares that 'the only problem in art is to achieve a balance between the subjective and the objective. But it is of the utmost importance that this problem should be solved, in the realm of plastic art – technically, as it were – and not in the realm of thought' (*MCWA*, p. 289). Kandinsky's and Mondrian's claims that their theories derive from their paintings exemplify this approach.

RHYTHMIC 'LANGUAGES'

Rimbaud, Mallarmé, Kandinsky and Mondrian aim to create new 'languages' whose primary function is not to convey meaning but to alter the receiver's experience of the medium. Ideals of rhythm and harmony form the basis of the search for a 'universal language' and ultimately for the transformation of reality itself. Rimbaud declares that 'le temps d'un langage universel viendra', a language which will be 'de l'âme pour l'âme, résumant tout, parfums, sons, couleurs, de la pensée accrochant la pensée et tirant' (*RO*, p. 349). He writes in 'A une Raison': 'Un coup de ton doigt sur le tambour décharge tous les sons et commence la nouvelle harmonie', and affirms that in the future, 'la Poésie ne rythmera plus l'action; elle *sera en avant*' (*RO*, p. 350). For Mallarmé, the poetic enterprise involves purifying language of 'le hasard' and enabling words themselves to embody 'l'ensemble des rapports existant dans tout, la Musique' (*MOC*, p. 368), where music can be understood 'dans le sens grec, au fond signifiant *Idée ou rythme entre les rapports*'.[6] He aspires to reach 'un compte exact de purs motifs rythmiques de l'être' (*MOC*, p. 345). Ultimately, the whole of reality could be subsumed into this rhythmic structure: poetry illuminates 'le rythme fondamental . . . du monde' and 'rejette, vain, le résidu' (*MOC*, p. 655). Kandinsky aspires to discover, through painting, a 'new universal language'.[7] He sees rhythm as the fundamental principle of pictorial composition, which links the visible with the invisible and unites the work of art with 'la pulsation cosmique' (*CB*, p. 235). For Mondrian, it is through 'the accentuation of rhythm' that 'the subject loses its importance in plastic art' and that art became 'the aesthetic expression of vitality' (*MCWA*, pp. 328–9). The 'difficult task of the new artist' is to 'realize the new harmony' (*MCWA*, pp. 113–14) which will link art with the universal.

Rhythm has been defined in terms of repetition and fixed patterns and of resistance to such patterns: in terms of objective, quantifiable structures and of subjective response: of temporal flow and of spatial patterns imposed on that flow. As argued in chapter 2 above, rhythm necessarily comprises tension between different modes of apprehension, and it is realized only through the receiver's participation in and enactment of tensions and resolutions between repetition and variation and between spatial and temporal patterns.[8] In poetry, virtual space can be brought into play when the reader is invited (for example through analogies and sound repetition) to link words which have been presented sequentially, while visual space can be foregrounded through the appearance of the poem on the page. In painting, virtual time can be foregrounded by suggested movement of the pictorial elements, and actual viewing time can be emphasized by structures (for example multiple centred and fragmented compositions) which invite sequential rather than simultaneous viewing.

CRUCIAL DIFFERENCES

The foregrounding of rhythm in both poetry and painting is closely associated with moves away from discursive meaning and figurative representation because it enables content to be created by the ontological transformation of the medium through its interaction with the receiver's imagination rather than by coded meanings. However, not only are rhythmic effects experienced in different ways in poetry and painting, but the poetic and pictorial mediums differ greatly in the extent to which they can depart from a coded (discursive or figurative) content while maintaining the capacity to arouse the imagining activity of the receiver. We have seen that in Rimbaud and Mallarmé, relationships between signifieds are crucial in evoking the rhythms of imaginary space, whereas in Kandinsky and Mondrian, rhythmic relationships between colours and forms can themselves be experienced as imaginary, even without the intermediary of figurative or iconographical coding. The signifier in painting is not so closely tied to a coded signified. On the other hand, painting experiences greater difficulties in breaking free of dependence on verbal language than does poetry from visual images (for example in the form of illustrations).

What, then, would be the equivalent of 'abstraction' in poetry? Not only abstract painting, but also the possibility of poetry which means nothing was envisaged in early Romanticism,[9] and it might be argued that it is only with the emergence of poetry based on the signifier with minimum reference to lexical signifieds that poetry directly parallels abstract painting. However, this parallel does not take sufficient account of the differences between the mediums concerned. Verbal language is highly codified, not simply at the level of syntax and lexical meanings, but even at the level of individual letters, which have fixed shapes and sounds. Moreover, the linguistic signified is an intrinsic part of the poetic medium, and if it is minimalized or excised, the medium is deprived of a crucial dimension of its signifying power.[10] Figurative and iconographical signifieds, on the other hand, are not an intrinsic part of the visual medium. Parallels between visual art composed of autonomous colours and forms and verbal art based on autonomous visual and aural 'signifiers' must therefore be treated with caution.

Concrete, Spatialist and Letterist poetry[11] have strong tendencies towards self-referentiality and tautology, emphasizing the visual and aural texture of the linguistic signifier. Mary Lewis Shaw writes: 'Concrete poetry can . . . be described as a kind of thickening or reification of the poetic sign . . . its meaning cannot be abstracted from its material form – "the medium is the message" . . . as the concrete value of a text becomes increasingly exploited, its semantic richness seems difficult to sustain.'[12] In the domain of the visual arts, this effect is much more closely paralleled by the 'literalism' of Minimalist art as defined by Fried than by the pictorial space of Kandinsky or Mondrian as described here. With reference to Pierre Garnier's aim to 'eliminate the connotative value' of words, Seaman observes that 'this effort of reduction of meaning corresponds somewhat to the trend toward minimal sculpture, and has much in common with an effort like Josef Albers' painting "White on White": avoiding complexities, it seeks first to define and present the isolated phenomenon'.[13] According to Garnier, 'le poète est en prise avec une langue qui ne représente plus rien qu'elle-même'.[14] Liselotte Gumpel refers to the 'strongly visual iconic base' of concrete poetry where words 'appear in exactly the spatial relations they signify, thus demonstrating their own optico-semantic tautology'.[15]

As Wendy Steiner has remarked, concrete poetry has claimed Mallarmé as its most important predecessor by 'stressing those aspects of his art that play into their program and ignoring the anticoncrete thrust of his work'. 'Un coup de Dés', although it is 'frequently mentioned as a crucial step toward the development of concrete poetry . . . could not be further from the concrete enterprise'.[16] 'Un coup de Dés' has a complex semantic dynamics which relies on an underlying syntactical structure. 'Il faut une garantie – la Syntaxe' (*MOC*, p. 385). The rhythmic movements performed in the act of reading, which are determined by the visual composition, are themselves bound up with the rhythms of imaginary space. Moreover, Mallarmé believed that poetry should preserve links with orality. 'Le vers et tout écrit au fond par cela qu'issu de la parole doit se montrer à même de subir l'épreuve orale ou d'affronter la diction comme une mode de présentation extérieure' (*MOC*, p. 855). Mary Lewis Shaw has proposed drawing a distinction between 'concrete' and 'abstract' poetry, where the latter 'uses circular semantic play to suspend the image-forming aspect of representation'.[17] This definition is interestingly close to Mondrian's conception of poetry, which was influenced by both Futurism and Dadaism. The De Stijl 'Literature Manifesto', published in *De Stijl* in 1920, was written by van Doesburg, Mondrian and Anthony Kok at a time when they were enthused by Dada.[18] It is critical of 'the predominance of associative and subjective sentiments' in poetry, and advocates giving a new significance to the word, using 'syntax, prosody, typography, arithmetic, orthography'.[19] Unbeknown to Mondrian, van Doesburg even published Dada poems in *De Stijl* under the pseudonym of I. K. Bonset. Under the same pseudonym, he published an article in 1921 in which he commented enthusiastically on the poetry of Rimbaud and Mallarmé.[20]

Mondrian's article on 'Neo-Plasticism: The General Principle of Plastic Equivalence' (1920) shows that his views differed from those of both the Futurists and the Dadaists. He argues that the Futurists place too much emphasis on sensation and not enough on intelligence and on the content and meaning of words. Of Dadaism he declares that 'it is not possible to free the word from [individual] thought by stringing words together without any connection between them, as the Dadaists wished'.[21] Mondrian believes that verbal art will be much slower to reach liberation than painting. In a very distant future, the word will be 're-created' and liberated from constraints. In the meantime, however, poetry should overcome its limitations through the association of contradictory ideas, which will free the word from specific meanings. 'The idea of the word will change in our consciousness to a contradictory meaning, for this alone can wrest the word away from its limitation . . . the limitation of the word is overcome, its content expanded.'[22] He specifies that to a greater extent than Neo-Plasticism, verbal art will use content in 'creating relationships of opposition'.[23]

Mondrian's theory of poetry is obviously very close to his pictorial aesthetics, with the crucial difference that he does not advocate excluding meanings in the same way as he excludes figurative objects: meanings are rather a part of the medium, which, like form and colour in Neo-Plastic painting, must be transposed from the particular to the universal through relationships of opposition. Kandinsky, on the other hand, believed in the possibility of 'nonobjective' poetry, 'by analogy with nonobjective painting' (*KCWA*, p. 469), which would be based on sound divorced from coded meanings. Like the pictorial medium, words would have to be analysed in order to discover their intrinsic suggestive ('inner') value. Sounds would be recombined, independently of meanings, to form 'nonexistent words'. Kandinsky is in favour of poetry where 'the meaning of the whole poem is eclipsed, as it were, by its resonance', and he speaks admiringly of Russian Futurist poets who 'wrote poetry consisting of nonexistent and newly created words' (*KCWA*, p. 468). Kandinsky refers here to his own stage composition, *The Yellow Sound*, where, he says, 'I introduced the resonance of vowels and consonants and also indistinct speech made up of nonexistent words' (*KCWA*, p. 469).

In practice, however, Kandinsky made extremely limited use of such effects in *The Yellow Sound* and in his collection of poems and woodcuts, *Sounds*, dating from 1912. His illogical juxtapositions and use of repetition recall aspects of Maeterlinck's

poetry, in whose work Kandinsky particularly admired the
'power of the word' (*KCWA*, p. 147) to evoke atmosphere
through resonance. Kandinsky's poems were popular with the
Dadaists,[24] and Hans Arp, who admired them greatly, wrote that
'Kandinsky's poetry lays bare the vacuousness of phenomena and
of reason' (*KCWA*, p. 292). The Dadaists themselves, however,
would use much more radical techniques. Kandinsky's later
poems, published in 1938 and 1939 (*KCWA*, pp. 810–12 and
837–9) are similar in many respects to his early ones. Interestingly, in *Point and Line to Plane*, written six years after the poetic
theory cited above, Kandinsky was much less dogmatic about
abstract poetry, admitting that 'the question as to the possibility
and limits of abstract poetry is a complex one' (*KCWA*, p. 621).
Ezra Pound, who felt strong affinities with Kandinsky's abstrac-
tionist theories, maintained that the poetic image, not pure
sound, was the poet's 'pigment'. 'The image is the poet's pigment;
with that in mind you can go ahead and apply Kandinsky, you
can transpose his chapter on the language of form and colour and
apply it in verse.'[25]

There is no simple answer to the question of what might
constitute a poetic equivalent of abstraction in painting, but
superficial parallels must be treated with caution. Parallels
between the poetry of Rimbaud and Mallarmé and the painting
of their contemporaries are similarly complex. Symbolist painting
continued to rely heavily on iconographical contexts, i.e. on
'literary' rather than 'pictorial' modes of signification,[26] while
Impressionism was more concerned with analysing and rendering
modes of perceiving objects than with transposing them to an
'imaginary' space. However, we saw in chapter 1 above that there
was a strong current in Symbolism which favoured 'pure' painting. Moreover, early abstract art combined elements of the
Symbolist aesthetic of suggestion and the Impressionist liberation
of colour and form in pursuing its aim of making the pictorial
medium an object of imaginary transformation. In fact, Impressionism itself was open to 'Symbolist' interpretations. Monet's
late paintings in particular lent themselves to such imaginative
responses, and it is not surprising that Mallarmé especially
admired Monet, to whom he wrote: 'Je mets ce que vous faites
au-dessus de tout.'[27] Mallarmé described a tree in a painting by
Monet as 'un paon brûlant le paysage de sa queue étalée'.[28] By
the early 1890s, it had become acceptable to link Impressionism
with Symbolism, largely as a result of Mirbeau's writings on
Monet. Mallarmé's fascination with Impressionism was closely
bound up with its dissolution of the object, as can be seen from his

longest piece on Impressionism, where light and air are described as 'plundering reality from the figures' in Manet's *Le Linge*: 'Everywhere the luminous and transparent atmosphere struggles with the figures, the dresses, and the foliage, and seems to take to itself some of their substance and solidity; whilst their contours, consumed by the hidden sun and wasted by space, tremble, melt, and evaporate into the surrounding atmosphere.'[29]

It is at this juncture of the Impressionist dissolution of the object and liberation of colour and a Symbolist aesthetics of suggestion that painting can be said to focus on an ontological transformation of the medium which leads directly into abstraction, and which is comparable to that which takes place in the poetry of Rimbaud and Mallarmé. However, parallels between this poetry and Impressionist paintings were closer for nineteenth-century spectators, who experienced the paintings very differently from how they are perceived today. At that time, spectators of Impressionist canvases found that the objects they depicted deviated very sharply from their everyday perceptions. As Bernard points out, contemporary descriptions of Impressionist colour are remarkably similar to the colour notations found in Rimbaud's *Illuminations*, and yet the *Illuminations* have not become familiar in the same way as Impressionist painting has. 'Aujourd'hui nous regardons les tableaux des Impressionistes comme parfaitement compréhensibles . . . il paraît douteux . . . que le monde *recréé* par Rimbaud . . . en vienne jamais à nous paraître entièrement compréhensible et perde ce caractère d'*étrangeté* foncière qui nous attire en même temps qu'il nous déconcerte.'[30] The passage of time has altered our view of Impressionist painting far more dramatically than it has our reading of Rimbaud's and Mallarmé's poetry, and has greatly reduced their similarities.[31]

TOTAL ART WORKS

According to Clement Greenberg, the 'common effort in each of the arts to expand the expressive resources of the medium'[32] accentuates their differences, since 'pure poetry strives for infinite suggestion' and 'pure plastic art for the minimum'.[33] We have already seen that Greenberg's theory does not in fact account for Kandinsky's and Mondrian's painting, which aims at the 'infinite suggestiveness' which Greenberg ascribes only to 'pure poetry'. Moreover, whereas Greenberg believes that each art form should remain within the confines of its own medium,[34] these poets and painters aim at developing modes of signifying which transcend the boundaries of their chosen medium and (with the exception of Rimbaud) move beyond the framework of the page or canvas in order to experiment with other art forms. These experiments are closely linked with the notion that the art work can function as a model for the creation of a 'total environment', where there would be a perfect interactive relationship between consciousness and the sensory world, an aspiration encouraged by transformations actually observed in the environment.

Although Rimbaud does not actually use different art forms, we have seen that the *Gesamtkunstwerk* figures prominently in the imaginary space of the *Illuminations*, enhancing the reader's awareness of the synaesthesic properties of textual space itself, where sound patterns, syntactical structures and rhythms work together to 'orchestrate', 'spatialize' and 'choreograph' the movement of reading. Dance plays a privileged role as an art form which involves movement in both time and space and which parallels the reader's own enactment of textual rhythms. The texts of 'Promontoire' and 'Villes I' and 'Villes II' evoke imaginary architectural and urban spaces which overwhelm and surround the 'spectator', while in texts such as 'Barbare' and 'Phrases', the rhythmic harmony of textual space is expanded in imaginary space to cosmic dimensions. Rimbaud's imaginary architectures are linked with the discourse of the superlative and the heterogeneous and the displacement of the opposition between the artificial and the natural which characterizes contemporary descriptions of urban spaces and especially the 'displays' of the recently developed 'grands magasins' and the World Fairs. A journalistic text of 1869, accompanied by an engraving, and describing the recently built 'Splendide Hôtel'[35] (in 'Après le Déluge', Rimbaud refers to the 'Splendide Hôtel', 'bâti dans le chaos de glaces et de nuit du pôle'), emphasizes its careful layout and rich ornamentation in a style which evokes both the logical manner in which Rimbaud frequently details the spatial distribution of objects (for example 'à gauche . . . à droite', in 'Mystique') and the foregrounding of aesthetic qualities which we have discussed in 'Promontoire'.

Contemporary descriptions of the 'grands magasins' emphasize their enormity and the heterogeneity of the objects on offer. These characteristics were accentuated at the World Fairs, and Mallarmé's account of the 'Exposition de Londres' in 1872, with its evocation of an 'architecture de féerie', flower displays whose patterns have the artificial aspect of a mosaic or an oriental carpet, buildings of 'vastes proportions' with 'innombrables fenêtres' and a complex exhibition space which makes it difficult to orientate oneself (*MOC*, pp. 680–6), not only sets up fascinating intertextual relationships with *Illuminations* such as 'Fleurs', 'Villes I', and 'Promontoire', but also emphasizes the ways in which Rimbaud's 'hallucination des mots' absorbs changes which were already taking place in the contemporary environment and the discourses with which they were connected, subjecting them to further imaginary and textual transformation.[36] Although Rimbaud also evokes negative aspects of this urban 'barbarie moderne' ('Villes II'), there is a strongly utopian element in the collapse of boundaries, semantic, sensory and spatio-temporal ('dans tous les sens') which it provokes. As Per Buvik writes of 'Villes II', 'on est partout et nulle part, dans la temporalité utopique'.[37] According to Marc Eli Blanchard, 'la ville entière apparaît comme un *objet d'art*: la séparation du poète (le sujet) et de la réalité dans laquelle il vit n'aurait plus d'actualité chez Rimbaud'.[38]

Moreover, theatrical imagery in the *Illuminations* draws the reader's attention to the capacity of textual space to become, in Mallarmé's words, 'un théâtre, inhérent à l'esprit' (*MOC*, p. 328). Wagner's concept of the *Gesamtkunstwerk* derives from Greek tragedy, and the model of poetry which corresponds most closely to Rimbaud's ideal is in fact the poetry of the Greeks. 'Toute poésie antique aboutit à la poésie grecque; Vie harmonieuse. – De la Grèce au mouvement romantique, – moyen âge, – il y a des lettrés, des versificateurs . . . En Grèce, ai-je dit, vers et lyres *rythment l'Action* . . . ce serait encore un peu la Poésie grecque . . . cette langue sera de l'âme pour l'âme, résumant tout . . . La Poésie ne rythmera plus l'action; elle *sera en avant*' (*RO*, pp. 347–50). Several poems evoke aspects of ancient Greece (see, for instance, 'Villes II', 'Antique'), and 'Fleurs', with its 'gradins d'or' and in particular, 'Scènes', suggest the setting of a Greek amphitheatre. In typically eclectic fashion, 'Scènes' contains references to diverse theatrical settings, some of which are evocative of Greek tragedy: 'la foule barbare évolue sous les arbres dépouillés', 'des scènes lyriques accompagnées de flûte et de tambour', 'La féerie manœuvre au sommet d'un amphithéâtre couronné par les taillis.'

Although Mallarmé believed in 'la pureté des genres',[39] he also believed that the arts were related through structural analogies, and favoured transpositions between them on this level. He held that 'les principales *ressources esthétiques* d'un art quelconque sont en droit transposables à un autre art'.[40] We saw in chapter 3 above that Mallarmé was fascinated by the possibility of transposing musical structures into poetry. After hearing a performance of Beethoven's Ninth Symphony he declared: 'Voilà, certes, le modèle des modèles, un type d'architecture spontanée s'appliquant à tous les arts.'[41] He envisaged painting primarily in terms of the formal structures which made it similar to music: 'la peinture restitue à ce voyant [an imaginary composer inspired by paintings in the Louvre] l'intuition de lignes, d'éclairage et de coloration ou le morceau d'orchestre, que, d'abord, elle est' (*MOC*, p. 860).

In fact, Mallarmé's fascination with theatre and performance led him to move beyond the boundaries of the written text. 'Hérodiade' and 'L'Après-midi d'un faune' were both originally written for the stage. In 1896, he started to rework 'Hérodiade' in dramatic form, a project which remained unfinished at his death. He also planned to write a play on Hamlet, whose hero was to be played by the poet himself.[42] Mallarmé saw the ideal actor as a priestlike figure, who, through the sacrifice of his own personality, acts as a channel for the divine presence. (See *MOC*, p. 396.) He was also fascinated by movement in space; hence his attraction to dance. 'La danse seule, du fait de ses évolutions, avec le mime me paraît nécessiter un espace réel, ou la scène' (*MOC*, p. 315). His experimentation with visual forms in poetry is motivated precisely by the desire to make of poetry a 'mise en scène spirituelle' (*MOC*, p. 455). Writing, for Mallarmé, is choreographical, just as dance is writing with the body (*MOC*, p. 307).

Mallarmé's 'Livre' was a radical gesture towards a new art form. The 'Livre' would have comprised both printed volumes for the public and performances for an élite. The numerical symmetry between the structure of the 'séances' and that of the printed volumes would ensure the unity of the printed and performed versions ('identité du Livre et de la Pièce' (129 A)).[43] The number of pages is linked with the number of guests: 'Chaque séance implique 24 feuillets, ou 3 feuilles (place triple) × 8. (autant que d'invités . . .' (107 A). Invitation cards would have been made of the same paper as the Book. In most of the accounts, the 'Séances d'interprétation de l'Œ. [*sic*]' (110 A) would have been attended by twenty-four 'invités' or 'assistants', divided into groups of eight, with Mallarmé himself being present as the twenty-fifth: not as the author, but as the 'opérateur' (90 A). His function was to present different orderings of the 'feuillets'. Thirty loose pages would be placed in six drawers of a lacquered cabinet, forming a diagonal line, five pages in each drawer (195 A). As master of ceremonies, Mallarmé could control the combinations, but he did not wish to be responsible for the meaning of the Book (201) or to be known as the author, but envisaged himself as the 'premier lecteur' (42 A).

The same elements would be used several times, since the pages would be mobile and could be combined in different ways. Even with a small number of basic elements it would be possible to create huge numbers of permutations. Readings would take place in pairs: in one version, Mallarmé envisaged a series of ten 'séances' with two readings each, involving ten different interpretations. The 'Livre' would create itself through its structure, whose 'confrontations' or symmetries could give rise to new entities. Different genres could be combined to create new ones: 'en rapprochant / la double face de ces deux genres / on en crée un troisième mixte . . . et de 4 on obtient 6, soit 1/3 en plus, les 2/3 seuls existant' (106 A). The entities created through these combinations would be generated by the structure itself. Similarly, the number 24 (or grouping of 8 × 3) creates a mysterious twenty-fifth page and a twenty-fifth guest, who is Mallarmé himself: 'une feuille idéale absente . . . la 25e comme moi' (112 A); 'moi 25e au nom de feuille pure, lueur' (128 A). In this way, the 'Livre' regenerates its own 'operator'. The universal, impersonal rhythms of the 'Livre' were envisaged as replacing contingent, finite existence, including that of individual consciousness, which, by losing itself in the impersonal rhythm of the 'Livre' ('le rythme même du livre, alors impersonnel et vivant': *MOC*, p. 633), would be enabled to transcend 'le hasard'. 'Tout, au monde, existe pour aboutir à un livre' (*MOC*, p. 378).

The 'Livre' would have both rivalled and exceeded the ambitions of the Wagnerian *Gesamtkunstwerk*, proving that poetry, not music, was the form which could contain 'l'ensemble des rapports existant dans tout' (*MOC*, p. 368). It is a 'genre suprême',[44] which oversteps the limits of art: it is modelled on magical rituals and also on liturgical structures, which, like solar mythology, follow the rhythms of the seasons, bringing about 'une assimilation humaine à la tétralogie de l'An' (*MOC*, p. 393). (See also *feuillet* 182.) For Mallarmé, the Catholic Mass remained the model of the perfect art work, a modern version of Greek tragedy (see *MOC*, p. 393), the 'prototype des cérémonials . . . par nul cadre encore dépassé' (*MOC*, pp. 394–6). In this ritual, the priest is an 'acteur effacé', whose task is to bring about the 'Présence réelle' through the consecration of the host, which is the climax of the Mass, and which permits 'notre communion ou part d'un à tous et de tous à un' (*MOC*, p. 394). I have argued elsewhere[45] that the transubstantiation of matter into divine presence which takes place in the ceremony of the Mass is the prototype of the 'transposition' which Mallarmé wished to operate by secular, poetic means.

Kandinsky, too, aspired to create a 'monumental' work of art, which would constitute a total sensory and spiritual experience.[46] He was influenced by Wagner's concept of the *Gesamtkunstwerk*, although he disagreed with Wagner on several counts, considering that he placed too much emphasis on 'external action' (plot), that he enriched the effect of one art form at the cost of subordinating others, and that he made too much use of parallel rather than contrasting effects of different means (see *KCWA*, pp. 261–5). Kandinsky was impressed by Maeterlinck's economical and suggestive use of scenery, which left room for the imagination of the spectator (see *KCWA*, p. 146). He was very interested in Skriabin's exploration of the correspondences between music and colour, and much admired his *Prometheus* (see *KCWA*, p. 159). He was also excited by Schoenberg's musical experiments, and Schoenberg, who, like Kandinsky, believed in the synaesthesia of sound and colour, was extremely impressed by Kandinsky's *Yellow Sound*, in which he saw a parallel with his own *Glücklicher Hand*.[47] There are also similarities between Kandinsky's *Yellow Sound* and works by Steiner and Schuré.[48] Peg Weiss' work on Kandinsky and the theatre has shown how much his theatre owes to the influence of the Munich Symbolist milieu, which emphasized anti-naturalism, the role of rhythm in communicating with the spectator and the importance of 'dematerializing' physical presence.[49] Kandinsky was aware of the ideas of George Fuchs, whose ideas on rhythm and movement were cited in chapter 1 above.

In addition to *Yellow Sound*, which was to have been performed in Fuchs' theatre, the Munich Künstlertheater, Kandinsky planned four other stage compositions, *Green Sound*, *Black and White*, *Black Figure* and *Violet*.[50] He designed stage sets and costumes for Moussorgsky's *Pictures at an Exhibition*, which was performed for the first time in 1928.[51] He collaborated in experiments in 'absolute dance' involving the composer Thomas von Hartmann (whose score for *Yellow Sound* has unfortunately been lost) and the dancer Alexander Sakharoff. He also designed murals for an octagonal room at the 1922 Juryfreie exhibition in Berlin, which was reconstructed at the Pompidou Centre in Paris in 1977,[52] and he produced ceramic murals for three walls of a music room which was part of the *Deutsche Bauaustellung* held in Berlin in 1931,[53] a reconstruction of which has been installed at Artcurial in Paris. Kandinsky wrote two essays on theatre: 'On Stage Composition' (*KCWA*, pp. 257–65) and 'Abstract Synthesis on the Stage' (*KCWA*, pp. 504–7). His 'Program for the Institute of Artistic Culture' (the Institute opened in Moscow in

1920, initially under Kandinsky) also contained a section on 'monumental art' and in 1927 he published an article entitled 'And, Some Remarks on Synthetic Art' (*KCWA*, pp. 708–18).

Kandinsky believed that 'the general uniting principle' of the arts was 'the effect on the psyche' (*KCWA*, p. 470). 'Monumental abstract art' could be produced by different art forms using the 'abstract, inner sound' of their elements working together in the theatre, which 'has the power of attracting all these languages to itself' (*KCWA*, p. 506). Different art forms should not imitate each other, but learn from each other how to use their own mediums to the best advantage (*KCWA*, p. 154). The abstract stage composition would have at its disposal the means of architecture (space and dimension), of painting (colour, especially coloured light), sculpture (individual spatial extension), music (organized sound), dance (organized movement) and poetry (the 'temporal and spatial extension of human words': *KCWA*, p. 506). Like painting itself, the abstract stage composition should make use of contrasting stimuli: 'contrasts and oppositions, that is our harmony'.[54] Kandinsky said of *Yellow Sound*: 'Some years ago I attempted to employ different art forms in one single work, according to the principle, not of parallelism, but of opposition' (*KCWA*, p. 713).

As their titles indicate, colour is an essential part of the stage compositions. Particularly in *Yellow Sound*, the prominent dramatic role played by coloured lights and the fact that the main protagonists (the giants) are themselves yellow suggest that, like the anthropomorphic shapes in Kandinsky's late paintings, they can be seen as 'personifications' of the colour yellow itself. In the theatre, more easily than in painting, coloured light can be detached from objects and used as an autonomous means of suggestion. In *Yellow Sound*, the role of plot in any conventional sense is reduced to a minimum and the 'dramatic' effects are created largely through the rhythmic interactions of changing colours, sounds and movements. Sometimes these effects are mutually reinforcing and sometimes contrasting, for example as indicated in the stage direction: 'these movements should not be in time to the music' (*KCWA*, p. 277). The non-naturalistic treatment of colour constitutes a kind of 'colour music', of which Skriabin is probably the best-known practitioner, but which was a fertile source of inspiration for artists, especially in Russia.[55]

Movement and dance also play a remarkably prominent role in *Yellow Sound*. Like Mallarmé, Kandinsky was fascinated by the suggestive power of gesture. In *Point and Line to Plane*, he used pictures of the dancer Palucca to illustrate aspects of pictorial dynamics.[56] Both Mallarmé and Kandinsky sought to infuse the visual form on the page/canvas with latent movement, but both were also irresistibly drawn to the 'espace réel' of the stage where movement could take place in both space and time. Referring to ancient Greek rites, Kandinsky remarks that 'certain gestures, distinguished by their extreme schematism, possess a superhuman power of expression' (*KCWA*, p. 467). The composer Thomas von Hartmann recounted that he and Kandinsky were interested in Greek dance. They had begun a remarkable experiment, where Kandinsky painted pictures based on a fairytale by Anderson, and together they tried to imagine an equivalent of the painting in the form of a ballet. Soon they were joined by the dancer Alexander Sakharoff, and they began work on a transposition of *Daphnis et Chloé*. Kandinsky later recalled: 'Dans une série d'aquarelles, le musicien en choisissait une qui, du point de vue musical, lui paraissait la plus claire. En l'absence du danseur, il jouait cette aquarelle. Puis arrivait le danseur; on lui jouait la musique, il la transformait en danse, et devinait ensuite laquelle des aquarelles il venait de danser.'[57] Nina Kandinsky recalls that 'jusqu'à sa mort, Kandinsky avait toujours désiré ardemment réaliser un grand ballet réunissant tous les média'. In 1939, together with the choreographer Massine, he was planning a staging of Beethoven's Ninth Symphony, which was sabotaged by the war.[58] Just before his death, he was planning a ballet for which he was to design the sets and Thomas von Hartmann was to compose the music.[59]

Kandinsky's ideal *Gesamtkunstwerk* creates a synaesthesic environment, a 'world' within which the spectator could live and move, like the peasant houses he described in Vologda. The goal is not to communicate an abstract meaning, but to create a new relationship between consciousness and the environment, where the spectator can experience the imaginary dimension of sensation. In the guide to the Berlin exhibition for which he designed the music-room murals, Kandinsky wrote that a space intended to bring people together 'for a special inner purpose . . . must have a special energy' and that since painting could serve as 'a kind of tuning-fork', it could affect or 'tune' people to that special purpose.[60] Like Kandinsky, Mondrian imagined a room where Neo-Plastic music would be performed, which would be 'neither a church nor a theatre, but a spatial structure': both performance and environment would contribute towards the realization of 'the true unity of the physical-spiritual' (*MCWA*, p. 163).

For Mondrian, the *Gesamtkunstwerk* is not an end in itself, but a means of recreating the environment. 'Everything has to be designed in accordance with *the one idea*, the *New Plastic conception* . . . all the arts automatically collaborate' (*MCWA*, p. 111). Theatre should be transformed in accordance with Neo-Plastic principles (*MCWA*, p. 147).[61] Mondrian himself designed the stage sets for Michel Seuphor's play, *L'Ephémère est éternel*. Opera would be transformed through the 'new music', and even musical instruments themselves would be modelled on Neo-Plastic principles (*MCWA*, p. 146). Mondrian envisaged that the structure of Neo-Plastic music would be based on the relationship between '*fundamental sound*' and 'fundamental nonsound', parallel to that between colour and non-colour in Neo-Plastic painting, and that it would arise from the opposition between the jazz band and the concert orchestra (*MCWA*, pp. 157 and 162). The composer Jacob van Domselaer in fact wrote music which was directly inspired by Mondrian's Neo-Plastic paintings.

Art forms would evolve by expanding to the maximum the expressive potential of their own medium. However, Mondrian envisaged the creation of a new art form which would combine time and space and which would be 'situated between painting and music'. He continued: 'because space and time are only different expressions of *the same thing*, in the Neo-Plastic conception, music is *plastic* (i.e. *expression in space*), and the *"plastic" (painting) is possible in time*' (*MCWA*, p. 163). Instead of being presented with a visual image which could be perceived all at once, the spectator would be shown images projected separately and sequentially, as in music. (See also discussion of 'colour music' above.) The ascetic Mondrian was a passionate devotee of the foxtrot and the Charleston, and we have seen that the titles of his last paintings attribute imaginary choreographical associations to the rhythms of pictorial space.[62] However, Mondrian envisaged that ultimately, performance and spectacle would become part of everyday life. 'Dance, theatre etc. as art, will disappear along with the dominating "expression" of tragedy and harmony: the movement of life itself will become harmonious' (*MCWA*, p. 168). The only art form which would not disappear in this evolutionary process was architecture, which played a crucial role in Mondrian's aesthetics throughout his career.

In 1926, Mondrian wrote that architectural structure, which manifests the vertical and horizontal lines and planes which remain hidden in nature, had a close affinity with Neo-Plasticism (*MCWA*, p. 210). Later he declared that the 'new reality' would be created by 'the unification of architecture, sculpture and painting' (*MCWA*, p. 299). He preferred painting to architecture because it was freer of external constraints. He also believed that

the modern city had already begun to transform the external
environment and that the home was more in need of change;
hence the importance of interior design. 'Whereas, especially in
the metropolis, the character of the street has been transformed
by the myriad artificial advertising lights, by coloured billboards,
by well-composed window displays, by utilitarian buildings – the
home, on the other hand, requires a special and conscious effort'
(*MCWA*, p. 209). He remarks that in French shopping streets
'the various facades *articulate* the street. Through black or white or
another definite colour, each is *distinct* from the other. Together
they form a *composition of colour planes*' (*MCWA*, p. 110). It is part
of the process of Neo-Plastic transformation that the city itself
should become a work of art composed of interacting planes.

The home can no longer be sealed, closed, separate; nor can the street
. . . Home and street must be viewed as the city, as a *unity formed by planes
composed in neutralizing opposition that destroys all exclusiveness* . . . the interior of the home [must be] *a construction of planes in colour and noncolour
unified with the furniture and household objects, which will be nothing in themselves
but which will function as constructive elements of the whole.* (*MCWA*, p. 212).

Mondrian put his principles of interior design into practice in
his Paris, London and New York studios. He considered the
studios as works of art in themselves and had photographs of them
published in art magazines. These environments presage the
disappearance of the easel painting. 'It will be possible for the
Abstract-Real "painting" to disappear as soon as we can bring its
beauty to equal expression through the colour articulation of the
room' (*MCWA*, p. 112). The appearance of the studios has been
well documented.[63] We already noted that Mondrian's paintings
frequently give the impression of extending beyond the canvas. V.
Locatelli points out that the studio décor 'gives the observer the
impression that he [is] somehow standing inside a painter's canvas'.[64] Rectangles of solid colour attached to the walls give the
walls themselves the appearance of Neo-Plastic paintings, and
items of furniture are positioned to function as space dividers.
Each particular plays a role in the overall structure, and the
Neo-Plastic canvas itself functions as an 'abstract surrogate of the
whole'.[65] Mondrian did not tolerate disturbances of this perfect
order: César Domela recounted that 'if you lit a cigarette in his
atelier and you put the box of matches down in another spot,
Mondrian would get up to put it back in the original position'.[66]
Everything in the studio conformed to the Neo-Plastic colour
scheme. Barbara Hepworth recalls a visit to Mondrian's London
studio: 'He served us tea on a white table with red and blue boxes
containing a few biscuits.'[67]

Mondrian himself observed of his studio that 'here, in this room, the abstract has become reality for me'.[68] The studios also produced a powerful impression on visitors. A journalist who visited his Paris atelier reports how when he later went into the metro station, it seemed to him as if the rectangular tunnels and trains and the division of walls into red and green colour planes reflected 'Mondrian's recipe', and when he was inside the studio he felt that: 'the oppressive aspect of modernity has been tamed, order has been brought into chaos, while the simplicity of the forms and colours create an impression of Apollonian peace'.[69] Many artists recorded their impressions of Mondrian's studio, and several responded by creating similar spaces in their own ateliers.[70] In 1983, the room interior which Mondrian had designed in 1926, commissioned by Ida Bienert in Dresden but never executed, was constructed in the Pace Gallery in New York. The effects on visitors as recorded by Harry Holtzman recall those produced by the studio interiors. 'The most surprising effect to so many is particularly in the felt reaction of the satisfying equilibrium, excitement and tranquillity in an environment completely free of "objects" or "decoration."'[71]

Despite their apparent success, both the studio interiors and the room design demonstrate the fundamentally problematic nature of Mondrian's project. His desire to order every detail in his studio stemmed from his belief that 'our surroundings must be in accord with our inner, vital force if we are to live in harmony' (*MCWA*, p. 346). However, the contingent and the particular cannot be eliminated without eliminating life itself. Moreover, the photographs which recorded the studio for posterity themselves present an artificial, contrived view. The studio in the rue de Départ, which was irregular in shape, was photographed to look rectangular. The room interior which Mondrian designed was to have been used as a study. However, according to Nancy Troy, apart from a small lamp and an oval table which Bienert asked Mondrian to include in the plans, 'the rest of the sparse furnishings seem to have been pressed up against the wall in an effort to integrate it with the overall Neo-Plastic design'. There is no provision for an adequate table, a desk, or chairs, and 'all the books were to be hidden behind the Neo-Plastic façade of the bookcase'.[72] Moreover, the room as it appears in colour photographs of the Pace Gallery installation has a strangely two-dimensional aspect which reflects Mondrian's hostility to volume.[73] Lissitsky commented on Mondrian's designs: 'it is really a still-life of a room, for viewing through a keyhole'.[74] An added sense of unreality is created by the surfaces, which correspond to

Mondrian's description in 'Home-Street-City': 'Surfaces will be smooth and bright, which will also relieve the roughness of the materials' (*MCWA*, p. 211). Clearly, Mondrian's aims were fundamentally incompatible with the exigencies of reality.

Not surprisingly, Mondrian found that Neo-Plastic principles could not be transferred to architecture as easily as he had hoped. In fact, although he considered architecture to be close to the principles of Neo-Plasticism, he also felt that it was too tied to volume and to corporeality and that it was too constrained by social and economic factors.[75] He therefore created a distinction between practical and experimental architecture.[76] He did not renounce the idea that Neo-Plastic principles could potentially be realized in architecture, but excluded any such possibility in the immediate present. 'Our external environment cannot yet be realized as the pure plastic expression of harmony . . . If the founders of Neo-Plasticism in painting succeeded in fully expressing the "new" plastic only at great sacrifice, to achieve this in the ordinary architecture of today is *virtually impossible*' (*MCWA* pp. 169–70). However, Mondrian refused to accept Oud's conclusion that painting and architecture would have to be separated, because he believed that Neo-Plastic principles could be realized in the architecture of the future.[77]

IMAGINING THE FUTURE

Rhythmic connections between textual/pictorial and imaginary space enable texts and pictures to be experienced as sites of harmonious interaction between sensory reality and imagining activity. At the same time, the complete integration of the medium and imagining activity remains an unrealizable goal, as does the universalization of this rhythmic relationship between consciousness and the sensory environment. Textual/pictorial spaces function as sites of 'negative presentation' whose utopian implications extend beyond the sphere of art itself. Andrew Bowie describes the 'aesthetic product' in Kantian aesthetics as 'a utopian symbol of the realisation of freedom: in it we can see or hear an image of what the world would be like if freedom were realised.'[78] In its most extreme manifestation, as exemplified in the work of Mallarmé and Mondrian, the art work itself can be envisaged as ultimately replacing reality, becoming a universal space which would exist 'à l'exception de tout' (*MOC*, p. 656). Mondrian desired to 'mondrianiser la terre entière; substituer à l'univers naturel où demeurent les hommes un univers néoplastique qui en réalise l'essence'.[79] In Mallarmé, the replacement of reality by art is shown to be necessarily fictive: art is an 'exception' to reality which shows us what might be achieved, but also the impossibility of achieving it.

According to Marcuse, 'Art cannot change the world, but it can contribute to changing the consciousness and drives of the men and women who could change the world.'[80] In Peircean terms, this aim involves the 'interpretant', which can be defined as a 'modification of consciousness' (v.485). Moreover, for Peirce, thinking is 'a kind of action' (VIII.191), and the ultimate truth which will end the infinite regression of signs[81] is seen as 'a modification of a person's tendency towards action' (v.476) or 'habit change' (v.476), where habit is a tendency to think and act in a certain way. Habit change involves modification of existing rules. 'Self-analysing habit' can be classified as a 'final logical interpretant' (v.491),[82] and logical interpretants are conceived of as existing in a 'conditional future' (v.483). Peirce declares that 'the future alone has primary reality' (VIII.194). His theory of truth rests on 'the notion of a COMMUNITY, without definite limits, and capable of a definite increase in knowledge' (v.311): final opinion must be based on general agreement (VIII.12). It is crucial to the poets and painters here that (as in the Peircean 'diagram' and the Kantian 'aesthetical idea') new insights are derived from sensory and material structures rather than from abstract and conceptual thought, but also that this process could form the basis for the constitution of a community of subjects predicated on this experience itself rather than on existing sets of values and class structures.

A key aspect of the utopian dimension of this poetry and painting is the desire to create a new public of readers/spectators whose attitude to the new art would be diametrically opposed to the accepted norms of bourgeois, materialist culture. Rimbaud's and Mallarmé's writing reacts against discursive and poetic norms, demanding a new kind of reading practice. Kandinsky and Mondrian were aware that their painting could not succeed without a new kind of spectator, and used their theoretical writings to further this aim. The first issue of *De Stijl* declared that its purpose was to develop modern man's sensitivity to the new art and to awaken the lay person's consciousness of beauty,[83] and the *De Stijl* declaration of 1922 stated: 'Today we stand between a society which does not need us and one which does not exist.'[84] Kandinsky's and Mondrian's involvement in collective artistic enterprises and their theosophical associations no doubt contributed to their optimism concerning the possibility of transforming the consciousness of the public.[85] Both saw their art as destined for a superior public of the future. According to Kandinsky, 'notre tâche est de créer "l'atmosphère" pour l'avènement de l'homme nouveau, supérieur' (*CB*, p. 204).[86] Mondrian preceded his essay of 1920, *Le Néo-plasticisme*, with the dedication 'Aux hommes futurs.'

In 'Alchimie du verbe', Rimbaud declares that 'je me flattais d'inventer un verbe poétique accessible, un jour ou l'autre, à tous les sens' (*RO*, p. 228), and in 'Adieu', he recounts: 'J'ai essayé d'inventer de nouvelles fleurs, de nouveaux astres, de nouvelles chairs, de nouvelles langues' (*RO*, p. 240). Rimbaud affirms that 'cet avenir sera matérialiste' (*RO*, p. 350), but his is a materialism of excess, a 'sensory surreality' which reveals the poverty of life as it is: 'la vraie vie est absente' (*RO*, p. 224). This recreation of reality involves transforming the whole of life and love itself: in the words of 'l'Epoux infernal', 'l'amour est à réinventer, on le sait' (*RO*, p. 224). It is poetry which shows the way forward for the transformation of life, by creating a rhythmic harmony which engages all the senses. 'L'amour' does not refer just to sexual love but to social relations, which will be regulated by a new harmony. 'Un coup de ton doigt sur le tambour décharge tous les sons et commence la nouvelle harmonie. / Un pas de toi, c'est la levée des nouveaux hommes et leur en-marche' ('A une Raison'). Ideally, through his work, the poet would be instrumental in the creation of these 'nouveaux hommes': poetry would be 'en avant de l'action'. Rimbaud, too, as we have seen, was influenced by mystical and utopian ideas. However, Kittang writes of Rimbaud that his poetic practice lacks a 'fondement social', and continues: 'L'opéra fabuleux monté par un Rimbaud . . . se trouve irrémédiablement coupé de la culture collective, et se joue par conséquent devant une salle terriblement vide.'[87] Both Rimbaud and Mallarmé are more sceptical about the potential success of their projects than Kandinsky or Mondrian, and Rimbaud takes delight in taunting his reader: 'je réservais la traduction' ('Alchimie du verbe'); 'J'ai seul la clef de cette parade sauvage' ('Parade'); 'Qu'est mon néant auprès de la stupeur qui vous attend?' ('Vies I').

Although as a young poet, Mallarmé was very concerned to exclude readers he deemed unsuitable, he also envisaged a new, more demanding role for readers, who would be called upon to experience 'cette joie délicieuse de croire qu'ils créent' (*MOC*, p. 869). Moreover, possibly influenced by the collectivist aspect of Wagner's *Gesamtkunstwerk* and by his jealousy of the capacity of music to move crowds, Mallarmé later accorded a more positive, quasi-mythical role to 'la foule'. 'La foule qui commence à tant nous surprendre . . . remplit envers les sons, sa fonction par excellence de gardienne de mystère! Le sien! elle confronte son riche mutisme à l'orchestre, où gît la collective grandeur' (*MOC*, p. 390). In 'Conflit' (1895), Mallarmé expressed his regret at the difficulty of communicating the value of his poetry to workers who could not see its usefulness, and wished that the scales would fall from their eyes: 'comme je voudrais que parmi l'obscurité qui court sur l'aveugle troupeau, aussi des points de clarté . . . se fixassent, malgré ces yeux scellés ne les distinguant pas' (*MOC*, p. 359). Mallarmé imagined ceremonies, 'les fêtes futures', where the crowd would be a 'protagoniste à son insu' and where each one would be 'circulairement le héros' (*MOC*, pp. 392–3). His plans for the distribution of the printed volumes of the 'Livre' show clearly his desire to reach a wide audience in addition to the élite who would attend the performances, although he must have been painfully aware of the gap between the reality and this future, imaginary public.

Of all these poets and painters, Mondrian was the most concerned with the application of his aesthetic principles to society. Art was the means of liberation from oppression (*MCWA*, p. 320), and mankind would have to be changed through art before other more direct forms of social action were taken. 'Today, however, the new spirit has nothing to gain from a total upheaval of society: as long as men themselves are not "new", there is no place for the "new"' (*MCWA*, p. 144). Mondrian believed that the transformation of the public through art was a prelude to more direct forms of social action, and that aesthetic principles could be translated into social terms. 'What is true in art must also be true in human life' (*MCWA*, p. 324). 'True socialism' is described as '*self-governed organizations composed of producers and consumers in equivalent mutual relationships*' (*MCWA*, p. 262). Neo-Plastic structures even provide a model for international relations. In the 'international order of the future', countries will be 'mutually equivalent', and 'there will be just frontiers, exactly in proportion to the value of each country in relationship to the whole federation. These frontiers will be clearly defined but not "closed"; there will be no customs, no work permits. "Foreigners" will not be viewed as aliens' (*MCWA*, p. 269). Family and country are seen as 'limiting forms' (*MCWA*, p. 269). Disabled members of society should be supported, since '*the essential value of each individual entitles him to an existence equivalent to that of others*' (*MCWA*, p. 267).

According to Jaffé, 'Mondrian's Utopia is based on aesthetic thought, whereas all the preceding Utopian conceptions were built on moral, social or political principles'.[88]However, despite his attention, unparalleled in the other poets and painters, to the detailed reconstruction of society along Neo-Plastic lines, Mondrian had no strategy, apart from Neo-Plastic painting itself, for creating this future. Towards the end of his life, he wrote: 'the oppressive forms of the present will be destroyed. It is not [foreseeable] either when nor how' (*MCWA*, p. 375). He remained resolute in his determination to steer clear of politics as expressed in a letter to van Doesburg in 1919.[89] It is significant that Mallarmé, Kandinsky and Mondrian, all of whom, though interested in the political in a broad sense, were opposed to close links between art and politics, had affinities with anarchism.[90] Rimbaud, whose earlier work shows more overt evidence of political interests than do the *Illuminations*,[91] was interested in the anarchist Vermersch.[92] Kandinsky defended the concept of anarchy and referred to contemporary art as 'anarchistic' (*KCWA*, p. 242). Although Mondrian did not have overtly anarchist sympathies, several of his articles were published in the journal *i 10*, whose editor he described as an anarchist and referred to their shared values as hostility to 'convention, capital-in-the-wrong sense, bourgeoisie etc.'.[93] He also quoted approvingly Marinetti's call 'Let us everywhere unleash and arouse the originality of the individual. Let all things be differentiated, transvalued, disproportioned', explaining that individualism still has a role to play in the present, and that 'full collectivism . . . is the dream of the future' (*MCWA*, p. 207).

The apparent contradictions in the work of these poets and painters between emphasis on individualism and universality and between destruction and creation, chaos and order, can be explained within the context of an aesthetic and socio-political ideal of an internally generated aesthetic order (Kandinsky's 'internal necessity') as opposed to one imposed from without, which is analogous to anarchist political aims. Mallarmé, who, after a bombing by the anarchist Vaillant, favourably compared the effects of the 'livre' with the use of weapons[94] and who acted as a character witness for Félix Fénéon when he was tried for anarchist activities, drew a clear parallel between social and literary structures. 'Dans une société sans stabilité, sans unité, il ne peut se créer d'art stable, d'art définitif. De cette organisation sociale inachevée, qui explique en même temps l'inquiétude des esprits, naît l'inexpliqué besoin d'individualité dont les manifestations littéraires présentes sont le reflet direct' (*MOC*, pp. 866–7). Even the structure of his 'Livre' had socio-political implications: 'c'est simplement "la symbolique du *bourgeois* ou ce qu'il est par rapport à l'Absolu''. Lui montrer qu'il n'existe pas indépendamment de l'Univers – dont il a cru se séparer – mais qu'il est une de ses fonctions, et une des plus viles – et ce qu'il représente, dans ce Développement. S'il le comprend, sa joie sera empoisonnée à jamais.'[95]

Anarchism's direct approach to the destruction of existing society short-circuited the problem of political strategies. Moreover, unlike socialism, anarchism was not based on class divisions, and the alienation of the bourgeois poet/artist from his own class led to a desire to found social coherence on artistic rather than social values. Mondrian saw the 'new man' as transcending class differences: 'it is from the *new man*, emerging from worker, bourgeoisie and aristocracy *but altogether different from them*, that the New Plastic will arise' (*MCWA*, p. 121). Mallarmé elaborated his ideas on society in a series of articles which appeared in 1895 in *La Revue blanche* (a journal which defended the causes of Symbolism, free verse and anarchy). Following the breakdown of religious and political cohesion, Mallarmé saw literature itself as the basis of social relations (see *MOC*, p. 420). We have already seen that he envisaged public festivals modelled on religious ceremonies and Greek tragedy which would unite the participants: 'notre communion ou part d'un à tous et de tous à un' (*MOC*, p. 394). This reflects precisely the ontology of the 'livre', where, as in the Eucharist, each part contains the whole. 'Mythe, l'éternel: la communion, par le livre. A chacun part totale' (*MOC*, p. 656). However, for Mallarmé, the 'Présence réelle' is not divine, but a fiction, and the ideal ceremony and society would have to be based on awareness of fiction. Ideally, the living would recognize their own non-existence ('ils n'ont pas lieu': *MOC*, p. 664; 'il n'est pas de Présent, non – un présent n'existe pas . . . mal informé celui qui se crierait son propre contemporain': *MOC*, p. 372), which is the condition of the possibility of a place for writing, a 'lieu d'écrire'. Mallarmé envisages that society could be governed by intellectuals, the 'Académiciens', but the real rulers would not be people, who are mere mortals, but books themselves: 'Que feront ici des vivants . . . On les veut immortels, en place que ce soit les ouvrages' (*MOC*, p. 418).[96] Here, as with Mondrian's ideal environment, exclusion of contingency would culminate in exclusion of life itself.

Clearly the concept of isomorphism of textual/pictorial and social structures raises fundamental ideological problems, some of which I shall briefly sketch before concluding. Firstly, there is the question of how successful these poetic/pictorial strategies are in their self-avowed aim of subverting bourgeois norms by purely

aesthetic means. In the case of Rimbaud and Mallarmé, it is often
held that resistance to models of communication which characterize bourgeois society is in itself subversive.[97] Rimbaud and
Mallarmé characterize their stance in terms of being 'en grève'.
'Travailler maintenant, jamais, jamais; je suis en grève' (*RO*,
p. 345); 'l'attitude du poëte dans une époque comme celle-ci, où
il est en grève devant la société, est de mettre de côté tous le
moyens viciés qui peuvent s'offrir à lui' (*MOC*, p. 870). The
refusal to explain, to communicate 'clearly' indicates a withdrawal of labour. This 'strike' can be seen as a protest against the
reduction of the work of art to communicative models based on
exchange values. Mallarmé notably compares direct communication or exchange of thoughts via 'l'emploi élémentaire du
discours' with the act of 'prendre ou mettre dans la main d'autrui
en silence une pièce de monnaie' (*MOC*, p. 368). Valéry suggests
that difficulty subverts facile consumerism. 'La lisibilité est la
qualité d'un texte qui en prévoit et en facilite la consommation.'[98]
In 'Villes II', Rimbaud speaks of 'la joie du travail nouveau', and
in 'Alchimie du verbe', he wonders: 'Quand irons-nous, par-delà
les grèves et les monts, saluer la naissance du travail nouveau'
('Matin'). However, discursive strategies alone are not sufficient
to subvert the norms of bourgeois society, especially in the context
of the integration of art into capitalist economic frameworks.

Rimbaud attempts to guard against this danger by anticipating
it within the text itself. In the *Illuminations*, not only is the reader
made aware of the fictive nature of the 'hallucination des mots',
but the utopian dimension of imaginary space is shown to be
reversible through the investment of the same words with positive
and negative connotations, and even to be part of the 'magie
bourgeoise' ('Soir historique') and the system of exchange values
from which it seeks to escape: nothing can elude the 'Solde', even
'les Corps sans prix', 'l'anarchie pour les masses' and 'ce qu'on ne
vendra jamais' ('Solde').[99] The Mallarmé of *La Dernière Mode* has
been accused of fetishizing the signifier,[100] and this critique is
pertinent to other parts of his work, including the 'Livre', where
the text is indeed conceived of as a self-sufficient, 'magical' object,
animated through its rhythm. 'Le sens enseveli se meut et dispose,
en chœur, des feuillets' (*MOC*, p. 372). In this way, it acquires
autonomous life: 'de mort il devient vie' (31 A) and has no need of
readers. 'Impersonnifié, le volume, autant qu'on s'en sépare
comme auteur, ne réclame approche de lecteur. Tel, sache, entre
les accessoires humains, il a lieu tout seul, fait, étant' (*MOC*,
p. 372). However, the magic of the fetish depends on 'the projection of consciousness into the object, and then a forgetting of that

act of projection',[101] and Mallarmé's irony does not allow the
reader to forget the interaction between textual and imaginary
space and the impossibility of the text existing alone, replacing
reality. 'Nous savons, captifs d'une formule absolue, que n'est que
ce qui est' (*MOC*, p. 647). It is only by acting as a 'supplément' to
this totality, by revealing what totality lacks, that writing can
exist. 'Signe! au gouffre centrale d'une spirituelle impossibilité
que rien ne soit exclusivement à tout' (*MOC*, p. 333). None the
less, it is ironic that the aesthetic object which defies petty bourgeois values and which transcends material reality through its
relation to imagining consciousness should come so close to being
the perfect commodity fetish, the 'magical object which contains
within itself the principle of its own value'[102] by erasing the
labour of imagination in its production and reception.

Kandinsky's and Mondrian's strategies of eliminating figurative objects and constructing pictorial spaces where forms and
colours can be imaginatively experienced as rhythmic relationships rather than as individual, material entities are inseparable
from their hostility to bourgeois materialism. According to Mondrian, 'overwhelming individualism' and 'a petty attachment to
material things' characterize the bourgeoisie (*MCWA*, p. 121),
and he declares that '*A concept of beauty free from materialism must
reshape our materialistic society*' (*MCWA*, p. 109). Apart from the
problem of whether aesthetic consciousness can in fact 'reshape'
society, this also raises the question of whether the overcoming of
materialism and individualism by ascribing properties of animation to the inanimate work of art does not once again involve the
attribution of 'magical' properties to the object, unless one maintains critical consciousness of one's own role in this process.
Moreover, in Mondrian, the elements of modernity singled out as
agents of destruction of the old reality (for example the flashing
advertisements and the fast rhythms of New York) themselves
epitomize the materialist society which the artist intends to
subvert, and which can appropriate his innovations. Mondrian's
uncritical approach to modernity, such as the machine culture
('the machine can free man from his state of slavery': *MCWA*,
p. 262) now seems unduly naïve and lacking in critical distance.
Raymond Williams takes a negative view of the avant-garde's
achievements in this respect. 'It was capitalism . . . that success-
fully integrated life and art in a new phase in which the commodity no longer feared culture because it had already incorporated
it . . . Practically effecting what the avant-gardists only dreamed,
capitalism may even have owed a direct debt to the former's
artefacts and technologies.'[103]

Furthermore, a problematic aspect of utopian thought which we have encountered here is its pseudo-universalism. Ruth Levitas has remarked that 'most utopias are portrayed as universal utopias', and 'most utopias conceived by men . . . subjugate women'.[104] Although all four poets and painters recognize the importance of the 'feminine' in aesthetic creation, they follow to greater or lesser degrees the by now well substantiated trend within Symbolism and Modernism for male writers/artists to appropriate the feminine as an attribute of the male creative imagination, with the aim of making it self-sufficient.[105] The male creative consciousness would find its apotheosis in fusing with the self-generating structure of an art work whose 'universality' is conceived of as androgynous and where the feminine principle is 'aufgehoben' in the masculine. The 'new man' referred to above is indeed a 'man', albeit one endowed with androgynous creativity. For Rimbaud, however, imagination's insatiable desire for the new is also a desire for difference, including gender difference: his utopian future is one where women are poets who discover their own 'imaginary spaces': 'Quand sera brisé l'infini servage de la femme, quand elle vivra pour elle et par elle . . . elle sera poète, elle aussi! La femme trouvera de l'inconnu! Ses mondes d'idées différeront-ils des nôtres? – Elle trouvera des choses étranges, insondables, repoussantes, délicieuses' (*RO*, p. 350).

The modelling of utopian social spaces on the relationship between textual/pictorial and imaginary space clearly comprises many dangers: at worst, the imposition of a pseudo-universal ideal order. Imagination and art works alone cannot provide criteria for social organization. However, the innovatory capacity of imagining activity, which is open to endless possibilities of 'imagining otherwise', affirming differences as well as synthesis, is crucial to the creation of new projects for 'liberation from oppression in art and life' (Mondrian, *MCWA*, p. 322). Moreover, capacity for critique, including self-critique, is a vital aspect of 'productive imagination', whose task Ricoeur sees as 'exploration of the possible': imagination here has a 'disruptive function' as 'an imagining of something else, the elsewhere', which is opposed to the 'process of identification that mirrors the order' which characterizes ideology.[106]

Utopian spaces opened up by imagining activity can introduce 'a sense of doubt that shatters the obvious'[107] by making us question assumptions previously taken for granted as immutable. The creation of rhythmic relationships between textual/pictorial and imaginary spaces opens up new sites of freedom and harmony, thereby critiquing existing reality ('la vraie vie est

Conclusion

I hope to have shown that imagination can be 'reconstructed' in the terms I have set out here, and that the concepts of imagining activity and imaginary space are crucial to appreciation of the art works which we have discussed.

As I stated earlier in this study, the extent of the semantic disruption which takes place in the poetry of Rimbaud and Mallarmé and the ways in which imaginary space is reflected in the textual space of their poems mark a culmination of Symbolist aesthetics, where it is the medium itself which becomes an object of aesthetic transformation. In painting, a similar process begins at the same period, but, for reasons which I have attempted to explain, the project of aesthetic transformation of the medium does not become the central issue in painting until somewhat later, when it leads to a radical modification of pictorial representation with the advent of abstraction in the early years of this century.

Given the restricted nature of the corpus of works which have been discussed in detail here, it is necessary to give some consideration to the questions of how representative these examples are and the status I wish to claim for them. At the outset, I placed this discussion in the context of theories of imagination and of the aesthetic. In particular, I stressed how the emergence of aesthetics as a discipline marked the recognition of a sphere of cognition particular to the senses, and showed how imagination played a crucial role in this sphere by operating in a sensory mode while challenging the relation of sense impressions to known objects and to conceptually definable meaning, even to the point of transgressing the boundaries of cognition and of the sensible by using images as 'negative presentations' of the inconceivable and of an absent supersensible. I also showed how access to the imaginary dimension of objects experienced through the senses was seen in terms of 'rhythm' and 'vibration', and we later saw the centrality of rhythm in linking imagining activity with the poetic/pictorial mediums.

Since these interactions are themselves central to the category of the 'aesthetic', they are of course by no means unique to the work of the poets and painters discussed here, which could be said to represent 'cas limites' in terms of the extent to which they aim at the imaginary transformation of the medium. However, there are important aspects of the function of imagining activity as described here which are historically relative. I have defined imaginary space as self-negating, owing to the innovatory and subversive nature of the signifying processes, which cannot be reduced to coded, identifiable objects, and which maintain the open-endedness of imagining activity and its dependence on the signifying processes themselves. Imagining activity is therefore bound up with the kind of disruptive signifying practices which are more prevalent in post-Romantic art than in earlier periods. We have also seen that disruption of established semiotic codes does not in itself guarantee stimulation of imagining activity or its focussing on the medium as an object of aesthetic transformation. The kind of effects which we have observed here cannot be attributed to all semantically disruptive works. The particular emphasis at the end of the last century and the beginning of this one on transforming perception of the artistic medium through its interaction with the imagination of the receiver, which is linked with a problematization of the ontological status of material objects, is undoubtedly connected with cultural circumstances and socio-economic factors pertaining at these periods. Further-more, the utopian dimension, the hope that the perfect relation-ship between receiver and art work could be extended to the environment as a whole, even the closely related concept of the *Gesamtkunstwerk*, can no longer be viewed in the same light after the events, artistic and political, of this century, and the increas-ingly sinister implications of the establishment of a 'new world order'.

On the other hand, the receiver's imaginative response to the medium, where the latter is experienced as a site of projection of new possibilities, in short, as an imaginary rather than simply an actual presence, is crucial to 'aesthetic' experience in a wider sense, especially in the context of non-verbal art forms, where the receiver's attention can more easily be focussed on the imaginary dimension of the medium rather than on conceptual content. Indeed, the foregrounding of rhythmic patterns which replace coded objects and act as a 'bridge' between the medium and imagining activity is relatively more developed in non-verbal and performative mediums, such as music and dance. It has emerged at several points during this study that the art of dance, which takes place in real as well as virtual time and space, in many ways provides a paradigm for the kind of spatio-temporal interactions which these poets and painters wished to exploit. Mallarmé was fascinated by new forms in dance, as were Kandinsky and Mondrian. Imaginary space could be described as 'choreographic', and dance itself is a privileged site of imaginary space.

I shall explore this space, and the figural role of dance as a paradigm for the aesthetic, in another place. For now, I shall simply recall Mallarmé's discernment, observing the dancer Loïe Fuller, of 'une spirituelle acrobatie' in 'le mouvement pur et le silence déplacé par le voltige' (*MOC*, p. 311), and end on a display of Rimbaud's textual 'choreography':

> J'ai tendu des cordes de clocher à clocher;
>   des guirlandes de fenêtre à fenêtre;
>   des chaînes d'or d'étoile à étoile,
> et je danse.
>
>   (Rimbaud, extract from 'Phrases', *Illuminations*)

Notes

INTRODUCTION

1 R. Jakobson, 'La Nouvelle poésie russe', in R. Jakobson, *Questions de poétique* (Paris: Seuil, 1973), p. 21.

2 R. Jakobson, 'The Contours of the Safe Conduct', in *Semiotics of Art*, ed. L. Matejka and I. R. Titunik (Cambridge, MA: MIT Press, 1976), p. 195. Jakobson refers to the influence of emerging abstract art on his theories in *Jakobson*, ed. R. Georgin (Lausanne: Editions l'Age d'Homme, 1978), p. 12. Mark Roskill's stimulating book, *Klee, Kandinsky and the Thought of their Time: A Critical Perspective* (Urbana: University of Illinois Press, 1992), which came to my attention while this manuscript was nearing completion, documents Kandinsky's collaboration with Jakobson (p. 90).

3 Firstly, in Lacan, the term is pejorative, since it denotes a state of consciousness where the subject is the victim of delusion, and secondly it has a very specific meaning within the framework of Lacanian psychoanalysis and cannot easily be applied outside the context of its relationship to the 'Real' and the 'Symbolic'. The ramifications of this conceptual edifice are enormous, and engagement with it would complicate the present discussion unnecessarily. For accounts of Lacan's use of the terms 'Imaginary', 'Real' and 'Symbolic', see Malcolm Bowie, *Lacan* (London: Fontana, 1991), and Anika Lemaire, *Jacques Lacan* (London: Routledge, 1977). Moreover, the term acquires additional pejorative connotations through its association with ideology within the context of Althusserian Marxism. 'Ideology is nothing other than the *imaginary* relation of individuals to their real conditions of existence; it teaches them to recognize (that is to misrecognize) themselves as free responsible individuals, and thus "voluntarily" to reproduce the dominant relations of production.' M. Moriarty, *Roland Barthes* (Cambridge: Polity Press, 1991), p. 171. See this book also for a very lucid exposition of the 'imaginary' in Barthes.

4 See discussion in chapter 1 below, p. 15.

5 This phrase is used by Hugo Friedrich in describing Rimbaud's poetry. See *The Structure of Modern Poetry from the Mid Nineteenth Century to the Mid Twentieth Century* (Evanston: Northwestern University Press, 1974), p. 56. Interestingly, Will Grohmann uses the term 'sensual unreality' of Kandinsky's painting. See W. Grohmann,

Wassily Kandinsky, Life and Work (London: Thames and Hudson, 1959), p. 246.

6 The term 'undecidable', used by Derrida, is not synonymous with 'ambiguous', but refers, by analogy with Gödel's discovery of undecidable propositions, to elements which suspend binary oppositions and which resist dialectical 'Aufhebung' or synthesis. On this topic, see R. Gasché, *The Tain of the Mirror, Derrida and the Philosophy of Reflection* (London: Harvard University Press, 1986), pp. 240–5.

7 The philosophical dilemma posed by the postmodern demise of imagination is debated in Richard Kearney's stimulating books, *The Wake of Imagination, Ideas of Creativity in Western Culture* (London: Hutchinson, 1988) and *Poetics of Imagining from Husserl to Lyotard* (London: Harper Collins, 1991). The association of discourses of the aesthetic and the sublime with the emergence of the bourgeois subject and social order is discussed in Terry Eagleton's *The Ideology of the Aesthetic* (Oxford: Blackwell, 1990).

8 These 'key moments' have of course been selected with a view to my own argument. I shall not attempt to cover all major elements of the philosophical background, such as the theories of Schopenhauer. On Schopenhauer's role in the aesthetics of Symbolism and abstraction, see Mark Cheetham, *The Rhetoric of Purity: Essentialist Theory and the Advent of Abstract Painting* (Cambridge University Press, 1991).

9 See, for instance, Cheetham, *Rhetoric of Purity* and P. Weiss, *Kandinsky in Munich: The Formative Jugendstil Years* (Princeton University Press, 1979).

10 See, for instance, C. Harrison, 'The Ratification of Abstract Art', in *Towards a New Art, Essays on the Background to Abstract Art 1910–20* (London: The Tate Gallery, 1980), pp. 146–55, and Cheetham, *Rhetoric of Purity*. Cheetham, whose book comprises extensive discussions of Kandinsky and Mondrian, sees his project as a 'critique of the absolutism of the rhetoric of purity along . . . postmodern lines' (p. 140).

11 On the possibility of a feminist aesthetics, see C. Battersby's incisive study, *Gender and Genius: Towards a Feminist Aesthetics* (London: The Women's Press, 1989), R. Felski, *Beyond Feminist Aesthetics: Feminist Literature and Social Change* (London: Hutchinson Radius, 1989) and *Journal of Aesthetics and Art Criticism*, 48 (1990, Feminist Aesthetics Issue), which includes articles on the gendering of the sublime. The question of a female imaginary is central to the work of Luce Irigaray. On this topic, see M. Whitford's stimulating study, *Luce Irigaray, Philosophy in the Feminine* (London: Routledge, 1991), pp. 62–70, 53–74 and 89–97.

12 I have recently edited, together with Penny Florence, a collection of essays entitled *Feminist Subjects, Multi-Media: Cultural Methodologies* (forthcoming, Manchester University Press), which addresses the issue of the positioning of female receivers over a wide range of media.

13 D. Scott, *Pictorialist Poetics: Poetry and the Visual Arts in 19th-Century France* (Cambridge University Press, 1988).

14 See, for instance, R. Barthes, 'Rhétorique de l'image', *Communications*, 4 (1964), pp. 40–51; U. Bayer, 'Zur Semiotik des Syntax-

begriffs in der Malerei', *Semiosis: Zeitschrift fur Semiotik und Ihre Anwendungen*, 17/18 (1980), pp. 143–52; H. Damisch, 'Huit thèses pour ou contre une sémiologie de la peinture', *Macula*, 2 (1974), pp. 17–23, and 'Sémiologie et iconographie', *Colloquio Artes*, 17 (1974), pp. 21–9; J.-M. Floch, 'Kandinsky: sémiotique d'un discours non-figuratif', *Communications* 34 (1981), pp. 135–59; L. Marin, *Etudes sémiologiques, écritures, peintures* (Paris: Klincksieck, 1971); M. Schapiro, 'Some Problems in the Semiotics of Visual Art: Field and Vehicle in Image-Signs', *Semiotica*, 1 (1979), pp. 223–42; F. Thürlemann, *Paul Klee, analyse sémiotique de trois peintures* (Lausanne: L'Age d'Homme, 1982); B. Uspensky, *The Semiotics of the Russian Icon* (Lisse: Peter de Ridder Press, 1976); D. Vallier, 'Malevitch et le modèle linguistique en peinture', *Critique* (1975), pp. 284–98, and J. Veltruský, 'Some Aspects of the Pictorial Sign', *Semiotics of Art*, ed. L. Matejka and I. R. Titunik (Cambridge, MA: MIT Press, 1976), pp. 245–65. Moreover, there is at present considerable interest in the issue of the 'language' of art history itself. See, in particular, *The Language of Art History*, ed. S. Kemal and I. Gaskell (Cambridge University Press, 1991), *Visual Theory, Painting and Interpretation*, ed. N. Bryson, M. N. Holly, and K. Moxey (Cambridge: Polity Press, 1991), and D. Preziosi, *Rethinking Art History, Meditations on a Coy Science* (London: Yale University Press, 1989).

I IMAGINATION AND IMAGINARY SPACE

1 C. Baudelaire, *Oeuvres complètes*, 2 vols., ed. Cl. Pichois, Bibliothèque de la Pléiade (Paris: Gallimard, 1975–6; hereafter, *BOC* I or II), II, p. 621.

2 I. Kant, *Critique of Judgement*, trans. J. H. Bernard (New York: Hafner Press, 1951; hereafter, *CJ*), p. 82/90. I shall be using this translation in preference to that by J. C. Meredith (*Kant's Critique of Aesthetic Judgement* (Oxford: Clarendon Press, 1952)), but since the latter is the standard edition, I shall give page references to both, in that order.

3 This mode of reflexivity has of course to be distinguished from reflexivity in the sense of self-referentiality, where the work is held to become its own object, without the involvement of imagination.

4 Kant, *Critique of Pure Reason*, trans. N. Kemp Smith (London: Macmillan, 1989; hereafter, *CPR*), A 702: B 730, p. 569. ('A' refers to the sections, as numbered by N. Kemp Smith, of the first edition of the *Critique*: 'B' refers to the second edition, both of which are included in this translation.)

5 See, for instance, J.-F. Lyotard, *Leçons sur l'analytique du sublime* (Paris: Galilée, 1991), p. 278.

6 Kant, *Anthropology from a Practical Point of View*, trans. V. L. Dowdell (London: Feffer and Simons, 1978), p. 146.

7 'The goal or aim of aesthetics is the perfection of sensory cognition as such'. Baumgarten's *Aesthetica*, cited in B. Poppe, *Alexander Gottlieb Baumgarten: Seine Bedeutung und Stellung in der Leibnitz-Wölffischen Philosophie und Seine Beziehungen zu Kant* (Borna-Leipzig: R. Noske, 1907,

translation mine), p. 40. Baumgarten's *Aesthetica* was published in 1750 and 1758, but many of the central ideas could already be found in his *Meditationes Philosophicae de Nonnullis ad Poema Pertinentibus*, published in 1735. Poppe points out (p. 450) that Baumgarten's concept of perfection ('Vollkommenheit') is strongly influenced by Wolff and Leibnitz.

8 Baumgarten argues that sensory cognition is perfected when the 'confused' ideas of sense acquire 'extensive clarity', i.e. become more complex and vivid by containing more than one sensate idea. A. Baumgarten, *Meditationes Philosophicae de Nonnullis ad Poema Pertinentibus*, trans. K. Aschenbrenner and W. B. Holther (Berkeley: University of California Press, 1954), p. 53. The term 'density' as used by Nelson Goodman, like Baumgarten's term 'extensive clarity', can qualify both verbal and non-verbal sign systems. See N. Goodman, *Languages of Art: An Approach to a Theory of Symbols* (Indianapolis: Hackett Publishing Company, 1976), p. 230.

9 Baumgarten, *Meditationes*, p. 53.

10 The Kantian sense of 'intuition' can be defined as a representation 'by means of which an object is presented to us as an appearance'. L. W. Beck, *Early German Philosophy: Kant and his Predecessors* (Cambridge, MA: the Belknap Press of Harvard University Press, 1969), p. 478.

11 M. Heidegger, *Kant and the Problem of Metaphysics* (London: Indiana University Press, 1972), p. 178. This is not, of course, what Kant actually said. Heidegger sees his task as that of 'bringing out what Kant intended to say' and believes that in order to do so he must 'necessarily resort to violence' (*ibid.*, pp. 206–7).

12 *Ibid.*, p. 173.

13 *Ibid.*, p. 170.

14 'No concept of the object lies at the basis of the judgement . . . the freedom of the imagination consists in the fact that it schematizes without any concept' (*CJ*, p. 129/143). Judgements of taste are disinterested (not oriented towards an external end) and universally valid (*CJ*, p. 54/60). Kant's claim that the pleasure produced by this harmony between the imagination and the understanding in judgements of taste is universal takes no account of cultural, historical or gender differences.

15 For instance, Kant argues that 'all our knowledge of God is merely symbolical' (*CJ*, p. 198/223).

16 T. Weiskel, *The Romantic Sublime: Studies in the Structure and Psychology of Transcendence* (Baltimore: Johns Hopkins University Press, 1976), p. 17.

17 E. Burke, cited in *ibid.*, p. 17.

18 Baumgarten, *Meditationes*, p. 52.

19 *Ibid.*, p. 53.

20 G. E. Lessing, *Laocoön, Nathan the Wise, Minna von Barnhelm*, trans. W. A. Steel (London: Dent, 1970), p. 14.

21 As remarked by Linda Nead in *The Female Nude* (London: Routledge, 1992), p. 29. The literature is too extensive to cite at length here, but it should be noted that the sublime has featured promi-

nently in the work of J. Derrida and J.-F. Lyotard. See, for instance, J. Derrida, *La Vérité en peinture* (Paris: Flammarion, 1978) and J.-F. Lyotard, *Leçons sur l'analytique du sublime*, and *The Postmodern Condition: A Report on Knowledge*, trans. G. Bennington and B. Massumi (Manchester University Press, 1984). See also J. Bernstein, *The Fate of Art: Aesthetic Alienation from Kant to Adorno and Derrida* (Cambridge: Polity Press, 1992); P. De Bolla, *The Discourse of the Sublime, Readings in History, Aesthetics, and the Subject* (Oxford: Blackwell, 1989); F. Ferguson, *Solitude and the Sublime* (London: Routledge, 1992), and J. Sychrava, *Idealism in Aesthetics: Schiller to Derrida* (Cambridge University Press, 1989).

22 Lyotard, *Postmodern Condition*, p. 79.

23 *Ibid.*, p. 81.

24 J.-P. Sartre, *L'Imaginaire, psychologie phénoménologique de l'imagination* (Paris: Gallimard, 1940; hereafter, *IM*), p. 118.

25 See, in particular: R. Ingarden, *The Cognition of the Literary Work of Art* (Evanston, IL: Northwestern University Press, 1973) and *The Literary Work of Art: An Investigation on the Borderlines of Ontology, Logic, and the Theory of Literature* (Evanston, IL: Northwestern University Press, 1973), and W. Iser, *The Act of Reading: A Theory of Aesthetic Response* (Baltimore: The Johns Hopkins University Press, 1978) and *The Implied Reader: Patterns of Communication in Prose Fiction From Bunyan to Beckett* (Baltimore: The Johns Hopkins University Press, 1974). On reader-response criticism generally, see *Reader-Response Criticism, From Formalism to Post-Structuralism*, ed. J. P. Tompkins (London: Johns Hopkins University Press, 1980).

26 See, for instance, J.-P. Richard, *Poésie et profondeur* (Paris: Seuil, 1955) and G. Poulet, *Les Métamorphoses du cercle* (Paris: Plon, 1961).

27 This is of course a crucial difference between the strictly structuralist and the phenomenological approach, which uses 'structuralist' methods of analysing relationships between images without wishing to confine itself to purely textual factors.

28 Iser, however, has emphasized the incompatibility of the imaginary with verbalization. 'The cardinal points of the text defy verbalization, and indeed it is only through these open structures within the linguistic patterning of the text that the imaginary can manifest its presence.' W. Iser, 'Feigning in Fiction', in *The Identity of the Literary Text*, ed. M. J. Valdés and Owen Miller (University of Toronto Press, 1985), p. 225.

29 See M. Merleau-Ponty, *La Prose du monde* (Paris: NRF Gallimard, 1969), p. 78 and p. 125.

30 G. Bachelard, *La Poétique de la rêverie* (Paris: Presses Universitaires de France, 1961), p. 1.

31 This concept of 'vécu' is not necessarily associated with a narrowly biographical approach. This distinction will be discussed in chapter 2 below.

32 *La Poétique de la rêverie*, p. 4.

33 J. Garelli, *La Gravitation poétique* (Paris: Mercure de France, 1960), p. 160.

34 P. Ricoeur, 'The Metaphorical Process as Cognition, Imagination and Feeling', *Critical Inquiry*, 5 (1978–9), p. 147.

35 *Ibid.*, p. 150.

36 *Ibid.*, p. 154.

37 *Ibid.*, p. 153.

38 *Ibid.*

39 In relation to painting, Sartre's analysis is in fact strongly biased towards figurative images, and he does not account for why non-figurative forms and colours should be perceived as 'objets' and 'choses'. In relation to music, he resorts to a rather Platonic explanation of the 'imaginaire' in terms of the distinction between a piece as performed, which is tied to the real, and the piece of which this performance is simply an interpretation or an 'analogon' (*IM*, pp. 138 ff.).

40 J. Derrida, *Marges de la philosophie* (Paris: Minuit, 1972), p. 196.

41 J. Derrida, *La Voix et le phénomène* (Paris: Presses Universitaires de France, 1967), p. 110, emphasis mine.

42 *Ibid.*, p. 111.

43 J. Derrida, *La Dissémination* (Paris: Seuil, 1972), p. 281.

44 *Ibid.*, p. 282.

45 G. Bachelard, *La Poétique de l'espace* (Paris: Presses Universitaires de France, 1958), p. 4.

46 *Ibid.*, p. 6.

47 *Ibid.*, p. 7.

48 Bachelard, *La Poétique de la rêverie*, p. 3.

49 'La poésie met le langage en état d'émergence', and the poetic image is an 'origine de conscience' (*La Poétique de l'espace*, pp. 10–11).

50 R. Kearney, *Poetics of Imagining from Husserl to Lyotard* (London: Harper and Collins Academic, 1991), p. 101.

51 P. Ricoeur, *Lectures on Ideology and Utopia* (New York: Columbia University Press, 1986), pp. 365–6.

52 *Ibid.*, p. 309.

53 M. Foucault, Introduction to L. Binswanger, *Le Rêve et l'existence* (Paris: Desclée, 1956), pp. 116–17.

54 J. Derrida, *Positions* (Paris: Minuit, 1972), p. 60. '*Aufhebung* literally means "lifting up"; but it also contains the double meaning of conservation and negation. For Hegel, dialectics is a process of *Aufhebung*: every concept is to be negated and lifted up to a higher sphere in which it is thereby conserved.' J. Derrida, *Margins of Philosophy*, trans. A. Bass (Sussex: Harvester, 1982), p. 20, n. 23.

55 Derrida, *Positions*, p. 39. See also J. Derrida, 'Economimesis', in S. Agacinski *et al.*, *Mimesis des articulations* (Paris: Aubier-Flammarion, 1975), p. 88, and the stimulating discussion by J. Bernstein in *The Fate of Art* of the parallels and differences between deconstruction and the sublime ('The Deconstructive Sublime', pp. 136–87).

56 J. Derrida, *De la grammatologie* (Paris: Minuit, 1967), pp. 263–4.

57 J. Derrida, *L'Écriture et la différance* (Paris: Seuil, 1967), p. 423.

58 Derrida treats consciousness in Husserlian terms of 'vouloir-dire' and sees it as unmediated presence. 'Le sujet comme conscience n'a

jamais pu s'annoncer autrement que comme présence à soi'
(Derrida, *Marges*, p. 17).

59 Derrida, *Positions*, p. 17, emphasis mine.

60 J. Engell points out that 'Coleridge had spoken of an imaginative
union of the *percipi* and the *percipere*, the "perceived" and the "perceiver". In short, what we now call "empathy" was very much alive
in the late Enlightenment, although the English word did not exist.'
J. Engell, *The Creative Imagination, Enlightenment to Romanticism*
(Harvard University Press, 1981), p. 157.

61 T. Lipps, *Asthetik: Psychologie des Schönen und der Kunst*, 2 vols.
(Hamburg: Leopold Voss, 1923, 1920 (first pub. 1903 and 1906);
hereafter, *AS* I or II), I, p. 226. All translations from Lipps are mine.

62 We shall see below that Kandinsky does not always succeed in
making these distinctions.

63 Compare Kandinsky's example of the conflict between the effect of
colours and that of the object to which they belong, cited in chapter
4 below, p. 119.

64 I shall discuss in more detail in the next chapter what is meant by the
concept of 'textual space'.

65 Hegel describes art as the spiritualization ('Vergeistigung') of
matter. G. W. F. Hegel, *Vorlesungen über die Asthetik* (Stuttgart:
Reclam, 1971), p. 87.

66 Lipps specifies that the condition of 'aesthetic contemplation' is that
'the sensuous is not there for its own sake, but is completely subordinate to the content, so that through the sensuous, I can perceive this
content and be completely given over to it' (*AS*, I, p. 535).

67 C. S. Peirce, *Collected Papers of Charles Sanders Peirce*, 8 vols., ed.
C. Hartshorne and P. Weiss, vols. I–VI; ed. A. W. Burks,
vols. VII–VIII (Cambridge, MA: Harvard University Press, 1931–
1958), VIII, p. 221. Hereafter references will be given in the text in
the customary form when referring to this work, i.e. volume number
followed by section number. This is not the place to attempt an
exposition of Peirce's complex theory of signs, and I aim here only to
draw attention to those aspects which are directly relevant to the
present discussion. A useful overview of Peirce's theory is given by J.
Chenu in his introduction to C. S. Peirce, *Textes anticartésiens* (Paris:
Aubier, 1984), pp. 11–170. The Peircean 'categories' are closely
related to Kant and also to Hegel and Aristotle (see I.300 and V.43).
On the philosophical background to Peircean semiotics, see B.
Altshuler, 'Peirce's Theory of Truth and his Early Idealism', in
Transactions of the C. S. Peirce Society, 16 (1980), pp. 118–39; K. O.
Appel, 'From Kant to Peirce: The Semiotical Transformation of
Transcendental Logic', in *Proceedings of the Third International Kant
Congress*, ed. L. W. Beck (Holland: Reidel, 1972), pp. 90–106; J. L.
Esposito, 'On the Origins and Foundations of Peirce's Semiotic',
Peirce Studies (1979), pp. 19–22, and M. G. Murphey, *The Develop-
ment of Peirce's Philosophy* (Cambridge, MA: Harvard University Press,
1961).

68 Peirce's distinction between the Dynamical Object, which is 'really
efficient but not immediately present' (VIII.343), and the Immediate

Object, which is 'the Object as the Sign represents it' (IV.536) could be explained in terms of the distinction between reference and meaning. Clearly, I am not in fact concerned here with referential objects. According to Peirce, signs themselves can be classified 'as to their own material nature, as to their relations to their objects, and as to their relations to their interpretants' (VIII.333). On the different categories arising out of these distinctions, see II.243 ff. and VIII.333 ff.

69 For different approaches to aesthetics based on semiotics, see, for instance, C. Morris, *Signification and Significance* (Cambridge, MA: MIT Press, 1964) and *Writings on the General Theory of Signs* (The Hague: Mouton, 1971), and J. Mukařovský, *The Word and Verbal Art* (New Haven: Yale University Press, 1977), *Structure, Sign and Function* (New Haven: Yale University Press, 1978), and *Aesthetic Function, Norm and Value as Social Facts* (Ann Arbor, MI: UMI Research Press, 1979).

70 Mondrian in fact uses the term 'intuitie', which will be discussed in chapter 5 below.

71 J. Moréas, *Les Premiers Armes du Symbolisme*, ed. M. Pakenham (Exeter University Press, 1973), p. 31. The term 'symbol' in this context of course has a very different meaning to the Peircean 'symbol'.

72 Cited in J. Kearns, *Symbolist Landscapes, The Place of Painting in the Poetry and Criticism of Mallarmé and his Circle* (London: Modern Humanities Research Association, 1989), pp. 32–3. On the term 'Synthetist', see especially H. R. Rookmaaker, *Synthetist Art Theories: Genesis and Nature of the Ideas on Art of Gauguin and his Circle* (Amsterdam: Swets and Zeitlinger, 1959). It is important to note the Neo-Platonic influence, especially on the painters. Sérusier wrote that 'Le mouvement auquel nous appartenons était antérieur aux influences allemandes. En philosophie nous parlions de Platon, d'Aristote, des néo-platoniciens et jamais de Kant.' (Cited in Rookmaaker, *Synthetist Art Theories*, p. 184).

73 Cited in Kearns, *Symbolist Landscapes*, p. 32.

74 T. Todorov, *Théories du symbole* (Paris: Seuil, 1977), p. 252.

75 Cited in A. Symons, *The Symbolist Movement in Literature* (London: Constable and Co., 1911), pp. 2–3.

76 Todorov, *Théories du symbole*, p. 252.

77 Baudelaire attributes the image of the dictionary to Delacroix (*BOC* II, p. 624). His theory of imagination is influenced by Coleridge via Edgar Allan Poe and also via the English writer, Mrs Crowe, whom he cites in the 'Salon de 1859' (*BOC* II, p. 624) in a passage which is taken almost directly from Coleridge. Coleridge's theories were themselves influenced by his readings of German Idealist philosophers.

78 R. Shattuck, 'Vibratory Organism: "crise de prose"', in *The Prose Poem in France: Theory and Practice*, ed. M. A. Caws and H. Riffaterre (Columbia University Press, 1983), pp. 28–9.

79 See K. Lankheit, 'Die Frühromantik und die Grundlagen der Gegenstandslosen Malerei', *Neue Heidelberger Jahrbücher* (1951), p. 69.

80 Cited in A. K. Wiedmann, *Romantic Roots in Modern Art, Romanticism and Expressionism: A Study in Comparative Aesthetics* (Surrey: Gresham Books/Unwin, 1979), p. 73. On music as a model for abstract painting, see P. Vergo, 'Music and Abstract Painting', in *Towards a New Art: Essays on the Background to Abstract Art 1910–20* (London: Tate Gallery, 1980), pp. 41–63.

81 Novalis, 'Monolog', in K. Pfefferkorn, *Novalis, A Romantic's Theory of Language and Poetry* (London: Yale University Press, 1988), p. 222, translation mine.

82 Cited in Lankheit, 'Die Frühromantik', p. 63, translation mine.

83 Cited in Wiedmann, *Romantic Roots*, p. 56.

84 Rimbaud writes to Demeny that 'la chanson est si peu souvent l'œuvre, c'est-à-dire la pensée chantée et *comprise* de l'auteur', leading on to the famous passage 'Car Je est un autre . . .' Rimbaud, *Oeuvres*, ed. S. Bernard and A. Guyaux (Paris: Gallimard, 1981; hereafter *RO*), p. 347. He argues the necessity of a 'dérèglement de *tous les sens*' (*RO*, p. 346). Mallarmé declares that 'l'œuvre pure implique la disparation élocutoire du poëte, qui cède l'initiative aux mots'. Mallarmé, *Oeuvres complètes*, ed. H. Mondor and G. Jean-Aubry, Bibliothèque de la Pléiade (Paris: Gallimard, 1945; hereafter *MOC*), p. 366. In response to criticism of his obscurity, he replies that 'il doit y avoir toujours énigme en poésie' (*MOC*, p. 869).

85 See *MOC*, p. 869.

86 'Pour garder une notion ineffaçable du Néant pur, j'ai dû imposer à mon cerveau la sensation du vide absolu.' Letter to Villiers de l'Isle-Adam, 24 September 1857, cxxix, *Correspondance*, 11 vols.; ed. H. Mondor and J.-P. Richard, vol. i; ed. H. Mondor and L. J. Austin, vols. ii and iii; ed. L. J. Austin, vols. iv–xi (Paris: Gallimard, 1959–85), i, p. 259.

87 Cited in S. Bernard, *Mallarmé et la musique* (Paris: Nizet, 1959), p. 75.

88 For a description of Mallarmé's 'Livre', see chapters 3 and 6 below.

89 On this topic, see A. Mercier, *Les Sources ésotériques et occultes de la poésie symboliste 1870–1914*, 2 vols., 1969–1974 (Paris: Nizet, 1969), i, p. 160, and E. Starkie, *Arthur Rimbaud* (London: Faber and Faber, 1961), pp. 106–7. According to Eliphas Lévi, the 'adepte' in magic becomes a 'voyant ou prophète'. *Histoire de la magie* (Chaumont: Ed. de la Maisnie, 1986), p. 61 (1st edn.; Paris: G. Ballière, 1860). Starkie, however, is not sufficiently critical in positing parallels between Lévi and Rimbaud. Indeed, one must exercise caution in making claims about Rimbaud's knowledge of esoteric doctrines, since we have no precise proof of his reading in this area, although we know that he was influenced by the occultism of his friend Charles Bretagne.

90 On this aspect of Fourier's thought, see P. Ricoeur, *Lectures on Ideology and Utopia* (New York: Columbia University Press, 1986), p. 302. On Rimbaud and Fourier, see G. Marcotte, *La Prose de Rimbaud* (Quebec: Boréal, 1989), p. 164. Marcotte also discusses Michelet and Saint-Simon. On occult connections, see also J. Gengoux, *La Pensée poétique de Rimbaud* (Paris: Nizet, 1950) and C. McIntosh, *Eliphas Lévi and the French Occult Revival* (London: Rider and Co., 1972).

91 See Mercier, *Les Sources ésotériques* I, p. 126. Schuré was influenced by Michelet (see *ibid.*, p. 59). I am grateful to the Musée Mallarmé for providing me with documentation on Mallarmé's library.

92 For fuller accounts of this topic, see C. Chassé, *Les Clés de Mallarmé* (Paris: Montaigne, 1954), pp. 14–35; D. Hampton Morris, 'The Creative Word: Mallarmé and Esoteric Theories of Language', *Language Quarterly*, 18 (1980), pp. 25–6 and p. 32; B. Léon-Dufour, 'Mallarmé et l'alphabet', *Cahiers de l'Association Internationale des Etudes Françaises*, 27 (1975), pp. 321–6 and p. 457; Mercier, *Les Sources ésotériques* I, and J. Scherer, *L'Expression littéraire dans l'œuvre de Mallarmé* (Paris: Droz, 1947), pp. 155–62. See also E. Lévi, *Dogme et rituel de la haute magie* (Paris: Germer Ballière, 1861). This book was recommended to Mallarmé by Villiers de l'Isle-Adam. According to Chassé, Mallarmé was a member of the Free Masons (Chassé, *Les Clés de Mallarmé*, p. 19).

93 See *MOC*, p. 662 and letter to Cazalis, cxxii, 14 May 1867, *Correspondance* I, p. 244. The term 'operator', which is used in the 'Livre', in fact designated the person in charge of magical rituals. See McIntosh, *Eliphas Lévi*, p. 22.

94 P. Valéry, *Ecrits divers sur Stéphane Mallarmé* (Paris: Gallimard, 1950), p. 39.

95 C. Mauclair, *L'Art en silence* (Paris: Ollendorff, 1901), p. 84.

96 G. Faure, *Lettres de Mallarmé à Aubanel et Mistral, précédées de Mallarmé à Tournon* (Saint-Félicien-en-Vivarais: Au Pigeonnier, 1924), p. 36. On Mallarmé and Hegel, see J. Langan, *Hegel and Mallarmé* (London: University Press of America, 1986), and my 'Mallarmé and Hegel, Speculation and the Poetics of Reflection', *French Cultural Studies*, 2 (1991), pp. 71–89.

97 In the French context, Balzac is a formative influence. Baudelaire writes: 'Balzac, ce grand esprit dévoré du légitime orgueil encyclopédique, a essayé de fondre en un système universel et définitif différentes idées tirées de Swedenborg, Mesmer, Marat, Goethe et Geoffroy Sainte-Hilaire' (*BOC* II, p. 248).

98 See J. A. Arguelles, *Charles Henry and the Formation of a Psychophysical Aesthetic* (University of Chicago Press, 1972), p. 99. Relevant works by Henry include 'Introduction à une esthétique scientifique', *La Revue Contemporaine*, 2 (1885), pp. 441–69, *Cercle chromatique* (Paris: Verdin, 1888), and *Harmonies de formes et de couleurs* (Paris: Hermann, 1891).

99 See Henry, 'Introduction', p. 443.

100 See E. Michoud, 'La Fin de l'iconographie, une nouvelle rhétorique du sensible', *Les Cahiers du Musée National d'Art Moderne* (1980), pp. 446–54.

101 See Rookmaaker, *Synthetist Art Theories*, pp. 92 and 169, and Arguelles, *Charles Henry*, p. 146.

102 Henry, 'Introduction', p. 445.

103 Denis, cited in Kearns, *Symbolist Landscapes*, p. 34.

104 Cited in *ibid.*, p. 35.

105 *Lettres de Gauguin à sa femme et à ses amis*, ed. M. Malingua (Paris: Grasset, 1946), p. 288.

106 Cited in Rookmaaker, *Synthetist Art Theories*, p. 103.

107 Cited in *ibid.*, p. 102.

108 G. Moreau, *L'Assembleur de rêves: écrits complets de Gustave Moreau*, ed. P.-L. Mathieu (Frontfroide: Bibliothèque Artistique et Littéraire, 1984), p. 39.

109 O. Redon, *A soi-même, journal (1867–1915)* (Paris: Corti, 1979), p. 27.

110 *L'Assembleur de rêves*, p. 39.

111 See P.-L. Mathieu, 'Gustave Moreau – du symbolisme à l'abstraction', *Revue de l'Université de Bruxelles, Littérature et Beaux-arts à la Fin du 19e Siècle*, 3 (1981), pp. 59–66.

112 I am indebted to Mme Geneviève Lacambre, curator of the Musée Gustave Moreau, for her helpfulness and for her useful comments on this question.

113 The connections between Symbolism and Impressionism are in fact closer than is often thought to be the case. This question will be discussed in chapter 6 below. Moreover, these connections were developed in the work of Neo-Impressionist painters such as Seurat and Signac, and the early work of both Kandinsky and Mondrian shows the influence of Neo-Impressionist techniques.

114 Cited in E. J. Garte, 'Kandinsky's Ideas on Changes in Modern Physics and their Implications for his Development', *Gazette des Beaux-Arts*, 110 (1987), p. 139.

115 Theosophy and Anthroposophy are concerned with access to supersensible knowledge, which can be achieved via the sensible world. For definitions, see M. Tuchman, ed., *The Spiritual in Art: Abstract Painting 1890–1985* (New York: Abbeville Press, 1986), pp. 369–70 and p. 388. For the sake of convenience I shall follow many other commentators in using the term Theosophy for both, and also for Christosophy. (M. H. J. Schoenmaekers, who influenced Mondrian, styled himself a 'Christosophist'.) The fullest examination of Kandinsky's connections with occultism is S. Ringbom's *The Sounding Cosmos, A Study in the Spiritualism of Kandinsky and Abstract Painting* (Åbo Akademi, 1970). See also R. Heller, 'Kandinsky and Traditions Apocalyptic', *Art Journal*, 43 (1983), pp. 19–26; S. Ringbom, 'Art in the Epoch of the Great Spiritual', *Journal of the Warburg and Courtauld Institutes*, 29 (1966), pp. 386–418; S. Ringbom, 'Kandinsky and das Okkulte' in *Kandinsky und München, Begegnungen und Wandlungen 1896–1914*, ed. A. Zweite (Munich: Prestel, 1982), pp. 85–101, and S. Ringbom, 'Die Steiner Annotationen Kandinskys', *ibid.*, pp. 102–5. The extent of the influence of the occult tradition on Kandinsky's work alleged by Ringbom has been contested by R.-C. Washton Long in *Kandinsky, The Development of an Abstract Style* (Oxford: Clarendon Press, 1980) and P. Weiss in *Kandinsky in Munich, The Formative Jugendstil Years* (Princeton University Press, 1979).

116 See, for instance, D. Gordon, *Expressionism, Art and Idea* (London: Yale University Press, 1987), ch. 2, and R. Sheppard, 'Kandinsky's *œuvre* 1900–1914: The *avant-garde* as rear guard', *Word and Image*, 6 (1990), pp. 41–67. For interesting discussions of the influence on

Kandinsky of Pan-Christian Universalism and of the symbolism of Moscow in Russian apocalyptic thought, see S. Behr, 'Wassily Kandinsky and Dimitrije Mitrinovic; Pan-Christian Universalism and the Yearbook "Towards the Mankind of the Future through Aryan Europe"', *Oxford Art Journal*, 15 (1992), pp. 81–8, and M. Werenskiold, 'Kandinsky's Moscow', *Art in America*, 77 (1989), pp. 96–111.

117 Cited in H. L. C. Jaffé, *De Stijl 1917–1931: The Dutch Contribution to Modern Art* (London: Harvard University Press, 1986), p. 61.

118 Cited in E. Hoek, 'Mondrian in Disneyland', *Art in America*, 77 (1989), p. 141.

119 This is documented by Sixten Ringbom in 'Kandinsky und das Okkulte', p. 92. See also R. Steiner, *Occult Science, An Outline* (London: Rudolf Steiner Press, 1969), p. 261 and *Die Stufen der Höheren Erkenntnis* (Dornach: Verlag der Rudolf Steiner Nachlass-verwaltigung, 1959), pp. 35–49.

120 Steiner, cited in Ringbom, *Sounding Cosmos*, p. 137 (translation mine).

121 R. Steiner, *Rudolf Steiner's Farbenlehre*, (Dornach, Switzerland: Philosophische-Anthroposophischer Verlag, 1929), p. 83, translation mine. Steiner, like Lipps, uses the term 'Miterlebnis'.

122 A. O. Eaves, *Die Kräfte der Farben* (Berlin: Talisman Bibliothek, 1906).

123 A. Besant and C. W. Leadbeater (London: The Theosophical Publishing Society, 1901).

124 This letter, written in French, is published in German translation in *Rudolf Steiner, Wenn die Erde Mond wird: Wandtafelzeichnungen zu Vorträgen 1919–24, mit ausgewählten Texten*, ed. W. Kugler (Cologne: Du Mont, 1992), p. 151. According to Seuphor, Mondrian's involvement with Theosophy began as early as 1899, and he was still reading books on Theosophy in 1934. M. Seuphor, *Piet Mondrian, Life and Work* (London: Thames and Hudson, 1957), pp. 53 and 57. Throughout his life he kept the document giving him membership of the Theosophical Society, which he joined in 1909, and which was then growing rapidly in Holland. See also R. Welsh, 'Mondrian and Theosophy', in *Piet Mondrian, 1872–1944, Centennial Exhibition* (New York: Solomon R. Guggenheim Museum, 1971), pp. 35–51 and P. Fingeston, 'Spirituality, Mysticism and Non-Objective Art', *Art Journal*, 21 (1961), pp. 2–7.

125 Seuphor, *Piet Mondrian*, p. 57. There is disagreement concerning the extent to which Mondrian took over ideas from Schoenmaekers. Mondrian wrote to van Doesburg in 1917: 'I have everything from the Secret Doctrine (Blavatsky), not from Schoenmaekers, although the latter says the same'. Cited in E. Hoek, 'Piet Mondrian', in *De Stijl 1917–1922, The Formative Years*, ed. E. Hoek (London: MIT Press, 1982), p. 49. However, see also Jaffé, *De Stijl 1917–1931*, pp. 56 ff. and Seuphor, *Piet Mondrian*, p. 134.

126 Seuphor, *Piet Mondrian*, p. 53.

127 Cited in Jaffé, *De Stijl 1917–1931*, p. 58. Naturally the male, active principle is seen as superior to the female, passive principle. Con-

nections between abstraction and misogyny will be discussed in chapter 5 below.

128 Cited in Welsh, 'Mondrian and Theosophy', pp. 48–9.

129 Schoenmaekers, cited in Jaffé, *De Stijl 1917–1931*, p. 56.

130 P. Mondrian, *The New Art – The New Life, The Collected Writings of Pier Mondrian*, ed. H. Holtzman and M. S. James (London: Thames and Hudson, 1987; hereafter, *MCWA*), p. 46.

131 Schoenmaekers, cited in Jaffé, *De Stijl 1917–1931*, p. 59.

132 Cited in *ibid.*, p. 56.

133 *Ibid.*, p. 60.

134 The latter was a Dutch philosopher who disseminated Neo-Hegelian ideas in Holland.

135 On this background, see J. Beckett, 'Discoursing on Dutch Modernism', *The Oxford Art Journal*, 6 (1983), p. 70. This very useful article situates the emergence of *De Stijl* in Holland in the context of Dutch art discourse at this period.

136 M. Pleynet, *Système de la peinture* (Paris: Seuil, 1977), pp. 129–30.

137 See C. Poling, *Kandinsky-Unterricht am Bauhaus: Farbenseminär und analytisches Zeichnen* (Weingarten: Kunstverlag Weingarten), 1982, p. 59.

138 See *ibid.*, p. 55.

139 See *ibid.*, pp. 53–4.

140 W. von Bezold, *Die Farbenlehre im Hinblick auf Kunst und Kunstgewerbe* (Braunschweig: George Westermann, 1877), pp. 233–5.

141 H. von Helmholtz, *Popular Scientific Lectures* (New York: Dover, 1962), p. 227. First published as *Populäre wissenschaftliche Vorträge*, 3 vols., 1865–76 (Braunschweig: F. Vieweg und Sohn). On Kandinsky and Helmholtz, see C. Poling, 'Kandinsky, Russian and Bauhaus Years, 1915–1933', in *Kandinsky: Russian and Bauhaus Years* (New York: Solomon R. Guggenheim Museum, 1983), p. 59, and Poling, *Kandinsky-Unterricht*, pp. 53 and 96.

142 On colour theory in relation to Delaunay as well as Kandinsky and Mondrian, see J. Gage, 'The psychological background to early modern colour: Kandinsky, Delaunay and Mondrian', in *Towards a New Art*, pp. 22–40. See also chapter 6, note 10 below.

143 *Jugendstil* is the German equivalent of Art Nouveau.

144 On rhythm and vibration in particular, see, for instance, J. Bowlt, 'Vasilii Kandinsky: The Russian Connection', in *The Life of Vasilii Kandinsky in Russian Art: A Study of On the Spiritual in Art*, ed. J. Bowlt and R. Washton Long (Newtonville, MA: Oriental Research Partners, 1980), p. 27; J. D. Fineberg, *Kandinsky in Paris 1906–7* (Ann Arbor, MI: UMI Research Press, 1984), p. 97, and Weiss, *Kandinsky in Munich*, p. 100. Weiss has investigated Kandinsky's relationships with Munich *Jugendstil* and Symbolism, while Washton Long has also devoted attention to Russian and French/Belgian influences (notably Maeterlinck) and to Biblical sources. Fineberg has explored the extent and effects of Kandinsky's involvement with the Symbolist group 'Tendances Nouvelles' between 1904 and 1910, and Bowlt has examined his connections with the Russian Symbolist milieu. See also M. Roskill, *Klee, Kandinsky and the*

Thought of Their Time (Urbana: University of Illinois Press, 1992); P. Weiss, 'Kandinsky and the Symbolist Heritage', *Art Journal*, 45 (1985), pp. 137–45; P. Weiss, 'Kandinsky: Symbolist Poetics and Theatre in Munich', *Pantheon*, 35 (1977), pp. 209–18, and P. Weiss, 'Kandinsky and the *Jugendstil* Arts and Crafts Movement', *The Burlington Magazine*, 117 (1975), pp. 270–9. On Mondrian and Symbolism, see C. Blotkamp, 'Annunciation of the New Mysticism: Dutch Symbolism and Early Abstraction', in *The Spiritual in Art: Abstract Painting 1890–1985*, ed. M. Tuchman (New York: Abbeville Press, 1986), pp. 89–111, and M. James, 'Mondrian and the Dutch Symbolists', *The Art Journal*, 23 (1963–4), pp. 103–11. On the influence of Symbolism in Holland at the turn of the century, see J. Beckett, 'The Netherlands', in *Abstraction: Towards a New Art, Painting 1910–20* (London: Tate Gallery, 1980), pp. 39–56.

145 Cited in Weiss, *Kandinsky in Munich*, p. 101.

146 H. Meschonnic, *Critique du rythme: anthropologie historique du langage* (Paris: Verdier, 1982), p. 500.

147 See Weiss, *Kandinsky in Munich*, pp. 43 ff.

148 The term 'inner necessity', used by Lipps, is a key phrase in *On the Spiritual in Art*. On this term, see P. Selz, *German Expressionist Painting* (Berkeley: University of California Press, 1957), p. 15, and A. Zweite, 'Kandinsky zwischen Tradition und Innovation', in *Kandinsky und München*, p. 173.

149 *Abstraktion und Einfühlung* (Münich: Piper and Co.). Worringer claimed to have met Kandinsky and it has been suggested that this meeting was significant for both men, but Kandinsky denied that such a meeting ever took place. See W. Grohmann, 'Festvortrag zum 100. Geburtstag von W. Kandinsky' in E. Hanfstaengl, *Wassily Kandinsky, Aquarelle und Zeichnungen im Lenbachhaus München* (Munich: Prestel Verlag/Städtische Galerie im Lenbachhaus, 1981), p. 9. In his correspondence with Kandinsky, Franz Marc manifests great enthusiasm for Worringer, to which Kandinsky does not respond. See *Wassily Kandinsky, Franz Marc, Briefwechsel*, ed. K. Lankheit (Munich: Piper, 1983), p. 136.

150 As remarked above, Lipps believes that 'if [colours] are colours of objects, then the aesthetic effect of the object to which the colour belongs will compete with the aesthetic effect of the colour' (*AS* 1, p. 448). See also chapter 4, p. 119 below.

151 Cited in Weiss, *Kandinsky in Munich*, p. 26. On Endell's links with Kandinsky, see *ibid.*, p. 34.

152 See Weiss, *Kandinsky in Munich*, pp. 36–7.

153 A. Roessler, *Neu-Dachau: Ludwig Dill, Adolf Hölzel, Arthur Langhauser* (Bielefeld and Leipzig: Velhagen and Klasing, Knackfuss Künstler Monographien, 1905), p. 117 (translation mine).

154 Roessler, *Neu-Dachau*, pp. 120–1. On van de Velde and Kandinsky, see Weiss, *Kandinsky in Munich*, p. 167, and on Charles Henry's influence on Van de Velde, see Arguelles, *Charles Henry*, p. 146.

155 As already pointed out, this is a crucial area in which the views of Kandinsky, and of Mondrian in particular, differ from my own. There is obviously an important sense in which they do give

credence to such a sphere. The subtleties of this question will be treated in more detail in chapters 4 and 5 below.

2 VERBAL HALLUCINATION; RIMBAUD'S POETICS OF RHYTHM

1 For a brief exposition of these issues, see S. Bernard, 'Le Problème des *Illuminations*', *RO*, 'Introduction', pp. liv–lxiv.

2 M. Jay, 'In the Empire of the Gaze: Foucault and the Denigration of Vision in 20th Century French Thought', *Postmodernism*, ICA Documents 4, (London: Institute of Contemporary Arts, 1986), p. 20.

3 *Ibid.*, p. 23.

4 J. Plessen, 'Stratégies pour une lecture du texte rimbaldien', *Rimbaud multiple*, Colloque de Cérisy (Gourdon: Bedon/Touzot, 1986), p. 176.

5 S. Bernard, *Le Poème en prose de Baudelaire jusqu'à nos jours* (Paris: Nizet, 1959), p. 184.

6 W. M. Frohock, *Rimbaud's Poetic Practice: Image and Theme in the Major Poems* (Cambridge, MA: Harvard University Press, 1963), p. 204.

7 J. P. Houston, *Patterns of Thought in Rimbaud and Mallarmé* (Lexington, KY: French Forum, 1980), p. 68.

8 T. Todorov, 'Une complication de texte, Les *Illuminations*', *Poétique*, 9 (1978), p. 241.

9 J. Plessen, 'Deux fois Rimbaud', *Littérature*, 11 (1973), p. 103.

10 Todorov, 'Une complication de texte', p. 204. This is not of course to say that biographical information cannot be used in more sophisticated and creative ways. Many of the most stimulating recent studies of the *Illuminations* analyse the texts in their socio-historical and cultural context, without however seeking a definite 'referent'. An outstanding example in the context of Rimbaud's early poetry is the work of Steve Murphy. Murphy relates Rimbaud's writing to political satire and to the techniques of caricature. Interestingly, Murphy emphasizes how Rimbaud makes of the text itself a visual caricature, commenting on 'L'Eclatante victoire de Sarrebrück' that 'l'image ne saurait être trouvée ailleurs que dans les mots qui composent le texte: l'image est le poème'. See *Rimbaud et la ménagerie impériale* (Lyon: Presses Universitaires de Lyon, 1991), p. 93. For further discussion of the ideological aspect of Rimbaud's poetry, see the closing pages of chapter 6 below. A notable aspect of recent publications on Rimbaud has been the highlighting of Rimbaud's identity as a 'voyageur' after the ending of his brief poetic 'career'. See, for instance, A. Borer, *Rimbaud en Abysinnie* (Paris: Seuil, 1984) and *Rimbaud d'Arabie* (Paris: Seuil, 1991).

11 M. Richter, 'Note de Mario Richter', in A. Fongaro, *Les Cahiers de littératures, sur Rimbaud, lire 'Illuminations'* (Toulouse: Publications de l'Université Toulouse-Le Mirail, 1985), p. 76.

12 J.-P. Richard, *Poésie et profondeur* (Paris: Seuil, 1955), p. 240.

13 *Ibid.*, p. 102.

14 *Ibid.*, p. 194.

15 *Ibid.*, p. 241.

16 Todorov, 'Une complication de texte', p. 244.
17 *Ibid.*, p. 248.
18 *Ibid.*, p. 252.
19 Lautréamont and Mallarmé spring to mind here. Valéry declared that Mallarmé introduced in France the notion of an 'auteur difficile', P. Valéry, *Ecrits divers sur Stéphane Mallarmé* (Paris: Gallimard, 1950), p. 36. Fongaro has shown that several of the examples of 'incoherence' picked out by Todorov can be satisfactorily explained, and has even pointed out an instance where Todorov misread the text. A. Fongaro, *Les Cahiers de littératures*, p. 7.
20 N. Wing, *Present Appearances: Aspects of Poetic Structure in Rimbaud's 'Illuminations'* (Mississippi University: Romance Monographs Inc., 1974), p. 46, emphasis mine.
21 *Ibid.*, p. 86.
22 M. Riffaterre, *Semiotics of Poetry* (London: Methuen, 1980), p. 42. This is not the place to attempt a definition of intertextuality. For a clear exposition of Riffaterre's brand of intertextuality (and others), see *Intertextuality: Theories and practices*, ed. M. Worton and J. Still (Manchester University Press, 1990).
23 Riffaterre, *Semiotics of Poetry*, p. 22.
24 *Ibid.*, p. 5.
25 *Ibid.*, p. 22. What this means in practice will become clearer when we look at Riffaterre's reading of 'Barbare'.
26 Riffaterre, 'Interpretation and Undecidability', *New Literary History*, 12 (1981), p. 233. 'Sociolect' refers here to conventionally accepted linguistic usages, while 'idiolect' is a linguistic usage particular to the individual poem.
27 Riffaterre, 'Interpretation and Undecidability', p. 238.
28 *Ibid.*, p. 90 (emphasis mine).
29 *Ibid.*, p. 148.
30 *Ibid.*, p. 228.
31 *Ibid.*
32 Riffaterre, 'Sur la sémiotique de l'obscurité en poésie: "Promontoire" de Rimbaud', *French Review*, 55 (1982), pp. 625–32.
33 Moreover, it is undeniable that Riffaterre, with a conjurer's skill, has produced remarkably coherent interpretations of seemingly recalcitrant texts through his 'intertextual' readings. A particularly striking example is his reading of 'Le Loup criait sous les feuilles', in 'Interpretation and Undecidability', pp. 229 ff. See also 'Sur la sémiotique de l'obscurité en poésie: "Promontoire" de Rimbaud'; 'The Making of the Text', in *Identity of the Literary Text*, ed. M. J. Valdés and O. Miller (London: University of Toronto, 1985), pp. 54–70, and 'Rimbaud intertextuel', *Parade sauvage, 'Rimbaud à la loupe'* (Charleville: Musée-Bibliothèque Rimbaud, 1990), pp. 93–105.
34 G. Genette, *Figures II* (Paris: Seuil, 1969), p. 45.
35 R. Jakobson, 'Closing Statement: Linguistics and Poetics', in *Style in Language*, ed. T. A. Sebeok (Cambridge, MA: MIT Press, 1960), p. 358.
36 Genette, *Figures II*, p. 45.
37 Kittang, *Discours et jeu*, p. 189.

38 *Ibid.*, p. 208.
39 *Ibid.*, p. 298.
40 *Ibid.*, p. 219.
41 *Ibid.*
42 *Ibid.*, p. 224.
43 *Ibid.*, p. 301.
44 *Ibid.*, p. 233.
45 *Ibid.*, p. 237.
46 *Ibid.*, p. 50. This view of Genette's will be discussed further in relation to Mallarmé and Derrida in chapter 3 below. Interestingly, Jacques Plessen, one of the critics with whom Kittang takes issue on this point, gave a very admiring account of Kittang's thesis (later published as *Discours et jeu*), in which he said that he had been convinced by Kittang's arguments. (See Plessen, 'Deux fois Rimbaud', p. 106).
47 Kittang, *Discours et jeu*, p. 50.
48 *Ibid.*, pp. 302–3, emphasis mine. We shall see in chapter 3 below that Derrida's objections to thematic criticism avoid this contradiction, since writing is not seen as a 'theme'.
49 André Guyaux emphasizes that Verlaine is in fact the principal authority for this title, since the word 'Illuminations' appears on the manuscripts only once, scribbled in pencil in an anonymous hand on a sheet which contains 'Promontoire'. Guyaux believes that Verlaine must have had good reason to use this title, but indicates that this provenance raises certain questions, for example whether its status was provisional or final. See A. Guyaux, *Poétique du fragment: essai sur les 'Illuminations' de Rimbaud* (Neuchâtel: La Baconnière, 1986), pp. 237–51.
50 See, for instance, S. Bernard, 'La Palette de Rimbaud', *Cahiers de l'Association Internationale des Etudes Françaises*, 12 (1960), pp. 105–19; R. Little, 'Rimbaud's "Mystique": Some Observations', *French Studies*, 26 (1972), pp. 285–8; L. Maranini, 'Lo spazio di Rimbaud', *Micromégas*, 9 (1982), pp. 127–53; R. Riese Hubert, 'La Technique de la peinture dans le poème en prose', *Cahiers de l'Association Internationale des Etudes Françaises*, 18 (1966), pp. 169–78; D. Scott, 'Rimbaud and Boucher: "Fête d'Hiver"', *Journal of European Studies*, 9 (1979), pp. 185–95. Maranini argues that Rimbaud's modernity makes him more of a contemporary than the Impressionists, and sees him as particularly close to Delaunay and Kandinsky. The question of whether Rimbaud and Mallarmé are closer to Impressionism or to abstract painting will be discussed in chapter 6 below.
51 On this subject, see David Scott, *Pictorialist Poetics: Poetry and the Visual Arts in Nineteenth-Century France* (Cambridge University Press, 1988), p. 133.
52 H. Friedrich, *The Structure of Modern Poetry from the Mid Nineteenth Century to the Mid Twentieth Century* (Evanston IL: Northwestern University Press, 1974), p. 56.
53 The *poème en prose* was established as a 'genre' by Aloysius Bertrand, whose *Gaspard de la Nuit* was published in 1842. (On *Gaspard de la Nuit* and its connections with the visual arts, see Scott, *Pictorialist Poetics*,

pp. 123–31). The first published examples of *vers libre* date from 1886: Laforgue and Kahn both claimed to be the first to use it, but Rimbaud could also lay claim to this honour, since two of the *Illuminations*, 'Marine' and 'Mouvement', which were published in 1886 but probably written in 1872–3, are in *vers libres*. Apart from these poems and 'Barbare', which is written in *versets*, all the texts of the *Illuminations* are prose poems.

54 This aspect of rhythm has been emphasized by the Russian Formalists, who point out that metre 'de-automatizes' perception of ordinary language, but could in turn become 'automatized', were it not for a tension between 'ordinary language and the esthetic norm'. V. Erlich, *Russian Formalism, History-Doctrine* (New Haven: Yale University Press, 1981), p. 215. Žirmunskij says that rhythm is created by 'the interaction between the natural characteristics of the linguistics medium and the metrical law' (M. Žirmunskij, *Introduction to Metrics: The Theory of Verse* (The Hague: Mouton, 1966), p. 23). The topic of rhythm is too vast to reference extensively here. In particular, see the interesting discussion in J. Mitry, *Esthétique et psychologie du cinéma*, 2 vols., 1963–5 (Paris: Editions Universitaires), I, pp. 287–328.

55 On this topic, see, for instance, A. Fongaro, *Segments numériques dans la prose d''Illuminations'* (Toulouse: Presses Universitaires de Mirail-Toulouse, 1993) and R. Little, 'Rimbaud's "Sonnet"', *The Modern Language Review*, 75 (1980), pp. 528–33.

56 W. J. T. Mitchell, 'Spatial Form in Literature: Towards a General Theory', in *The Language of Images*, ed. W. J. T. Mitchell (University of Chicago Press, 1980), p. 276.

57 See Mitchell, 'Spatial Form in Literature', p. 280. I have argued in more detail the case concerning the interaction between space and time in rhythm in my 'Rhythmic Structures and Imaginary Space in Rimbaud, Mallarmé, Kandinsky and Mondrian', in *Word and Image Interactions*, ed. M. Heusser (Basel: Wiese Verlag, 1993), pp. 143–56. There is a large body of literature on space and time in poetry and painting. In addition to Mitchell's 'Spatial Form in Literature', which contains a useful account of the recent history of this debate, see W. Holtz, 'Spatial Form in Modern Literature: A Reconsideration', *Critical Inquiry*, 4 (1977/8), pp. 276–80; R. Arnheim, 'A Stricture on Space and Time', *Critical Inquiry*, 4 (1977/8), pp. 645–55, and J. McClain, 'Time in the Visual Arts: Lessing and Modern Criticism', *Journal of Aesthetics and Art Criticism*, 43 (1985), pp. 41–58.

58 P. Valéry, *Cahiers*, 2 vols., ed. J. Robinson-Valéry (Paris: Gallimard, 1973, 1974), I, p. 1351.

59 *Ibid.*, p. 1341.

60 *Ibid.*, p. 1310.

61 On this topic, see A. Guyaux, *Poétique du fragment*, pp. 151–61. A crucial advance in Rimbaud studies in recent years has been the publication of facsimiles of the manuscripts. See Cl. Zissmann, *Ce que révèle le manuscrit des 'Illuminations'* (Paris: Le bossu Bitor, 1989), R. Pierrot, *Manuscrits autographes des 'Illuminations' d'Arthur Rimbaud*

(Paris: Ramsay, 1984), and A. Guyaux, *Poétique du fragment*. Moreover, A. Guyaux's edition of 1985 (Neuchâtel, La Baconnière), like Zissmann's, approximates the visual layout of the manuscript versions and comprises commentaries on the ambiguities of the manuscripts. My quotes are based on the texts of this edition.

62 'Interpretation and Undecidability', p. 236. My reading does, however, confirm the implications of this interpretation, which also has a political dimension, as we shall see below.

63 Todorov comments: 'Bien des titres de textes, qu'on comprend toujours comme des substantifs décrivant l'être référent, pourraient se lire aussi comme des adjectifs qualifiant le ton, le style, la nature du texte même: n'est-ce pas un texte *barbare* qui porte ce titre, un exercice dans le genre barbare?' (Todorov, 'Une complication de texte', p. 251). Kittang describes the beginning of 'Barbare' as an 'ouverture brisant tout cadre spatio-temporel et existentiel, et désignant en fin de compte l'espace propre, multidimensionnel, du jeu scriptural' (Kittang, *Discours et jeu*, p. 299). See also Wing, *Present Appearances*, pp. 76–7.

64 Riffaterre, 'Interpretation and Undecidability', p. 236.

65 The *verset*, intermediate between a syllabic verse line and a paragraph of prose, is a verse line in the sense of Claudel's definition: 'une idée isolée par du blanc'. P. Claudel, *Oeuvres en prose*, ed. J. Petit and C. Galpérine (Paris: Gallimard, 1965), p. 3. According to S. Bernard, whereas the *vers libre* is a 'loosening' of the structure of classical verse, the *verset* is 'plutôt une prose qui se resserre' (*Le poème en prose*, p. 592).

66 In the manuscript, the circumflex accents have been omitted from these 'o's. One may speculate as to whether this omission was deliberate, in order to emphasize their roundness. Until recently, editors of the *Illuminations* have corrected this 'error'. André Guyaux's 1985 edition and Claude Zissmann's 1989 edition, however, follow the manuscript in omitting the accents. See A. Guyaux, *Arthur Rimbaud, 'Illuminations'* (Neuchâtel: La Baconnière, 1985), and Zissmann, *Ce que révèle le manuscrit des 'Illuminations'*.

67 See E. Starkie, *Arthur Rimbaud* (London: Faber and Faber, 1961), p. 207.

68 Letter to Paul Demeny, 15 May 1871, *RO*, p. 348.

69 Cited in H. Wetzel, 'Un texte opaque et son interprétation socio-historique: "Barbare" de Rimbaud', in *Romantisme*, 12 (1983), p. 130. Wetzel also points out that during the Commune uprising, the 'dangerous' classes were often branded as 'barbarians'. On the interaction between masculine/feminine paradigms in Michelet's *La Sorcière* and its relation to 'Barbare', see my '"L'Hallucination des mots": Textual and Imaginary Space in Rimbaud's "Barbare"', *Forum for Modern Language Studies*, 28 (1992), pp. 29–41.

70 H. Morier, *Dictionnaire de poétique et de rhétorique* (Paris: Presses Universitaires de France, 1961), pp. 808–11. It is interesting that Baudelaire's poem 'Harmonie du soir', which, like 'Barbare', foregrounds circular, rotating movement, is written in an irregular 'pantoum' form.

71 Strictly speaking, in verse, a mute 'e' preceded by a vowel should only occur at the end of a line, where there would be no question of pronouncing it. The influence of the alexandrine in French verse is such that it can still be felt in free verse and in prose poetry. On metrical patterns in the *Illuminations*, see M. Dominicy, '"Les Ponts", analyse linguistique', in *Lectures de Rimbaud*, ed. A. Guyaux (Université de Bruxelles, 1982), pp. 109–23.

72 P. Broome, 'From Vision to Catastrophe in Rimbaud's *Illuminations*' *Forum for Modern Language Studies*, 15 (1979), p. 362.

73 Friedrich, *The Structure of Modern Poetry*, p. 63.

74 N. Wing, 'Rimbaud's "Les Ponts", "Parades", "Scènes": The Poem as Performance', *The French Review*, 46 (1972/3), p. 512.

75 A. Felsch, *Arthur Rimbaud, Poetische Struktur und Kontext: Paradigmatische Analyse und Interpretation einiger 'Illuminations'* (Bonn: Bouvier, 1977), p. 379, translation mine.

76 *Ibid.*

77 A. Py, in A. Rimbaud, *Illuminations*, ed. A. Py (Geneva: Droz, 1967), p. 126.

78 Wing, *Present Appearances*, p. 142.

79 This question will be discussed in chapter 6 below.

80 Friedrich, *Structure of Modern Poetry*, p. 63.

81 P. Underwood has suggested connections between 'Les Ponts' and illustration: see Rimbaud, *Illuminations*, ed. A. Py, p. 125.

82 Compare Dominicy's division of 'Les Ponts' into rhythmically significant units ('"Les Ponts", analyse linguistique', p. 155). However, this division is based on metrics rather than punctuation, and Dominicy does not explore connections between rhythmic patterns in textual and imaginary space.

83 Compare discussion of linear dynamism in chapter 1 above, p. 20.

84 R. Kloepfer and U. Oomen, *Sprachliche Konstituenten Moderner Dichtung: Entwurf einer Descriptiven Poetik* (Bad Homberg: Atheneum, 1970), p. 157, translation mine.

85 Theatrical imagery will be discussed further in chapter 6 below.

86 See, for instance, G. M. Macklin, 'The Theatrical Imagination of Arthur Rimbaud', *Forum for Modern Language Studies*, 23 (1987), pp. 131–50, which contains a wide range of references to other studies on this topic.

87 Kittang, *Discours et jeu*, p. 232.

88 Compare discussion of the sublime in chapter 1 above, pp. 9 ff.

3 REFLECTIONS IN BLACK AND WHITE; MALLARMÉ AND THE ACT OF WRITING

1 His influence on Jakobson has already been referred to in the introduction. Barthes declared that 'all we can do is repeat Mallarmé'. Cited in R. G. Cohn, 'Epistemology and Literary Theory', in *Writing in a Modern Temper: Essays on Literature and Thought in Honour of Henri Peyre*, ed. M. A. Caws (Saratoga: Anma Libri; Stanford French and Italian Studies, 1984), p. 5. Derrida attributes the emergence of 'la question de la littérarité', which he regards as 'un

progrès décisif de ce demi-siècle', partly to the Russian Formalists, but also to 'une certaine transformation de la pratique littéraire elle-même'. He affirms that certain texts, such as those of Mallarmé, Artaud, Bataille and Sollers, 'opèrent, dans leur mouvement même, la manifestation et la déconstruction pratique de la *représentation* qu'on se faisait de la littérature'. J. Derrida, *Positions* (Paris: Minuit, 1972), pp. 93–4. See also note 7 below.

2 A. Thibaudet, 'Réflexions sur la littérature: Mallarmé et Rimbaud', *Nouvelle Revue Française*, 18 (1922), pp. 199–206.

3 See J.-P. Richard, *L'Univers imaginaire de Mallarmé* (Paris: Seuil, 1961).

4 G. Genette, 'Bonheur de Mallarmé', in *Figures I* (Paris: Seuil 1966), p. 94. This 'vécu' is not necessarily of the kind open to biographical analysis, but it is seen as pre-textual. (See discussion in chapter 2 above, p. 43).

5 Genette, 'Bonheur de Mallarmé', p. 93.

6 *Ibid.*, p. 99.

7 Derrida, *La Dissémination* (Paris: Seuil, 1972), pp. 199–317. On intertextual relationships between Mallarmé and Derrida, see M. Riffaterre, 'La Trace de l'intertexte', *La Pensée, Revue de Rationalisme Moderne*, 215 (1980), pp. 4–18. R. G. Cohn notes of Derrida that 'all his concepts are out of Mallarmé: *trace, pli, blanc,* bipolar *indécidable* and tetrapolar *différance,* all are first in the master'. R. G. Cohn, 'Epistemology and Literary Theory', in *Writing in a Modern Temper*, p. 22.

8 Derrida, *La Dissémination*, p. 277.

9 *Ibid.*, pp. 279–80.

10 See Derrida, *De la grammatologie* (Paris: Minuit, 1967), p. 227 and *Positions*, p. 117.

11 Derrida, *La Dissémination*, p. 236.

12 *Ibid.*, p. 239.

13 *Ibid.*, p. 292.

14 *Ibid.*, p. 297.

15 *Ibid.*, p. 239.

16 *Ibid.*, p. 266.

17 M. Riffaterre, 'On Deciphering Mallarmé', *The Georgia Review*, 19 (1975), p. 76.

18 *Ibid.*, p. 80.

19 P. Valéry, *Ecrits divers sur Stéphane Mallarmé* (Paris: Gallimard, 1950), pp. 57 and 139.

20 Letter to A. Mockel, 28 September 1891, mclxv, *Correspondance* (11 vols., ed. H. Mondor and J.-P. Richard, vol. I; ed. H. Mondor and L. J. Austin, vols. II and III; ed. L. Austin, vols. IV–XI; Paris: Gallimard, 1959–85), IV, p. 310.

21 H. Friedrich, *The Structure of Modern Poetry from the Mid Nineteenth Century to the Mid Twentieth Century* (Evanston IL: Northwestern University Press, 1974), p. 46.

22 Letter to Odilon Redon, 2 February 1885, cdxvii, *Correspondance* II, p. 280. The lithograph in question is 'Dans mon rêve, j'ai vu un visage de mystère', from the series *Hommage à Goya*.

23 Letter to Cazalis, April 1866, civ, *Correspondance* I, p. 208.

24 Letter to Cazalis, 18 February 1869, clvii, *Correspondance* I, p. 301.

25 Valéry, *Ecrits divers*, p. 73.

26 Jacques Scherer, *Le 'Livre' de Mallarmé* (Paris: Gallimard, 1957; revised version, 1977).

27 We noted in chapter 1 above the relevance to the 'Livre' of Mallarmé's interest in the occult. The details of the 'Livre' will be discussed further in chapter 6 below.

28 Letter to Cazalis, 14 May 1867, cxxii, *Correspondance* I, p. 242.

29 'Je redeviens un littérateur pur et simple. Mon œuvre n'est plus un mythe.' (Letter to Cazalis, 3 March 1871, clxxxv, *Correspondance* I, p. 342).

30 Cited in S. Bernard, *Mallarmé et la musique* (Paris: Nizet, 1959), p. 75.

31 On Mallarmé and illustration, see my 'Illustration, Present or Absent: Reflecting Reflexivity in Mallarmé's "Sonnet en yx"', *Journal of European Studies*, 19 (1989), pp. 311–29.

32 Valéry, *Ecrits divers*, p. 86.

33 See also note 87, chapter 1 above.

34 Valéry, *Ecrits divers*, p. 71.

35 *Ibid.*, pp. 36 and 118.

36 Some of the fans on which Mallarmé wrote verses are black, elegantly inscribed in white ink. For details, see *Stéphane Mallarmé, Oeuvres complètes, 'Poésies'*, ed. C. P. Barbier and C. G. Millan (Paris: Flammarion, 1983), p. 560.

37 See A. E. Chisholm, 'Mallarmé: "Le vierge, le vivace"', *French Studies*, 16 (1962), p. 363 and E. Noulet, *L'Oeuvre poétique de Stéphane Mallarmé* (Brussels: Jacques Antoine, 1974), p. 263.

38 T. Hampton, 'At the Sign of the Swan', *Romanic Review*, 73 (1982), p. 448. There have been many excellent commentaries on this sonnet and I have deliberately refrained from discussing features frequently analysed by other commentators, such as the repetition of 'i' sounds.

39 This paradox has been admirably analysed by Malcolm Bowie in *Mallarmé and the Art of Being Difficult* (Cambridge University Press, 1978), pp. 9–16.

40 *Ibid.*, p. 10.

41 See, for instance, Bowie, *Mallarmé and the Art of Being Difficult*, p. 11; J. R. Lawler, 'A Reading of Mallarmé's "Le vierge, le vivace et le bel aujourd'hui"', *AUMLA (Journal of the Australasian Universities Language and Literature Association)* 9 (1958), p. 83, and E. Noulet, *L'Oeuvre poétique*, p. 264.

42 See L. J. Austin, 'How Ambiguous is Mallarmé? Reflections on the Captive Swan', in *Literature and Society: Studies in Nineteenth and Twentieth Century French Literature Presented to R. J. North*, ed. C. A. Burns (Birmingham: Goodman, 1980), pp. 112–13.

43 *MOC*, pp. 1163–278. For an interesting discussion of Mallarmé and myth, see P. Renauld, 'Mallarmé et le mythe', *Revue d'Histoire Littéraire de la France*, 73 (1973), pp. 48–68. See also B. Marchal's extremely valuable study, *La Religion de Mallarmé* (Paris: Corti, 1988).

44 See, in particular, E. Burt, 'Mallarmé's "Sonnet en *yx*": The

Ambiguities of Speculation', *Yale French Studies*, 54 (1977), pp. 55–82; R. Dragonetti, 'La Littérature et la lettre: introduction au "Sonnet en -yx" de Mallarmé', *Lingua et Stile*, 4 (1969), pp. 205–22; O. Paz, 'Stéphane Mallarmé: Sonnet in "ix"', *Delos*, 4 (1970), pp. 14–28; D. Scott, *Sonnet Theory and Practice in 19th-Century France: Sonnets on the Sonnet* (Hull: University of Hull, 1977), pp. 61–6.

45 I have argued this in more detail in 'Mallarmé et la transformation esthétique du langage, à l'exemple de "Ses purs ongles"', *French Forum*, 15 (1990), pp. 203–20.

46 'The inner rhythm of a sonnet should be like that of a drama': W. Mönch, *Das Sonett, Gestalt und Geschichte* (Heidelberg: F. H. Kerle Verlag, 1955), p. 37 (translation mine).

47 Scott, *Sonnet Theory and Practice*, p. 66.

48 Compare his description of the dancer, who combines whirling movement with stillness: 'tout obéit à une impulsion fugace en tourbillons, elle résume, par le vouloir aux extrémités éperdu de chaque aile et darde sa statuette, stricte, debout' (*MOC*, p. 309).

49 Letter to Cazalis, 18 July 1868, cxli, *Correspondance* I, p. 279.

50 Letter to Lefébure, 20 March 1870, clxxi, *ibid.*, p. 318.

51 Cited in H. Mondor, *Autres précisions sur Mallarmé et inédits* (Paris: Gallimard, 1961), p. 234.

52 Letter to Cazalis, 18 July 1868, cxli, *Correspondance* I, p. 278.

53 *Ibid.*, p. 279.

54 'L'adjectif "pur" s'applique presque toujours dans l'œuvre de Mallarmé à un foyer de lumière.' In G. Davies, *Mallarmé et le drame solaire* (Paris: Corti, 1959), p. 126.

55 For an interesting discussion of the 'Phénix' image, see G. Robb, 'The Phoenix of Mallarmé's "Sonnet en -yx"', *French Studies Bulletin*, 24 (1987), pp. 13–15 and C. Chadwick, 'Mallarmé le Phénix', *French Studies Bulletin*, 25 (1987/8), p. 16.

56 Compare Mallarmé's comment, cited in chapter 1, note 86 above, that he experienced the 'Néant' through sensation.

57 Letter to Cazalis, 18 July 1868, cxli, *Correspondance* I, p. 279. On 'Ses purs ongles' and illustration, see my 'Illustration, Present or Absent'. Mallarmé's sonnet was not in fact included in the collection *Sonnets et eaux-fortes*.

58 See D. Mihram, 'The Abortive Didot/Vollard Edition of *Un Coup de Dés*', *French Studies*, 33 (1979), p. 42. Mallarmé was very impressed by Redon's use of black, which inspired fear in him. 'Selon Redon lui-même, Mallarmé avait *peur* de ses noirs' (J.-P. Richard, *L'Univers imaginaire de Mallarmé*), p. 510.

59 D. Scott, *Pictorialist Poetics: Poetry and the Visual Arts in Nineteenth-Century France* (Cambridge University Press, 1988), p. 85.

60 To what must surely be the most laughable of these, Leconte de Lisle's suggestion that by 'ptyx' (in the first version of the sonnet) Mallarmé meant a piano, we owe Mallarmé's reply: 'Nullement, mon cher maître . . . j'avais simplement besoin d'une rime à Styx; n'en trouvant pas, j'ai créé un instrument de musique nouveau: or, c'est bien clair, le ptyx est insolite, puisqu'il n'y en a pas; il résonne

bien, puisqu'il rime; et ce n'en est pas moins un vaisseau d'inanité, puisqu'il n'a jamais existé!' Cited in *Oeuvres complètes de Mallarmé* (ed. C. P. Barbier and C. G. Millan), p. 222.

61 Letter to Lefébure, 3 May 1868, cxxxviii, *Correspondance* I, p. 274.

62 See H. G. Liddell and R. Scott, *A Greek–English Lexicon* (Oxford: Clarendon Press, 1864).

63 Taking this analogy a little further, one could associate the 'x' with the celestial space of the constellation and the 'o' with the terrestrial space of the mirror, an association which finds a parallel in a Taoist diagram which represents the union of earth and sky by the constellation of the Great Bear at the centre of a spiral. See L. Legeza, *Magie du Tao* (Paris: Chêne, 1976), p. 113. This yin/yang relationship also involves gender roles, about which there is much to be said concerning this sonnet. See, for instance, J.-P. Richard's 'Feu rué, feu scintillé: note sur le fantasme et l'écriture', *Littérature* 17 (1975), pp. 84–105.

64 Letter to Cazalis, 18 July 1868, cxli, *Correspondance* I, p. 278.

65 Mallarmé wrote to Rodenbach: 'ne reste aucune réalité: elle s'est évaporée en écrit'. Letter to G. Rodenbach, 25 March 1888, dcxvi, *Correspondance* III, p. 177.

66 Mallarmé attached great importance to the initial letter of the line of verse. He wrote to E. Champsaur: 'Je ne vous haïs qu'en raison de la majuscule ôtée, au vers, la lettre d'attaque y a, selon moi, la même importance que la rime, et on ne saurait trop fortement la marquer'. Cited in Richard, *L'Univers imaginaire*, p. 576.

67 Letter to Cazalis, July 1866, cx, *Correspondance* I, p. 220.

68 He described the 'Vénus de Milo' and 'la Joconde' as 'les deux grandes scintillations de la Beauté sur la Terre' and his own 'Œuvre, tel qu'il est rêvé, la troisième' (letter to Lefébure, 17 May 1867, cxxiii, *Correspondance* I, p. 246).

69 Mallarmé refers to the 'Grande Ourse' in a letter to Cazalis, which describes the scene as it might appear in an etching: 'une chambre avec personne dedans . . . sans meubles, sinon l'ébauche plausible de vagues consoles, un cadre belliqueux et agonisant, de miroir appendu au fond, avec sa réflexion, stellaire et incompréhensible, de la Grande Ourse, qui relie au ciel seul ce logis abandonné du monde'. (18 July, cxli, *Correspondance* I, p. 279).

70 E. Lévi, *Dogme et rituel de la haute magie* (Paris: Germer Baillière, 1861), p. 312.

71 *Ibid.*, pp. 195 and 200.

72 The title is normally written with a capital 'C', but I am following here the typography of the title page of the Ronat edition: *Un coup de Dés jamais n'abolira le Hasard*, ed. M. Ronat and T. Papp (Paris: Change Errant/d'Atelier, 1980), which corresponds to that of the proofs.

73 Ronat, for instance, asserts that 'le "Coup de Dés" apparaît – sinon comme un fragment, car ses pages ne sont pas mobiles – comme une préfiguration du Livre, du Grand Œuvre dont Mallarmé a rêvé toute sa vie' ('"Cette architecture spontanée et magique"', in *Un coup de Dés*, p. 4). The experimental form of 'Un coup de Dés' and its

image of the constellation have appealed to artists as well as writers. This is not the place to cite numerous examples, but an interesting and little known case in point is that of the Belgian artist Marcel Broodthaers, who declared that 'Mallarmé est à la source de l'art contemporain . . . Il invente inconsciemment l'espace moderne.' *Broodthaers, Writings, Interviews, Photographs*, ed. B. H. D. Buchloh (Cambridge, MA: MIT Press, 1987), p. 110. Broodthaer's book, *'Un coup de dés jamais n'abolira le hasard', Image*, a visual translation of Mallarmé's text, appeared in 1969.

74 The folio page would have measured 57 × 38 cm. for a double spread, 28.5 × 38 cm. for a single spread. See J.-C. Lebenstejn, 'Note relative au "Coup de Dés"', *Critique*, 36 (1980), p. 640.

75 See *ibid.*, pp. 633–59.

76 An ingenious 'typographical' translation of the poem into English by Neil Crawford, which also 'translates' the proportions of the written text and the space of the page, accompanied by aquatints by Ian Tyson, has been published by the Tetrad Press (London, 1985). I am very grateful to Neil Crawford and Ian Tyson for permitting me to consult their copies of the Harvard proofs.

77 Ronat, '"Cette architecture"', p. 3.

78 *Ibid.*

79 See, in particular, R. G. Cohn, 'A propos du "Coup de Dés"', *Critique*, 38 (1982), pp. 92–3.

80 Mallarmé was critical of the lack of variety in newspaper layout, and compared newspapers unfavourably with the 'livre' (*MOC*, p. 379 and p. 381). See C. Poggi, 'Mallarmé, Picasso, and the Newspaper as Commodity', *Yale Journal of Criticism*, 1 (1987), pp. 133–51. On typography as a lexical element in 'Un coup de Dés', see V. La Charité, 'Mallarmé's *Livre*: The Graphomatics of the Text', *Symposium*, 34 (1980), p. 257. See also G. Blanchard, 'Mallarmé et la typographie', *Techniques graphiques*, 32–3 (1960), pp. 156–66.

81 Letter to E. Deman, 7 April 1891, mlxxxiv, *Correspondance* IV, p. 219.

82 Cited in C. Mauclair, *Mallarmé chez lui* (Paris: Grasset, 1935), p. 116.

83 Facsimiles of proofs have been published by R. G. Cohn in *Mallarmé's Masterwork, New Findings* (The Hague: Mouton, 1966), pp. 89–111. It is ironically appropriate to this text that the dispersal of the proofs corrected by Mallarmé means that the definitive text remains elusive. For a useful discussion of the situation see D. Mihram, 'The Abortive Didot/Vollard Edition of *Un Coup de Dés*'.

84 These are not necessarily the same, since the typographical point measurement applies only to the block of metal on which the letter sits (its 'corps'), not to the letter itself. The Ronat edition duplicates as closely as possible the visual appearance of the text in the proofs. The typographical measurements in question are disputed. While Ronat finds five different sizes, La Charité finds seven, and does not follow the French system of measurement. (La Charité, *Dynamics of Space*, p. 52.) (Surprisingly, Ronat's article, '"Cette architecture spontanée et magique"' reveals some ignorance of typography, for instance when she gives as page measurements what are in fact

measurements of the maximum height and width of the page area covered by text; 27 × 36 cm. for a double page.) Having examined sets of copies of the Harvard proofs and the set held at the Bibliothèque Nationale, I would speculate that there are in fact six typographical sizes. However, the point size cannot be definitively established while uncertainties remain concerning the exact cutting of the face used. The late Mitsou Ronat reported that the original type founts were made specially for 'Un coup de Dés', and have not survived (conversation with Ronat). Neil Crawford informs me that the largest series (series 1) is set in a titling face very similar to 48D Initiales Thorey, but could also be a recutting of the late eighteenth-century Initiales Firmin Didot, the word 'POEME' (series 2) is set in a face closely resembling both the Fonderie Beaudoire's 30D Initiales Maigre and 32D Initiales Thorey (though I found it was also very similar to 24D Initiales Firmin Didot), and the poet's name (series 4) appears in a face similar to 20D Initiales Demi Maigre. These findings contradict Ronat's classification of series 1 as 60, series 2 as 36, and series 4 as 24 (all multiples of 12). I am very grateful to Neil Crawford for his generous sharing of his expertise in this area.

85 M. Blanchot, *Le Livre à venir* (Paris: Gallimard, 1959), p. 284.

86 'Le hasard n'entame pas un vers, c'est la grande chose' (letter to François Coppée, 5 December 1866, cxix, *Correspondance* I, p. 234).

87 B. Johnson, *Défigurations du langage poétique, la seconde révolution baude-lairienne* (Paris: Flammarion, 1979), pp. 175–91. On Mallarmé's manipulation of binary division and its relation to gender differences, see my 'Mallarmé as "Maître": The (En)gendering of Genre in "Un coup de Dés"', *Journal of the Institute of Romance Studies*, 1 (1992), pp. 439–52.

88 A double '//' denotes a break across the central margin from left to right.

89 See facsimiles of Mallarmé's corrections to the proofs, in Cohn, *Mallarmé's Masterwork*, pp. 108–9.

90 *Ibid.*, pp. 101–5.

91 Pierre Duplan, 'Pour une sémiologie de la lettre', in *L'Espace et la lettre*, ed. A.-M. Christin (Paris: Union Générale d'Editions, 1977), pp. 324–37.

92 See Cohn, *Mallarmé's Masterwork*, p. 105.

93 Mallarmé was very interested in Hamlet. Hamlet's costume was frequently based on Delacroix's lithographs, in which his entire outfit was black. In his article on Hamlet, Mallarmé cited de Banville's lines: '"Tu sens courir par la nuit dérisoire, / Sur ton front pâle aussi blanc que du lait, / Le vent qui fait voler ta plume noire"' (*MOC*, p. 299). See also C. Chassé, 'Le Thème de Hamlet chez Mallarmé', *Revue des Sciences Humaines*, 78 (1955), pp. 157–69.

94 J. Scherer, *Le 'Livre' de Mallarmé* (Paris: Gallimard, 1977), *feuillet* 59 (B). The alchemists to whom Mallarmé referred as his ancestors symbolized the Great Work by the figure of the androgyne, and I have shown elsewhere (see my 'Mallarmé as "Maître"') that the potential apotheosis of the 'Maître' figure can be linked with the figure of the male androgyne.

4 PUTTING THE SPECTATOR IN THE PICTURE; KANDINSKY'S PICTORIAL WORLD

1 W. Kandinsky, *Complete Writings on Art*, 2 vols., ed. K. Lindsay and P. Vergo (London: Faber and Faber, 1982; hereafter, *KCWA*), p. 369.

2 Kandinsky, *Cours du Bauhaus* (Paris: Denoël/Gonthier, 1975; hereafter, *CB*), p. 226.

3 For a brief summary of the controversy surrounding this date, see C. Derouet and J. Boissel, *Kandinsky: œuvres de Vassily Kandinsky (1866–1944)* (Paris: Centre Georges Pompidou, 1984), p. 100.

4 T. Messer, 'Introduction', in V. Barnett, *Kandinsky at the Guggenheim*, ed. V. Barnett (New York: Abbeville Press, 1983), p. 12.

5 V. Barnett, 'The Essential Unity of Kandinsky's Pictorial Modes', in *Kandinsky at the Guggenheim*, p. 44.

6 Kandinsky, 'La Valeur d'une œuvre concrète', *XXe Siècle* (1939, supplement to nos. 5–6, 1938), no page numbers. Cited here in the original owing to errors in English version reproduced in *KCWA*.

7 R. Korn, *Kandinsky und die Theorie der Abstrakten Malerei* (Berlin: Henschelverlag, 1960), p. 12.

8 M. Pleynet, *Système de la peinture* (Paris: Seuil, 1977), p. 164. See also Cheetham, *The Rhetoric of Purity, Essentialist Theory and the Advent of Abstract Painting* (Cambridge University Press, 1991), and R. Sheppard, 'Kandinsky's œuvre 1900–14; The *avant-garde* as rearguard', *Word and Image*, 6 (1990), pp. 41–67. Mark Roskill argues that 'with Kandinsky, the theory and the practice stem from very different compulsions'. *Klee, Kandinsky and the Thought of their Time, A Critical Perspective* (Urbana: University of Illinois Press, 1993), p. 40. See also p. 191.

9 This case is argued in relation to early abstraction by W. J. T. Mitchell, in '*Ut Pictura Theoria*: Abstract Painting and the Repression of Language', *Critical Inquiry*, 15 (1989), pp. 348–71.

10 Kandinsky's nephew, the philosopher Alexandre Kojève, wrote to his uncle in 1929 that the real debate about art was not whether it should be figurative or abstract (since 'representing reality' had never really been the aim of art), but whether it expressed the subjective emotions of the artist or described objective beauty: the debate, according to Kojève, came down to an opposition between subjective idealism and Platonic realism. 'Deux lettres inédites d'Alexandre Kojève à Vassily Kandinsky', *Kandinsky, album de l'exposition* (Paris: Centre Georges Pompidou, 1984), p. 64.

11 F. Thürlemann, *Kandinsky über Kandinsky, Der Künstler als Interpret eigener Werke* (Bern: Benteli, 1986). Thürlemann's work will be discussed below in relation to Kandinsky's *Composition IV*.

12 H. K. Roethel, in collaboration with J. K. Benjamin, *Kandinsky* (Oxford: Phaidon, 1979), p. 82.

13 Cited in C. Derouet, 'Notes et documents sur les dernières années du peintre Vassily Kandinsky', *Les Cahiers du Musée National d'Art Moderne: Paris–Paris 1937–1957* (1982), p. 48. See Baudelaire's comment: 'La meilleure critique est celle qui est amusante et poéti-

que; non pas celle-ci, froide et algébrique, qui, sous prétexte de tout expliquer, n'a ni haine ni amour . . . Ainsi le meilleur compte rendu d'un tableau pourra être un sonnet ou une élégie' (*BOC* II, p. 418).

14 23 October 1935, Bauhaus Archiv Nr. 3721/1–28.

15 Cited in Roethel and Benjamin, *Kandinsky* , p. 13.

16 There is an extensive literature on this subject. See introduction, note 13 above. On abstract art as a language, see S. Bann, 'Abstract Art – a Language?', in *Towards a New Art, Essays on the Background to Abstract Art 1910–1920* (London: The Tate Gallery, 1980), pp. 125–45.

17 See C. V. Poling, 'Kandinsky au Bauhaus, théorie de la couleur et grammaire picturale', *Change* 26/27 (1976), p. 202.

18 Cited in Derouet, 'Notes et documents', p. 97.

19 Letter of 1944, cited in *ibid.*, p. 99.

20 C.-P. Bru, *Esthétique de l'abstraction* (Paris: Presses Universitaires de France, 1955), p. 82.

21 C. Greenberg, 'Modernist Painting', *Art and Literature*, 4 (1965), p. 198.

22 W. Grohmann, *Wassily Kandinsky, Life and Work* (London: Thames and Hudson, 1959), p. 246. Note similarity with Friedrich's description of Rimbaud's poetry as a 'sensory unreality'. H. Friedrich, *The Structure of Modern Poetry from the Mid Nineteenth Century to the Mid Twentieth Century* (Evanston, IL: Northwestern University Press, 1974), p. 56.

23 'La Valeur d'une œuvre concrète', no page numbers.

24 A. K. Wiedmann, *Romantic Roots in Modern Art, Romanticism and Expressionism: A Study in Comparative Aesthetics* (Surrey: Gresham Books, 1979), p. 125.

25 The influence of *Jugendstil* can be seen especially in Kandinsky's graphic work. There is no space here to discuss Kandinsky's early work in detail. On the Munich period, see in particular R.-C. Washton Long, *Kandinsky, The Development of an Abstract Style* (Oxford: Clarendon Press, 1980), and P. Weiss, *Kandinsky in Munich, The Formative Jugendstil Years* (Princeton University Press, 1979).

26 On this period, see V. E. Barnett, *Kandinsky and Sweden, Malmö 1914, Stockholm 1916* (Malmö Konsthall, 1989.) Kandinsky had considerable exposure to the latest styles in painting. He had seen the French Impressionists' Exhibition in Moscow in 1895 (where he was so struck by Monet) and after settling in Munich, he moved in avant-garde circles and in 1901 founded an artistic group called the Phalanx, which held exhibitions of modern art. He exhibited at the Salon d'Automne in Paris every year from 1904–10 and lived in Paris from May 1906 to June 1907.

27 Only ten of Kandinsky's paintings bear the title *Composition*. Compositions are paintings which expressed feelings that Kandinsky had been forming over a long period of time and which had been clearly worked out on the basis of preliminary sketches. (See *KCWA*, p. 218.)

28 H. K. Roethel and J. K. Benjamin, *Kandinsky: Catalogue Raisonné of the Oil Paintings*, 2 vols.; 1900–15, vol. I; 1916–44, vol. II (London:

Sotheby, 1982 and 1984; hereafter, *RB*), pl. 361. For paintings not in this catalogue, other sources will be given where appropriate. References to the *Catalogue Raisonné* will also be given for paintings reproduced here, designated as 'figure'.

29 P. Vergo, *Kandinsky Cossacks* (London: The Tate Gallery, 1986).

30 See Washton Long, *Kandinsky*.

31 See J.-M. Floch, 'Sémiotique d'un discours plastique non-figuratif', *Communications*, 34 (1981), pp. 135–58 and Thürlemann, *Kandinsky über Kandinsky*, pp. 90–114.

32 Thürlemann, *Kandinsky*, p. 109. (All translations from Thürlemann are mine.)

33 *Ibid.*, p. 113.

34 *Ibid.*, p. 144.

35 This diagram is identical to Kandinsky's second sketch for the composition. See *Die Zeichnungen Wassily Kandinsky*, intro. P. Volboudt (Cologne: Du Mont Schauberg, 1974), drawing no. 19. Six drawings for *Composition IV* are reproduced in Vergo, *Kandinsky Cossacks*, p. 10.

36 The scientific basis for this principle, which had a powerful impact on painters, was established by E. Chevreul in his book *De la loi du contraste simultané des couleurs et de l'assortiment des objets colorés, considérés d'après cette loi dans ses rapports avec la peinture* (Paris: Pitois-Levrault, 1839).

37 Colours nearer the red-yellow end of the spectrum are commonly described as warm, while those nearer the blue-green end are described as cool. These epithets are linked with the tendency of warm colours to advance and cool ones to recede. Kandinsky commented on this technique: 'I would let cold come to the fore and drive warm into the background. I would treat the individual tones likewise, cooling the warmer tones, warming the cold, so that even one single colour was raised to the level of a composition' (*KCWA*, p. 397).

38 In his commentary, Kandinsky says that the principal contrast is the juxtaposition of 'bright-sweet-cold tone with angular movement (battle)' (*KCWA*, p. 384).

39 Compare with the two upright figures with haloes in the painting on glass, *Composition with Saints*, 1911. (Reproduced in Washton Long, *Kandinsky*, pl. 82.)

40 See *Improvisation 27 (Garden of Love II)*, 1912, *RB*, pl. 430 and *Section of Composition II*, 1910, *RB*, pl. 325.

41 Compare with the figure with skull and crossbones and a large flower in the glass painting, *All Saints Day I*, 1911 (colour pl. 83 in Roethel and Benjamin, *Kandinsky*).

42 See *Horsemen of the Apocalypse I*, 1911 (*RB*, pl. 423).

43 The image of a walled city or fortress dates back to Kandinsky's fairytale-like pictures in a *pointilliste* style, where the towers are capped with minarets. In the Munich paintings, it is connected with the heavenly Jerusalem of the Apocalypse, and also suggests the vision of Moscow as the third Rome.

44 The *Blue Rider* was formed by Kandinsky and Franz Marc in 1909, after disagreements with the *Neue Künstlervereinigung München*. The almanac appeared in 1912. See *The Blaue Reiter Almanac*, edited by Wassily Kandinsky and Franz Marc, ed. K. Lankheit (London: Thames and Hudson, 1974) and H. K. Roethel, *The Blue Rider* (New York: Praeger, 1971). The cover illustration is reproduced in Roethel and Benjamin, *Kandinsky*, colour pl. 17.

45 See P. Vergo, *Kandinsky Cossacks* (London: Tate Gallery, 1986), p. 19.

46 See Washton Long, *Kandinsky*, pp. 181–2.

47 There is an interesting parallel here with the determination of critics to find an interpretation of Mallarmé's 'ptyx'.

48 Roethel and Benjamin, *Kandinsky*, p. 124.

49 Poling, 'Kandinsky au Bauhaus', p. 203.

50 Cited in Grohmann, *Wassily Kandinsky*, p. 187.

51 *Ibid.*, p. 188.

52 'I love circles today in the way that previously I loved, e.g. horses – perhaps even more, since I find in the circle more inner possibilities, which is the reason why the circle has replaced the horse' (*KCWA*, p. 740).

53 See his sketchbooks of 1903–4 (Städtische Galerie im Lenbachhaus, GMS 330 and 331), and *Kandinsky und München, Begegnungen und Wandlungen 1896–1914*, ed. A. Zweite (Munich: Prestel, 1982), figures 22, 27, 28, 161, 170, 173, 174, 180, 181. Kandinsky's experiments with different mediums will be discussed in chapter 6 below.

54 See V. E. Barnett, 'Kandinsky and Science: The Introduction of Biological Images in the Paris Period', in *Kandinsky in Paris: 1934–1944* (New York: Solomon R. Guggenheim Museum, 1985), pp. 61–87.

55 These aspects of Kandinsky's Parisian style have often been compared with the work of Arp and Miró, who were among his friends in Paris. On Kandinsky's relationship to biomorphic Surrealism and the influence of science, see J. Weiss, 'Late Kandinsky, From Apocalypse to Perpetual Motion', *Art in America*, 73 (1985), pp. 118–25. See also S. W. Hayter, 'The Language of Kandinsky', *Magazine of Art*, 38 (1945), pp. 178–9, and F. F. Stella, 'Commentaire du tableau "Complexité-simple – Ambiguité"', *Kandinsky, album de l'exposition* (Paris: Centre Georges Pompidou, 1984), pp. 84–90.

56 German titles have been translated: French titles will be given in French.

57 See colour reproduction in Barnett, *Kandinsky at the Guggenheim*, pl. 165.

58 *Ibid.*, p. 255.

59 See, for instance, Grohmann, *Wassily Kandinsky*, p. 246.

60 Felix Thürlemann, 'Le Figuratif au service de l'abstrait', in *Collection les grandes expositions, Vassily Kandinsky* (Paris: Beaux-Arts Magazine, 1985), p. 18.

5 BETWEEN THE LINES; FORM AND TRANSFORMATION IN MONDRIAN

1 Mondrian. cited in J. J. Sweeney, 'Mondrian, the Dutch and De Stijl', *Art News*, 50 (1951), p. 25.
2 See H. Henkels, *Mondrian, From Figuration to Abstraction* (London: Thames and Hudson, 1988), p. 187.
3 Cited in H. L. C. Jaffé, *De Stijl 1917–1931, The Dutch Contribution to Modern Art* (London: Harvard University Press, 1986), p. 50.
4 M. Seuphor, *Piet Mondrian, Life and Work* (London: Thames and Hudson, 1957), p. 160. After he ceased being a figurative painter, Mondrian professed dislike for natural objects such as trees and flowers. It is also reported that on more than one occasion, when he was visiting friends, Mondrian asked to change places so that he would not have to see the trees. Nina Kandinsky recounts: 'La visite de Piet Mondrian chez nous est restée pour moi inoubliable. C'était par une journée resplendissante de printemps. Les marronniers devant notre immeuble étaient en fleurs, et Kandinsky avait placé la petite table à thé de façon à ce que, de sa place, Mondrian put voir cette magnifique splendeur fleurie.' Mondrian was so disgusted at the sight of the trees that he changed places with Kandinsky, with his back to the window. On another occasion, after visiting Mondrian in his studio, Kandinsky remarked to his wife: 'Je ne comprends vraiment pas comment il peut peindre dans cette uniformité de couleur.' N. Kandinsky, *Kandinsky et moi* (Paris: Flammarion, 1978), pp. 202–3. Kandinsky did not have a great deal of sympathy for Mondrian's approach, finding him 'a little narrow-minded', although 'very intelligent'. Letter to Zervos, 24 April 1931, cited in C. Derouet, 'Kandinsky in Paris: 1934–1944', *Kandinsky in Paris: 1934–1944* (New York: Solomon R. Guggenheim Museum, 1985), p. 44.
5 M. Butor, 'Notes autour de Mondrian', in M. G. Ottolenghi, *Tout l'œuvre peint de Mondrian* (Paris: Flammarion, 1976), p. 5.
6 D. Craven, 'Towards a Newer Virgil, Mondrian De-mythologized', *Praxis: A Journal of Radical Perspectives on the Arts*, 4 (1978), p. 242. See also M. Pleynet, *Système de la peinture* (Paris: Seuil, 1977), p. 164.
7 C. Greenberg, 'Modernist Painting', *Art and Literature*, 4 (1965), p. 198.
8 H. Rosenberg, *Art on the Edge* (London: Macmillan, 1975), p. 44. This topic will be discussed further in the final chapter below.
9 M. Cheetham, *The Rhetoric of Purity, Essentialist Theory and the Advent of Abstract Painting* (Cambridge University Press, 1991), p. 125. Although Mondrian favours an androgynous model of creativity, this model is not symmetrical, in that a woman can 'never completely [be] an artist'. Mondrian, *Two Mondrian Sketchbooks, 1912–1914*, ed. R. Welsh and J. Joosten (Amsterdam: Meulenhoff International, 1969), p. 34. It would, however, be absurd to reject abstraction *per se* on such grounds. The feminist project involves not only exposing misogynist ideologies but also appropriating and transforming modes of expression from which women have been excluded.

10 See Seuphor, *Piet Mondrian*, p. 114.

11 Cited in Henkels, *Mondrian*, p. 40.

12 M. Roweli, 'Interview with Charmion von Wiegand', in *Piet Mondrian 1872–1944, Centennial Exhibition* (New York, Solomon R. Guggenheim Museum, 1971), p. 82.

13 Mondrian, 'De l'art abstrait. Réponse de Piet Mondrian.' *Cahiers d'Art*, 6 (1931), p. 43.

14 See chapter 1, note 118 above.

15 Greenberg, 'Modernist Painting', p. 198.

16 M. Fried, 'Art and Objecthood', *Artforum*, 6 (1967), p. 20.

17 Y.-A. Bois, 'Piet Mondrian, "New York City"', *Critical Inquiry*, 14 (1987/8), p. 259.

18 *Ibid.*, p. 263. This approach develops the arguments of H. Damisch in *Fenêtre jaune cadmium ou les dessous de la peinture* (Paris: Seuil, 1984).

19 Cited in *ibid.*, p. 260.

20 *Ibid.*, pp. 261–2.

21 *Ibid.*, p. 262.

22 *Ibid.*, p. 258.

23 Fried, 'Art and Objecthood', p. 20.

24 Robert Morris, cited in *ibid.*, p. 15.

25 Letter to Cazalis, 14 May 1867, cxxii, *Correspondance*, 11 vols., ed. H. Mondor and J.-P. Richard, vol. i; ed. H. Mondor and L. J. Austin, vols. ii and iii; ed. L. J. Austin, vols. iv–xi (Paris: Gallimard, 1959–85), i, p. 240.

26 These notes are in Mondrian's English.

27 Hegel, *Hegel's Aesthetics*, 2 vols., trans. T. M. Knox (Oxford: Clarendon Press, 1975), i, p. 57.

28 Welsh suggests that the term 'beelding' is best translated as 'form-giving'. R. Welsh, 'Mondrian and Theosophy', in *Piet Mondrian, 1872–1944, Centennial Exhibition* (New York: Solomon R. Guggenheim Museum, 1971), p. 35. On problems in translating Mondrian's terminology, see the very interesting study by I. Rike, 'Piet Mondrian's *Nieuwe Beelding* in English', in *Translation Data 7* (Amsterdam: Instituut voor Vertaalwetenschap, 1991).

29 Cited in Henkels, *Mondrian*, p. 199.

30 See J. Beckett, 'Discoursing on Dutch Modernism', *Oxford Art Journal*, 6 (1983), p. 70.

31 Cited in J. Beckett, 'The Netherlands', in *Abstraction: Towards a New Art, Painting 1910–20* (London: Tate Gallery, 1980), p. 40.

32 See Mondrian, *MCWA*, p. 63.

33 Cited in Henkels, *Mondrian*, p. 199.

34 See Jaffé, *De Stijl 1917–1931*, p. 54.

35 See, however, R. Welsh, *Piet Mondrian's Early Career, The Naturalistic Periods* (London: Garland, 1977).

36 See *Dune V*, 1910, reproduced in M. G. Ottolenghi, *Tout l'œuvre peint de Piet Mondrian*, intro. M. Butor (Paris: Flammarion, 1976), colour pl. xix, and also *Dune I*, 1909 and *Dune IV*, 1909–10, reproduced in J. Meuris, *Mondrian* (Paris: Nouvelles Editions Françaises, 1991), colour pls. 101 and 103. Although Ottolenghi has a fuller catalogue, with more colour plates, the most commonly used catalogue for

Mondrian's paintings is still the one drawn up by Seuphor, in *Piet Mondrian*, which is more widely available. Where possible, I shall give both sources here, using the French edition of M. Seuphor, *Piet Mondrian* (Paris: Flammarion, 1970), which has an updated catalogue. Catalogue numbers in Seuphor are designated as *S*, Ottolenghi as *O*. Paintings reproduced here will also be referenced in Ottolenghi.

37 On Mondrian and Abstract Expressionism, see B. Rose, 'Mondrian in New York', *Artforum*, 10 (1971), p. 58.

38 K. S. Champa, *Mondrian Studies* (University of Chicago Press, 1985), p. 12.

39 See Welsh, 'Mondrian and Theosophy', p. 49.

40 Cited in M. James, 'The Realism Behind Mondrian's Geometry', *Art News*, 56 (1957), p. 35.

41 Mondrian's working method, which involves progression in logical stages, means that his *œuvre* is best examined as a continuum. The prominence of series paintings in his work exemplifies this approach.

42 See E. Hoek, 'Piet Mondrian', in *De Stijl: The Formative Years, 1917–1922*, ed. E. Hoek (Cambridge, MA: MIT Press, 1986), p. 44.

43 I. Tomassoni, *Mondrian* (London: Hamlyn, 1970), p. 30.

44 There have been several misplaced attempts to prove the existence of a geometrical basis for Mondrian's paintings. On this topic, see A. Hill, 'Art and Mathesis: Mondrian's structures', *Leonardo*, 1 (1968), pp. 233–42, and I. C. McManus *et al.*, 'Experimenting with Mondrian – The Aesthetics of Composition', *Perception*, 19 (1990), p. 278, an article which discusses the production of 'quasi-Mondrians' by computer. Other examples of such compositions are reproduced in Meuris, *Mondrian*, p. 220.

45 Mondrian, cited in C. Ragghianti, *Mondrian e l'arte del xx secolo* (Milan: Edizioni di Communità, 1963), p. 293 (translation mine). This function could be compared with that of the Mallarmean 'pli'.

46 R. Krauss, 'Grids', in *The Originality of the Avant-Garde and Other Modernist Myths* (Cambridge, MA: MIT Press, 1985), p. 19.

47 Champa, *Mondrian Studies*, p. 90.

48 Mondrian, in *De Stijl*, ed. H. L. C. Jaffé (London: Thames and Hudson, 1970), p. 226.

49 Champa, *Mondrian Studies*, p. 105.

50 M. Butor, 'Le carré et son habitant', *Nouvelle Revue Française*, 17 (1961), p. 324.

51 I follow Saxon in using the term 'diamond' rather than 'lozenge', since all the interior angles in Mondrian's diamonds are right angles, whereas a proper lozenge has two obtuse angles. See E. Saxon, 'On Mondrian's Diamonds', *Artforum*, 18 (1979), p. 40.

52 Mondrian's instructions for hanging one of his diamond compositions very high on the wall, in a position corresponding to that of escutcheons in churches, confirms that there is a connection here. See E. A. Carmean, *Mondrian, The Diamond Compositions* (Washington: National Gallery of Art, 1979), p. 52.

53 See C. Blotkamp, 'Mondrian's First Diamond Compositions', *Artforum*, 18 (1979), p. 38.

54 The influence of the latter development has been contested by Carmean, *Mondrian*, p. 34.
55 Cited in Blotkamp, 'Mondrian's First Diamond Compositions', p. 36.
56 Mondrian in fact creates a remarkable 'double contrapuntal' effect in two diamond compositions, *Composition with Black and Blue*, 1926 (*O 365*) and *Composition with Two Lines*, 1921 (*O 405*), where, in an incredibly spare composition, the internal cropped rectangle generates a diagonal axis which runs parallel to the sides of the diamond.
57 Butor, 'Le Carré et son habitant', p. 325.
58 Interestingly, these linear patterns are very similar to a diagram used by Kandinsky in *Point and Line to Plane* to illustrate complex rhythm. (See *KCWA*, p. 614.)
59 In the 1920s he had used strips of transparent paper. See Carmean, *Mondrian*, p. 58.
60 M. Roweli, 'Interview with Charmion von Wiegand', in *Piet Mondrian 1872–1944* (New York: Solomon R. Guggenheim Museum, 1971), p. 82.
61 See *MCWA*, p. 217.
62 For a useful discussion of this comparison, see K. von Maur, 'Mondrian and Music', *Mondrian* (Stuttgart: Staatsgalerie Stuttgart, 1980), pp. 287–311).
63 Roweli, 'Interview with Charmion von Wiegand', p. 80.
64 Mondrian, cited in Carmean, *Mondrian*, p. 63. I am most grateful to the owners of this painting for allowing me to view it.
65 J. J. Sweeney, 'Piet Mondrian', *The Museum of Modern Art Bulletin*, 12 (1945), p. 12.
66 C. Argan, cited in R. Tomassoni, *Mondrian* (London: Hamlyn, 1970), p. 47.

6 UNIVERSAL EXCEPTIONS; SITES OF IMAGINARY SPACE

1 Peirce's concept of the 'diagram' is similar in some respects to the Sartrean 'schema'. For Sartre, as we saw earlier, the image, which is constituted by a pre-existing 'savoir', has no innovatory capacity. The schema is 'intermédiaire entre l'image et le signe' (*IM*, p. 64). It can be apprehended through a 'conscience d'image' or a 'conscience de signe', where the former is 'irréfléchie', the latter 'réflexif' (*IM*, pp. 209 and 203). For Sartre, however, these modes of signification and consciousness are incompatible, and the 'conscience de signe' is superior to the 'conscience d'image', which is a 'dégradation de la pensée' (*IM*, p. 225), endangering it with infinite regression, which must be overcome in order to reach 'l'idée pure' (*IM*, p. 225).
2 In Peirce's case, this does not derive from a view of the imagination as a creative faculty, but from a view of truth which accords central importance to hypothesis and abduction as means of gaining knowledge. 'The essence of an induction is that it infers from one set of facts another set of similar facts, whereas hypothesis [and abduction] infers from one set of facts to another' (II.642). Moreover, for Peirce,

the 'Form of the Icon, which is also its object, must be logically possible' (iv.531). Unlike Kant, Peirce does not believe in the existence of 'unpresentable' ideas, and although the ultimate realization of truth is hypothetical and in the realm of the 'conditional future' (v.483), it is located in real time.

3 See chapter 1, note 86 above.

4 Letter to Lefébure, 17 May 1867, cxxiii, *Correspondance*, 11 vols., ed. H. Mondor and J.-P. Richard, vol. i; ed. H. Mondor and L. J. Austin, vols. ii and iii; ed. L. Austin, vols. iv–xi (Paris: Gallimard, 1959–85), i, p. 249.

5 Cited by Valéry in 'Degas danse dessin' in *Oeuvres*, 2 vols.; ed. J. Hytier (Bibliothèque de la Pléiade; Paris: Gallimard, 1960), ii, p. 1208.

6 See chapter 1, note 87 above.

7 Cited in K. Roethel and J. K. Benjamin, *Kandinsky* (Oxford: Phaidon, 1979), p. 13.

8 Compare Valéry: 'C'est ce que J'ajoute à la suite des perceptions enregistrables qui construit le rythme . . . Introduction de notion subjective [*sic*]'. (See chapter 2 above, note 58.)

9 Novalis imagined 'poems which are melodious and full of beautiful words but destitute of meaning or connection'. Cited in A. K. Wiedmann, *Romantic Roots in Modern Art, Romanticism and Expressionism: A Study in Comparative Aesthetics* (Surrey: Graham Books/ Unwin, 1979), p. 57.

10 Raymond Williams goes so far as to say that a true pictorial analogy with the 'deliberate exclusion or devaluing of all or any referential meaning' in poetry would be 'a decision by painters to give up paint'. R. Williams, *The Politics of Modernism, Against the New Conformists*, ed. Tony Pinkney (London: Verso, 1989), p. 69. Apollinaire's projected title for his collection *Calligrammes*, 'I too am a Painter', is in fact justified less by his picture poems, where drawing in words proves an awkward half-way house between poetry and painting, than in those poems which utilize *linguistic* techniques of juxtaposition intended to parallel the 'simultanist' aesthetic of the Cubists and Delaunay. The linguistic signified plays a far greater role in these poems than does the figurative object in Delaunay, and its resources prove invaluable in establishing connections with the painting, as can be seen for instance in the colour imagery of the poem 'Les Fenêtres', inspired by Delaunay's paintings of the same name.

11 The concrete poetry movement was co-founded in the 1950s by Eric Gomringer in Switzerland and the Noigandres group in Brazil. Letterist poetry was founded by Isidore Isou in Paris in 1942. Pierre Garnier founded the Spatialist movement in Paris in the sixties. See D. Seaman, *Concrete Poetry in France* (Ann Arbor, mi: UMI Research Press, 1981).

12 M. Lewis Shaw, 'Concrete and Abstract Poetry: The World as Text and the Text as World', *Visible Language*, 23 (1989), p. 29 and p. 34. It is also the case, however, that concrete poetry can work in very different ways, and can suggest the invisible rather than the visible or tangible.

13 Seaman, *Concrete Poetry*, p. 271.

14 Garnier, *Spatialisme et poésie concrète* (Paris: Garnier, 1968), p. 23.

15 L. Gumpel, *'Concrete' Poetry from East and West Germany* (London: Yale University Press, 1976), p. 102.

16 W. Steiner, '*Res Poetica*: The Problematics of the Concrete Program', *New Literary History*, 12 (1981), p. 537.

17 M. Lewis Shaw, 'Concrete and Abstract Poetry', pp. 29–30. Shaw in fact cites 'Un coup de Dés' as an example of abstract poetry. See also W. Bohn, 'Marius de Zayas and abstraction' in W. Bohn, *The Aesthetics of Visual Poetry 1914–1928* (Cambridge University Press, 1986), pp. 185–203. On the concept of abstract poetry in relation to Kandinsky, see R. Sheppard, 'Kandinsky's Early Aesthetic Theory: Some Examples of Its Influence and some Implications for the Theory and Practice of Abstract Poetry', *Journal of European Studies*, 5 (1975), pp. 19–40. This question is also discussed by H. Brinkmann in his excellent study of Kandinsky's poetry, 'Wassily Kandinsky als Dichter' (Ph.D., University of Cologne, 1980). The uses of the term 'concrete' and 'abstract' with reference to Kandinsky are complicated by the fact that Kandinsky was increasingly unhappy with the application of the epithet 'abstract' to painting, and proposed using instead the terms 'real' (*KCWA*, p. 785) and 'concrete' (*KCWA*, p. 817).

18 *De Stijl* also published works by Schwitters, Arp and Ball.

19 'Manifesto II from *De Stijl* 1920; Literature', in J. Baljeu, *Theo van Doesburg* (London: Studio Vista, 1974), pp. 10–11.

20 Van Doesburg is critical of what he sees as the role of language as an intermediary between the writer and the reader, but he is particularly admiring of the visual ('beeldend') properties of their poetry. 'Mallarmé and Rimbaud already express themselves more visually [*beeldend*] in poetry, creating images in the word. They search, in order to find at the correct moment, the contrasting word which totally characterizes their mental perception. They also know how to be silent at the correct moment. They create wordless poetry . . . They break the prosody and render every logical continuing movement of our brains impossible. They are mental materialists because they recognize the identity of letter and spirit.' 'Inleiding tot de nieuwe Verskunst', *De Stijl*, 4 (1921), p. 24 (translation mine).

21 P. Mondrian, *Neue Gestaltung* (Berlin: Florian Kupferberg Verlag, 1974), p. 21. I am translating here from the German version of this essay, which was published in German by the Bauhaus in 1925. An English translation of the French version of the essay can be found in *MCWA*, pp. 132–47.

22 *Ibid.*, p. 17.

23 *Ibid.*, p. 18.

24 On Kandinsky and Dada, see R. Sheppard, 'Kandinsky's Early Aesthetic Theory', and for a fruitful discussion of *Sounds*, including relations between image and text, see R. Sheppard, 'Kandinsky's *Klänge*: An Interpretation', *German Life and Letters*, 33 (1979–80), pp. 134–46, and R. Sheppard, 'Kandinsky's *œuvre* 1900–14: The *avant-garde* as rear guard', *Word and Image*, 6 (1990), pp. 41–67. On

this topic, and also on the relation between Kandinsky's poetry and Expressionism, Futurism and Symbolism, see H. Brinkmann, *Wassily Kandinsky als Dichter*.

25 Pound, cited in Sheppard, 'Kandinsky's Early Aesthetic Theory', p. 25.

26 Symbolist painting is currently less fashionable than either Impressionism or abstraction, a situation which can be explained at least in part by the prominence of iconography drawn from 'literary' contexts with which many late twentieth-century spectators are unfamiliar.

27 Letter to Monet, 18 June 1888, dclxiii, *Correspondance* III, p. 212. According to Valéry, what attracted Mallarmé to Monet was 'la merveille d'une transposition *sensuelle et spirituelle* consommée sur la toile'. Cited in J. Kearns, 'Symbolist Landscapes' (Ph.D. University of Warwick, 1976), p. 198, emphasis mine. Monet himself had no Symbolist aspirations, but his assertion that landscape is undermined by constant variations of light and air corresponds interestingly to the features of Impressionist painting singled out by Mallarmé. See P. H. Tucker, *Monet in the '90's, The Series Paintings* (London: Museum of Fine Arts, Boston/Yale University Press, 1989), pp. 102–3.

28 Cited in W. Fowlie, 'Monet and the Painters of his Age', *The Southern Review*, 2 (1966), p. 545.

29 'The Impressionists and Edouard Manet', in P. Florence, *Mallarmé, Manet and Redon, Visual and Aural Signs and the Generation of Meaning* (Cambridge University Press, 1986), pp. 11–21. This article was published in English, in a translation approved by Mallarmé: the original is lost. Although these lines were written about Manet, Monet was far more radical in the respects which Mallarmé describes, and the late Monet is often seen as a precursor of abstraction. (Note Kandinsky's response to Monet's *Haystack* painting, cited in chapter 1 above.) There would be a great deal more to say about the relationship between Mallarmé and Monet. See, for instance, Tucker, *Monet in the '90s*, pp. 101–4; J. Kearns, *Symbolist Landscapes, The Place of Painting in the Poetry and Criticism of Mallarmé and his Circle* (London: Modern Humanities Research Association, 1989) pp. 46–7; and J. House, *Monet, Nature into Art* (London: Yale University Press, 1986), pp. 223–5.

30 S. Bernard, 'Rimbaud, Proust et les impressionnistes', *Revue des Sciences Humaines*, 78 (1955), pp. 261–2.

31 This phenomenon raises interesting questions about differences over time between receivers' adaptation to innovations in different mediums. These remarks apply less to Symbolist painting, especially to pictures such as those of Redon, whose strangely disturbing qualities are unaffected by changing habits of perception.

32 C. Greenberg, 'Towards a Newer Laocoon', *Partisan Review*, 7 (1940), p. 303.

33 *Ibid.*, p. 307.

34 'The arts lie safe now, each within its "legitimate" boundaries, and free trade has been replaced by autarchy' (*ibid.*, p. 305). The

analogy with power here is significant: I have argued elsewhere that genre boundaries are charged with ideological implications. See my 'Mallarmé as "Maître": The (En)gendering of Genre in "Un coup de Dés"', *Journal of the Institute of Romance Studies*, 1 (1992), pp. 439–52.

35 See M. Pakenham, 'Et le Splendide Hôtel fut bâti dans le chaos de glaces et de nuit du pôle', in *Parade sauvage, colloque no 2, Rimbaud à la loupe* (Charleville-Mezières: Musée-Bibliothèque Rimbaud, 1990), pp. 157–63. Riffaterre remarks that 'l'hôtel de luxe, institution qui se développe sous le Second Empire, est au centre d'une nouvelle thématique du spectacle du Beau proposé au regard'. See M. Riffaterre, 'Sur la sémiotique de l'obscurité en poésie', *The French Review*, 55 (1982), p. 631.

36 On this context of the *Illuminations*, especially in relation to the 'parc Second Empire', the 'grand magasin' and the 'Expositions Universelles', see Y. Vadé, 'Le Paysan de Londres', *Revue d'Histoire Littéraire de la France*, 92 (1992), pp. 951–66, and on the influence of the 'grande ville' in specifically visual terms, see D. Scott, 'La ville illustrée dans les *Illuminations* de Rimbaud', *Revue d'Histoire Littéraire de la France*, 92 (1992), pp. 967–81.

37 P. Buvik, 'Les Villes de Rimbaud. Poésie et thématique des descriptions urbaines dans les *Illuminations*', *Parade sauvage*, 5 (1988), p. 83. The utopian aspect of the work of all four poets and painters will be discussed in chapter 6 below.

38 Cited in *ibid.*, p. 82.

39 Cited in S. Bernard, *Mallarmé et la musique* (Paris: Nizet, 1959), p. 66.

40 Cited in G. Delfel, *L'Esthétique de Stéphane Mallarmé* (Paris: Flammarion, 1951), p. 116.

41 Cited in Bernard, *Mallarmé et la musique*, p. 44. Note the association of music and architecture, a characteristic which we have observed in the *Illuminations*, in Kandinsky's *Accord réciproque* and in Mondrian's *Broadway Boogie-Woogie*. Kandinsky makes several references to Beethoven in his theoretical writings.

42 See P. Gilbert Lewis, *The Aesthetics of Stéphane Mallarmé in Relation to His Public* (New Jersey: Associated University Presses, 1976), p. 92.

43 *Feuillets* are cited here in the text as numbered by Scherer in *Le 'Livre' de Mallarmé* (Paris: Gallimard, 1977). There are different versions of these symmetrical structures. Compare *feuillet* 127 (A). Mary Lewis Shaw's *Performance in the Texts of Mallarmé, The Passage From Art to Ritual*, which appeared as this manuscript was going to press, comprises a detailed discussion of the 'Livre' as 'performance'.

44 B. Marchal, *La Religion de Mallarmé* (Paris: Corti, 1988), p. 506.

45 'Mallarmé et la transformation esthétique du langage', *French Forum*, 15 (1990), pp. 203–20.

46 Both Mallarmé and Kandinsky were also interested in less exalted means of integrating art and life. In 1874, Mallarmé produced, single-handed, eight numbers of a fashion magazine, *La Dernière Mode*. His poems inscribed on fans have already been referred to in chapter 3 above. On the 'day to day' aspect of Mallarmé's aesthetics, see R. Dragonetti, *Un fantôme dans le kiosque, Mallarmé et l'esthétique du*

quotidien (Paris: Seuil, 1992). As a young artist, Kandinsky designed dresses for Gabriele Münter and painted brightly coloured pictures on furniture. See *Kandinsky und München, Begegnungen und Wandlungen 1896–1914*, ed. A. Zweite (Munich: Prestel, 1982), pp. 244 and 316–18.

47 See A. Teichmann, 'Klang–Farbe–Ausdruck: Zum synästhetischen Prinzip bei Wassili Kandinsky und Arnold Schoenberg', *Beiträge zur Kunstwissenschaft*, 32 (1990), pp. 204–13. For a discussion of Kandinsky's relation to Schönberg with reference to Laban's theories of dance, see V. Preston Dunlop, 'Laban, Schönberg, Kandinsky', in *Danses tracées, dessins et notations des chorégraphes* (Paris: Dis-Voir, 1991), pp. 133–50.

48 See R.-C. Washton Long, 'Kandinsky and Abstraction: The Role of the Hidden Image', *Artforum*, 11 (1972), pp. 42–4.

49 See P. Weiss, 'Kandinsky: Symbolist Poetics and Theater in Munich', *Pantheon*, 35 (1977), pp. 209–18 and P. Weiss, *Kandinsky in Munich: The Formative Jugendstil Years* (Princeton University Press, 1979), chapter 9.

50 For background to this, see S. Alyson Stein, 'Kandinsky and Abstract Stage Composition, Practice and Theory, 1909–12', *Art Journal*, 43 (1983), pp. 61–6; J. Hahl-Koch, 'Kandinsky et le théâtre – Quelques aperçus', in *Wassily Kandinsky à Munich, Collection Städtische Galerie im Lenbachhaus* (Munich: Prestel Verlag/Städtische Galerie im Lenbachhaus, 1976), pp. 53–9, and N. Kandinsky, *Kandinsky et moi* (Paris: Flammarion, 1978), pp. 178–81. *Yellow Sound* and a fragment of *Violet* are published in the English edition of the *Complete Writings on Art*. *Green Sound*, *Black and White* and *Violet* are published in W. Kandinsky, *Ecrits complets*, 2 vols., ed. P. Sers (Paris: Denoël-Gonthier, 1975), III, *La Synthèse des arts*. *Violet* was performed for the first time during the Festival of Expressionism in Manchester in 1992.

51 See C. Derouet and J. Boissel, *Kandinsky, œuvres de Vassily Kandinsky (1866–1944)* (Paris: Centre Georges Pompidou, 1985), pp. 232–3 and reproductions, pp. 308–17.

52 See *ibid.*, pp. 250–4.

53 See C. Poling, *Kandinsky: Russian and Bauhaus Years, 1915–33* (New York: Solomon R. Guggenheim Museum, 1983), pp. 80–1 and *RB*, pls. 999–1001.

54 Cited in J. Langner, ''Gegensätze und Widersprüche: dass ist unsere Harmonie'' – Zu Kandinsky's expressionistischer Abstraktion', *Kandinsky und München*, p. 106.

55 See, for instance, B. M. Galeyev, 'The Fire of *Prometheus*: Music-Kinetic Experiments in the USSR', *Leonardo*, 21 (1988), pp. 383–96.

56 Before dancing, Palucca would relax by meditating in front of a diamond-shaped Mondrian composition. See H. Henkels, 'The Other Side of a Still Life', in *Mondriaan/Aanwinsten/Acquisitions 1979–1988*, ed. H. Henkels (The Hague: Gemeentemuseum, 1988), p. 14.

57 Cited in J. Hahl-Koch, 'Kandinsky et le théâtre', *Wassily Kandinsky à Munich*, p. 54.

58 N. Kandinsky, *Kandinsky et moi*, p. 181. Note Mallarmé's interest in the same symphony.

59 See J. Lassaigne, *Kandinsky: A Biographical and Critical Study* (Geneva: Skira, 1964), p. 10.

60 Cited in C. Poling, *Kandinsky-Unterricht am Bauhaus: Farbenseminär und Analytisches Zeichnen* (Weingarten: Kunstverlag Weingarten, 1982), p. 81, translation mine. For reproductions, see *RB*, pls. 999–1001.

61 See N. Troy, 'Piet Mondrian's Atelier', *Arts Magazine*, 53 (1978), p. 85, and M. Seuphor, *Piet Mondrian, Life and Work* (London: Thames and Hudson, 1957), p. 194. Mondrian also collaborated with Seuphor on a picture-poem, for which Seuphor provided the text (see Seuphor, *Piet Mondrian*, pp. 194–5), and he wrote to van Doesburg in 1919 that he was writing a play inspired by his studio design. See V. Locatelli, 'Mondrian e De Stijl: tra "astrazzione" e Architettura', *Abitare*, 290 (1990), p. 215.

62 It is noteworthy that all four poets and artists accord a privileged role to dance. Arguably dance, even more than music, is the prototype of the avant-garde art work.

63 See, for instance, H. Holtzman, *Mondrian, The Process Works* (New York: The Pace Gallery, 1983), pp. 3–5; Troy, 'Piet Mondrian's Atelier'; H. Henkels, *Mondrian, From Figuration to Abstraction* (London: Thames and Hudson, 1988); N. Troy, *The De Stijl Environment* (London: MIT Press, 1983), pp. 135–41; M. Friedman, 'Mondrian's Paris Atelier, 1926–31', in *De Stijl: 1917–1931, Visions of Utopia*, ed. M. Friedman (Oxford: Phaidon, 1982), pp. 80–5, and Locatelli, 'Mondrian e De Stijl', pp. 211–15.

64 Locatelli, *ibid.*, p. 213.

65 Mondrian, cited in Troy, 'Piet Mondrian's Atelier', p. 84.

66 Cited in *ibid.*, p. 87.

67 W. Nicholson, B. Hepworth, N. Gabo, H. Read, B. Nicholson, N. Gabo, 'Reminiscences of Mondrian', *Studio International*, 172 (1966), p. 288.

68 Cited in Locatelli, 'Mondrian e De Stijl', p. 213.

69 Cited in Henkels, *Mondrian*, p. 185.

70 See Troy, 'Piet Mondrian's Atelier', p. 86, and Henkels, *Mondrian*, p. 191.

71 Holtzman, *Mondrian*, p. 5.

72 N. Troy, 'Piet Mondrian's Design for the "Salon de Madame B . . . à Dresden"', *Art Bulletin*, 62 (1980), p. 642.

73 See Holtzman, *Mondrian*, p. 16.

74 Cited in Troy, 'Piet Mondrian's Design', p. 643.

75 See Y.-A. Bois, 'Mondrian et la théorie de l'architecture', *Revue de l'Art*, 53 (1981), pp. 40–2.

76 See letter from Mondrian to J. J. P. Oud, one of the architects associated with De Stijl, cited in Bois, 'Mondrian', p. 45.

77 See letter from Mondrian to Oud, cited in *ibid.*, p. 46.

78 A. Bowie, *Aesthetics and Subjectivity from Kant to Nietzsche* (Manchester University Press, 1990), p. 47.

79 J.-Cl. Lebenstejn, 'Mondrian, la fin de l'art', *Critique*, 39 (1983), p. 895.

80 Cited in R. Levitas, *The Concept of Utopia* (London: Philip Allan, 1990), p. 148.

81 According to Peirce, 'every thought is a sign' (1.538), and this leads to 'infinite regression' (1.339).

82 These interpretants are 'final' in that they represent 'that which *would finally* be decided if consideration of the matter were carried so far that an ultimate opinion were reached' (VIII.184). On Peirce's categories of interpretants, see V.491, VIII.184, VIII.314, VIII.343. On this topic, see U. Eco, *The Role of the Reader* (Bloomington: Indiana University Press, 1979), pp. 191–9 and D. Greenlee, *Peirce's Concept of Sign* (The Hague: Mouton, 1973), pp. 117 ff.

83 See P. A. Roedl, 'Abstrakte Kunst und der Traum von der rezeptiven Gesellschaft', in *Festschrift Klaus Lankheit* (Cologne: Du Mont Schauberg, 1973), p. 73.

84 *De Stijl*, ed. H. L. C. Jaffé (London: Thames and Hudson, 1970), p. 174.

85 Kandinsky was involved in founding several artists' groups (the 'Phalanx', the 'Neue Künstlervereinigung', the 'Blue Rider') as well as initiating and participating in many official artistic enterprises in Russia from 1918 to 1921 and teaching at the Bauhaus from 1922 to 1933. Mondrian co-founded the 'Modern Art Circle' in Amsterdam in 1910 and was involved with the 'De Stijl' group from 1917 to 1927; in 1930 he exhibited with the 'Cercle et Carré' group in Paris and contributed to its journal. Differences of opinion of course frequently existed within such groups.

86 The 'new man' was a central concept of Expressionist aesthetics.

87 A. Kittang, *Discours et jeu* (Grenoble: Presses Universitaires de Grenoble, 1975), p. 344.

88 H. L. C. Jaffé, *De Stijl, 1917–31, The Dutch Contribution to Modern Art* (London: Harvard University Press, 1986), p. 132.

89 See passage cited in P. Overy, *De Stijl* (London: Thames and Hudson, 1991), p. 33.

90 Space precludes detailed treatment of this background here. Interest in anarchist and utopian ideas was widespread amongst intellectuals and artists in the Symbolist period. See, in particular, R. D. Sonn, *Anarchism and Cultural Politics in Fin de Siècle France* (London: University of Nebraska Press, 1989). Rimbaud's connections with the anarchist Vermersch are discussed in A. Jouffroy, *Arthur Rimbaud et la liberté libre* (Monaco, Editions du Rocher, 1991). On the vexed question of Rimbaud and the Commune, the reader is referred to S. Murphy, *Le Premier Rimbaud* (Lyon: Presses Universitaires de Lyon/ CNRS, 1990). See also K. Ross, *The Emergence of Social Space: Rimbaud and the Paris Commune* (London: Macmillan, 1988). On Mallarmé and anarchism, see A. Lebois, 'Stéphane Mallarmé et la politique', *Mercure de France*, 374 (1948), pp. 70–8 and J. Montférier, 'Symbolisme et anarchie', *Revue d'Histoire Littéraire de la France*, 65 (1965), pp. 233–8. On Kandinsky and anarchism, see Y. F. Heibel, '"They Danced on Volcanoes": Kandinsky's Breakthrough to Abstraction, the German Avant-garde and the Eve of the First World War', *Art History*, 12 (1989), pp. 342–61, R. Sheppard, 'Kandinsky's *œuvre* 1900–14: The *avant-garde* as rear-guard', *Word and Image*, 6 (1990), pp. 41–67; R.-C. Washton Long, 'Occultism, Anar-

chism and Abstraction: Kandinsky's Art of the Future', *Art Journal*, 46 (1987), pp. 38–45, and R.-C. Washton Long, 'Expressionism, Abstraction and the Search for Utopia in Germany', in *The Spiritual in Art: Abstract Painting 1890–1985*, ed. M. Tuchman (New York: Abbeville Press, 1986), pp. 201–17. See also D. Kuspit, 'Utopian Protest in Early Abstract Art', *Art Journal*, 29 (1970), pp. 430–7. On the political climates in Germany and Holland which favoured both anarchist ideas and the growth of artists' collectives, see P. Jelavich, 'München als Kulturzentrum: Politik und die Künste', in *Kandinsky und München*, p. 25; R. Heller, 'Confronting Contradictions: Artists and their Institutions in Wilhelmine and Weimar Germany', in *Art in Germany 1909–1936, From Expressionism to Resistance*, ed. R. Heller (Munich: Prestel, 1990), pp. 17–24, and Jaffé, *De Stijl*, pp. 76–7.

91 On the political dimension of Rimbaud's poetry, see, in particular, S. Murphy, *Le Premier Rimbaud* and *Rimbaud et la ménagerie impériale* (Lyon: Presses Universitaires de Lyon/CNRS, 1991).

92 See A. Jouffroy, *Arthur Rimbaud et la liberté libre*, and *Arthur Rimbaud, œuvre-vie*, ed. A. Borer (Evreux: Arléa, 1991).

93 See Henkels, *Mondrian*, p. 210.

94 'Je ne pense pas qu'on puisse se servir d'arme plus efficace que la littérature', cited in *Correspondance*, VI, p. 287. On this subject, see also L. Hill, 'Blanchot and Mallarmé', *Modern Language Notes*, 105 (1990), pp. 908 and 913. Compare Mondrian's comment to van Doesburg in sending him his article 'The Manifestation of Neo-Plasticism in Music': 'Enclosed is another bombshell I would like to load into your gun ... Think how people will be appalled to see everything shot away' (*MCWA*, p. 148).

95 Letter to Villiers, 30 September 1867, *Correspondance*, I, p. 261.

96 On the background to this idea and the move to a 'modèle aristocratique', see B. Marchal, *La Religion de Mallarmé* (Paris: Corti, 1988), p. 537. On Mallarmé and artistic aristocracy, see also K. Newmark, 'Beneath the Lace: Mallarmé, the State, and the Foundation of Letters', *Yale French Studies*, 77 (1990), pp. 243–75, and J.-P. Sartre, *Mallarmé, la lucidité et sa face d'ombre* (Paris: Gallimard, 1986).

97 See, for instance, A. Kittang, *Discours et jeu*, J.-L. Baudry, 'Le Texte de Rimbaud', *Tel quel* (1968), pp. 46–53, and J. Kristeva, *La Révolution du langage poétique* (Paris: Seuil, 1974).

98 Cited in A. Guyaux, *Duplicitées de Rimbaud* (Paris/Geneva: Champion/Slatkine, 1991), p. 202.

99 On this topic, see A. J. Ahearn, 'Explosions of the Real: Rimbaud's Ecstatic and Political Subversions', *Stanford French Review*, 9 (1985), pp. 71–81.

100 See L. Frappier-Mazur, 'Narcisse travesti: poétique et idéologie dans *La Dernière mode* de Mallarmé', *French Forum*, 11 (1986), pp. 41–57.

101 W. J. T. Mitchell, *Iconology, Image, Text, Ideology* (London: University of Chicago Press, 1986), p. 193. Compare comments in chapter 1, p. 19 above, concerning Derrida's attribution of the effects of desire to the text itself.

Select bibliography

IMAGINATION, AESTHETICS, ART THEORY

Arguelles, J. A. *Charles Henry and the Formation of a Psychophysical Aesthetic*. University of Chicago Press, 1972.

Bachelard, G. *La Poétique de l'espace*. Paris: Presses Universitaires de France, 1958.

La Poétique de la rêverie. Paris: Presses Universitaires de France, 1961.

Baudelaire, Ch. *Oeuvres complètes* (2 vols., ed. Cl. Pichois, Bibliothèque de la Pléiade). Paris: Gallimard, 1975–6.

Baumgarten, A. *Meditationes Philosophicae de Nonnullis ad Poema Pertinentibus* (trans. K. Aschenbrenner and W. B. Holther). Berkeley: University of California Press, 1954.

Bernstein, J. *The Fate of Art: Aesthetic Alienation from Kant to Adorno and Derrida*. Cambridge: Polity Press, 1992.

Bowie, A. *Aesthetics and Subjectivity from Kant to Nietzsche*. Manchester University Press, 1990.

Bru, Ch.-P. *Esthétique de l'abstraction*. Paris: Presses Universitaires de France, 1955.

Engell, J. *The Creative Imagination, Enlightenment to Romanticism*. Harvard University Press, 1981.

Foucault, M. 'Introduction', L. Binswanger, *Le Rêve et l'existence*. Paris: Desclée, 1956, pp. 9–128.

Garelli, J. *La Gravitation poétique*. Paris: Mercure de France, 1960.

Hegel, G. W. F. *Vorlesungen über die Asthetik*. Stuttgart: Reclam, 1971.

Hegel's Aesthetics (2 vols., trans. T. M. Knox). Oxford: Clarendon Press, 1975.

Henry, Ch. 'Introduction à une esthétique scientifique', *La Revue Contemporaine*, 2 (1885), pp. 441–69.

Jay, M. 'In the Empire of the Gaze: Foucault and the Denigration of Vision in 20th Century French Thought', in *Postmodernism*, ICA Documents 4. London: Institute of Contemporary Arts, 1986, pp. 19–24.

Kearney, R. *The Wake of Imagination, Ideas of Creativity in Western Culture*. London: Hutchinson, 1988.

Poetics of Imagining from Husserl to Lyotard. London: Harper Collins, 1991.

Lankheit, K. 'Die Frühromantik und die Grundlagen der Gegenstandslosen Malerei', *Neue Heidelberger Jahrbücher* (1951), pp. 55–90.

271

Lipps, T. *Asthetik: Psychologie des Schönen und der Kunst* (2 vols.).
    Hamburg: Leopold Voss, 1923 and 1920 (first pub. 1903 and 1906).
Lyotard, J.-F. *Leçons sur l'analytique du sublime.* Paris: Galilée, 1991.
    The Postmodern Condition, A Report on Knowledge (trans. G. Bennington
    and B. Massumi). Manchester University Press, 1984 (first pub.
    1979).
Merleau-Ponty, M. *L'Œil et l'esprit.* Paris: Gallimard, 1964.
    La Prose du monde. Paris: Gallimard, 1969.
Mitchell, W. J. T. *Iconology, Image, Text, Ideology.* University of Chicago
    Press, 1986.
    'Ut Pictura Theoria: Abstract Painting and the Repression of Lan-
    guage', *Critical Inquiry,* 15 (1988/9), pp. 348–71.
Mitry, J. *Esthétique et psychologie du cinéma* (2 vols.). Paris: Editions
    Universitaires, 1963–5.
Poppe, B. *Alexander Gottlieb Baumgarten: Seine Bedeutung und Stellung in der
    Leibnitz-Wölffischen Philosophie und Seine Beziehungen zu Kant.* Borna-
    Leipzig: R. Noske, 1907.
Ricœur, P. 'The Metaphorical Process as Cognition, Imagination and
    Feeling', *Critical Inquiry,* 5 (1978–9), pp. 143–59.
Sartre, J.-P. *L'Imaginaire, psychologie phénoménologique de l'imagination.*
    Paris: Gallimard, 1940.
Todorov, T. *Théories du symbole.* Paris: Seuil, 1977.
Tate Gallery *Towards a New Art, Essays on the Background to Abstract Art
    1910–20.* London: The Tate Gallery, 1980.
Weiskel, T. *The Romantic Sublime: Studies in the Structure and Psychology of
    Transcendence.* Baltimore: Johns Hopkins University Press, 1976.
Williams, R. *The Politics of Modernism, Against the New Conformists.*
    London: Verso, 1989.
Worringer, W. *Abstraktion und Einfühlung.* Munich: Piper and Co.,
    1908.

KANT

Heidegger, M. *Kant and the Problem of Metaphysics.* London: Indiana
    University Press, 1972.
Kant, I. *Anthropology from a Practical Point of View* (trans. V. L. Dowdell).
    London: Feffer and Simons, 1978.
    Critique of Judgement (trans. J. H. Bernard). New York: Hafner Press,
    1951.
    Kant's Critique of Aesthetic Judgement (trans. J. C. Meredith). Oxford,
    Clarendon Press, 1952.
    Critique of Pure Reason (trans. N. Kemp Smith). London: Macmillan,
    1989.

PEIRCE

Peirce, C. S. *Collected Papers of Charles Sanders Peirce* (8 vols., ed. C.
    Hartshorne and P. Weiss, vols. I–VI; ed. A. W. Burks, vols. VII–VIII).
    Cambridge, MA: Harvard University Press, 1931–58.

DERRIDA

Derrida, J. *La Dissémination*. Paris: Seuil, 1972.
  'Economimesis', in S. Agacinski *et al.*, *Mimesis des articulations*. Paris: Aubier-Flammarion, 1975, pp. 57–93.
  L'Écriture et la différance. Paris: Seuil, 1967.
  De la grammatologie. Paris: Minuit, 1967.
  Marges de la philosophie. Paris: Minuit, 1972.
  Positions. Paris: Minuit, 1972.
  La Vérité en peinture. Paris: Flammarion, 1978.
  La Voix et le phénomène. Paris: Presses Universitaires de France, 1967.

POETICS

Bernard, S. *Le Poème en prose de Baudelaire jusqu'à nos jours*. Paris: Nizet, 1959.
Caws M. A. and Riffaterre H. (eds.) *The Prose Poem in France: Theory and Practice*. Columbia University Press, 1983.
Claudel, P. *Oeuvres en prose* (ed. J. Petit and C. Galpérine). Paris: Gallimard, 1965.
Erlich, V. *Russian Formalism, History-Doctrine*. New Haven: Yale University Press, 1981.
Friedrich, H. *The Structure of Modern Poetry from the Mid Nineteenth Century to the Mid Twentieth Century*. Evanston, IL: Northwestern University Press, 1974.
Genette, G. *Figures II*. Paris: Seuil, 1969.
Iser, W. 'Feigning in Fiction', in *The Identity of the Literary Text* (ed. M. J. Valdés and O. Miller). University of Toronto Press, 1985, pp. 204–30.
Jakobson, R. 'The Contours of the Safe Conduct', in *Semiotics of Art* (ed. L. Matejka and I. R. Titunik). Cambridge, MA: MIT Press, 1976, pp. 188–97.
  'Closing Statement: Linguistics and Poetics', in *Style in Language* (ed. T. A. Sebeok). Cambridge, MA: MIT Press, 1960, pp. 350–77.
  'Entretien avec Roman Jakobson', in *Jakobson* (ed. R. Georgin). Lausanne: Editions l'Age d'Homme, 1978, pp. 11–28.
  Questions de poétique. Paris: Seuil, 1973.
Meschonnic, H. *Critique du rythme: anthropologie historique du langage*. Paris: Verdier, 1982.
Morier, M. *Dictionnaire de poétique et de rhétorique*. Paris: Presses Universitaires de France, 1961.
Riffaterre, M. *Semiotics of Poetry*. London: Methuen, 1980.
Scott, D. *Pictorialist Poetics: Poetry and the Visual Arts in 19th-Century France*. Cambridge University Press, 1988.
Tompkins, J. P. (ed.) *Reader-Response Criticism, From Formalism to Post-Structuralism*. London: Johns Hopkins University Press, 1980.
Valéry, P. *Cahiers* (2 vols., ed. J. Robinson-Valéry). Paris: Gallimard, 1973–4.
Worton, M. and Still, J. (eds.) *Intertextuality: Theories and Practices*. Manchester University Press, 1990.

Žirmunskij, M. *Introduction to Metrics, The Theory of Verse.* The Hague: Mouton, 1966.

SPACE AND TIME IN POETRY AND PAINTING

Arnheim, R. 'A Stricture on Space and Time', *Critical Inquiry*, 4 (1977/8), pp. 645–55.
Genette, G. *Figures II.* Paris: Seuil, 1969.
Greenberg, C. 'Towards a Newer Laocoon', *Partisan Review*, 7 (1940), pp. 296–310.
Holtz, W. 'Spatial Form in Modern Literature: A Reconsideration', *Critical Inquiry*, 4 (1977/8), pp. 276–80.
Lessing, G. E. *Laocoön, Nathan the Wise, Minna von Barnhelm* (trans. W. A. Steel). London: Dent, 1970.
McClain, J. 'Time in the Visual Arts: Lessing and Modern Criticism', *Journal of Aesthetics and Art Criticism*, 43 (1985), pp. 41–58.
Mitchell, W. J. T. 'Spatial Form in Literature: Towards a General Theory', in *The Language of Images* (ed. W. J. T. Mitchell). University of Chicago Press, 1980, pp. 271–301.
Reynolds, D. A. 'Rhythmic Structures and Imaginary Space in Rimbaud, Mallarmé, Kandinsky and Mondrian', in *Word and Image Interactions* (ed. M. Heusser). Basel: Wiese Verlag, 1993, pp. 143–56.

SPATIAL AND CONCRETE POETRY

Garnier, P. *Spatialisme et poésie concrète.* Paris: Garnier, 1968.
Gumpel, L. *'Concrete' Poetry from East and West Germany.* London: Yale University Press, 1976.
Seaman, D. *Concrete Poetry in France.* Ann Arbor, MI: UMI Research Press, 1981.
Shaw, M. Lewis 'Concrete and Abstract Poetry: The World as Text and the Text as World', *Visible Language*, 23 (1989), pp. 29–44.
Steiner, W. '*Res Poetica*: The Problematics of the Concrete Program', *New Literary History*, 12 (1981), pp. 529–45.
Van Doesburg, T. (Bonset, I. K.) 'Inleiding tot de nieuwe Verskunst', *De Stijl*, 4 (1921), pp. 24–6.

RIMBAUD

Ahearn, A. J. 'Explosions of the Real: Rimbaud's Ecstatic and Political Subversions', *Stanford French Review*, 9 (1985), pp. 71–81.
Bernard, S. 'La palette de Rimbaud', *Cahiers de l'Association Internationale des Etudes Françaises*, 12 (1960), pp. 105–19.
'Rimbaud, Proust et les impressionistes', *Revue des Sciences Humaines*, 78 (1955), pp. 257–62.
Broome, P. 'From Vision to Catastrophe in Rimbaud's *Illuminations*', *Forum for Modern Language Studies*, 15 (1979), pp. 361–79.
Buvik, B. 'Les Villes de Rimbaud. Poésie et thématique des descriptions urbaines dans les *Illuminations*', *Parade sauvage*, 5 (1988), pp. 76–87.

Dominicy, M. '"Les Ponts", analyse linguistique', in *Lectures de Rimbaud* (ed. A. Guyaux). Université de Bruxelles, 1982, pp. 109–23.

Felsch, A. *Arthur Rimbaud, Poetische Struktur und Kontext: Paradigmatische Analyse und Interpretationen einiger Illuminations*. Bonn: Bouvier, 1977.

Fongaro, A. *Les Cahiers de littératures, sur Rimbaud, lire 'Illuminations'*. Université de Toulouse-Le Mirail, 1985.

Frohock, W. M. *Rimbaud's Poetic Practice: Image and Theme in the Major Poems*. Cambridge, MA: Harvard University Press, 1963.

Gengoux, J. *La Pensée poétique de Rimbaud*. Paris: Nizet, 1950.

Guyaux, A. *Duplicités de Rimbaud*. Paris/Geneva: Champion/Slatkine, 1991.

    Poétique du fragment: essai sur les 'Illuminations' de Rimbaud. Neuchâtel: La Baconnière, 1986.

Houston, J. P. *Patterns of Thought in Rimbaud and Mallarmé*. Lexington, KY: French Forum, 1980.

Hubert, R. Riese 'La Technique de la peinture dans le poème en prose', *Cahiers de l'Association Internationale des Etudes Françaises*, 18 (1966), pp. 169–78.

Kittang, A. *Discours et jeu: essai d'analyse des textes d'Arthur Rimbaud*. Presses Universitaires de Grenoble, 1975.

Kloepfer, R. and Oomen, U. *Sprachliche Konstituenten Moderner Dichtung: Entwurf einer Descriptiven Poetik*. Bad Homberg: Atheneum, 1970.

Little, R. 'Rimbaud's "Mystique": Some Observations'. *French Studies*, 26 (1972), pp. 285–8.

Macklin, G. M. 'The Theatrical Imagination of Arthur Rimbaud'. *Forum for Modern Language Studies*, 23 (1987), pp. 131–50.

Maranini, L. 'Lo spazio di Rimbaud', *Micromégas*, 9 (1982), pp. 127–53.

Marcotte, G. *La Prose de Rimbaud*. Québec: Boréal, 1989.

Pakenham, M. 'Et le Splendide Hôtel fut bâti dans le chaos de glaces et de nuit du pôle', in *Parade sauvage, colloque no. 2, Rimbaud à la loupe*. Charleville-Mezières: Musée-Bibliothèque Rimbaud, 1990, pp. 157–63.

Plessen, J. 'Stratégies pour une lecture du texte rimbaldien', in *Rimbaud multiple*, Colloque de Cérisy. Gourdon: Bedon/Touzot, 1986, pp. 170–88.

    'Deux fois Rimbaud', *Littérature*, 11 (1973), pp. 102–8.

Reynolds, D. A. '"L'Hallucination des mots": Textual and Imaginary Space in Rimbaud's "Barbare"', *Forum for Modern Language Studies*, 28 (1992), pp. 29–41.

Richard, J.-P. *Poésie et profondeur*. Paris: Seuil, 1955.

Richter, M. 'Note de Mario Richter', in *Les Cahiers de littératures, sur Rimbaud, lire 'Illuminations'* (ed. A. Fongaro). Publications de l'Université de Toulouse-Le Mirail, 1985, p. 76.

Riffaterre, M. 'Interpretation and Undecidability', *New Literary History*, 12 (1981), pp. 227–43.

    'The Making of the Text', in *Identity of the Literary Text* (ed. M. J. Valdés and O. Miller). London: University of Toronto, 1985, pp. 54–70.

    'Rimbaud intertextuel', *Parade sauvage, 'Rimbaud à la loupe'*. Charleville: Musée-Bibliothèque Rimbaud, 1990, pp. 93–105.

'Sur la sémiotique de l'obscurité en poésie: "Promontoire" de Rimbaud', *French Review*, 55 (1982), pp. 625–32.

Rimbaud, A. *Illuminations* (ed. A. Guyaux). Neuchâtel: La Baconnière, 1985.

Illuminations (ed. A. Py). Geneva: Droz, 1967.

Ce que révèle le manuscrit des 'Illuminations' (ed. Cl. Zissmann). Paris: Le bossu Bitor, 1989.

Manuscrits autographes des 'Illuminations' d'Arthur Rimbaud (ed. R. Pierrot). Paris: Ramsay, 1984.

Oeuvres complètes (ed. S. Bernard and A. Guyaux). Paris: Gallimard, 1981.

Scott, D. 'Rimbaud and Boucher: "Fête d'Hiver"', *Journal of European Studies*, 9 (1979), pp. 185–95.

'La Ville illustrée dans les *Illuminations* de Rimbaud', *Revue d'Histoire Littéraire de la France*, 92 (1992), pp. 967–81.

Starkie, E. *Arthur Rimbaud*. London: Faber and Faber, 1961.

Todorov, T. 'Une complication de texte: les *Illuminations*', *Poétique*, 9 (1978), pp. 241–53.

Vadé, Y. 'Le Paysan de Londres'. *Revue d'Histoire Littéraire de la France*, 92 (1992), pp. 951–66.

Wetzel, H. 'Un texte opaque et son interprétation socio-historique: "Barbare" de Rimbaud'. *Romantisme*, 12 (1983), pp. 127–41.

Wing, N. *Present Appearances: Aspects of Poetic Structure in Rimbaud's 'Illuminations'*. Mississippi University, 1974.

'Rimbaud's "Les Ponts", "Parade", "Scènes": The Poem as Performance', *The French Review*, 46 (1972/3), pp. 506–21.

MALLARME

Austin, L. J. 'How ambiguous is Mallarmé? Reflections on the Captive Swan', in *Literature and Society: Studies in 19th and 20th Century French Literature Presented to R. J. North* (ed. C. A. Burns). Birmingham: Goodman, 1980, pp. 112–13.

Bernard, S. *Mallarmé et la musique*. Paris: Nizet, 1959.

Blanchard, G. 'Mallarmé et la typographie', *Techniques Graphiques*, 32–3 (1960), pp. 156–66.

Blanchot, M. *Le Livre à venir*. Paris: Gallimard, 1959.

Bowie, M. *Mallarmé and the Art of Being Difficult*. Cambridge University Press, 1978.

Burt, E. 'Mallarmé's "Sonnet en *yx*": The Ambiguities of Speculation', *Yale French Studies*, 54 (1977), pp. 55–82.

Chadwick, C. 'Mallarmé le Phénix', *French Studies Bulletin*, 25 (1987/8), p. 16.

Chassé, Ch. *Les Clés de Mallarmé*. Paris: Montaigne, 1954.

'Le Thème de Hamlet chez Mallarmé', *Revue des Sciences Humaines*, 78 (1955), pp. 157–69.

Chisholm, A. E. 'Mallarmé: "Le vierge, le vivace"', *French Studies*, 16 (1962), pp. 359–63.

Cohn, R. G. 'Epistemology and Literary Theory', in *Writing in a Modern Temper: Essays on Literature and Thought in Honour of Henri Peyre* (ed. M. A. Caws). Saratoga: Anma Libri, 1984.

Mallarmé's Masterwork, New Findings. The Hague: Mouton, 1966.

'A propos du "Coup de dés"', *Critique*, 38 (1982), pp. 92–3.

Davies, G. *Mallarmé et le drame solaire*. Paris: Corti, 1959.

Delfel, G. *L'Esthétique de Stéphane Mallarmé*. Paris: Flammarion, 1951.

Dragonetti, R. 'La Littérature et la lettre: introduction au "Sonnet en -yx" de Mallarmé', *Lingua e Stile*, 4 (1969), pp. 205–22.

Un Fantôme dans le kiosque, Mallarmé et l'esthétique du quotidien. Paris: Seuil, 1992.

Duplan, P. 'Pour une sémiologie de la lettre', in *L'Espace et la lettre* (ed. A.-M. Christin). Paris: Union Générale d'Editions, 1977, pp. 324–37.

Florence, P. *Mallarmé, Manet and Redon: Visual and Aural Signs and the Generation of Meaning*. Cambridge University Press, 1986.

Frappier-Mazur, L. 'Narcisse travesti: poétique et idéologie dans *La Dernière mode* de Mallarmé', *French Forum*, 11 (1986), pp. 41–57.

Genette, G. 'Bonheur de Mallarmé' in G. Genette, *Figures I*. Paris: Seuil 1966, pp. 91–100.

Hampton, T. 'At the Sign of the Swan', *Romanic Review*, 73 (1982), pp. 438–51.

Houston, J. P. *Patterns of Thought in Rimbaud and Mallarmé*. Lexington, KY: French Forum, 1980.

Johnson, B. *Défigurations du langage poétique, la seconde révolution baudelairienne*. Paris: Flammarion, 1979.

La Charité, V. *The Dynamics of Space: Mallarmé's 'Un Coup de dés jamais n'abolira le hasard'*. Kentucky: French Forum, 1987.

'Mallarmé's *Livre*: The Graphomatics of the Text', *Symposium*, 34 (1980), pp. 249–59.

Langan, J. *Hegel and Mallarmé*. London: University Press of America, 1986.

Lebenstejn, J.-Cl. 'Note relative au "Coup de Dés"', *Critique*, 36 (1980), pp. 633–59.

Léon-Dufour, B. 'Mallarmé et l'alphabet' in *Cahiers de l'Association Internationale des Etudes Françaises*, 27 (1975), pp. 321–6 and discussion 455–60.

Lewis, P. G. *The Aesthetics of Stéphane Mallarmé in Relation to His Public*. New Jersey: Associated University Presses, 1976.

Mallarmé, S. *Oeuvres complètes* (ed. H. Mondor and G. Jean-Aubry, Bibliothèque de la Pléiade). Paris: Gallimard, 1945.

Stéphane Mallarmé, Oeuvres complètes, Poésies (ed. C. P. Barbier and C. G. Millan). Paris: Flammarion, 1983.

'Un coup de Dés' (ed. M. Ronat). Paris: Change Errant/d'Atelier, 1980.

'A Cast of Dice' (trans. N. Crawford). London: Tetrad Press, 1985.

'The Impressionists and Edouard Manet', in P. Florence, *Mallarmé, Manet and Redon, Visual and Aural Signs and the Generation of Meaning*. Cambridge University Press, 1986, pp. 11–21.

Correspondance (11 vols., ed. H. Mondor and J.-P. Richard, vol. I; ed. H. Mondor and L. J. Austin, vols. II and III; ed. L. J. Austin, vols. IV–XI). Paris: Gallimard, 1959–85.

Marchal, B. *La Religion de Mallarmé*. Paris: Corti, 1988.

Mauclair, C. *L'Art en silence*. Paris: Ollendorff, 1901.

Mallarmé chez lui. Paris: Grasset, 1935.

Mihram, D. 'The Abortive Didot/Vollard Edition of *Un coup de Dés*', *French Studies* 33 (1979), pp. 39–56.

Morris, D. Hampton 'Mallarmé and Esoteric Theories of Language', *Language Quarterly*, 18 (1980), pp. 25–6 and p. 32.

Noulet, E. *L'Oeuvre poétique de Stéphane Mallarmé.* Brussels: Jacques Antoine, 1974.

Paz, O. 'Stéphane Mallarmé: Sonnet in "ix"', *Delos*, 4 (1970), pp. 14–28.

Reynolds, D. A. 'Illustration, Present or Absent: Reflecting Reflexivity in Mallarmé's "Sonnet en yx"', *Journal of European Studies*, 19 (1989), pp. 311–29.

'Mallarmé and Hegel, Speculation and the Poetics of Reflection', *French Cultural Studies*, 2 (1991), pp. 71–89.

'Mallarmé et la transformation esthétique du langage, à l'exemple de "Ses purs ongles"', in *French Forum*, 15 (1990), pp. 203–20.

'Mallarmé as "Maître": The (En)gendering of Genre in "Un coup de Dés"', *Journal of the Institute of Romance Studies*, 1 (1992), pp. 439–52.

Richard, J.-P. *L'Univers imaginaire de Mallarmé.* Paris: Seuil, 1961.

'Feu rué, feu scintillé: note sur le fantasme et l'écriture', *Littérature*, 17 (1975), pp. 84–105.

Riffaterre, M. 'La Trace de l'intertexte', *La Pensée, revue de rationalisme moderne*, 215 (1980), pp. 4–18.

'On Deciphering Mallarmé', *The Georgia Review*, 19 (1975), pp. 75–91.

Robb, G. 'The Phoenix of Mallarmé's "Sonnet en -yx"', *French Studies Bulletin*, 24 (1987), pp. 13–15.

Scherer, J. *Le 'Livre' de Mallarmé.* Paris: Gallimard, 1977.

L'Expression littéraire dans l'œuvre de Mallarmé. Paris: Droz, 1947.

Scott, D. *Sonnet Theory and Practice in 19th Century France: Sonnets on the Sonnet.* University of Hull, 1977.

Shaw, M. Lewis, *Performance in the Texts of Mallarmé: The Passage from Art to Ritual.* The Pennsylvania State University Press, 1993.

Thibaudet, A. 'Réflexions sur la littérature: Mallarmé et Rimbaud', *Nouvelle Revue Française*, 18 (1922), pp. 199–206.

Valéry, P. *Ecrits divers sur Stéphane Mallarmé.* Paris: Gallimard, 1950.

CONTEXTS OF SYMBOLISM

Gauguin, P. *Lettres de Gauguin à sa femme et à ses amis* (ed. M. Malingua). Paris: Grasset, 1946.

Kearns, J. *Symbolist Landscapes: The Place of Painting in the Poetry and Criticism of Mallarmé and his Circle.* London: Modern Humanities Research Association, 1989.

Lévi, E. *Histoire de la magie.* Chaumont: éd. de la Maisnie, 1986 (first pub. 1860).

Dogme et rituel de la haute magie. Paris: Germer Baillière, 1861.

Mathieu, P.-L. 'Gustave Moreau – du symbolisme à l'abstraction', *Revue de l'Université de Bruxelles*, Special issue on *Littérature et Beaux-Arts à la Fin du 19e siècle*, 3 (1981), pp. 59–66.

McIntosh, C. *Eliphas Lévi and the French Occult Revival*. London: Rider and Co., 1972.

Mercier, A. *Les Sources ésotériques et occultes de la poésie symboliste 1870–1914* (2 vols.). Paris: Nizet, 1969–74.

Michoud, E. 'La Fin de l'iconographie, une nouvelle rhétorique du sensible', *Les Cahiers du Musée National d'Art Moderne* (1980), pp. 446–54.

Moréas, J. *Les premiers armes du Symbolisme* (ed. M. Pakenham). Exeter University Press, 1973.

Moreau, G. *L'Assembleur de rêves: écrits complets de Gustave Moreau* (ed. P.-L. Mathieu). Fontfroide: Bibliothèque artistique et littérature, 1984.

Redon, O. *A soi-même, Journal (1807–1915)*. Paris: Corti, 1979.

Rookmaaker, H. R. *Synthetist Art Theories: Genesis and Nature of the Ideas on Art of Gauguin and His Circle*. Amsterdam: Swets and Zeitlinger, 1959.

KANDINSKY

Barnett, V. 'Kandinsky and Science: The Introduction of Biological Images in the Paris Period', in *Kandinsky in Paris: 1934–44*. New York: Solomon R. Guggenheim Museum, 1985, pp. 61–87.

'The Essential Unity of Kandinsky's Pictorial Modes', in V. Barnett, *Kandinsky at the Guggenheim*. New York: Abbeville Press, 1983, pp. 19–56.

Bowlt, J. and Washton Long, R.-C. (eds.) *The Life of Vasilii Kandinsky in Russian Art: A Study of On the Spiritual in Art*. Newtonville, MA: Oriental Research Partners, 1980.

Brinkmann, H. *Wassily Kandinsky als Dichter*. Ph.D., University of Cologne, 1980.

Derouet, C. and Boissel, J. *Kandinsky, Oeuvres de Vassily Kandinsky 1866–1944*. Paris: Centre Georges Pompidou, 1985.

Derouet, C. 'Notes et documents sur les dernières années du peintre Vassily Kandinsky', *Les Cahiers du Musée National d'Art Moderne*, Special Issue on *Paris–Paris 1937–1957* (1982), pp. 84–107.

Fineberg, J. D. *Kandinsky in Paris 1906–7*. Ann Arbor, MI: UMI Research Press, 1984 (first pub. 1975).

Floch, J.-M. 'Kandinsky: sémiotique d'un discours non-figuratif', *Communications*, 34 (1981), pp. 135–58.

Galeyev, B. M. 'The Fire of Prometheus: Music-Kinetic Experiments in the USSR'. *Leonardo*, 21 (1988), pp. 383–96.

Garte, E. J. 'Kandinsky's Ideas on Changes in Modern Physics and their Implications for his Development', *Gazette des Beaux-Arts*, 110 (1987), pp. 137–44.

Gordon, D. *Expressionism, Art and Idea*. New Haven and London: Yale University Press, 1987.

Grohmann, W. *Wassily Kandinsky, Life and Work*. London: Thames and Hudson, 1959.

Hahl-Koch, J. 'Kandinsky et le théâtre – Quelques aperçus', in *Wassily Kandinsky à Munich, Collection Städtische Galerie im Lenbachhaus*. Munich: Städtische Galerie im Lenbachhaus, 1976, pp. 53–9.

Kandinsky, N. *Kandinsky et moi*. Paris: Flammarion, 1978.

Kandinsky, W. *Complete Writings on Art* (2 vols., ed. K. Lindsay and P. Vergo). London: Faber and Faber, 1982.

Cours du Bauhaus. Paris: Denoël/Gonthier, 1975.

Ecrits complets (2 vols., ed. P. Sers). Paris: Denoël/Gonthier, 1970–5.

'La Valeur d'une œuvre concrète', *XXe Siècle*, 5–6 (1938), pp. 48–9; supplement to 5–6 (1939), no page numbers.

Kojève, A. 'Deux lettres inédites d'Alexandre Kojève à Vassily Kandinsky', in *Kandinsky, album de l'exposition*. Paris: Centre Georges Pompidou, 1984, pp. 64–70.

Korn, R. *Kandinsky und die Theorie der Abstrakten Malerei*. Berlin: Henschelverlag, 1960.

Long, R.-C. Washton *Kandinsky, The Development of an Abstract Style*. Oxford: Clarendon Press, 1980.

'Kandinsky and Abstraction: The Role of the Hidden Image', *Artforum*, 11 (1972), pp. 42–9.

Messer, T. 'Introduction', *Kandinsky at the Guggenheim* (ed. V. Barnett). New York: Abbeville Press, 1983, pp. 9–17.

Poling, C. *Kandinsky-Unterricht am Bauhaus: Farbenseminär und analytisches Zeichnen*. Weingarten: Kunstverlag Weingarten, 1982.

(*Kandinsky's Teaching at the Bauhaus: Colour Theory and Analytical Drawing*. New York: Rizzoli, 1986.)

Kandinsky: Russian and Bauhaus Years. New York: Solomon R. Guggenheim Museum, 1983.

'Kandinsky au Bauhaus, théorie de la couleur et grammaire picturale', *Change*, special issue on *La peinture*, 26/27 (1976), pp. 194–208.

Roessler, A. *Neu-Dachau: Ludwig Dill, Adolf Hölzel, Arthur Langhammer*. Bielefeld and Leipzig: Velhagen and Klasing, Knackfuss Künstler Monographien, 1905.

Roethel, H. K., in collaboration with J. K. Benjamin, *Kandinsky*. Oxford: Phaidon, 1979.

Roethel, H. K. and Benjamin, J. K. (eds.) *Kandinsky: catalogue raisonné of the oil paintings* (2 vols.; 1900–15, vol. I; 1916–44, vol. II). London: Sotheby, 1982–4.

Roskill, M. *Klee, Kandinsky and the Thought of Their Time: a Critical Perspective*. Urbana: University of Illinois Press, 1992.

Selz, P. *German Expressionist Painting*. Berkeley: University of California Press, 1957.

Sheppard, R. 'Kandinsky's Early Aesthetic Theory: Some Examples of Its Influence and some Implications for the Theory and Practice of Abstract Poetry', *Journal of European Studies*, 5 (1975), pp. 19–40.

'Kandinsky's *Klänge*: An Interpretation', *German Life and Letters*, 33 (1979–80), pp. 134–46.

'Kandinsky's œuvre 1900–14: The *avant-garde* as rear guard', *Word and Image*, 6 (1990), pp. 41–67.

Stein, S. Alyson 'Kandinsky and Abstract Stage Composition, Practice and Theory, 1909–12', *Art Journal*, 43 (1983), pp. 61–6.

Teichmann, A. 'Klang, Farbe, Ausdruck: Zum Synästhetischen Prinzip bei Wassily Kandinsky und Arnold Schönberg', *Beiträge zur Kunstwissenschaft*, 32 (1990), pp. 204–13.

Thürlemann, F. *Kandinsky über Kandinsky, Der Künstler als Interpret eigener Werke*. Bern: Benteli, 1986.

'Le Figuratif au service de l'abstrait', in *Collection les grandes expositions, Vassily Kandinsky*. Paris: Beaux-Arts Magazine, 1985, pp. 17–18.

Vergo, P. *Kandinsky Cossacks*. London: The Tate Gallery, 1986.

Weiss, P. *Kandinsky in Munich: The Formative Jugendstil Years*. Princeton University Press, 1979.

'Kandinsky and the *Jugendstil* Arts and Crafts Movement', *The Burlington Magazine*, 117 (1975), pp. 270–9.

'Kandinsky and the Symbolist Heritage', *Art Journal*, 45 (1985), pp. 137–45.

'Kandinsky: Symbolist Poetics and Theatre in Munich', *Pantheon*, 35 (1977), pp. 209–18.

Wiedmann, A. K. *Romantic Roots in Modern Art, Romanticism and Expressionism: A Study in Comparative Aesthetics*. Surrey: Gresham Books/Unwin, 1979.

Zweite, A. (ed.) *Kandinsky und München: Begegnungen und Wandlungen 1896–1914*. Munich: Prestel Verlag, 1982.

MONDRIAN

Beckett, J. 'Discoursing on Dutch Modernism', *Oxford Art Journal*, 6 (1983), pp. 67–79.

'The Netherlands', in *Abstraction: Towards a New Art, Painting 1910–1920*. London: Tate Gallery, 1980, pp. 39–56.

Blotkamp, C. 'Annunciation of the New Mysticism: Dutch Symbolism and Early Abstraction', in *The Spiritual in Art: Abstract Painting 1890–1985* (ed. M. Tuchman). New York: Abbeville Press, 1986, pp. 89–111.

'Mondrian's First Diamond Compositions', *Artforum*, 18 (1979), pp. 33–9.

Bois, Y.-A. 'Mondrian et la théorie de l'architecture', *Revue de l'Art*, 53 (1981), pp. 39–52.

'Piet Mondrian, "New York City"', *Critical Inquiry*, 14 (1987-8), pp. 244–77.

Butor, M. 'Le Carré et son habitant', *Nouvelle Revue Française*, 17 (1961), pp. 119–27 and 315–27.

'Notes autour de Mondrian', in M. G. Ottolenghi, *Tout l'œuvre peint de Mondrian*. Paris: Flammarion, 1976, pp. 5–9.

Carmean, E. A. *Mondrian, The Diamond Compositions*. Washington: National Gallery of Art, 1979.

Champa, K. S. *Mondrian Studies*. University of Chicago Press, 1985.

Cheetham, M. A. *The Rhetoric of Purity: Essentialist Theory and the Advent of Abstract Painting*. Cambridge University Press, 1991.

Craven, D. 'Towards a Newer Virgil, Mondrian De-mythologized', *Praxis: A Journal of Radical Perspectives on the Arts*, 4 (1978), pp. 235–48.

Fried, M. 'Art and Objecthood', *Artforum*, 6 (1967), pp. 12–24.

Greenberg, C. 'Modernist Painting', *Art and Literature*, 4 (1965), pp. 193–201.

Henkels, H. *Mondrian, From Figuration to Abstraction*. London: Thames and Hudson, 1988.

Hoek, E. 'Mondrian in Disneyland', *Art in America*, 77 (1989), pp. 136–43.

Hoek, E. (ed.) *De Stijl 1917–22: The Formative Years*. London: MIT Press, 1982.

Holtzman, H. *Mondrian, The Process Works*. New York: The Pace Gallery, 1983.

Jaffé, H. L. C. *De Stijl 1917–1931: The Dutch Contribution to Modern Art*. London: Harvard University Press, 1986.

Jaffé, H. L. C. (ed.) *De Stijl*. London: Thames and Hudson, 1970.

James, M. 'Mondrian and the Dutch Symbolists', *Art Journal*, 23 (1963), pp. 103–11.

'The Realism Behind Mondrian's Geometry', *Art News*, 56 (1957), pp. 34–7.

Krauss, R. 'Grids', in *The Originality of the Avant-Garde and Other Modernist Myths*. Cambridge, MA: MIT Press, 1985, pp. 8–22.

Lebenstejn, J.-Cl. 'Mondrian, la fin de l'art', *Critique*, 39 (1983), pp. 893–912.

Locatelli, V. 'Mondrian et De Stijl: tra "astrazzione" e Architettura', *Abitare*, 290 (1990), pp. 211–15.

Meuris, J. *Mondrian*. Paris: Nouvelles Editions Françaises, 1991.

Mondrian, P. *The New Art – The New Life, The Collected Writings of Piet Mondrian* (ed. H. Holtzman and M. S. James). London: Thames and Hudson, 1987.

'De l'art abstrait. Réponse de Piet Mondrian', *Cahiers d'Art*, 6 (1931), pp. 41–3.

Neue Gestaltung. Berlin: Florian Kupferberg Verlag, 1974 (first pub. 1925).

Nicholson, W., *et al.* 'Reminiscences of Mondrian', *Studio International*, 172 (1966), pp. 286–92.

Ottolenghi, M. G. *Tout l'œuvre peint de Piet Mondrian*. Paris: Flammarion, 1976.

Overy, P. *De Stijl*. London: Thames and Hudson, 1991.

Pleynet, M. *Système de la peinture*. Paris: Seuil, 1977.

Rose, B. 'Mondrian in New York', *Artforum*, 10 (1971), pp. 54–63.

Rosenberg, H. *Art on the Edge*. London: Macmillan, 1975.

Roweli, M. 'Interview with Piet Mondrian', in *Piet Mondrian 1872–1944, Centennial Exhibition*. New York: Solomon R. Guggenheim Museum, 1971, pp. 77–87.

Saxon, E. 'On Mondrian's Diamonds', *Artforum*, 18 (1979), pp. 40–5.

Seuphor, M. *Piet Mondrian, Life and Work*. London: Thames and Hudson, 1957.

Piet Mondrian, sa vie, son œuvre. Paris: Flammarion, 1970.

Sweeney, J. J. 'Piet Mondrian', *The Museum of Modern Art Bulletin*, 12 (1945), pp. 2–12.

'Mondrian, the Dutch and De Stijl', *Art News*, 50 (1951), p. 25 and pp. 62–3.

Tomassoni, I. *Mondrian*. London: Hamlyn, 1970.

Troy, N. 'Piet Mondrian's Atelier', *Arts Magazine*, 53 (1978), pp. 82–7.

'Piet Mondrian's Design for the "Salon de Madame B . . . à Dresden"', *Art Bulletin*, 62 (1980), pp. 640–7.

The De Stijl Environment. London: MIT Press, 1983.

Von Maur, K. 'Mondrian and Music', in *Mondrian*. Stuttgart: Staatsgalerie Stuttgart, 1980, pp. 287–311.

Welsh, R. *Piet Mondrian's Early Career, The Naturalistic Periods*. London: Garland, 1977.

Welsh, R. and Joosten, J. (eds.) *Two Mondrian Sketchbooks, 1912–14*. Amsterdam: Meulenhoff International, 1969.

THEOSOPHICAL/MYSTICAL CONTEXTS OF ABSTRACTION

Besant, A. and Leadbeater, C. W. *Thought Forms*. London: The Theosophical Publishing Society, 1901.

Eaves, A. O. *Die Kräfte der Farben*. Berlin: Talisman Bibliothek, 1906.

Fingeston, P. 'Spirituality, Mysticism and Non-Objective Art', *Art Journal*, 21 (1961), pp. 2–7.

Heller, R. 'Kandinsky and Traditions Apocalyptic', *Art Journal*, 43 (1983), pp. 19–26.

Ringbom, S. 'Art in the Epoch of the Great Spiritual', *Journal of the Warburg and Courtauld Institutes*, 29 (1966), pp. 386–418.

The Sounding Cosmos, A Study in the Spiritualism of Kandinsky and Abstract Painting. Abo Akademi, 1970.

'Kandinsky und das Okkulte', in *Kandinsky und München: Begegnungen und Wandlungen 1896–1914* (ed. A. Zweite). Munich: Prestel Verlag, 1982, pp. 85–101.

'Die Steiner Annotationen Kandinskys', in *Kandinsky und München: Begegnungen und Wandlungen 1896–1914* (ed. A. Zweite). Munich: Prestel Verlag, 1982, pp. 102–5.

Steiner, R. *Occult Science, An Outline*. London: Rudolf Steiner Press, 1969.

Die Stufen der Höheren Erkenntnis. Dornach: Verlag der Rudolf Steiner Nachlassverwaltigung, 1959.

Rudolph Steiner's Farbenlehre. Dornach: Philosophischer-Anthroposophischer Verlag, 1929.

Tuchman, M. (ed.) *The Spiritual in Art: Abstract Painting 1890–1985*. New York: Abbeville Press, 1986.

Welsh, R. 'Mondrian and Theosophy', in *Piet Mondrian 1872–1944, Centennial Exhibition*. New York: Solomon R. Guggenheim Museum, 1971, pp. 35–51.

UTOPIANISM

Friedman, M. (ed.) *De Stijl: 1917–1931, Visions of Utopia*. Oxford: Phaidon Press, 1982.

Kuspit, D. 'Utopian Protest in Early Abstract Art', *Art Journal*, 29 (1970), pp. 430–7.

Levitas, R. *The Concept of Utopia*. London: Philip Allan, 1990.

Ricoeur, P. *Lectures on Ideology and Utopia*. New York: Columbia University Press, 1986.

Roedl, P. A. 'Abstrakte Kunst und der Traum von der rezeptiven Gesellschaft', *Festschrift Klaus Lankheit*. Cologne: Du Mont Schauberg, 1973, pp. 66–77.

Washton, Long, R.-C. 'Expressionism, Abstraction and the Search for Utopia in Germany', in *The Spiritual in Art: Abstract Painting 1890– 1985* (ed. M. Tuchman). New York: Abbeville Press, 1986, pp. 201–17.

Index

Cambridge Studies in French

GENERAL EDITOR: Malcolm Bowie (*All Souls College, Oxford*)
EDITORIAL BOARD: R. Howard Bloch (*University of California, Berkeley*), Terence Cave (*St John's College, Oxford*), Ross Chambers (*University of Michigan*), Antoine Compagnon (*Columbia University*), Peter France (*University of Edinburgh*), Toril Moi (*Duke University*), Naomi Schor (*Harvard University*)

Also in the series (* denotes titles now out of print)

Art Center College of Design
Library
1700 Lida Street
Pasadena, Calif. 91103

Art Center College of Design
Library
1700 Lida Street
Pasadena, Calif. 91103